THE INDIAN FAMILY: CHANGE AND PERSISTENCE

THE INDIAN FAMILY: CHANGE AND PERSISTENCE

Edited by

DR. PARIMAL KUMAR ROY

GYAN PUBLISHING HOUSE
NEW DELHI-110002

THE INDIAN FAMILY: CHANGE AND PERSISTENCE
(*Health and Planning*)

ISBN : 81-212-0706-1

Published in 2000 in India by
Gyan Publishing House,
5, Ansari Road, Darya Ganj
New Delhi-110 002

Phone: 3282060, 3261060 Fax: (011)-3285914
E-mail: gyanbook@del2.vsnl.net.in
Visit Our Web Site At http://www.gyanbooks.com

Laser Typesetting at A.S. Printers, Delhi

Printed at Mehra Offset Press, Delhi

CONTENTS

	List of Contributors		vii
	Publishers Permission		ix
	Acknowledgements		xi
	Introduction	*P.K. Roy*	1

PART–I

FAMILY RELATIONS AND SOCIAL CHANGE

1.	Industrialisation and the "Fitness" of Nuclear Family: A Case Study in India	*P.K. Roy*	19
2.	Structure and Organization and Indian Family: The Emerging Patterns	*K.Gupta*	37
3.	Some Observations on the Study of Family Change in India	*R.K. Bhadra*	59
4.	The Domestic Cycle in India: Natural History of a Will-o'-the Wisp	*S.A. Freed and R.S. Freed*	73
5.	Changes in the Indian Family: An Examination of Some Assumption	*A.M. Shah*	99
6.	Changing Family Types in India	*S.A. Freed and R.S. Freed*	113

PART–II

FAMILY COHESION AND KIN NETWORKS

7.	The Extended Family as an Independent Factor in Social Change: A Case Study from India	*G.H. Conklin*	137
8.	Industrialization and the Indian Joint Family	*R. Owens*	153

9. The Adaptive Extended Family 191
A.A. Khatri

10. Urban Kinship Ties in South India: A Case Study 211
G.N. Ramu

11. Trends in North Indian Urban Kinship: The Matrilateral Asymmetry Hypothesis 229
S.J. Vatuk

PART–III
VARIATIONS IN FAMILY STRUCTURE AND RELATIONS

12. The Hindu Family and Development 257
T.N. Madan

13. Urbanization and Family Types in a North Indian Village 281
S.A. Freed and R.S. Freed

14. Family Structure in Village Lonikand, India: 1819, 1958, 1967 303
P.M. Kolenda

15. Family Structure and Classes in Four Villages 329
P.K. Bose

16. Some Aspects of Household Organization and Family Structures in Calcutta 349
P. Chakrabarty and S. Bhowmick

Bibliography 365

Index 397

LIST OF CONTRIBUTORS

The following biographical details are as of the time when permission to reprint was first obtained.

Dr. R.K. Bhadra, Reader, Department of Sociology and Social Anthropology, University of North Bengal, India.

Dr. P.K. Bose, Senior Fellow, Centre for Social Studies, South Gujarat University Campus, Surat, India.

Dr. S. Bhowmick is associated with the Sociological Research Unit, Indian Statistical Institute, Calcutta, India.

Dr. P. Chakrabarty, Associate Professor, Sociological Research Unit, Indian Statistical Institute, Calcutta, India.

Professor H.H. Conklin, Professor of Sociology, Department of Sociology, North Carolina Central University, U.S.A.

Dr. R.S. Freed, Research Associate at the American Museum of Natural History, New York, U.S.A.

Dr. S.A. Freed, Curator at the American Museum of Natural History, New York, U.S.A.

Dr. K. Gupta, Principal, Hindu Kanya Mahavidyalaya, Sitapur, U.P., India.

Dr. A.A. Khatri, Associate Professor of Sociology, Department of Sociology, School of Behavioral Sciences, University of Alabama at Birmingham, U.S.A.

Professor P.M. Kolenda, Professor of Anthropology, Department of Anthropology, University of Houston, U.S.A.

Professor T.N. Madan, Professor of Sociology, Institute of Economic Growth, Delhi, India.

Dr. R. Owens, Department of Anthropology, University of Texas, U.S.A.

Professor G.N. Ramu, Professor of Sociology, Department of Sociology, University of Manitoba, Canada.

Dr. P.K. Roy, Senior Lecturer in Sociology, Monash University Gippsland Campus, Churchill, Victoria, Australia.

Professor A.M. Shah, Professor of Sociology, Department of Sociology, University of Delhi, India.

Professor S.J. Vatuk, Professor of Anthropology, Department of Anthropology, University of Illinois, U.S.A.

PUBLISHERS PERMISSIONS

For permission to reprint copyright material the editor and the publisher are indebted to the original publishers for the following articles:

1. P.K. Roy: "Industrialisation and the "Fitness" of Nuclear Family: A Case Study in India". *Journal of Comparative Family Studies*, 1974, Vol. 5: 74-86. Reproduced by permission of the *Journal of Comparative Family Studies.*

2. K. Gupta: "Structure and Organization of Indian Family: The Emerging Patterns". *International Journal of Contemporary Sociology*, 1973, Vol. 10: 163-182. Reproduced by permission of the *International Journal of Contemporary Sociology.*

3. R.K. Bhadra: "Some Observations on the Study of Family Change in India". *Man in India*, 1977, Vol. 57: 44-59. Reproduced by permission of *Man in India.*

4. S.A. Freed and R.S. Freed: "The Domestic Cycle in India: Natural History of a Will-o-the Wisp". *American Ethnologist*, 1983, Vol. 10, No. 2: 312-324. Reproduced by permission of the American Anthropological Association from American Ethnologist 10:2, 1983. Not for further reproduction.

5. A.M. Shah: "Changes in the Indian Family: An Examination of Some Assumption". *Economic and Political Weekly*, 1968, Vol. 3: 127-134. By permission of the author.

6. S.A.Freed and R.S. Freed: "Changing Family Types in India". *Ethnology*, 1982, Vol. 21: 189-202. Reproduced by permission of Ethnologist.

7. G.H. Conklin: "The Extended Family as an Independent Factor in Social Change: A Case Study from India". *Journal of Marriage and the Family*, 1974, Vol. 36: 798-804. Reproduced by permission of the National Council on Family Relations.

8. R. Owens: "Industrialization and the Indian Joint Family". *Ethnology*, 1971, Vol. 10: 223-250. Reproduced by permission of Ethnologist.

9. A.A. Khatri: "The Adaptive Extended Family Today". *Journal of Marriage and the Family*, 1975, Vol. 37: 633-642. Reproduced by permission of the National Council on Family Relations.

10. G.N. Ramu: "Urban Kinship Ties in South India: A Case Study". *Journal of Marriage and the Family*, 1974, Vol. 36: 619-627. Reproduced by permission of the National Council on Family Relations.

11. S.J.Vatuk: "Trends in North Indian Urban Kinship: The Matrilateral Asymmetry Hypothesis". *Southwestern Journal of Anthropology*, 1971, Vol. 27: 287-307. Reproduced by permission of the Journal of Anthropological Research, published by the University of New Mexico.

12. T.N. Madan: "The Hindu Family and Development". *Journal of Social and Economic Studies*, 1976, Vol. 4, No. 2: 211-231. Reproduced by permission of the *Journal of Social and Economic Studies*, A.N. Sinha Institue of Social Studies.

13. S.A. Freed and R.S. Freed: "Urbanization and Family Types in a North Indian Village". *Southwestern Journal of Anthropology*, 1969, Vol. 25: 342-359. Reproduced by permission of the *Journal of Anthropological Research*, published by the University of New Mexico.

14. P.M. Kolenda: "Family Structure in Village Lonikand, India: 1819,1958, 1967". *Contributions to Indian Sociology*, New Series, 1970, Vol. 4: 50-72. Reproduced by permission of the Contributions to Indian Sociology.

15. P.K. Bose: "Family Structure and Classes in Four Villages". *Man in India*, 1978, Vol. 58: 151-170. Reproduced by permission of Man in India.

16. P. Chakrabarty and S. Bhowmick: "Some Aspects of Household Organization and Family Structures in Calcutta". *Eastern Anthropologist*, 1983, Vol. 36, No. 1: 31-44. Reproduced by permission of the Eastern Anthroplogist, Ethnographic and Folk Culture Society.

ACKNOWLEDGEMENTS

I wish to express my appreciation to all the authors who gave permission to reprint their papers in this volume. While every care has been taken to trace and acknowledge copyright, some authors could not be traced or located. I am deeply indebted to the contributors of this volume who took an interest in my project and their advice and support regarding the publication of this book.

My sincere thanks to my colleagues Dr. Harry Ballis and Mr Ian Hamilton for their comments and assistance they provided during the preparation of the manuscript. I would like to acknowledge the assistance and support received from the School of Communications, Humanities and Social Sciences. I have also received valuable assistance and support from a number of people and wish to thank particularly the following: Colin Thornby, Luisa Viggiano and John Schmuttermaier. My special thanks go to Mr Randhir Singh Gill for typing some chapters and for his moral support. I am grateful to Dr. Peter Harwood, Dean of Faculty of Arts, Auckland University of Technology, New Zealand for his encouragement and support. I am especially appreciative of the constant support and help received from my wife Sikha Roy and her assistance including the tasks of typing, proof reading, and helping to prepare the bibliography. Without her constant sources of encouragement and help throughout this venture, I would not have been able to complete this volume. I want to express my thanks to Mr Amit Garg, Director of Publication, Gyan Publishing House, New Delhi, India for his assistance and patience.

Introduction

Parimal Roy

A considerable body of sociological literature has appeared in recent decades regarding the effects of modern forces on the extended and nuclear family, both in rural and urban areas in different parts of the world. The changes brought about by industrialization, urbanization and other modern forces have raised questions in the minds of sociologists and anthropologists and other researchers over the status of the "isolated nuclear family" and the viability of joint or extended family networks in India (see Kolenda, 1968; Freed and Freed, 1969, 1982). A great number of studies have been produced over the years examining the relationship of family types to variables such as ownership of property, caste, education, type of employment, industrialization, and urbanization in India. Is the joint family more a characteristic of landed castes than landless castes? Is it mainly found in rural areas and not in urban-industrial areas? Is the joint family more a feature of higher castes than of lower castes, and more common among the upper class than the lower class? These questions have been raised by many researchers and are persued in detail in this volume.

This book aims at facilitating a better understanding of the changing structure and functions of the family and wider kin networks in India, and to inspire further research on this subject. The book aims to provide readers with an overview of major theoretical paradigms, regarding the effects of contemporary social change on the extended and nuclear family in both rural and urban areas in India. The readings deliberately draw on research conducted during the 1970s and 1980s, a period of profound and unprecedented social change both in India and elsewhere. The selected readings attempt to show, in considerable detail, the friction between traditional family ideals held by our forebears and the values espoused by the present generations. I am particularly concerned in this collection of readings with highlighting the continuity between contemporary views and those in the relatively recent past.

This introduction focuses on the themes of continuity and change and reviews some studies which are not included in this volume. My intention is to provide a context for the book, and a framework to facilitate a better understanding of the work of the authors represented in the selections. Another very important consideration in my choice of readings is that recent research on Indian family reported in journals does not cover the subject matter in detail. Existing texts are topic-bound and limited in scope. The rationale adopted for this book is the desire to provide a broad appreciation of how recent research on family in India that has developed over a time period, serves to recapitulate the perspectives of a previous generation.

Due to the rapid rate of publications in this field during the last two decades, the task of selection was rather difficult in view of an inevitable limitation of space. Because of this, it has been impossible to include no more than a small sample of good selections of writings. Selections are based on the criteria of readability, diversity and pedagogical usefulness. I have included an extensive bibliography on family and kinship network in India. These references may be useful for those students of families who might wish to pursue further research on specific aspect of the family.

The selections in this book are presented in three parts, each containing a careful selection of readings. The first part is concerned with the relationship between the process of industrialization and the changing structure of the family. It focuses on the debate concerning the emergence of an "isolated nuclear family" and the persistence of extended or joint family in India. Findings from various studies included in this part provide support for each of the alternative views mentioned above. While the proportion of nuclear families varies from region to region, the sentiment with regard to extended family remains high in some regions. The intention of this section is to show the diversity and complexity of the issues regarding industrialization and family. In this connection Goode (1963: 110) has pointed out that both family and industry are interacting variables, "neither fully determine the other, although both fully influence each other."

The second part includes selections that describe the significance of extended family and kinship obligations in everyday life and on special occasions despite the influence of industrialization and other modern forces on family life. Most of the studies contained in this part claimed that universal family change due to industrialization is still questionable, as there has been no demonstration of an unilineal determinate relationship between the two variables. Conklin's (1977) study of the modernising effects of factory employment on family roles in an industrial area of South India, for example, demonstrated that factory employment did not appear to alter workers' family values. He provided evidence that factory employment, modern education, urbanization or industrialization have not resulted in exclusion of kin but "rather to increased tolerance of different role patterns of all kin within the extended family" (p. 325).

The third part focuses on variations in family types. Studies included in this part have suggested that industrialization and other modern forces do not lead to the singular evolution of the small nuclear family. Families differ across geographical locations, by castes and religious groups, by economic and social classes. These families are adapting to the changing environment, however, industrialization or any other modern forces are not affecting the wide variety of families in the same way.

Family Relations and Social Change

Within the past century, the people of India have been strongly affected by the worldwide tides of social change. Such change had occurred as a result of the establishment of the British rule in India, the impact of Christianity, social movements, modern education, western values, the impact of industrialization, a share in the new economic opportunities and the modern political ideas. Modern forces such as industrialization, urbanisation, education, occupational differentiation, do seem to correlate with an increasing proportion of nuclear families and many studies have emphasized the effects of these forces on the family structure and functions. Kurian (1961: 129), for example, has pointed out that "better communications, education, and work outside the home as a result of the growth of towns and industries, have assisted the basic functions to transform themselves to fit into the newly developing social and economic structure". Beals' (1955: 91-92) study showed a trend towards reference for nuclear families as a result of modern education, new urban-industrial occupations, development of market cash economies, and changes in the family law dealing with joint property. In this connection, Kapadia (1951: 238) stated that "...the net results of the administration of the Hindu law by British courts were the disintegration of the joint family organization, and the assertion of the individual's inherent right in the property held by the head of the family". Beals supported such a theory in his research in South India. He (1955: 92) argued that "the change in the legal position of the joint family, and the use of law courts, explains why all but one of large families divided after 1920. By 1953 it had become almost customary for families to divide as soon as the children reached maturity".

The rural to urban migration because of population pressure on land also added to the weakening of the joint family. There are now a large number of factories in cities that recruit workers from villages. In an intensive survey on the impact of urbanization of the tribal and non-tribal social life in Ranchi city, Vidyarthi (1969) has shown that urbanization has brought many changes in the ways of life of the tribal population. He stated that the general change is noticed in the occupational sphere and this, in turn, changes other aspects of social life (p. 312). He (1969: 308) also asserted that "changes in the family organization, social solidarity, and conventional discipline are clearly evident in day-to-day life of the tribal migrants". Bailey (1957), in his account of an Orissa village, emphasized that changes have been brought about in the village by the arrival of political administration and the development of commercial economy. He argued that the breakdown of the joint family system in the village was due to diverse occupations (see also Bailey 1960: 325).

Morrison (1959) also observed in his study of Badlapur that the greater acceptance of nuclear families among rural people was a response to the impact of modern education, urbanization, industrialization and modern values. He indicated that only six per cent of the total sample was living in joint families, eight per cent of the total was quasi-joint families and 85 per cent of the total were nuclear families. He noted that although the nuclear family was found in all status levels, it was more so among upper and middle classes. "Many of the sons of the landlord class have entered into non-agricultural livelihoods, and have established their own nuclear families" (pp. 48-49). There was a significant correlation between education and the size of the family. Morrison (1959: 66) stated that:

> "The proportions of joint familism and quasi-joint familism decrease as education increases, while the proportions of nuclear familism increase as educational attainment increases... The data show that the representation of the uneducated is above the village average in the joint and quasi-joint families. But the uneducated are below average in proportional representation among nuclear families".

Orenstein's (1960) research of 59 villages in Poona provided further evidence of this. He examined the relationship of agricultural technology to family type. He found that families with more technological advances in agriculture were much less likely to have joint families. He suggested that families with more technological advances in agriculture get more of their income in cash. The family members are likely to get divided further because the distribution of income leads to quarrels and both the cash income and irrigated lands are readily divisible. Some indication of these trends can be seen in other studies as well (see Epstein, 1962; Beals, 1955). A study conducted by Desai (1964) in Mahuva, a town in South Gujarat showed that of 423 families surveyed, about 95 per cent of the families practised some kind of jointness. Of the 95 per cent, 21 per cent practised jointness in the traditional sense. The remainder percentage of various types of jointness were: 30 per cent marginally joint, 17 per cent joint in terms of property and 27 per cent jointness by way of mutual obligations. He (p. 146) stated that the greater jointness was associated with business and agricultural castes. Those people having non-traditional occupations have a slightly lesser degree of jointness than those do with the traditional types. Desai (1964: 119) indicated that common ownership of property was the main factor, which helped to maintain jointness (see details in Chapter 1: Roy). Gore (1968: 77-91) investigated whether industrialization and urbanization led to a greater acceptance of nuclear family norms. His sample was based on 399 Aggarwal families from urban fringe and rural areas in Delhi who followed their traditional occupations such as banking and commerce. He also obtained information from 100 additional families of professionals and office workers who did not follow traditional occupations. These families showed less favour for joint family living and were more eager to change than those who followed traditional occupations (details of Gore's findings are provided in Chapter 1: Roy).

Ross' (1961) research among the traditional middle and upper class urban Hindu family in Bangalore, provided further evidence of the impact of industrialization on the family. She discussed how the various factors such as increased pressure on land, modern education, western influences, new techniques of mass communications, increased employment opportunities in towns and cities have contributed to break up the traditional large joint family and how these factors have affected the role relationships within the family and wider kinship network. Inkeles (1969) focused on a similar perspective. In his study of the process of modernization from six developing countries, he argued that factory work was a significant factor in bringing social change including changing individual's attitudes, values and behaviour.

In the first selection Roy examines the impact of industrialization on rural and urban families. Research efforts in this study were geared to an explanatory analysis of people's attitudes toward family living. Similar to many studies mentioned above, Roy found that those who followed non-traditional occupations showed less favour for jointness. Gupta and Bhadra (Selections 2 and 3), present a general review of family organization in India. Many studies reviewed by them showed certain amounts of change in the family structure and relationships and a trend toward an increase in the proportion of nuclear families. Freed and Freed (Selection 4) evaluated the concept of the "domestic cycle" in a north Indian village by an analysis of the sequence of changes that domestic groups have undergone. These changes in the structure of many families were influenced by cultural values, economic circumstances of each family, the particular personalities of its members and demographic events. They pointed out that although such causal complexity tended to preclude the existence of a single domestic cycle for a majority of families, there were however, 'significant regularities such as the frequent evolution of nuclear families into lineal joint families'.

Some researchers have noted that large and joint households exist despite the impact of industrialization and urbanization on the household. Shah (Selection 5) presents a general review of theory and research concerning changes in the Indian family. He states that industrialization and urbanization do not lead to disintegration of joint family and there is no point in postulating a single line of change for the entire Indian society. This position has been documented by Freed and Freed (Selection 6) in their study of a rural area. They found that the joint family systems are more common among rural people. However, they claimed that the current trend towards the joint family may prove to be temporary and it is quite likely that investigations elsewhere in India will show different trends.

Family Cohesion and Kin Networks

The purpose of this section is to show that participation in a modern industrial economy does not necessarily imply the complete dissolution of all extended kin groups beyond the immediate family. Many studies (Owens, 1971; Ramu, 1973, 1974; Vatuk, 1971; Khatri, 1975; Conklin, 1974, 1976, 1977; Chekki, 1974) have demonstrated with some variations in emphasis that in modern India the nuclear family of husband, wife and unmarried children has maintained relationships with wider sets of kin who did not share the same household. A few studies that are not included in this book due to space limitations have shown that the proportion of nuclear households has increased among many groups, more because of economic factors than because of any contempt of joint family obligations. Singer (1968), for example, in his study of nineteen leading industrialists in Chennai city, found that there were more nuclear households than joint households among industrial leaders in the city. His findings, however, questioned the hypothesis that the small nuclear family is brought about by modern industrial economy. In this connection, he (1968: 438) remarked, "Families living in nuclear households continue to maintain numerous joint family obligations and for the most part, continue to subscribe to the norms of that system". He asserted that the social obligations and interactions were more intense and frequent among the members of the leading industrialists. When the members of families met on such occasions as festivals, weddings, funerals, feasts, etc., then this did not prove jointness. It is difficult to refuse to meet these obligations, since they may have to resort to the same dependency at some time. For their part, these people also place some value on their own group life, partly because they feel more at ease within this setting. Singer himself commented that many of the practices associated with traditional joint family system "offer some distinct advantages for organizing an industrial enterprise" (Singer 1968: 445). He (1968: 441-442) further suggested: "All major company decisions are discussed at informal meetings of brothers, which take place at least once a month. These decisions require complete consensus, on the assumption that if anyone has a reasonable proposal he should be able to persuade the others". Singer's study is supported by Ramu (1973), Vatuk (1979), Gould (1968), Conklin (1974, 1976, and 1977), Shah (1974), Owens (1971) and Roy (1984) who provided empirical evidence of interlocking kin networks and the importance of joint family ties in the economic development. Chekki (1974) suggested that in Dharwar literacy did not weaken kin relationships because literacy helped some families to keep records of their kin more efficiently. Kapadia (1958, 1959) made a similar observation in his research in India. He presented evidence that the small nuclear family was not socially isolated from kin, the joint family provided very enduring and significant sources of sociability; it helped in economic and other crises, and provided refuge and advice. He (1959: 261) stated that "even in those cases where the property is divided and the income of the members of the family is not pooled... the constituent families maintain their connections through mutual cooperation and rights and obligations other than those of property".

In Selection 7, Conklin emphasized that joint households and kinship network meet the needs of economic development, and that education, modernization, economic development and other modern forces did not constitute a barrier to kin relationships and joint household participation. Instead, joint households and kinship network provided the needs of economic development.

The existence of conjugal family in a separate household closely linked within a matrix of reciprocal relations among extended kinship lines has gained increasing empirical and theoretical support from a number of other studies in India. Selections 8, 9 and 10 by Owens, Khatri and Ramu respectively provided evidence of interlocking networks created by families with commercial and business interests, families with common property, laws of succession, intermarriage between families of industrialists and also the involvement of family members and outside kin in family decision-making. These studies within commercial and industrial areas have found viable extended family systems. The observations made by Ramu (1973:253) in south India revealed that "the more successful business firms in Kolar Gold field (situated in Mysore State) were those owned by coparceners. These business firms came into existence after collective decision of the coparceners to convert family property into capital for new family enterprise". Owens' (Selection 8) study in an urban area of Howrah city among families of entrepreneurs and non-entrepreneurs demonstrated that coparcenary joint family provided an aid in modern business practices. Khatri's (Selection 9) Study in Ahmedabad showed that the majority of respondents from nuclear, extended and joint households and from various socio-economic strata were in favour of extended family living. He found that there was a high degree of kin involvement in family-decision making. In Selection 10, Ramu noted that the closeness of kin relationship was a matter of personal factors and personal preferences and there was "no institutional compulsion to maintain close ties with certain relatives". Close contacts and relationships were more frequent between the respondent and 'most significant kin'.

The essay by Vatuk (Selection 11) is somewhat different but particularly useful where the author analyses the changing kinship practices in urban India from the viewpoint of the 'matrilateral asymmetry' hypothesis which developed in the study of western urban kinship system. The emergence of matrilateral kinship ties in traditionally patrilineal and patrilocal societies had been hypothesised by many theorists as a result of industrialisation and other changes in societies. Several studies of family life in western societies have shown a tendency toward matrilateral asymmetry in interaction between members of the nuclear family and extended kin of the two spouses. Vatuk presented evidence of the emergence of matrilateral kinship ties in her study of kinship interaction in a city of Western Uttar Pradesh. She underlined the supportive role of the matrilateral kin in providing material aid, advice and services in everyday life. She pointed out that these supports by wife's kin to the neo-locally resident couple were clearly greater than in the traditional patriarchal rural society.

Variations in Family Structure and Relations

The above studies in part two have provided a broad outline of family groupings and the strength of kinship ties in modern India. The third section includes a sampling of works that focused specifically on the variations in family types. These studies claimed that industrialization is not a homogeneous process but rather one which creates a variety of opportunities that do not necessarily lead to increasing incidence of nuclear families. These studies have provided evidence of the prevalence of divergent types of families in India. Many researchers have gathered large amounts of material regarding the relationship of castes, ownership of property, class, education, industrialization and urbanization to family types. They have questioned some of the prevailing notions that the nuclear family emerges under the impetus of modern forces. Barnabas (1957: 16-20), for example, found that traditionally joint households were more frequent among the high caste Hindus than among the lower castes. He stated that "there is little motivation or impetus for the lower castes to maintain a join family, since they rarely possess landed property". Lewis (1958: 17-18) also found in his study of Rampur, Delhi, that all castes have some joint families. However, his data showed that both ownership of land and caste status had high correlation with family type. The landowning castes had the highest proportion (66.6 per cent) of extended family but among the lower castes the nuclear family predominated. In a similar vein, Mandelbaum (1968: 32-34) argued that, 'the more property there is to divide, the more difficult the separation' (c.f. Freed and Freed, 1969:356). Sen (1965) and Sarma (1964) contain a somewhat similar conclusion in two studies of different villages in West Bengal. They reported that 'owner-cultivators had a higher proportion of joint families than people who had followed non-agricultural occupations' (c.f. Freed and Freed, 1969:356). Sengupta's (1958) study of three villages in three different districts in West Bengal demonstrated that lower castes who belonged to lower classes tended to establish separate households than higher castes. Mandelbaum (1957: 247), Beteille (1964: 239), Morrison (1959) have shown that the joint family was least characteristic of lower castes than of higher castes, more characteristic of landowning castes than of landless castes, and more prevalent in rural areas. Mandelbaum (1959: 67) argued that the joint family was more characteristic of upper castes and upper strata of society than of the lower and poorer strata and to be found more in rural areas (see also Gupta, 1973). Dube (1963: 197) on the other hand maintained that it was an "urban phenomenon, confined mostly to upper caste groups in traditional small towns". In what segments of the population joint family and kin obligations were most apparent, both of them argued that in rural areas the joint family was characteristic of upper castes rather than of lower castes. Shah (1974) reached a similar conclusion indicating that in urban areas, higher castes continued to maintain old patterns and traditions. He (1974: 151) concluded that "in modern small towns and older sections of enlarged towns have more or less the same traditional characteristics". Carroll (1975) and Gupta (1973) have provided more evidence of the divergent types of families in India.

Madan (Selection 12) has questioned the assertion made by many researchers that occupational diversification, urbanization and industrialization have altered the traditional joint family structure of India. He acknowledged the fact that while some changes have taken place in this structure, different families have responded differently to external forces, however, this does not necessarily mean that the joint family is an impediment to social and economic development in India. Freed and Freed (Selection 13) have argued that high caste and landowning families are more likely to be joint than low caste and landless ones.

Kolenda (Selection 14) provided one of the most informative accounts of family types in India carried out since 1949. Her comparative data of 26 studies on the frequency of various types of families from many regions of India showed regional variations in family structure. From the analysis of quantitative data, she found that the joint family was more characteristic of higher castes than for the untouchable castes. Bose (Selection 15) in his study of four West Bengal villages has noted that there existed a strong relationship between class status and family structure. He proved that agricultural labourers had the highest percentage of nuclear families than the landowners. Chakrabarti and Bhowmick (Selection 16) have presented evidence concerning variations in family structure in Calcutta. Family types differed across state of origin by community, religious and occupational groups, education and age.

The foregoing analysis has attempted to present in brief a major trend in family research in India. In spite of considerable writings and research on the changing structure of family, kinship networks and the variation in family types, the literature in these areas are scattered in various journals. There is a severe lack of general reader bringing together facts and theoretical issues concerning the relationships between social change and the family system in India. The book in general will be useful to anyone interested in understanding and appreciating the change and continuity of Indian family.

BIBLIOGRAPHY

Bailey, F.G.: 1957: *Caste and the Economic Frontier*. Manchester: Manchester University Press.

————: 1960: "The joint family in India". *Economic Weekly*, Vol. 20 (February), 345-52.

Barnabas, A.P.: 1957: "Patterns of rural family". *Bulletin of the Christian Institute for the Study of Society*, Vol. 4 (September), pp. 16-25.

Beals, A.R.: 1955: "Interplay among factors of change in a Mysore village". pp. 78-102 in McKim Marriott (Ed.), *Village India*. Chicago: Chicago University Press.

Beteille, A.: 1964: "Family and social change in India and other south Asian countries". *Economic Weekly*, Vol. 16, pp. 237-44.

Bose, P.K.: 1978: "Family structure and classes in four villages". *Man in India*, Vol. 58, pp. 151-70.

Bhadra, R.K.: "Some observations on the study of family change in India". *Man in India*, Vol. 57 (January-March), pp. 44-59.

Caldwell, J.C., P.H. Reddy and P. Caldwell: 1984: "The determinants of family structuro in rural south India". *Journal of Marriage and the Family*, Vol. 46 (February), pp. 215-29.

Carroll, J.J.: "Field research on urbanisation and family change in India". *Man in India*, Vol. 55, pp. 339-54.

Chakrabarty, P. and S. Bhowmick: 1983: "Some aspects of household organisation and family structures in Calcutta". *Eastern Anthropologist*, Vol. 36, No. 1, pp. 31-44.

Chekki, D.A.: 1974: *Modernisation and Kin Network*. Leiden: E.J. Brill.

Conklin, G.H.: 1974: "The extended family as an independent factor in sociai chance". *Journal of Marriage and the Family*, Vol. 36 (November), pp. 798-804.

———: 1976: "The household in urban India". *Journal of Marriage and the Family*, Voi. 38 (November), pp. 771-79.

———: 1977: "Family modernisation values and factory employment: An example from South India". *Journal of Comparative Family Studies*, Vol. 8 (Autumn), pp. 315-26

Desai, I.P.: 1964: *Some Aspects of Family in Mahuva*. New York: Asia Publishing House.

Dube, S.C.: 1963: "Men's and women's roles in India : A sociological review", in B. Ward (Ed.), *Women in the New Asia*. UNESCO.

Epstein, T.S.: 1962: *Economic Development and Social Change in South India*. Manchester: Manchester University Press.

Freed, S.A. and R.S. Freed: 1969: "Urbanisation and family types in a North Indian village". *South Western Journal of Anthropology*, Vol. 25 (Winter), pp. 432-59.

———: 1982: "Changing family types in India". *Ethnology*, Vol. 21 (July), pp. 189-202.

———: 1983: "The domestic cycle in India: natural history of a will-o-the wisp". *American Ethnologist*, Vol.10, No. 2, pp. 312-24.

Goode, W.J.: 1963: *World Revolution and Family Patterns*. New York: The Free Press of Glencoe.

Gore, M.S.: 1968: *Urbanisation and Family Change*. New York: Humanities Press.

Gould, H.A.: "Time dimension and structural change in an Indian kinship system : Problem of conceptual refinement". pp. 413-21 in M. Singer and B.S. Cohn (Eds.), *Structure and Change in Indian Society*. Chicago: Aldine.

Gupta, K.: "Structure and organization of Indian family: The emerging patterns". *International Journal of Contemporary Sociology*, Vol.10, (October); 163-82.

Inkeles, A.: 1969: "Making men modern". *American Journal of Sociology*, Vol. 75 (September), pp. 208-25.

Kapadia, K.M.: 1958: *Marriage and Family in India*. 2nd ed., London: Oxford University Press.

———: 1959: "The family in transition". *Sociological Bulletin*, Vol. 8, pp. 68-99.

Kolenda, P.M.: 1968: "Region, caste, and family structure: A comparative study of the Indian joint family". pp. 339-96 in M. Singer and B.S. Cohn (Eds.), *Structure and Change in Indian Society*. Chicago: Aldine.

———: 1970: "Family structure in village Lonikand, India: 1819, 1958 and 1967". *Contributions to Indian Sociology*, Vol. 4, pp. 50-72.

Khatri, A.A.: 1975 : "The adaptive extended family in India today". *Journal of Marriage and the Family*, Vol. 37 (August), pp. 633-42.

Kurian, G.: 1961: *The Indian Family in Transition*. The Hague, Mouton.

Lewis, O.: *Village Life in North India*. Urbana: University of Illinios Press.

Madan, T.N.: 1976: "The Hindu Family and Development". *Journal of Social and Economic Studies*, Vol. 4, No. 2, pp. 211-31.

Mandelbaum, D.G.: 1957: "The family in India". *In Introduction to Civilization of India: Changing Dimensions of Indian Society and Culture*. Chicago: University of Chicago Press.

———: "The family in India". pp. 167-200 in R.N. Anshen (Ed.), The Family Its Function and Destiny. New York: Harper and Row.

———: 1968: *"Family, jati, village"*. pp. 29-50 in M. Singer and B.S. Cohn (Eds.), *Structure and Change in Indian Society*. Chicago: Aidine.

Morrison, W.A.: 1959: "Family types in Badlapur: An analysis of a changing institution in Maharashtrian village". *Socio- logical Bulletin*, Vol. 8, pp. 45-67.

Orenstein, H.: 1960: "Irrigation, settlement pattern and social organization". pp. 318-23 in A.F.C. Wallace (Ed.), *Selected Papers of the Fifth*

International Congress of Anthropological and Ethnological Sciences. Philadelphia, University of Pennsylvania Press.

Owens, R.: "Industrialization and the Indian joint family". *Ethnology*, Vol. 20 (April), pp. 223-50.

Parmar, S.B.S.: 1979: "Jointness and nuclearity of the Hindu family in rural settings". *Eastern Anthropologist*, Vol. 32 (July-September), pp. 193-199.

Ross, A.D.: 1961: *The Hindu Family in its Urban Setting*. Toronto: University of Toronto Press.

Ramu, G.N.: 1973: "Family structure and entrepreneurship: An Indian case". *Journal of Comparative Family Studies*, Vol. 4 (Autumn), pp. 240-56.

————: 1974: "Urban kinship ties in south India". *Journal of Marriage and the Family*, Vol. 36 (August), pp. 619-27.

Rao, M.S.A.: 1968: "Occupational diversification and joint household organization. *Contributions to Indian Sociology*, Vol. 2 (December), pp. 98-111.

Rao, N.J. Usha: 1973: "Family patterns in an urban setting: A case study in 'Pataliputra Colony', Patna (Bihar)". *Journal of Social Research*, Vol. 16 (September), pp. 35 52.

Roy, P.K.: "Industrialization and the 'fitness' of nuclear family". *Journal of Comparative Family Studies*, Vol. 5 (Spring), pp. 74-83.

————: 1983: "The structure and change of the family in India: A review of research and theory". *International Journal of Asian Studies*, Vol. 3, No.1, pp. 22-33.

————: 1984: "Extended kinship ties in Malaysia." *Journal of Comparative Family Studies*, Vol. 15, No. 2, pp. 175-94.

Sarma, J.: 1964: "The nuclearization of joint family households in West Bengal". *Man in India*, 44, pp. 193-206.

Sen, L.K.: 1965: "Family in four Indian villages". *Man in India*, Vol. 45, pp. 1-16.

Sengupta, S.: 1958: "Family organization in West Bengal: Its nature and dynamics". *Eonomic Weekly*, Vol. 10, pp. 384-89.

Shah, A.M.: 1968: "Changes in the Indian family: An examination of some assumptions". *Economic and Political Weekly*, Vol. 3, pp. 127-34.

————: 1974: *The Household Dimension of the Family in India*. Berkeley: University of California Press.

Singer, M.: 1968: "The Indian joint family in modern industry". pp. 423-52 (Eds.), in M. Singer and B. Cohn (Eds.), *Structure and Change in Indian Society*. Chicago: Aldine.

Vatuk, S.J.: 1971: "Trends in north Indian urban kinship: The matrilateral asymmetry hypothesis". *Southwestern Journal of Anthropology*, Vol. 27, pp. 287-307.

————: 1979: *Kinship and Urbanization*. Berkeley: California Press.

Vidyarthi, L.P.: 1969: *Cultural Configuration of Ranchi: Survey of an Emerging Industrial city of Tribal Bihar*. Calcutta: Bookland.

Yadava, J.S.: 1966: "Changing family structure in Delhi village, *The Anthropologist*, Vol. 13, pp. 21-29.

(Note: A part of this introduction has appeared in the International *Journal of Asian Studies*, Vol. 3, No. 1, 1983).

PART - I

FAMILY RELATIONS AND SOCIAL CHANGE

1

Industrialization and 'Fitness' of Nuclear Family: A Case Study

P.K. Roy

The Indian family is gradually modifying itself to 'fit' into the technological civilization structure. In this chapter attention is directed to the hypothesis that when large scale industrialization takes place, the family structure would move away from the extended type toward the nuclear type. But in this study the author is also concerned to see, not only whether extended families were increasingly giving place to nuclear families in the urban industrial areas, but also to what extent kinship has declined in importance in industrially affected rural and urban areas. The layout of this chapter contains the theoretical background of the study, the setting of the subjects studied, industrialization and family identification, attitudes towards family size, and lastly, a brief summary.

Theoretical Background

Whether the extended or joint family has undergone any changes due to industrialization and urbanization and whether the nuclear family is functional for urban industrial society, are questions which have received both theoretical and research interest in recent years. Two alternative views are held.

One school of thought argues that the nuclear family is functionally suited for urban industrial society. Many researchers

(Parsons, 1943, 1955, 1961; Ogburn and Nimkoff, 1950; Burgess and Locke, 1953; Weber, 1950; Goode, 1963, 1964, 1968) concentrate on this approach. Goode (1963, 1964) affirms that family systems throughout the world are generally moving in the direction of conjugal pattern, and notes the lack of 'fit' between the extended family and industrialization. He (1964: 109) notes that the integration of the family weakens because the wage job is an individualistic affair, and also because members of the kin group no longer live close together. Parsons (1949) seems to go further in suggesting that the isolated nuclear family is the only type, which is functional for urban industrial society. Stuckert (1960) notes that as industrialization has moved forward the individual is more likely to be able to make his own way without his kin. A number of studies in India show that the extended family is very important in rural areas and that the nuclear or conjugal family stands as a relatively independent unit in urban localities (Mandelbaum, 1957: 247; Beteille, 1964: 239; Morrison, 1959). Davis (1949), Loomis and Beegle (1951), and Burgess and Locke (1953) held that the disintegration of the extended family has proceeded further in the city than in the country. On this point, Davis (1949: 422-23) writing of the effects of industrialization on the family notes that "modern society, characterized by an elaborate industrial technology, a high degree of urbanisation, and a greater amount of geographical and social mobility, has sheered away the extended kinship bonds." Viewing industrialization, urbanization, education and occupational differentiation as new sources of change, Ross (1961: 28-31) anticipates gradual breakdown of the joint family and the emergence of the nuclear family. The relevance of these views to the situation which the author studied in India will be seen later. Some other views of the effects of industrialization and urbanization on the family structure will also be examined later in the chapter.

The second school of thought argues that the family has not changed as radically as has been argued by the first school. Along this line of investigation, S.M. Greenfield (1961) argues that the small nuclear family exists without industrialization and urbanization. Erwin H. Johnson (1960) questioned the hypothesis that the small nuclear family is brought about by industrialization and urbanization. After examining data from modern Japan he

(1960: 13) notes that the "traditional family, in fact, had not and does not have to give way under urban or industrial influences." Litwak (1969) suggests that occupational mobility due to industrialization has not destroyed the extended family. He (1969: 72-73) asserts that "because technological improvements in communications systems have minimised the socially disruptive forces of geographical distance and because an extended family can provide important aid to nuclear families without interfering with the occupational system", a sort of 'modified extended family' has survived. A few studies of the Western family, underline the supportive role of the bilateral extended kin in providing material aid, advice, and services both in everyday life and on special occasions (Bott, 1957; Mogey, 1956, 1964; Young and Willmott, 1957; Sussman and Burchinal, 1962).

These arguments have provided a continuing debate on the effects of modern forces on the extended and nuclear family in India and elsewhere. It is important to observe the change in different regions of India, and with the data thus collected, to make a comparative study in order to find the general trend. Let us compare a few studies. The observations made by Kapadia (1959) in his works in Bombay and Gujarat (western part of India), in the writings of Srinivas (1956), and Ross (1961) for the erstwhile state of Mysore and the city of Bangalore, respectively, the material available in Kurian's (1961) writing for Kerala (all these studies were conducted in south India), Desai (1964) for Mahuva and Morrison (1959) for Badlapur (west India), Gore's (1968) and Kapoor's (1965) observations near Delhi, all indicate with some variations in emphasis, a certain amount of change in the family structure and relationships.

Kapadia's different studies give information on such things as family size, family composition, and attributes to marriage and divorce. It would appear from a comparison that the change recorded in attitudes is probably greater in the present sample than in Kapadia's. Ross (1961), Gore (1968) and Kurian (1961) present some data to show the direction of familial change. Their data, especially on the position of women, family authority and aspirations show similar change with the author's data. Kapadia (1959), and Desai (1964) seem to assess their materials differently. They observe that the joint family has been affected by "the impact of various forces stemming from economic progress." But then Kapadia (1959:264) goes on to conclude, "Despite the clashes between different generations . . . there is a strong feeling for the joint family in the generation that is coming up." He also suggests that the joint family will make adjustments to change and survive 'the strains and stress'. Ross (1961:297), on the other hand, argues convincingly in her study of the Hindu urban family in India that "if a full complement of technological change impinges on the family structure, it will alter."

Desai (1964: 68-69) in his study of Mahuva, a town in south Gujarat, indicates that, except 5 per cent of the sample of 423 families, about 95 per cent of the families practise some kind of jointness, the percentage of various types being: 21 traditionally joint, 30 marginally joint, 17 joint in terms of property, and 27 joint by way of mutual obligations. He (p. 146) states that the greater jointness is associated with business and agricultural castes and people having new types of occupational relations have a lesser degree of jointness than those with traditional types. This is similar to the situation the author studied in India—those people having non-traditional occupations showed less favour for jointness. Desai indicates that common ownership of property is the main factor, which helps to maintain jointness. Long settled families showed a higher degree of jointness than the new immigrant families (p. 119). The actual types of family distribution in Mahuva are 61 per cent nuclear and 39 per cent joint. The reasons for family, separation are mainly due to occupational diversification and other circumstantial reasons rather than domestic quarrels (pp. 52-53).

Gore (1968) attempts to determine whether an increase in industrialization and urbanization leads to a greater acceptance of nuclear family norms. Gore's sample is based on 399 Aggarwal families in Delhi area, including urban and rural residents and some 'fringe' villages near the city. Responses were also obtained from 100 additional families of men in professions and office workers who did not follow the traditional occupations. These are not the families of the locally born, most of them are migrants from rural areas pursuing white-collar occupations in the city (pp. 90-91, 101-02). Their educational level was much higher than the average main sample. The population in the main sample (i.e., 399 Aggarwal families) follow their traditional occupations such as commerce, money-lending or allied occupations such as banking and stock market speculation. The level of education and the degree of occupational differentiation among them are low. They conform to the pattern of joint family living in behaviour, role perception and attitudes. The additional sample, however, indicates that urban residence, non-traditional occupations and education "do seem to introduce a certain measure of variation" (p. 232). These people showed less favour for joint family living.

Despite the differences in the appraisal of future trends, all these authors agree that some change is taking place in the joint family system in India because of occupational diversification.

The author does not refute the notion that the extended family is dysfunctional for the industrial system, nor does he maintain that the isolated nuclear family invariably emerges under the impact of industrialization and urbanization. What he has observed from the answers to questions about preference in family size and about kin recognition is that the majority (especially the urban people) were in favour of small families and indeed most of them were living in small family units during the time of the field investigation. The general trend, as observed in the present study, shows a desire for change. The author's own data support the ideas of the first school of thought as to the 'fitness' (Goode) of the nuclear family and to 'narrower range of kin recognition' (Parsons) to the industrial situation.

At present the Indian families are facing the full impact of the rapidly changing conditions which have accompanied growing industrialization. As Kurian (1961:129) points out, "better communications, education, and work outside the home as a result of the growth of towns and industries, have assisted the basic functions to transform themselves to fit into the newly developing social and economic structure." It is in the rural areas too, that the people are coming in close contact with urban influences. Many scholars (Dube, 1955; Beals, 1955; Barnabas, 1957; Bailey, 1957; Morrison, 1959) have done research in Indian villages and these studies suggest that most people do not live in joint families.

The Setting

This piece is concerned with the study of 725 rural and urban families in and around Ranchi—a city, in the eastern part of India. The process of industrialization at Ranchi is a recent development. The development of a heavy engineering factory, insulator factory and some other industries has contributed to changing the old Ranchi into an important industrial city. Industrialization has brought enormous changes in land use, population, economy and socio-cultural life. The most vitally affected were the inhabitants of 28 villages living on the site chosen for the construction of the heavy engineering factory, who had to be evacuated and resettled in a completely different place. This not only meant that they had to leave their houses and villages which had been established for several generations, but it also necessitated a change in their general pattern of life. In order to enable the economically and socially displaced people to work in the new industrial setting, the resettlement areas were located quite close to the industrial centre. The economic functions of the resettled families, in particular, were most directly and most radically affected by the technological development in Ranchi.

Of the 28 displaced villages, three resettlement villages, comprising a total of 391 families, were selected for the study, and a total of 693 persons interviewed. In addition, four villages of Ranchi which were not uprooted by the industrial project were selected for the study. These included 228 families. From these families, a total of 312 respondents were interviewed. It should be noted that the aim was not to conduct a community study of villages per se, but to draw data from communities in order to test some of the basic theoretical notions about the socio-economic impact of industrialization on families. In each family, the household head and those members who were working in the heavy engineering factory at the time of this survey were interviewed. An additional sample of 106 migrant families were randomly selected and a total of 225 persons interviewed. These people came from different parts of India for various types of skilled and unskilled work. Thus, a total of 1230 persons from 725 families were interviewed. This study is based on twelve months' fieldwork (from February 1964 to February 1965).

A questionnaire was used to obtain information. This questionnaire was prepared in the standard form of a structured, largely close-ended interview schedule. Many questions were open-ended, in an attempt to get more qualitative information. In this chapter important findings of other studies are reviewed so that the author's results might be placed within the total perspective of present knowledge of the effect of Industrial and technological change on the rural and urban families.

Industrialization and Family Identification

The main aim of this section is to examine the extent to which kinship has declined in importance in Ranchi and nearby industrially affected rural and urban areas. The traditionally strong family ties have been weakened because family members, like brothers and sisters, may be working in different and far distant places. Whereas previously the members of a family, all lived together in one house or in the same village or town, now they are widely scattered. This happened in Ranchi when the villagers had to leave their native villages and resettle in completely different places. Not ali members of one particular village resettled in the same area. Even some of the members of the same extended family went to different areas in search of jobs. These new nuclear families find and create new relationships with other people in the localities where they work and so gradually loosen their ties and contacts with their own families.

In the pre-industrialization period, the source of income was mainly from agriculture, and economic status and prestige depended on the size of arable land holdings. Due to sudden change in the economy, some people were attracted to new and economically advantageous occupations while others were forced to adapt to new types of jobs. The industrial occupation necessitates individual mobility, both physical and occupational, so relatives may be separated from one another both geographically and socially. Because of geographical mobility it is not possible to interact with a wider kin group. The geographical distribution of occupations may contribute indirectly to the breakup of the extended family relationships. Parsons (1949) suggests that occupational mobility is antithetical to extended family relations. LeMasters (1954) notes that families that have not experienced social class mobility are those families "in which the aged parents live with their grown children with considerable consensus and mutual enjoyment." Stuckert (1960) reports that vertical mobility is also associated with less visitation of extended families, less family identification, less use of family as a reference group and lesser concern for family unity. The author's own data support these views.

The following discussion on industrialization and family identification in and around Ranchi touches on all these different aspects of the above mentioned theoretical framework, though with varying degrees of emphasis. In this part of the research the independent variable is 'occupational mobility' and the dependent variable is what is called 'extended family identification'. The concept 'family identification' has been used to refer to the kin ties, the frequency of, kinds of, and occasions for contact, and the attributes of closeness and obligation. In the course of the fieldwork detailed information was collected on the frequency and type of contact between the respondents and their kin. All respondents were divided into two categories: those who had more contact, closeness and obligation with extended family were classified as 'high identification' and those who had lesser contact, proximity and obligation with extended family were classified as 'low identification'. The following tables test two hypotheses of the present study. Hypothesis I–that there will be a positive relationship between high occupational mobility and low identification with extended family, and, hypothesis II–that geographical distance, to some extent, leads to a loss of extended family identification.

TABLE 1

Occupational Mobility and Extended Family Identification

	Occupational Mobility[1]					
Extended Family	*High*		*Low*		*Total*	
Identification	*No.*	*Per cent*	*No.*	*Per cent*	*No.*	*Per cent*
High	240	19.5	310	25.2	550	44.7
Low	527	42.8	153	12.5	680	55.3
Total	767	62.3	46.3	37.7	1230	100.0

$X^2 = 129.9$

D.F. = 1

Level of significance = 0.05

The above table shows that persons with high occupational

mobility have a lower identification with their extended families than persons with low occupational mobility. Thus, in hypothesis I, in which persons of high occupational mobility are more likely to have less identification with extended family than those of low occupational mobility, is given support. Those who are in permanent jobs and have nothing to do with their place of origin appear to have a restricted range of contacts with their relatives because they seldom get adequate holidays to visit them and as a result their kinship network becomes loose-knit. The only exception is among those who make visits to aged parents who live alone and who have some work to do in the village during the agricultural season.

The following table shows that individuals who work in factories, far away from their hometowns, have less identification with the extended family than those who live close to their homes.

TABLE 2

The Geographical Distance and Extended Family Identification

Extended Family Identification	Geographical Mobility: Live Far Away No.	Per cent	Life Close No.	Per cent	Total No.	Per cent
High	30	2.4	520	42.3	550	44.7
Low	195	15.8	485	39.5	680	55.3
Total	225	18.2	1005	81.8	1230	100.0

X^2= 85.8

D.F. = 1

Level of significance – 0.05

Of the total respondents in this study, 42.3 per cent with relatives living close by received one or more family visits per month. In contrast, only 2.4 per cent of those with no such nearby relatives received visits this often. Thus, in hypothesis II, in which geographical distance does lead to a loss of extended family identification, is given support. Table 2 shows that those who are geographically distant from their relatives are not likely to retain their extended family identification. This result occurred whether they were high or low in their occupational mobility. This is a relatively strong confirmation of hypothesis II as mentioned above.

A considerable body of theory has arisen regarding the extended and nuclear families in both rural and urban areas in different parts of the world. Some of the relevant literature has already been discussed. There is also considerable literature showing the effects of industrialization and other modern forces on the extended family whether it is rural or urban. These theoretical propositions are relevant in the present study. Although the author has presented his findings mainly with reference to a specific locality, the processes appear relevant in a wider context.

Different scholars of family organization suggest that people are individualized in the city that they have little or no time to spend with members of their extended families. (Martindale and E. Monachesi, 1951; Bossard, 1948; Nimkoff, 1947; Ross, 1961). Moore (1965: 86) writes: "The principal cause of the breaking of large kinship organizations is the extensive mobility required by industrialization. This mobility is geographical, involving a concomitant physical separation of kinsmen." Linton (1949), Parsons (1943) and Bales (1955) also support the position that the nuclear family is highly functional in urban industrial society. Parsons suggests that the nuclear family system consisting of husband, wife and children is ideally suited to the demands of occupational and geographical mobility which are inherent in modern industrial society. The conclusion reached by different theorists are that demands associated with occupational and geographical mobility have brought about a family pattern in urban areas consisting of relatively isolated nuclear family units which operate without much support from the extended kinship system. Furthermore, the small nuclear family is ideally suited to meet the requirements of an industrial society for a mobile workforce. All these researchers make the point that individual members of the family participate in extended family activities less in urban areas than in rural areas and that there is consistent decline in such participation as one goes from rural to urban areas. These theoretical propositions by different authors support the two hypotheses of the present study that occupational and geographical mobility is antithetical to extended family relations in Ranchi.

Attitudes Toward Family Size

The previous section provided a broad outline of the effects of industrialization on family identification. This section views the same phenomena from a different angle. Here the emphasis is on the attitudes of the sample population towards family size. This section provides first, a brief description of the different sizes and membership patterns of households of the sample population, which will help us to see the differences in attitudes among the rural and urban respondents.

The data regarding the size and composition of the family indicate some differences among rural and urban sectors. The urban and migrant groups have typically nuclear characteristics: that is, small size of family. Let us now see the structure and size of the family of the present sample population. As mentioned earlier, the dominant pattern of family structure among the urban and migrant groups in the present sample is nuclear. A few families are seen as minimal extended which generally consisted of husband, and wife—parents and unmarried children. This is shown in Table 3.

Having described the actual family size, it is of interest now to consider the attitudes of the sample population towards family size. Respondents were asked which type of family they would prefer–large or small. To begin with, it was found that there was a difference in the way in which the rural people responded to this question as compared to local urban and in-migrant respondents. Some respondents from rural areas (especially older people) were in favour of extended family living, whereas, the respondents from local urban and migrant groups preferred to have nuclear families (see Table 4). As was expected, the migrant group was mostly composed of nuclear families, who had left their parents and other dependent family members in their native places. Table 4 shows the differences in their attitudes.

TABLE 3

Distribution of Size of Families According to Rural and Urban Sectors

Size of Family	*Migrants*		*Local Urban*		*Rural*	
	No.	*Per cent*	*No.*	*Per cent*	*No.*	*Per cent*
1-3	55	51.8	84	21.5	25	10.9
4-6	45	42.5	167	42.7	104	45.6
7-9	6	5.7	103	26.4	71	31.2
10 and above	—	—	37	9.4	28	12.3
Total	106	100.0	391	100.0	228	100.0

TABLE 4
Perference in Family size

Preference	*Migrants*		*Local Urban Group*		*Rural Group*	
	No.	*Per cent*	*No.*	*Per cent*	*No.*	*Per cent*
Nuclear	210	93.3	510	73.5	127	40.7
Large	15	6.7	183	26.5	185	59.3
Total	225	100.0	693	100.0	312	100.0

These figures show that immigrant and urban people are relatively more eager to have a nuclear family. Preference for small size also varies with the nature of a person's job. Preferences for small size families are much higher among permanent workers than among seasonal or temporary workers. These, in turn, have higher preferences for living in small families than those who are unemployed. The unemployed who cannot afford to live by, themselves, prefer to stay with other members of their family. The permanent workers are far more satisfied with their existing small families. It is of interest to compare those who want to live in a nuclear family with those who want to stay with different members in a large family. Informants, who were most keen to have smaller families, in most cases, had permanent jobs. Low income respondents were less willing to have this. Age also affects people's attitudes to family living, and the desirability and the nature of change. Some older people preferred to live in large families. They do not want to lose their extended family identification. Younger people on the other hand, expressed a wish for small families and most of them preferred to live in towns rather than in the villages.

If we analyse the reasons for choosing a nuclear family unit, we see that city residents find it more difficult to allow relatives to stay with them owing to the limited facilities for accommodating them in the city and the high rents demanded to get a housing large enough for an extended family. This is not a problem of great magnitude for the rural residents, as life in the village is much simpler and accommodation is fairly easy to obtain. The change of attitude in the urban and immigrant groups is to be expected but many rural people also showed a strong liking for small nuclear families. Not only that, the movement of persons from one place to another has rapidly increased due to industrialization. Migration—seasonal and of long duration, always takes place which helps the family to break down to nuclear type. Table 5 gives the breakdown of the reasons for choosing a nuclear family unit.

TABLE 5
Reasons for Choosing the Nuclear Family

Reasons	*Migrants*		*Local Urban*		*Rural*	
	No.	*Per cent*	*No.*	*Per cent*	*No.*	*Per cent*
Shortage of accommodation and high rents	59	28.0	206	40.4	5	3.9
Easy to support each member	52	24.8	92	18.1	47	37.1
Greater freedom	42	20.0	90	17.6	30	23.6
To give more attention to children	37	17.6	82	16.1	22	17.3
Easy to move	20	9.6	40	7.8	23	18.1
Total	210	100.0	510	100.0	127	100.0

Economic factors have probably been the main cause for the increasing number of family separations. As Ross (1961: 41) mentioned, "the inability of the land to support the growing population has forced many sons to leave home to seek their livelihood in the growing cities". Freedom from interference by other family members is another cause of the separation of the extended family household and preference for the nuclear or small family. This leads to another important reason for choosing the nuclear family—to avoid conflict between family members arising out of jealousy and quarrels. Kapadia (1959) gives evidence that the introduction of certain social security programmes such as pensions, provident funds, savings in banks and post office, sale of insurance, has given the individual a little more security and in turn diminishes his dependence on the joint family. The small size of the family has an important bearing on the process of industrialization and the willingness of the present sample population to accept and initiate change. The most important characteristic of the ideal-type nuclear family is that it excludes a wide range of kin groups from its everyday affairs. The couple cannot count on a large number of kinsmen for help, just as these latter cannot call on the couple for services. As Goode notes, the ideal type of conjugal family demonstrably does 'fit' the central demands of an industrial system. He (1968:242) goes on to say that "an individual with a limited kin network is facilitated in selecting the industrial job best suited to his skill. He can invest only in himself, not in his kin. He can change his style of life more easily". The accepted notions of strong family ties thus show growing weakness. This weakness is more clearly demonstrated through the attitudes of some of the people who have relatives staying with them.

Summary

In this chapter an examination has been made of the impact of industrialization on rural and urban families in and around Ranchi. In the discussion of industrialization and family change, case material has been presented and the general trend as observed in the present study, shows a desire for change, and this has materialised to some extent due to changes in the different spheres of the lives of the people. The relevance of the 'fitness' of the nuclear family and the 'narrower range of kin recognition' which have developed have also been considered. The extensive mobility, both geographical and economic, the weakening of extended family identification and the reshaping of the family form into a nuclear type as a consequence of industrialization are shown in the present investigation.

The findings have been presented mainly with reference to a particular area of India, yet the changes that were observed have parallels in other parts of India too. Goode (1963) notes that family, change in India is not yet great but the direction of the change is clear, a greater emphasis being laid on the conjugal bond. Much of Goode's argument is applicable to the present study. The new ways of earning a living and widespread education are affecting people's ideas about their families.

Notes

1. 'Occupational mobility,' has been measured here in two ways: (a) comparing the occupations of the respondents and the respondent's father and (b) relation of last occupation of the sample wage earners before moving to the present occupation. To measure the occupational mobility, all respondents were divided into two categories: (1) High occupational mobility: Those who have

changed their occupations from agriculture to non-agriculture, manual to non-manual, semi-skilled to skilled, clerical to administrative. It involves significant change in income and prestige. (2) Low occupational mobility: Those who have changed their occupations from agriculture, labour, sweeper, domestic servants and other traditional occupations to unskilled manual work. It does not involve significant change in income and prestige.

2. Mainly migrants. It may be expected that the migrant who came to Ranchi from elsewhere may not maintain closer and more intimate ties with those relatives who remained in the previous place of residence.
3. Since the chi square value of 129.9 for Table 1 and 85.8 for Table 2 is beyond the required limit of 3.841 (on 0.05 significance level) we conclude that the observed value is much greater than the expected frequency and the finding is consistent with the research hypothesis that occupational and geographical mobility reduces extended family contact.

REFERENCES

Bailey, F.G.: 1957. *Caste and the Economic Frontier*. Manchester: Manchester, University Press.

Barnabas, A.P.: 1957: "Patterns of Rural Family." *Bulletin of the Christian Institute for the Study of Society*, Vol. 4.

Beals, A.R.: 1955: "Interplay, Among Factors of Change in a Mysore Village," in *McKim Marriott (ed.), Village India*. Chicago: Chicago University Press.

Beteille. A.: 1964: "Family and Social Change in India and South Asian Countries." *Economic Weekly*, 16.

Bossard, J.H.S.: 1948: *The Sociology of Child Development*. New York: Harper.

Bott, E.: 1957: *Family and Social Network*. London: Tavistock Publications.

Burgess, E.W. and H.J. Locke: 1953: *The Family*. New York: American Book Company.

Davis, K.: 1949: *Human Society*. New York: Macmillan.

Desai, I.P.: 1964: *Some Aspects of Family in Mahuva*. Bombay: Asia Publishing House.

Dube, S.C.: 1955: *Indian Village*, London: Routledge and Kegan Paul.

Goode, W.J.: 1963: *World Revolution and Family Patterns*. New York: The Free Press.

————: 1964: *The Family,* New Jersey: Prentice-Hall Inc., Englewood Cliffs.

————: 1968: "*Industrialisation* and *Family Change,*" in B.F. Hoselitz and W.E. Moore (eds.), *Industrialisation and Society*. UNESCO: Mouton.

Gore, M.S.: 1968: *Urbanisation and Family Change*. New York: Humanities Press.

Greenfield, S.M.: 1961: "Industrialisation and the Family in Sociological Theory." *American Journal of Sociology*, 67.

Johnson, E.H.: 1960: "The Stem Family and its Extensions in Modern Japan." (Paper presented at the Annual Meeting of the American Anthropological Association, Minneapolis, Minnesota).

Kapadia, K.M.: 1959: *Marriage and Family in India*. Bombay: Oxford.

Kapoor, S.: 1965: "Family and Kinship Groups Among the Khatris in Delhi." *Sociological Bulletin,* 14.

Kurian, G.: 1961: *The Indian Family in Transition*. Mouton and Co.

LeMasters, E.E.: 1954: "Social Class Mobility and Family Integration." *Marriage and Family Living*, 16.

Linton, R., 1949: "The Natural History of the Family," in R.N. Anshen (ed.), *The Family: Its Function and Destiny*. New York: Harper.

Litwak, E.: 1969: "Geographic Mobility and Extended Family Cohesion," in J.N. Edwards (ed.), *The Family and Change*. New York: Alfred A. Knopf.

Loomis. P. and J.A. Beegle: 1951, *Rural Social System*. New York: Prentice-Hall Inc., Englewood Cliffs.

Mandelbaum, D.: 1957, "The Family in India," in *Introduction to Civilization of India; Changing Dimensions of Indian Society and Culture*. Chicago: University of Chicago Press.

Martindale, D. and E. Monachesi: 1951, *Elements of Sociology*. New York: Harper.

Mogey, J.M.: 1956, *Family and Neighbourhood*. Oxford: Oxford University Press.

————: 1964, "Family and Community in Urban Industrial Societies," *in H.T. Christensen (ed.), Handbook of Marriage and the Family.* Chicago: Rand McNally and Co.

Moore, W. E.: 1965: *The Impact of Industry*. New Jersey,: Prentice-Hall Inc., Englewood Cliffs.

Morrison, W.A., 1959: "Family Types in Badlapur: An Analysis of a Changing Institution in a Maharashtrian Village." *Sociological Bulletin*, 8.

Nimkoff, M.: 1947: *Marriage and Family*. New York: Houghton Mifflin.

Obgurn, W.F. and M.F. Nimkoff: 1950, *Sociology*. Boston: Houghton Mifflin.

———: 1949: "The Social Structure of the Family," in R.N. Anshen (ed.), *The Family: Its Function and Destiny*. New York: Harper and Row.

Parsons, T. and R.M. Bales: 1955: *Family Socialisation and Process*. Glencoe, Illinois: The Free Press.

Parsons, T.: 1943: "The Kinship System of the Contemporary United States." *American Anthropologist*, 45.

———: 1961: Introduction to Part Two: "Differentiation and Variation in Social Structures," in T. Parsons et al (ed.), *Theories of Society*. New York: The Free Press.

Ross, A.D.: 1961: *The Hindu Family in its Urban Setting* Toronto: University of Toronto Press.

Srinivas, M.N.: 1956, "Industrialisation and Urbanisation of Rural Areas." *Sociological Bulletin*, V. No. 2.

Stuckert, R.P.: 1960: "Occupational Mobility and Family Relationships," in N.W. Bell and E.F. Vogel (eds.), *A Modern Introduction to Family*. London: Routledge and Kegan Paul.

Sussman, M.B. and L.G. Burchinal: 1962, "Kin Family Network: Unheralded Structure in Current Conceptualisations of Family Functioning." *Marriage and Family Living*, 24.

Weber, Max: 1950, *General Economic History*. Glencoe, Illinois: The Free Press.

Young, M. and P. Willmott: 1957: *Family and Kinship in East London*. London: Routledge and Kegan Paul.

2

Structure and Organization of Indian Family: The Emerging Patterns

Smt. Kuntesh Gupta

A characteristic feature of family studies in India since 1955 onwards has been to classify the structure and organization of families into several family patterns, rather than following a simple dichotomy of joint and nuclear families or a simple trichotomy of joint, transitional and nuclear families. This practice was adopted by scholars for reasons of the difficulties involved in defining the joint or the nuclear family. Moreover, it was commonly observed that the traditional joint family was undergoing characteristic changes, but doubts were expressed whether it was transforming into western type nuclear family. To resolve this problem some scholars preferred to talk of the extended family as also of transitional family. But scholars did not agree on the precise definitions of either extended family or transitional family or nuclear family. Some preferred to term a changing family structure as "intermediate family". Anthropologists avoided to use the term "joint" or "nuclear" but preferred the use of "joint extended family" and "elementary family". Scholars like Mayer (1960) and Chauhan (1957) preferred the use of "kutumb" in preference to joint or extended types of family structures. Chauhan stressed the usage of "unit family" to designate what the members of a local society considered their own family to be (1957:38). This term was meant by him to indicate all the variations of nuclear family either in the manner of its extensions or depletions which were considered in the village setting to reflect the villager's idea of that unit and its role in the community.

This tendency resulted in giving up the traditional concept of Hindu joint family as also rejecting the pure type of nuclear family. Instead, attempts were made in all subsequent studies dating back to 1955 or 1956, to classify families into varying patterns, either based on residence or kinship, or generation depth or marriage or family relationships, or a mixture of these patterns.

Therefore, if one wants to get an idea of the structure and organization of Indian family, as it is emerging over the past decades, it is no longer valid for him to think in terms of joint or nuclear or extended or transitory types of families. One can get an idea about the Indian family system of today only in terms of varying and emerging patterns of family living. An attempt has been made here to review the various family patterns as adopted by Indian scholars of the past two decades towards an understanding of the emerging structure and organization of Indian family.

The ball for rejecting the old style joint family was set rolling by Desai (1955: 97-106), who subjected to severe criticism the census data on family types. He expressed the view that the opinions about the joint family today were largely the subjective reflections of the individuals based on extremely limited and partial observations and largely conditioned by the socio-economic strata to which they belonged. To substantiate his point, he referred to the census publications. The Census Commissioner of India gave the following percentage of different types of households for the whole of India :

Type of Household	*Number of Household in a Typical Village*	*Typical Town*
Small	33	38
Medium	44	41
Large	17	16
Very Large	6	5
Total	100	100

His observations on the above table were as follows:

Of the four types, medium households were the most numerous, which was what one would expect. That very large households with 10 or more members (numbering only about one in sixteen was) also not unexpected. But it seemed a little surprising that every third household in a village should be a 'small household' with three members or less. Such a large proportion of small households was a prima facie indication that families did not continue to be 'joint' according to the traditional custom of the country and the habit of breaking away from the joint family and setting up separate households was quite strong (Census 1951, I, Pt. I-A: 50). Desai criticized this view on two counts: (1) that the statistics indicated that the joint family was still the major type of family structure in India (1955: 116); and (2) that the size of the household was not a valid indicator of whether it contained a nuclear or joint family (1956: 144). Desai detected similar faults in Bombay Census data as also in other census reports.

Therefore, Desai (1956) collected data of about 25,000 inhabitants living in about 4,800 households in a small town in Saurashtra and showed that it was the relationship between the members of a household among themselves and with those of another household that determined the type of the family of that household. He selected a few such relationships such as kinship, generation depth, property, income and the mutual cooperation. He called a household a nuclear family if it was composed of a group of parents and their unmarried children or of the husband, wife and unmarried children, unrelated to their other kin through or by property or income or the rights and obligations pertaining to them and as are expected of those related by kinship. He called that household a joint family which had greater generation depth (i.e. three or more) than the nuclear family and the members of which were related to one another by property, income and mutual rights and obligations. The members might be related collaterally or lineally. In between these two he distinguished three more groups: (1) A household which was nuclear family in composition, but which was related to another nuclear or joint family in all or some of these respects in which the members of a joint family were usually related. (2) A household, the members of which were nuclear in composition and who were unrelated through property or income, but by other rights and obligations to another nuclear or joint family with which ties of kinship obtained. (3) A household which consisted of either father or mother only living with a married son or daughter with or without children or a group consisting of father and mother with married sons without children having property and income in common. Each of these types, including the joint family, will have sub-types according to the kin with whom they had relationship and also according to the marital status of sons of the head of the household.

On the basis of the above classification Desai concluded that the husband-wife-children group was predominant in the residential and compositional pattern of the families. He also concluded that the criteria of co-residence, commensality, size and the relations within the household were not very significant. What mattered was the property, income, and the rights and obligations between persons within the household and the kin without it. (Desai, 1956: 156). Regarding the radius of kinship relations coming within the circle of jointness, Desai found the lineal depth of relationship being largely among father, son, and grandson. The collateral relationships were found between a man and his paternal uncle and his own brothers (1956: 156).

Mention may here be made of the village studies conducted by Dube (1955), Morrison (1959), Gould (1959, 1966) and Lewis (1960). These studies used fewer categories of family types. They mostly depended upon the classification of nuclear family and joint family. Lewis (1958), however, added a category of "single person" family and another of "supplemental collateral" (one parent with married sons). In these studies 120, 641, 43 and 150 families were studied respectively. These studies revealed that in the Gangetic plain area, there were 54 to 56 per cent joint (with supplemented nuclear) families, while in Central India, this percentage was 14 to 18.5 per cent and 14 per cent respectively.

Kulkarni (1960) studied family patterns in Gokak Taluka in the Belgaum district. The Taluka was divided in eight zones. He studied only four zones, which differed from one another not only in their geographical environment, but also in density of population, in occupational structure and the caste patterns. In all 1401 family heads were interviewed on a 5 per cent random sample basis. For purpose of his analysis, Kulkarni made a distinction between joint and separated families on the basis of property ownership, between the members of two or more generations in a family such as ego, his son and his grandson all being major and earning members and/or married staying together under one roof or between male siblings who were major and earning members and/or married. Thus, he designated a separate family as one in which the movable and immovable property and residence were not shared in common and that a legal separation of property had taken place resulting also in the separation of residence. Both joint and separate families were broken into 14 patterns: Head with (1) wife and children only; (2) parent or parents; (3) father's brother and or his wife; (4) brother and or unmarried sister; (5) married brother and his family; (6) married son and his family; (7) parents with brother and or unmarried sister; (8) parents with married brother; (9) parents with brother and married son; (10) parents with married son; (11) married brother and son; (12) sister and widowed daughter; (13) sister's children; and (14) others. Kulkarni found that, of these fourteen categories of the family composition in the four zones, the first eleven had persons related to the head of the family directly. The last three referred to unusual circumstances. The nuclear family consisting of the head, his wife and their children was found to be common to all the thirteen categories. It was found that the nuclear family, considering all the 14 categories, was the single majority type in all the zones. Next to nuclear family, it was the nuclear family with ego's parent or parents that was the highest (17.1 per cent). The third and fourth in numerical strength were those where ego and his married son and his family stayed together and where married brothers stayed together without the parents in more families than with parents in all the zones (1960: 80-81).

Leela Dube (1960) in her study of families in northern Madhya Pradesh villages suggested a different model of family classification. She considered residence as the determining factor. People sharing a common residence constitutes a household. She classified families as: (1) Simple family consists of father, mother and children. (2) Incomplete family, missing any of the three components of the simple family. It may be composed of the conjugal unit or may be disintegrated simple family. The family might also have some adjuncts and or adhesions. The adhesions were the remnants of an earlier larger group. The adjuncts were those who did not belong to the patrilineal family. They might be affinal relatives, or the married daughters who might come back to reside with parents after being widowed or divorced. (3) Compound family and (4) Extended family formed by extensions of the simple family or the compound family. The extensions might be both vertical and lateral.

Driver (1962:119) also felt that our findings about family structures in India were likely to be influenced by the manner in which we defined a joint family. He classified family structure into nuclear and joint, but sub-divided them further into simple and complex types on the basis of their composition. The simple nuclear family consisted of head male and his wife. The complex nuclear family included one parent. The simple joint family had three categories, consisting, in addition to head male and spouse, of (i) both parents, (ii) either brother(s) or son(s); (iii) either brother(s) or son(s) and one parent. The complex joint family consisted of, in addition to head male and his spouse, of (i) brother(s) and son(s); (ii) brother(s), son(s) and one parent; (iii) both parents, and either brother(s) or son(s) and (iv) both parents, brother(s) and son(s). Driver (1962:115) studied 2314 couples of Nagpur District and found that the joint family structure was not widespread in Central India. The joint family was usually found to be simple in form i.e., one consisting of the couple and one other married pair (either collateral or lineal of the male head). Furthermore, joint family was found to be less prominent among younger couples and highly educated people than older people and those without education.

Basu (1962) studied 285 families in Kanchanpur village of Bardhaman District, West Bengal. He classified families into: (1) single person; (2) sub-nuclear; (3) nuclear; (4) lineal and lineal-collateral; (5) collateral joint; and (6) other joint (which included a married daughter or married sister's family). He found that the proportion of joint families was 39 per cent.

Gore (1968) attempted to differentiate between joint and nuclear families in their behaviour patterns and attitudes. He felt that the division of families into joint and nuclear was somewhat crude and arbitrary. Therefore, on some points, he made a further distinction between lineal and joint families (where the eldest male was the father of the adult males) and the fraternal joint families (where the eldest male was the eldest of the brothers). He found that in some attributes the joint and the nuclear families differed in their distributions (1968: 229-230). Thus he identified the following basic types of household relationships: (1) husband, wife and unmarried children (pure nuclear); (2) husband, wife, children and unmarried and non-earning brothers (regarded as 'nuclear'); (3) husband, wife, children, with widowed mother as dependent or with other dependents who were not coparceners ('nuclear'); (4) husband, wife, children (married and unmarried) (father-son of lineal joint family); (5) husband, wife, children (unmarried and married) and unmarried brothers (fraternal joint family); (6) husband, wife, married sons, married brothers and their families, i.e., combination of 'lineal' and 'fraternal' joint families (1968:94). In an earlier study (1962) he identified family types as: (1) rural nuclear; (2) rural joint; (3) fringe nuclear; (4) fringe joint; (5) urban immigrant joint; (6) urban immigrant nuclear; (7) urban local nuclear; and (8) urban joint.

Gore (1968: 235) studied 499 families and found that in the urban areas and among more educated groups in India the fraternal joint family was less common than the lineal joint family. The nuclear household, immediately upon marriage, was not commonly established. Such households were established only as a result of family division after the death of parents or as a result of migration to the city. He suggested that fraternal or collateral joint family was never the most common form of the family.

Das and Banerjee (1963:16-18) provided nine categories for the classification of tribal families. These are: (1) nuclear; (2) vertical extended; (3) lateral extended; (4) vertical lateral; (5) nuclear and adhesion; (6) vertical extended with adhesion; (7) lateral with adhesion; (8) intermediary and (9) broken.

The authors collected data about 3141 tribals living in 554 households in three zones, in various districts of West Bengal in 1962. They found that most of the tribal families belonged to nuclear type, consisting of husband, wife and their unmarried children. The second predominant group was the vertical extended families. In one zone of the State, however, nuclear family unit, consisting of husband and wife was more prevalent, particularly amongst Bhil tribes as Babhas and Lepchas, etc., who lived separately with separate kitchen after marriage.

Sarma (1964: 200) identified (1) nuclear families which included single-person and supplemented nuclear where unmarried brother or sister of married brother was present; (2) joint families with parents which included lineal-collateral, supplemented collateral, supplemented nuclear where only one married son and one parent were present; (3) joint families with brothers (collateral joint), and (4) joint families with others i.e., relatives of wife cr mother. Her sample was based on 593 families in four villages in Bardhaman district in West Bengal. She found that in all the four villages, the nuclear type was most common (56 per cent). Only 28 per cent families were joint with parents, 10 per cent joint with brothers and 6 per cent with others.

Bandyopadhyay and Chattopadhyay (1964:25) suggested the following classification of families: (1) 'male' single-member type; (2) 'female' single-member type; (3) conjugal type; (4) sibling type; (5) elementary; (6) joint; (7) male single-member with kin; (8) female single-member with kin; (9) conjugal with kin; (10) sibling with kin; (11) elementary family type with kin; (12) joint with kin; and (13) kindred.

A number of studies on family structure were conducted by the Human Factor Studies of the Central Arid Zone Research Institute, Jodhpur, Rajasthan (Bose and Saxena, 1964b, 1965a and 1965b; Malhotra and Sen, 1964) . In studies of two districts, Jalor and Barmer, the term "joint" family was used to include supplemented nuclear families and the "nuclear" to include single-person and sub-nuclear households. In both districts the proportions of joint families were found to be close to, but somewhat less than half. Since these figures also included supplemented nuclear families, it could be assumed that considerably less than one-half were joint families. In another study of a village Korna, 36 miles from Jodhpur, Bose, Malhotra and Bharara (1963:122) found that the proportion of joint families was somewhat higher in Korna than Jalor district.

Pakrasi (1965) classified family types as: (1) non-familial unit (man); (2) non-familial unit (woman); (3) conjugal; (4) elementary; (5) extended; (6) non-familial (man) complex; (7) non-familial (woman) complex; (8) conjugal complex; (9) elementary complex, and (10) extended complex. Jha and Chatterjee (1965: 64-72) in their study of seven families in a polyandrous community of Dehradun, found that four families were living in traditional extended households consisted of grandfather, grandmother, married sons, their wives and children. In the remaining three families, only two generations were living together.

Sen (1965: 1-16) investigated 609 families of four isolated villages of West Bengal and classified families into nuclear and extended types. The nuclear families outnumbered the extended types.

Madan (1965) instead of classifying families preferred to classify households as follows: (1) Single-member households; (2) Two-member households; (3) One parent and his or her children; (4) Nuclear families; (5) Household in a transitional phase between nuclear and extended families; (6) Pattern families; (7) Surviving kin from paternal extended families after the grandfather's death; (8) Families in a transitional phase likely to grow into fraternal-extended families; and (9) Fraternal extended families. He found that a large number (29 to 30 per cent) of Kashmiri pandits lived in fraternal-extended families and the next (26 per cent) lived in supplemental nuclear families, lying between nuclear and extended types. There were also cases where the family was composed of a head, his married son or sons or son's wives, and unmarried children.

Kapoor (1965: 54-63) classified household composition on the basis of generation depth and lateral extension as follows: (1) one generation; (2) two generation units; (3) three generation units; (4) four generation units; (5) two or more brothers and their unmarried children; and (6) two brothers, their father's brother's widows and their brother.

Ahuja (1966:31) studied 415 Bhil families and classified into (1) independent nuclear; (2) dependent nuclear; (3) small-size joint; and (4) intermediate-size joint. He subdivided dependent nuclear families further into (a) those families where dependence was because of joint tilling of land; and (b) those families where there was no joint tilling but the members were subservient to the leadership and authority of the ancestors. He considered a nuclear family, as independent if the family of procreation was neither subject to the authority of any of his relatives nor economically dependent upon them. He found that the dependent family was the dominant type among the Bhils (77.1 per cent).

Bose (1966: 169) classified nuclear families into (a) uni-member; (b) husband wife; (c) husband, wife with children; and (d) widowed head with children. Of 274 such families, 230 were found to be of the husband-wife with children type. Then he distinguished between families with additional kin of (a) widowed parents; (b) wives and children of married sons with/without parent; (c) sisters and brothers without their spouses and children with/without parent; (d) sisters and brothers without their wives and children and brothers with their wives and children with/without parent; and (e) others (including relatives in addition to above). Of 530 such families the greatest number (115) was those families with additional kin of wives and children of married sons with/without parent.

Sengupta (1966:217) studied 177 Mahali families of 12 villages in Midnapur district. He classified families into (1) elementary; (2) joint/ extended; (3) intermediate; and (4) polygynous. He found that the elementary family was the most dominant type (72-81 per cent).

Berreman (1963:150) in his study of 79 families of a polygynous community in Sirkanda of Sub-Himalayan region in U.P. indicated that a simple polygynous family was composed of a man, his two wives and their unmarried children. A supplemented polygynous family was composed of simple polygynous family plus some unmarried, widowed, and divorced relatives of the head or of his wives, other than their unmarried children. A sub-polygynous family was usually composed of a woman, one of the wives of a man living elsewhere (perhaps with his other wife), and her unmarried children. A supplemented sub-polygynous was such a household plus an unmarried, divorced, or widowed relatives other than one of the children. A polygynous lineal or collateral household included at least one component family composed of a man and two wives. Berreman found that 33 per cent of families living in less than nuclear type, 24 per cent in nuclear and 16 percent in supplemented families.

Mayer (1960) also adopted an almost similar classification in his study of 196 families of Ramkheri village in Madhya Pradesh, except he did not consider the supplemented sub-nuclear, supplemented sub-polygynous, supplemented polygynous, polygynous and lineal, polygynous and collateral, lineal collateral and supplemented lineal-collateral types. He found that 41.5 per cent of the families were nuclear and 18 per cent were supplemented nuclear type.

Gough (1956) and Ray (1956) classified families into (1) single person; (2) nuclear; (3) supplemented nuclear; and (4) joint. Ray included some supplemented families also under the 'joint' category.

Hitchcock (1956), Kolenda (1968) and Mencher (1962) classified families as (1) supplemental lineal collateral; (2) lineal collateral; (3) lineal; (4) supplemental lineal; (5) supplemented collateral; (6) collateral; (7) supplemental nuclear; (8) nuclear; (9) supplemented sub-nuclear; (10) sub-nuclear; (11) single-person; and (12) other. While Kolenda found a case of supplemental sub-nuclear family in her study of untouchable of Khalapar, Hitchcock and Mencher did not find any of this type in their studies of Rajputs of Khalapar and Nayyars of Angadi village in Kerala respectively. The collateral type was absent in Kolenda's study and present in Hitchcock's. Again, lineal and supplemental lineal was common in Hitchcock's and Mencher's studies but not found by Kolenda. Hitchcock mentioned supplemental lineal collateral only. These authors found that nuclear (36 per cent) and supplemental nuclear (25 per cent) were predominant family types among Rajputs and Chuhras (38 percent and 32 per cent respectively) and lineal type among Nayyars (42 per cent and 29 per cent in two different tracts).

Cohen (1961) and Singh (1962) classified families into lineal, collateral, other joint, nuclear, and single-person types. The data revealed a large difference between the Thakurs and Chamars in the proportion of collateral joint families.

Shahani (1961) studied 258 high school students from three large high castes in Baroda: the Brahmins, Baniyas and Patidars. They classified families into nuclear, supplemental sub-nuclear, sub-nuclear, and joint. It was found that there was high proportion of joint families among the Patidars (66 per cent) and the low proportion among the Baniyas (37 per cent) while 43 percent of the Brahmins were living in joint families.

Woodruff (1959) and Dumont (1967) studied 207 families among untouchable Paraiyans of Bangalore and 26 families of Pramalai Kallar of Madurai district. They classified families as (1) single-person; (2) sub-nuclear; (3) nuclear; (4) supplemental nuclear; (5) joint, and (6) other. They found that nuclear family was the dominant type.

The above review of about 22,500 Indian families in different parts and communities of the country, shows the tendency among scholars to classify families into varying types. The 'joint' family has not been taken as the broad and single category for purposes of analysis but broken into several units. These units are (1) collateral joint family; (2) supplemental collateral joint family; (3) lineal joint family; (4) supplemental lineal joint family; (5) lineal collateral joint family; (6) supplemental lineal-collateral joint family; (7) small size joint; (8) intermediate size joint; (9) fraternal; (10) fraternal joint; (11) lineal-fraternal joint; (12) other joint. Similarly 'nuclear' category has been classified into several sub-categories, such as: (1) pure nuclear of the single-person–either 'male' or 'female' type; (2) nuclear; (3) supplemental nuclear; (4) sub-nuclear; (5) supplemental sub-nuclear; (6) incomplete; (7) conjugal; (8) sibling; (9) 'male' or 'female' single-person with kin; (10) conjugal with kin; (11) sibling with kin; (12) two-member type; (13) transitional; (14) surviving kin; (15) independent nuclear; (16) dependent nuclear; (17) widowed members and children; etc. Evidently many of these categories overlap and could be collapsed into a few broad sub-categories.

Families have also been classified according to extensions, such as vertical extension and lateral extension, with or without adhesions.

The above review of studies of varying types of families suggests that the traditional Hindu joint family changing into other type of nuclear families. The findings of about 22,500 families show that it is the nuclear or elementary type, which is emerging in modern India. Only in very few cases, lineal joint family or vertical extended family and fraternal-extended types were found. Where joint families were found to be common, it included nuclear, supplemented nuclear or supplemented sub-nuclear categories, thus rendering the traditional 'joint' category quite obsolete and breaking away.

But it would be a mistake to take these family types as various family patterns. In fact, a 'family pattern' is characterized by a number of roles, which are different from the roles of members in other family patterns. Thus, in India, one finds families of different patterns (Karve: 1964: 47). The majority of people have a patrilineal, patrilocal family. Whereas, in the extreme south-west of Kerala and the Kasi Hills in the north-east, one finds matrilineal families. In the case of the patrilineal family, various patterns are followed as regard number of mates and the types of mates. Among the cis-Himalayan tribes, Todas of Nilgiri Hills and Asari caste of Kerala, "patrilocal polyandrous" families are found. In North India, in the States of Punjab, U.P., Bihar, Bengal, Assam, Orissa, parts of M.P., Rajasthan and Gujarat, the patrilineal family is patrilocal and rules of marriage do not allow marriages of blood relatives upto at least the third generation either in the father's or the mother's line. Some parts of Maharashtra, Gujarat, Orissa, M.P., Andhra Pradesh, Tamil Nadu, Karnatak, Kerala have also a patrilineal and patrilocal family. This type of family, however, differs from that of the north in one fundamental respect. The only rule of marriage is not to marry outside one's own clan, and quite close relatives very often marry each other.

In Kerala, the family is matrilineal and matrilocal. A family consists of a woman, her siblings (her brothers and sisters), her own children and children of the sisters and the children of the female descendants. No spouses either of the males or the females form a regular part of the household. No instance of polyandry was noticed among such matrilineal families (Karvey, 1964: 50). In north-east India, the Khasi matrilineal family differs from the matrilineal family of Kerala, as much as that a man after his marriage comes to live in his wife's village with his wife's family. After a few years, the husband and wife build a separate 'hut' but the husband maintains his wife and children, though his mother has rights over his acquired property and on his death he is buried along with his mother's family in the mother's village only.

The family pattern of the Muslims of India more or less tends to be like that of the region in which they dwell. The same can be said of Christians in India.

The characteristic of "jointness" varies from one family pattern to another. Thus, in patrilineal group, a Hindu joint family consists of a man and his brothers, all their wives, their married sons with their wives and children and the unmarried daughters in each generation. Again, in many cases, even when the family members live together, status considerations tend to arise within the family depending on the property share of different branches of the family.

Greater emphasis has been laid by the family sociologists to study this feature of "jointness" of the family, irrespective of its pattern, under varying conditions of change. Goode (1963) has held that most parts of the world are undergoing a family revolution. Almost everywhere, in the future, he predicts, the predominant type of family will be nuclear in structure, made up of parents and their unmarried children. Larger families that include grandparents, unmarried or widowed uncles and aunts, married children, their spouses and unmarried children, and other more distant kin are likely to disappear as industrialization, urbanization and westernization gather momentum. Talcott Parsons, who has long inclined toward the same view, has put it this way: "There has been a historic trend to whittle down the size of kinship units in the general direction of isolating the nuclear family (Parsons, 1961: 257).

Various scholars (Parsons, 1953:116; Weber, 1950: III Wirth, 1938; Linton,1952:84; Ogburn and Nimkoff, 1950:469-73; Burgess and Locke, 1953:26-27) have argued that the nuclear family is functionally appropriate for a modern urban industrial economy and that the nuclear family form will develop wherever a modern industrial economy is established. This hypothesis, then, has stimulated much research (see Greenfield, 1961; Arensberg, 1955, 1960; Johnson, 1964; Nimkoff and Middleton, 1960; Litwak, 1960; Sussman, 1963; Young and Willmott, 1957). In India also a number of studies have been guided by this hypothesis (see Desai, 1964; Gore, 1961; Kapoor, 1965; Morrison, 1959; Ross, 1961; Sarma, 1964; Shahani, 1961).

Studies conducted in the area of family sociology both in India and elsewhere suggest three points.

First, the modern forces such as industrialization, urbanization and westernization do seem to correlate with, a trend toward increasing proportions of nuclear families and decreasing proportions of joint families. In India, factors that appear to be related to this trend are (a) western secular education; (b) modern salaried occupations; (c) development of market cash economy, displacing agrarian subsistence economy (Bailey, 1957; Epstein, 1967: 307); and (d) changes in family law or legal practices relating to joint property (Beals, 1955: 86-87, 91-92 ; Gough, 1952: 79-81; Mencher, 1962). Partly as a result of population pressure on land, there has been an influx of people, including the more educated people into cities (Gough, 1956: 831-832; Ray, 1956: 9; Madan, 1965: 145-151 ; Singh, 1962: 44-77). When men goto the city leaving their wives and children in the village, their departure may actually seem to strengthen the joint family as Basu (1962: 90) suggests, or it may lead to break-up through various processes, among which are the inequality of earnings of brothers, leading to envy and resentment and the eventual division of households. The men who come alone in search of employment in cities eventually bring their wives and children once they had secured employment and establish their own homes in cities.

Second, industrialization, modernization and westernization in their various manifestations may serve to strengthen the joint family because an economic base has been provided to support a joint family or because more hands are needed in a new family enterprise or because kin can help one another in the striving for upward mobility (Johnson, 1964; Friedl, 1964: 574).

Third, westernization, industrialization and urbanization may not take place at the same rate.

We have little quantitative evidence on the distribution of family types during early time periods to be used as a standard for measuring family change in India. Only there is some such evidence provided by Ghurya (1960 and Coats, 1823:182). From genealogies, Hitchcock (1956:155) was able to make a retrospective estimate of family structure in 1901 for a section of a village jati of Rajputs. Gould (1966:10) has reported two sets of statistics on family structure for the village, collected in 1954-55 and 1959-60.

The common belief is that Indians generally live in 'joint' families under varying patterns, or extended families. Karve (1953: 10-12) suggests that it is the larger or smaller joint family that is typical of India. Dube '(1952: 213), on the other hand, suggests that the nuclear family or smaller joint family is typical. Karve

(1953) says that in the north, at least, the joint family divides at the time of its founder's death, and divides, not into nuclear families but into smaller joint families. Dube (1959: 213) states that, in villages, children who have grown up and who have "a degree of economic self-sufficiency" break away earlier, presumably before the father's death, and that a complete joint family of any type is rare. Again, Mandelbaum (1957: 247) suggests that the joint family tends to be a rural phenomenon. Dube (1963: 197) suggests that it is an "urban phenomenon, confined mostly to upper-caste groups in traditional small towns". The two writers agree that in rural areas the joint family is characteristic of upper castes rather than of lower castes and those who accept western culture are less likely to live in joint families.

Dube and Beteille (1964:239) say that the joint family is characteristic of landowning groups rather than of landless groups. Mandelbaum says that it is a characteristic of "wealthier strata of society".

The most recent study about family patterns comes from Godwin (1972), who identifies such patterns as: (1) Household or the Chulah group; (2) Joint Residential Household groups; (3) The Nuclear or Conjugal Residential Household; (4) The Sub-nuclear Residential Household; (5) The Single-Person Residential Household; (6) The "other" Household. He describes the structure, jointness and role expectations. He found that 'occupation' accounted for a change in the traditional family pattern. The area of "jointness" has suffered on this account. This was particularly so when daughters and wives began to take up jobs outside the home and gradually freeze all their wages or income. It was further accentuated when wives began working, often earning as much—if not more—as the husband. They were understandably reluctant to share, or handover their salary to the father-in-law or the eldest brother-in-law. He further, found separate chulah as almost the rule. This was the norm especially where married brothers were living in a joint residence, though to a lesser degree where parents and their married sons were living co-residentially. The reasons for this were found to be mainly economic, and especially dependent on the relations between the daughter-in-law and the other members of the house.

Godwin (1972:115-116) further, found the element of jointness in the socio-religious spheres of life, whether co-residential or not. But the youths were beginning to resist this area of conformity.

Another significant observation made by Godwin (1972:118-122) is in respect of changes in role expectations. With the impact of forces of modernization/westernization, there were significant changes in the position of the wife and mother in the family, and especially her relations with her husband. With the increase of education among women, their taking up occupations outside the home before marriage, and their exposure to various modern values through the mass communication media they were unconsciously beginning to make more and more decisions for themselves. They were developing a more independent judgement in areas formerly denied to them. This naturally brought about changes in the husband's role-expectations of the wife. It called for mutual readjustments and highlighted new tensions in the home.

Parent-children relationship also got affected in respect of role-expectations. Daughters were traditionally expected to help in household duties. But with education and independent occupation and earning they too, were beginning to unconciously seek greater say in the family. While the tendency among grown daughters was towards greater independence and more extra family life, that of the son was in some ways towards more family participation. Whereas, traditionally, sons were allowed greater freedom, contributing little to family and household life as such, the tendency in modern families is that like the husband and father, they, should also contribute to family life.

One other special area mentioned by Godwin in which inter-personal relationships were changing radically was that of the young versus elders. Children and young people were less willing to listen to conform to the advice or orders of older people and often treated the very old rather harshly.

From the above it is apparent that one of the most important areas concerning Indian family that requires systematic investigation is the family structure. Taking for granted the separation of some significant forces of change, viz., industrialization, westernization and modernization, the question needs to be investigated is what sorts of family patterns are now emerging. Since scholars are divided on the issue of whether joint family or the nuclear family is the dominant type in India today and they display a tendency to delineate varying types between these two extremes, it may be examined what family types are characteristic of specific family patterns now emerging in a given region or locality or community. We have seen that the forces of change are bringing out changes in role expectations of different family members as also in the inter-personal relationships. Therefore, it needs to be examined as to what changes in role expectations and inter-personal relations correspond to family patterns and family types? In terms of the forces of change, the impact of modern secular education, increasing occupational differentiation, caste differentiation, socio-economic status, etc. on varying family patterns also needs a closer examination. An examination of these questions is likely to provide a fuller picture of modern Indian family in any region.

REFERENCES

Arensberg, C.M.: 1955: "American Communities". *American Anthropologist,* Vol. 66, pp. 1143-62.

Ahuja, R.: 1966: "Family patterns among Bhils". *Eastern Anthropologist,* Vol. 19, pp. 29-42.

Bailey, F.G.: 1957: *Caste and the Economic Frontier* (Manchester: Manchester University Press).

Bandyopadhyay, S. and K. Chattopadhyay: 1964: "A Method of Classifying Family Structures". *Indian Sociological Bulletin,* Vol. II, pp. 22-23.

Basu, Tara Krishna: 1969: *The Bengal Peasant From Time to Time* (New York and Calcutta: Asia Publishing House).

Beals, A.R.: 1955: "Interplay among factors of change in a Mysore village". pp. 78-102 in McKim Marriott (ed.), *Village India*. (Chicago: Chicago University Press).

Berreman, Gerald D.: 1963: *Hindus of the Himalayas.* Los Angeles: University of California Press.

Beteille, A.: 1964: "Family and social change in India and other South Asian countries". *Economic Weekly*, Vol. 16, pp. 237-44.

Bose, A.B.: 1963a: "The structure and composition of rural families". *Indian Journal of Social Work*, 234, pp. 352-58.

————: 1963b: "The size and composition of households in dispersed dwellings". *Journal of Family Welfare*, Vol. 10, pp. 24-31.

———: 1964a: "Age of head and composition of rural joint households". *Indian Journal of Social Research,* Vol. 5, pp. 229-38.

———: 1964b: "Composition of rural households in Rajasthan". *Indian Journal of Social Research,* Vol. 5, pp. 299-308.

———: 1965a: "Composition and size of rural joint households". *Indian Journal of Social Research,* Vol. 6, pp. 30-40.

———: 1965b: "Some characteristics of rural nuclear households". *Man in India*, Vol. 45, pp. 195-200.

———: 1966: "Rural family organization in Western Rajasthan". *Eastern Anthropologist*, Vol. 19, pp. 163-75.

Bose, A.B., S.P. Malhotra and L.P. Bharara:1963: "Socio-economic difference in dispersed dwellings". *Man in India*, Vol. 48, pp. 119-130.

Bose, A.B. and P.C. Saxena: "Composition and size of rural joint households in Rajasthan (Studies in Households III)". *Indian Journal of Social Research*, Vol. 5, No. 2, pp. 299-308.

Burgess, E.W. and H.J. Locke: 1953: *The Family*. New York: American Book Company.

Chauhan, B.R.: 1960: "Family and household in a Rajasthan village". *Indian Sociologist.*

Coats, Thomas: 1823: "Account of the present state of the township of Lony". *Transactions of Literary Society of Bombay*, 3, pp. 172-64

Das, A.K. and S.K. Banerjee: 1963: "The Family of Tribals of West Bengal Static and Dynamic Aspects of Composition". *Bulletin of the Cultural Research Institute*, 2 (1), pp. 12-20.

Desai, I.P.: 1955: "Symposium: caste and joint family". *Sociological Bulletin*, Vol. 4, pp. 85-146.

———: 1956: "The joint family in India: an analysis". *Sociological Bulletin*, Vol. 5, pp. 144-56.

———: 1964: *Some Aspects of Family in Mahuva.* New York: Asia Publishing House.

Driver, E.D.: 1962: "Family structure and socioeconomic status in central 1ndia". *Sociological Bulletin*, Vol 11, pp. 112-20

Dube, L.:1960: "Towards a typology of family". *Sixth All India Sociological Conference*, Saugar.

Dube, S.C.: 1955: *Indian Village*. London: Routledge And Kegan Paul.

———: 1959: "Social structure and change in Indian peasant communities", in A.R. Desai (ed.) *Rural Sociology in India.* Bombay: Indian Society of Agricultural Economics, Vora and Co.

Dube, S.C.: 1963: "Men's and women's roles in India: A sociological review". In B. Ward (ed.), *Women in the New Asia*. UNESCO.

Dumont, L.: 1951: "Kinship and alliance among the Pramalai Kallar". *Eastern Anthropologist*, Vol. 4, pp. 3-26.

Epstein, T.S.: 1962: *Economic Development and Social Change in South India*. Manchester: Manchester University Press.

Friedl, E.: 1964: "Lagging emulation in post-peasant society", *American Anthropologist*, 66, pp. 559-86.

Ghurey, G.S.: 1960: *After a Century and Quarter.* (Bombay: Popular Book Co.

Godwin, C.J.: 1972: *Change and Continuity.* Bombay: Tata McGraw-Hill Co. Ltd.

————: "Notes on the family among the Dimasa Kachari". *Man in India*, Vol. 45, pp. 17-27.

Goode, W.J.: 1968: *World Revolution and Family Patterns.* London: The Free Press of Glencoe, Collier-Macmillan.

Gore, M.S.: 1962: "The husband-wife and the mother-son relationships". *Sociological Bulletin*, Vol. II, pp. 91-102.

————: 1968: *Urbanisation and Family Change*. New York: Humanities Press.

Gough, E.K.: 1952: "Changing kinship usages in the settings of political and economic change among the Nairs of Malabar". *Journal of the Royal Anthropological Institute,* Vol. 82, pp. 71-88.

Gough, E.K.: 1956: "Brahmin kinship in a Tamil village". *American Anthropologist,* Vol. 58, pp. 826-53.

Gould, H.A.: 1968: "Time dimension and structural change in an Indian kinship system: A problem of conceptual refinement". pp. 413-22 in M. Singer and B.S. Cohn (eds.), *Structure and Change in Indian Society*, Chicago: Aldine.

Greenfield, S.M.: 1961: "Industrialization and family in sociological theory". *American Journal of Sociology,* 47, pp. 312-22.

Hitchcock, J.T.: 1956: *The Rajputs of Khalapar: A Study of Kinship, Social Stratification and Politics,* Ph.D. Dissertation.

Johnson, E.: 1964: "The stem family and its extension in present-day Japan". *American Anthropologist*, 66, pp. 839-51.

Jha, J.C. and B.B. Chatterjee: 1965: "Changing family in a Polyandrous community". *Eastern Anthropologist,* 18 (2), pp. 64-72.

Kapoor, S.: 1965: "Family and kinship groups among the Khatris in Delhi". *Sociological Bulletin*, Vol. 14, pp. 54-63.

Karve, I.: 1953: *Kinship Organization in India*. Poona: Deccan College.

————: 1964: "Family in India " In B. N. Varma (ed.) *Contemporary India*. Bombay: Asia Publishing.

Kolenda, P.: 1968: "Region, caste and family structure: A comparative study of the Indian joint family". pp. 339-96 in M. Singer and B.S. Cohn (Eds.), *Structure and Change in Indian Society*. Chicago: Aldine.

Lewis, O.: 1958: Village Life in Northern India. Urbana: University of Illinois Press.

Linton, R.: 1952: "Cultural and Personality Factors Affecting Economic Growth". In B.F. Hoselitz (ed.) *The Progress of Underdeveloped Areas*. Chicago: University of Chicago Press.

Madan, T.N.: 1965: *Family and Kinship: A Study of the Pandits of the Rural Kashmir.* New York: Asia Publishing House

Malhotra, S.P. and M. L.A. Sen: 1964: "A comparative study of the socio-economic characteristics of nuclear and joint households (II)". *Journal of Family Welfare,* pp. 21-32.

Mandelbaum, D.G.: 1957: "The family in India". In *Introduction to Civilization of India: Changing Dimensions of Indian Society and Culture.* Chicago: University of Chicago Press.

Mayer, A.C.: 1960: *Caste and Kinship in Central India: A Village and it Regions.* London: Routledge and Kegan Paul.

Mancher, J.P.: 1962: "Changing familial roles among South Malabar Nayars". *Southwestern Journal of Anthropology,* 18, pp. 230-45.

Morrison, W.A.: 1959: "Family types in Badlapur: An analysis of changing institution in a Maharashtrian village". *Sociological Bulletin*, Vol. 8, pp. 45-67.

Nimkoff, M.F.: 1959: "Family in India: Some problems concerning research on the changing family in India". *Sociological Bulletin,* Vol. 8, pp. 32-39.

Nimkoff, M.F. and M.S. Gore: 1959: "Social bases of the Hindu joint family". *Sociology and Social Research,* XLIV, pp. 27-36.

Nimkoff, M.F., and R. Middleton: 1960: "Types of families and types of economy". *American Journal of Sociology*, 66, pp. 215-25.

Ogburn, W.F. and F. Nimkoff: 1950: *Sociology*. Boston: Houghton Miffin.

Pakrasi, K.: 1965: "On some aspects of family structure of the refugees of West Bengal". *Sociological Bulletin,* Vol. 12, pp. 18-20.

Parsons, T.: 1961: Introduction to part two: "Differentiation and variation in social structures", in T. Parsons, et.al., *Theories of Society.* New York: Free Press of Glencoe.

Ray, A.D.: 1956: "A Brahmin village of the Sasna type in the district of Puri, Orissa". *Man in India,* 36, pp. 7-16.

Ross, A.D.: 1961: *The Hindu Family in its Urban Setting*. Toronto: University of Toronto Press.

Sarma, J.: 1951: "Formal and informal relations in the Hindu joint household of Bengal" *Man in India*, Vol. 31, pp. 51-71.

———: 1964: "The nuclearization of joint family households in West Bengal". *Man in India*, Vol. 44, pp. 198-206.

Sen, L.K.: 1965: "Family in four Indian villages". *Man in India*, Vol. 45, pp. 1-16.

Sengupta, S.K.: 1966: "A study of Mahali families". *Eastern Anthropologist*, XIX (30), pp. 215-24.

Shahani, Savitri: 1961: "The Joint Family: A Case Study," *Economic Weekly*, 13: pp. 1823-28.

Singh, R.D.: 1962: "Family Organisation in a North Indian Village: A Study in Culture, Change," *Ph.D. Dimertation*, Cornell.

Sussman, M.B.: 1963: "The isolated nuclear family: fact or fiction". In M.B. Sussman (ed.) *Sourcebook in Marriage and the Family*. Boston: Houghton, Miffin.

Weber, M.: 1950: *General Economic History*. Glencoe: The Free Press.

Wirth, L.: 1938: "Urbanism as a way of life". *American Journal of Sociology*, 40, pp. 1-24.

Young, M. and P. Willmott: 1957: *Family and Kinship in East London*. London: Routledge and Kegan Paul.

Woodruff, G.M.: 1959: An Adidravida Settlement in Bangalore, India. *Unpublished Ph.D. dissertation*, Radcliffe College.

Acknowledgement is due to my research supervisor, Professor G.C. Hallen for his invaluable inspiration in preparing this paper.

3

Some Observations on the Study of Family Change in India

Ranajit K. Bhadra

Abstract: Recently there has been a tendency among a few scholars to show the Indian joint family with its adaptable capacity in the Industrial-Urban Environment. Thus, they deny the nuclearization of the joint family and as a result, it has created confusion in the study of family change, terms and concepts of the family, etc. All these, subsequently, create obstacles in developing a generalized methodological technique. Finally, the inadequate methodology appears as obstacles to find out the real picture of family dynamics. The author has critically evaluated a few of such studies and discussed the methodology which, he feels, would be helpful for further research.

In pre-British India joint family was the norm of the agrarian society. The widest expression for this family was 'subcaste' consisting of a few joint families which intermarried and interdined among themselves (Panikkar, 1955). The agrarian economy without developed methods of agro-technology needed more hands for working in the economic field, which led the society to practise family with more members. The rapid development of technology and industry in the British period brought urbanization and westernization, and gradually displaced the agrarian economy, which brought several changes in the traditional family. It is a known fact that most of the social relationships have an economic component and many social relations are directly connected with economic activities (Firth, 1971).

Most of the sociologists noted that industrialization, urbanization and westernization brought about changes in the family life in India. Also many of them disagreed on this point and thought that joint family was still persisting in the new economic environment. In this chapter an attempt has been made (a) to examine some of the studies of family change in India, (b) to test the basic terms and concepts of the family and (c) to reconsider the methods for these studies.

I

In order to evaluate such explanations it is necessary to discuss some studies where persistence of joint family in the industrial-urban environment has been shown.

Singer (1968) argues that it is impossible to support the nuclearization of the joint family, because larger number of censuses, statistical survey and case studies support the persistence of joint family. "Jointness" in these studies is very complex and multidimensional in nature, which includes common houses and food, common festivals, common property and the maintenance of kin-ties even between separate households. He emphasizes on distinctiveness of different types of joint family, i.e., lineal, collateral and others, and different types of nuclear family. According to him movement of the sons of industrial leaders from the parental home and establishment of neolocal residence do not indicate towards breakdown of joint family; because, contact is maintained between the 'family of orientation' and 'family of procreation' through rites of passage, festivals and ceremonies; and they maintain the joint family obligations and continue to subscribe to the norms of that system. According to him, structural change and structural persistence are both occurring simultaneously and the joint family is adapting itself functionally in the new urban-industrial environment.

Singer's study is inadequate for depending only on the nineteen industrialist families to test his hypothesis excluding the industrial employees and labourers and various other workers in the city area. A generalized picture of societal norm is impossible to obtain from such small sample families of equal economic status. Industrialization, sometimes, might not bring about any change in the industrialist families but it, possibly, brings about changes in the families of other employees and neighbours living in its environment. Industrialization and urbanization bear several inter-related characteristics like compact urban areas, small houses, non-traditional occupations, money and market economy, etc. which are enough for bringing divisions in the joint family.

To show the impact of urbanization on the joint family, Gore (1968) asserts that the urban joint family is larger than the rural one. It is clear that all these dependants are very temporary, as family members have come either for higher education or for seeking jobs in the city. He mentions that even after breakdown of the families, brothers always help each other in emergency and an elder brother has an important role in the decision-making process in the family of his younger brother. Helping a brother and advising him in family affairs do not indicate any feature of persistence of joint family. These may be considered as remnants of the traditional joint family customs, which they could not shake off immediately. It is questionable here that has he measured the degree of changes of such behaviours among the brothers? Has he seen the factors, which have changed these interpersonal relations? Let us take an example to nullify Gore's view. Sometimes in our society it is found that maternal uncle also takes part in decision-making and helps in time to his sister's children, of course, if he resides close to them. But it does not mean that he is a member of the family of his sister's children. If it happens, our patriarchal society would lose its distinguishing features.

Gore points out that in respect of family preference most of the urban respondents prefer nuclear family than the rural respondents. Regarding decision-making process in the family no change is seen in the urban areas. He (1968: 232) concludes: "One is that the sample as a whole still largely conforms to the pattern of joint family living in behaviour, role perception and attitudes. The second is that within this overall pattern of conformity urban residence and education do seem to introduce a certain measure of awareness of the difficulties of joint family living, a tendency to verbal 'non-conformity' in replies to additional question, and a hesitant assertion of the importance of the conjugal tie; but they also indicate a simultaneous assertion of traditional pattern of behaviour in the acceptance of familial obligations, limitation of the decision-making role of the individual parent in the family".

Gore (1968: 232) comments that "the findings thus support limited change". The emphasis on 'limited', however, rather than a 'change' is questionable. What does he mean by limited change? He is not clear about it. For his study, Gore uses only a detailed questionnaire, which is no doubt a good method to find out the structural characteristics of the family, but in respect of some other aspects of the family it raises doubt regarding capability of collecting real data. A simple questionnaire schedule is not proper to find out the reality of "whether the nuclear as well as joint households in the urban areas showed characteristic differences in acceptance of familial obligations, in the pattern of authority, and in the attitudes to the institution of marriage etc."

II

The extremely diversified nature of studies on the family has created ambiguity and confusion in the concept of family types in India. What would be the proper definition of nuclear as well as joint families? If some other varieties of families are found, what sort of terminology and definitions should be used?

Ross (1967: 34) proposes: "... it was thought appropriate to classify the sample of families in terms of the number of generations living in one household; the presence and absence of married couples; and the number of dependent members". In this way four types of family are found: large joint family (Type A), small joint family (Type B), the nuclear family (Type C), and the nuclear family with dependants (Type D).

Actually the large joint family as mentioned by Ross, is rarely found today. She has considered visiting relatives and married pregnant daughters as members of this family. It is questionable why these temporary persons are included as family members. Her nuclear family with dependants is composed of a man, his wife and their children with one or more dependants. But she has not mentioned whether there is any joint family with dependants or not. If we examine with a correct definition of nuclear family, we can not say her "Type D" family as a nuclear family. The

Type A and *Type B* are actually joint families, but she has made it complicated by distinguishing into two types.

Mandelbaum (1949) mentions a household group having three types of composition, which includes three-or-four generations.

Karve (1953) also follows the same three-or-four generation's formula for defining joint family. Actually, this type of family bears so many complications regarding the concept of the joint family.

Dube (1955) tells us about three types of family. His first one is 'elementary family' or the 'house', which consists only of the husband, wife, their sons and unmarried daughters. He does not mention whether these sons are married or unmarried. In other case one or both parents, unmarried brothers and unmarried sisters may also belong to this unit. It is actually not a nuclear family because it includes more members than that of nuclear family. But he does not include this type in the joint family or in other category. His second type of social unit is 'extended or allied family' and third one is still larger group comprising near kin from the parental side.

Bailey (1957) has mentioned joint family as a 'joint property group' and states that sons may establish new houses in their working place away from the father's working place but they may remain in the joint family in respect of common property, earnings, expenses, etc. I do not understand how the two established families located in two different places maintain on common earnings and sharing common expenses. Shah (1964) argues on this point: "In the same way, if a man and his married son live in a single household and also manage their property jointly, will he not consider this group a joint family?"

Nicholas (1961) also follows the same principle in describing family of West Bengal villages and refers to joint family as property-holding group and an extended family as a unit of "co-residence or the use of certain kinds of family kinship terms outside the nuclear family".

Gore (1968: 87) defines: "The term nuclear was applied to the family units consisting primarily of husband, wife and their children. In some cases, other dependents were present, but none of these was an independent earner in his own right. In no case was an additional married couple present in the nuclear family unit. In no case was a male dependent in the family, the father, brother or an agnatic relation of the husband in the family". His definition is too complicated. Who are these mentioned dependents in the nuclear family? He does not explain clearly here. According to the correct definition it is not a nuclear family.

Gore (1968: 87) says: "The term joint was applied to the families where generally there were at least two married couples living in common residence and where the males were related as father-son or as brother-brother, and in a few cases, as uncle-nephew. In other cases, a family was included in the joint stratum where there was only one married couple, but where the head of the family was either the widowed father, father's brothers, or elder brother of the married male in the family, where the father, father's brother, or elder brother was economically active". Here Gore has given emphasis on the common property and the authoritative pattern. But he has confused the definition as he mentions "families where the widowed mother stayed with her married son was considered nuclear". But one can argue that a widowed mother is not always regarded as dependent. In many cases she holds authority in the son's family similar to that of her deceased husband.

Singer (1970) proposes different types of nuclear and joint families, i.e., lineal, collateral and others. Cohn (1961) defines joint family as eating from one *Chulah*. He says: "This means sharing property and rights, pocket-book, larder, debts, labour and usually one head".

Madan (1965) finds different types of familial situation among Pandits of Kashmir and has classified the families into eight different types. His fourth category is 'two-generation' household in a transitional phase between nuclear and paternal extended or fraternal extended families. The fifth category is 'three-generation' family. The sixth category of family is in a transitional phase and likely to grow into fraternal-extended families. Some of them are 'two-generation' and some are 'three-generation' households. The seventh category is fraternal-extended families and eighth category of household is of type which are differentially constituted owing to the occurrence of certain events, like the unusual early death of an adult member, or the unusual non-occurrence of certain events, like marriage or partition.

III

The above discussion on the terms and concepts of Indian family reveals a diversified and complex picture, which hinders to draw any conclusion. Now the problem is that why they do not find similar types of family pattern all over India except some minor regional variations? It is evident from the findings that there are some families that cannot be classified as nuclear family or joint family. Therefore, one can easily assume that there are, perhaps, trends of disintegration in the family patterns and if it is true, how it has happened. To answer this question we will discuss the traditional Indian family patterns.

Early Sanskrit literature provides evidence of the existence of joint family in the past. In this connection Karve (1953: 21) states that stories of the classics like the *Mahabharata* and the *Ramayana* show how stable the joint family system has been down through the ages. She (1953: 21) writes that "the Mahabharata family is found today all over India and a Mahabharata battle is being fought in most joint families. The ideas of status, duties and rights of members of the joint family are those inherited from any deeply rooted in the tradition of these epics".

The historical evidence supports the prevalence of joint family in the past. If it was a general trend of the traditional Hindu family structure, why some of the present studies show such disintegration in it? Kolenda (1968) argues: "What is the typical Indian family? An estimate based on ten studies suggested that not until a community has 30 per cent joint families does the majority of the population live in joint families". Nearly every study shows that nuclear family is the most common residential form of India. It is not difficult to assume that Indian family is changing. A question naturally arises, here, why the traditional family has been changing and why there is great controversy among the scholars regarding it. Desai (1964) points out that Hindu joint family system has always been changing which is evident from the history of changes in such matters as the rules of exogamy, the laws of succession and inheritance and the composition of its households. It is the general assumption that industrialization and urbanization have brought dynamism in the Indian family structure, and there are some supporting evidence to this view. Goode (1963) mentions that industrialization and urbanization have some impact on the family and most part of the world are undergoing a family revolution, and in future nuclear family will be the norm of every society. Levey (1949) also provides evidence that industrialization and urbanization have brought revolutionary changes in the traditional joint family system in China. Ancient China and India had the same pattern of agrarian economy and both of them had joint family as the smallest kinship and social unit. So it can be said that in India industrialization and urbanization have brought about changes in the traditional family pattern, i.e., from joint to nuclear. Ross (1967), Desai (1964) point out that the joint family in India has been affected by the new economic structure of the society.

IV

Principal family types, which are found in most societies, are nuclear and joint or extended which are two extreme family types, because there is no family smaller than nuclear and bigger than joint family (Murdock, 1965). But from the above discussion we find that many authors have emphasized on different types of families that cannot be categorized into these above two types. But all these family types fall in place between the nuclear and joint families. Madan's (1965) first, second and third categories can be said to be nuclear family, but one difficulty is that he includes husband's father's sister's son's son in this nuclear family. As soon as their sons are included in the family as a member, this family cannot be regarded as nuclear. His other categories like fourth, fifth, sixth, seventh and eighth are joint families. In fact, these various types of family creates problems in family study.

Ross' (1967) four types of family also create confusion in the family study, because the Type-A and Type-B are joint families, but Type-C is nuclear family and Type-D is not at all nuclear family. These types of family actually fall in the intermediate position between the nuclear and joint families. Gore (1968) mentions two types of families but he has included other members in the same nuclear family. His nuclear family with other members, is not nuclear family, because it can be placed in the same intermediate position between the nuclear and the joint families.

So in almost all family studies we find nuclear and joint

families along with some other families belong to the intermediate category. It would be proper if it is termed as 'Transitional family unit', because it indicates breaking down of the family from joint to nuclear. Therefore its structures appears to be informal in nature which varies from society to society according to its transitional phases.

To support this transitional family unit it is necessary to define the nuclear and joint families. When the family is composed of a couple and unmarried children, i.e., presence of two generations, it can be called nuclear family. And it may also be less than two generations. In this respect a couple without child, or persons of same generation only like uterine brother and sister, or widow and widower with married children can form a nuclear family. Karve (1953: 8) defines that a "joint family is a group of family members who generally live under one roof, eat food cooked at one hearth, hold property in common and participate in common family worship and are related to each other as some particular type of kindred". According to this definition of joint family, it is assumed that change in any of the above conditions means disintegration in the system itself. It is generally found that changes in the above first and second conditions bring changes in the structure of the unit. But according to Bailey (1957), Nicholas(1961), Agarwala (1955), and Madan (1965) 'Joint Family' term should be used only for the joint property group. Thus, they confuse the concept of joint family, because they strongly support that Indian family is unchanging. Agarwala (1955) says that It is inessential for members of the joint family to live in one place and eat in a common kitchen. He mentions that family members may live in any distant place like Calcutta, Madras and Bombay for business purposes, but their property is commonly held and they belong to the joint family. But it is not a joint family; actually it is a nuclear family attached to the family of orientation through some sentiments, obligations, etc., but not physically and demographically. If demographic aspect is one of the main features of family structure, one should not neglect the physical feature of the family. As, for example, a man has left his parental village home and establishes a new residence with his wife at his working place in the town. His father maintains his own family by cultivating the family land. This man also maintains his family by his earning and deposits some money in the bank for using in times of necessity. He brings certain amount of crops from his father for annual consumption of his family. But he attends all social and religious functions in his village home together with his parent's family. In this situation why it cannot be seen as two families, i.e., parent's family and son's nuclear family. Shift from parental residence means eating in separate hearth, eating in separate hearth means maintenance of new separate family (i.e., expenditure, bank deposit, etc.). Getting crops from parent's family means division of property indirectly, because it is difficult for him to cultivate land from the town. So structurally these are two family units. Another such problem is with Bailey's (1957) usage of 'common property'. What does he mean by common property? Is it only landed property or cash property (i.e., cash in bank)? If it is cash in a bank, then the problem is when a man deposits money in the bank in town for future necessities, it is not regarded as common property. It is individual property of that particular person.

As social facts are functionally interrelated with each other, change in one aspect brings about change in other aspects also. So family change in this aspect (i.e., physical and demographic) brings changes in other aspects of the family life like sentiment, behavioural pattern, decision-making process, authoritative pattern, system of power, rights, duties, etc. So we should consider the multidimensional characters of family life. Williams (1951) has shown that economic structure affects the family. Economy of the industrialized and urbanized society is in many ways incompatible with a stable family structure. Economic competition and market economy cause strains to the family solidarity by exerting pressure both towards reduction in size and towards insulating certain family roles from the competitive matrix. Williams (1951) writes: "Still more generally, the removal of economic production from the home radically affects the total pattern of family relations. It would seem that the most important fact is not the loss of economic functions as such but the reduction in intrafamily...interaction centred upon purposeful common goals, and effective patterns".

Thus, all the families, which cannot be classified as nuclear or joint, are termed as 'transitional families'. Gore's (1968) findings are similar to this category. Still today, people in India cannot fully leave their traditional family obligations as these are deeply rooted in their sentiments. Dependants, which are found in the town and city families, are due to earlier joint family obligations and sentiments, and all these dependants are purely temporary members in such families. It will be wrong to conclude that behavioural pattern and family obligation do not show any change today. Gore (1968: 108) argues: "In few cases, their younger brother had come to join them in the city in search of a livelihood. In some cases, marriage of younger brothers led to the establishment of joint families". Has he considered here the separation of such brothers from the elder brother's family after their marriage?

V

To establish a scientific truth it requires universal applicability of the methods. If a large number of family types are revealed from the studies due to application of different methods, it creates considerable problems in family research. The methodology automatically suffers from the lack of adequate techniques. If we consider the following three types of families according to the Indian context, such as, (i) Joint family, (ii) Transitional family and (iii) Nuclear family, it can be used anywhere in India, and through this it is possible to develop better methods and techniques for the study of family types as well as its changes under any impact. It will not be wise to prefer several types of family, because it creates complexity in the study of family types and also of its dynamic aspects. To study the family types, this method will facilitate us to understand the trends of dynamic aspects of the Indian family. The transitional family will indicate (a) whether the joint family is breaking down to a nuclear family or not, or (b) whether it is a new type of family or not or (c) whether there is any 'structural persistence' of the joint family in the new industrial-urban environment or not.

Studies on the family change in India are very few and most of them suffer from poor methodological techniques. Ross' (1967: 22) study on the change of the Hindu family can be considered as one of the best. She has pointed out: "All these studies and the many controversies over whether family structures are changing or not, point out the complexity of the processes of industrialization and urbanization, and show the necessity of analysing the many variables in the total situations in which each family is found, before definite trends can be established as predicted".

In the study of family change in India the most important task is to find out–what were the typical traditional family types and their compositions, and what types were the norm of the society? The second task is to find out the roles of the family members. If a researcher knows all these necessary information, he/she can compare the family of the past with that of the present. Through this study it will be easy to understand whether it is 'normal development process' or change. It is easily understandable from the earlier discussion that the present day family change is not a normal development process; because normal development process does not create any conflict in the family affairs. But nowadays family conflicts, such as conflict of hierarchy, role conflict, changing role of women, parent-child relations, sexual frustration, etc. are very common in the industrial-urban society. At the same time one should not neglect the very common features like the present-day economic crisis and family conflict which lead to breakdown of the family. So the family change should also be examined through the various factors of conflict situations.

Though in this short chapter it is very difficult to present a detailed methodology, an attempt has been made to discuss some of the methods and techniques of data collection for the family study. Simple questionnaire method for collection of data in all aspects of family study is insufficient enough, because it suffers from many drawbacks. In certain aspects of family study this method is unable to collect reliable data as mentioned above. Conklin's (1969) study on the family type in 26 villages in rural Mysore reveals such drawback in the application of questionnaire method. His questions are: (a) "Do you think there are more or fewer joint families today as in the past?" (b) "Do you think children today are as well-behaved as in the past?" These types of unscientific questions cannot reveal the reality of the social life. The investigator should always consider the psychological aspects of the human being at the time of data collection. To elicit answers to such questions the researcher(s) should ask the respondents indirectly. So both formal and informal types of interviews are necessary to collect data regarding certain aspects of human life. Observational method is also essential for confirmation of the collected data and to bring richness in it. This method also gives fruitful results especially in the study of changing roles of family members, authoritative pattern, decision-making process, power and status, attitudes towards marriage, etc.

Rivers (1910) says the genealogical method is also important for obtaining data regarding kinship system and wider social structure. The genealogical method offers a powerful means of gathering data for the study of both structural change and structural persistence of family system. It is an appropriate method for the study of what happens to the joint family in an urban and industrial setting. But it needs avoidance of synchronic restriction of the genealogical method (Singer, 1970). The "family history" approach can also provide a fruitful result in the study of family change (Singer, 1970).

REFERENCES

Agarwala, B.R.: 1955: "In a mobile commercial community", in Symposium: Caste and Joint Family. *Sociological Bulletin*, Vol. IV, No. 2. The joint family in India: a frame work for discussion. *Economic Weekly*, 12, 18.

Bailey, F.G.: 1957: *Caste and Economic Frontier*, Manchester University Press.

Cohn, B.S.: 1961: "Chamar family in a Northern India village– a structural contingent". *Economic Weekly*, Special No. July.

Conklin, G.H.: 1969: "Social change and the joint family – the causes of research biases". *Economic and Political Weekly*, Vol. 4, No. 36.

Desai, I.P.: 1955: "Symposium on caste and joint family: an analysis". *Sociological Bulletin*, Vol. 4, No. 2.

————: 1956: "The joint family in India: an analysis. *Sociological Bulletin*, Vol. 5, No. 2.

————: 1964: *Some Aspects of Family in Mahuva. A Sociological Study of Jointness in a Small Town*. Bombay: Asia Publishing House.

Dube, S.C.: 1955: *Indian Village*. London, Routledge and Kegan Paul.

Firth, R.: 1971: *Elements of Social Organisation*. London: Tavistock.

Goode, W.J.: 1963: *World Revolution and Family Patterns*. London: The Free Press of Glencoe.

Gore, M.S.: 1968: *Urbanization and Family Change*. Bombay.

Karve, I.: 1953: *Kinship Organization in India*. Poona: Deccan College.

Kolenda, P.M.: 1968: "Region, caste and family structure: A comparative study of the Indian joint family." In M. Singer and B.S. Cohn (eds.) *Structure and Change in Indian Society*. Aldine Publishing Company.

Levey, Jr. M.J.: 1949: *The Family Revolution in Modern China*. Cambridge, Mass.: Havard University Press.

Madan, T.N.: 1965: *Family and Kinship: A Study of the Pandits of Rural Kashmir*. Bombay: Asia Publishing House.

Mandelbaum, D.G.: 1949: "The Family in India". In R. Anshen (ed.), *Family: Its Function and Destiny*, N.Y. Harper.

Murdock, G.P.: 1965: *Social Structure*. N.Y.: Free Press.

Nicholas, R.W.: 1961: "Economy of family types in two West Bengal villages". *Economic Weekly*, Vol. 13.

Panikkar, K.M.: 1955: *Hindu Society at the Cross Road*. Bombay.

Rivers, W.H.R.: 1910: "The genealogical method of Anthropological inquiry". *Sociological Review*, Vol. 8.

Ross, A.D.: 1967: *The Hindu Family in its Urban Settings*. Toronto: University of Toronto Press.

Saha, A.M.: 1964: "Basic terms and concepts in the study of family in India". *Indian Economic and Social History Review*, Vol. 1, No. 3.

——————: 1970: "Changes in the Indian family: An examination of some assumptions". *Economic and Political Weekly*, Vol. 3.

Singer, M.: 1970: "The Indian joint family in modern industry. In M.Singer and B.S. Cohn (Eds.) Structure and Change in Indian Society. Aldine Publishing Company.

Williams, M.R.: 1951: *American Society*. N. Y.: Alfred A. Knoff.

4

The Domestic Cycle in India: Natural History of a Will-o'-the-Wisp

Stanley A. Freed
Ruth S. Freed

The concept of the domestic cycle is evaluated by an analysis of the changes that domestic groups have undergone in the Indian village of Shanti Nagar during a 19-year period. Diversity of family histories precludes the existence of a single domestic cycle, or even of two or three dominant cycles. There are, however, significant regularities, such as the frequent evolution of nuclear families into lineal joint families. [India, social structure, domestic cycle, family types, peasant society]

Ever since the appearance of the volume of essays entitled *The Developmental Cycle in Domestic Groups* (Goody, 1958), the developmental cycle, also known as the family cycle or the domestic cycle, has been a staple of anthropological *analysis.*[1] Delineating what has remained the basic definition of the domestic cycle, Fortes (1958:2) tells us that, "The domestic group goes through a cycle of development analogous to the growth cycle of a living organism." The cycle implicitly has a beginning and an end and there is "a regular sequence of changes during the cycle which culminates in the dissolution of the original unit and its replacement by one or more units of the same kind." Fortes

(1958:3) suggests that the classification of families by types creates confusion, "But when it is recognized that these so-called types are in fact phases in the developmental cycle of a single general form for each society, the confusion vanishes." The main stages in the developmental cycle are, according to Fortes (1958:4-5), the establishment of the unit; its expansion, principally by the birth of children, the dispersion of component units, which may overlap the stage of expansion as children marry and leave their natal family; the replacement phase, when new family members replace those who die or *depart*; and finally, the end of the cycle, marked by the death of the founding parents. The characteristics of the domestic cycle are, therefore, that it is like the growth cycle of an organism; there is one typical form for each society; there is a regular sequence of changes during the cycle; and it has a beginning when the founders are young and an end when the founders die.

It is so reasonable and appealing to think in terms of a domestic cycle that the extent to which it exists has never been seriously questioned. The concept seems reasonable because domestic groups are composed of people, who can be said to pass through a life cycle from birth to infancy, childhood, maturity, old age, and death. Therefore, by analogy, families must have a similar cycle. The concept is also appealing because to some extent it shifts the focus of analysis from structure to process. Anthropologists generally extol the study of process and are predisposed to welcome any apparent analytical contribution in this regard.

However, the concept of the domestic cycle has proven difficult to use analytically. The main problem that generally becomes apparent when one attempts to use it in analyzing empirical data is that a single domestic cycle, or even a typical one, often cannot be found. This problem was not initially recognized because most early studies of the domestic cycle were based on data collected at one point in time. The common procedure was to identify family types and then to arrange them in logical order to yield a domestic developmental cycle. When diachronic data from two points in time became available, however, they often revealed many possible cycles through which a family might pass. The experience of Otterbein (1970) is instructive. Based on the frequency distribution of family types at one point in time and also on adult life histories, he proposed a typical domestic cycle for the Andros household. Data from a second census taken seven years after the first one failed to confirm the "typical" cycle; in fact, there were about 40 possible cycles. It is fair to ask whether the concept of the domestic cycle has any meaning in a society where the analysis of diachronic census data fails to reveal a single cycle, a typical cycle, or even two or three "typical" cycles.

We propose to evaluate the concept of the domestic cycle by an analysis of the sequence of changes that domestic groups have undergone in the north Indian village that we call Shanti Nagar. Our analysis is based both on censuses and on holistic ethnographic data that we collected in 1958-59 and 1977-78. The approximately 19-year interval between the two studies allows sufficient time for changes to have taken place in the structure of most village families. Our analysis shows that these changes form a varied and complex set of transformations. They can be understood best by the realization that family structure is influenced by cultural values that foster specific family types, by the disparate economic circumstances of each family, by the particular personalities of its members, and by demographic events, the relative timing of which is largely a matter of chance. Such causal complexity tends to preclude the emergence of a domestic cycle in the generally accepted sense of the term.

Shanti Nagar: Basic Information

Shanti Nagar is located in the Union Territory of Delhi, north-west of the City of Delhi. As is typical of the region, the village consists of a compact habitation site surrounded by cultivated fields. The population, all Hindus, totaled 799 persons in 1958-59, of whom 392 were females and 407 were males, in 1977-78 there were 629 females and 695 males, for a total of 1324 persons. There were 110 families in 1958-59 and 176 in 1977-78. Although agriculture was the principal occupation, many men had salaried urban jobs. Men often practised more than one occupation, a frequent combination being farming and urban employment. Most women also had two principal occupations: agricultural work and housework. The castes that were most populous in Shanti Nagar were Brahman Priest, Jat Farmer, Cola Potter, Chamar

Leatherworker, and Chuhra Sweeper, all well represented in the villages of the Union Territory of Delhi and neighbouring states. A description of the village as it was in 1958-59 may be found in a series of monographs that have appeared in the last several years (S. Freed and R. Freed 1976, 1978; R. Freed and S. Freed 1979, 1980, 1981).

In the interval between our two periods of research in Shanti Nagar, a number of social and economic trends had become established: the educational level had risen dramatically; there had been a substantial increase in salaried urban occupations; the technological level of agriculture was considerably higher; and the villagers were more deeply involved in markets outside of Shanti Nagar, owing largely to the construction of the immense Delhi Vegetable Market just to the north of Delhi and within easy reach of the farmers of Shanti Nagar. Despite changes in technology and occupation, cultural values in the domain of family life and kinship, which fostered the joint family in its various forms, persisted essentially unchanged. There were, however, sometimes modifications in family life that tended to ameliorate the lot of younger family members; one example was the establishment of a separate room or apartment for a young couple in a joint family dwelling.

Family Types

Although there are many classifications of Indian family types, all of them are recognized nuclear families and joint families. The nuclear family is almost always defined as a domestic unit based on a husband and wife; the joint family is generally defined as a unit based on two or more related nuclear families. The Indian joint family is usually patrilineal and patrilocal and/or virilocal. It emphasizes filial and fraternal solidarity and, based on the *Mitakshara* (a 12th-century legal text), each male family member is entitled to an equal share of the family property (Mandelbaum 1970:35).[2]

Both nuclear and joint families can assume a variety of forms. We have found Kolenda's (1968:346-348, 356) classification of Indian family types to be the most useful. It identifies a sufficient number of types to do justice to the ethnographic situation and yet is not overly elaborated, it fits the Shanti Nagar data quite well, and the descriptive names used for each category make it easy to visualize the structure of a family with considerable precision from its type. Kolenda derives her types pragmatically from the distinctions most frequently used by 26 researchers who provided her with all the relevant ethnographic data then available. These distinctions are based on a few principles, namely, marriage, lineality collaterality, and supplementation, most of which are commonly emphasized in kinship studies. As Kolenda notes, researchers have used other principles, such as number of generations represented in a family, whether a married couple has children, and whether a couple has been ceremonially married, but none of them has been used often enough, in her estimation, to justify using any of them in her classification. Kolenda's system has proved to be a landmark in the study of the Indian family and appears to be coming gradually into general use.

Kolenda defines the nuclear family as a married couple with or without unmarried children, the subnuclear family as a fragment of a former nuclear family e.g., a widow or widower and unmarried children, and a joint family as at least two married couples related either lineally e.g., a father, mother, and their married son or collaterally e.g., two married brothers or cousins. Any unmarried family members who are not children of any of the married couples of a family supplement the family. The three basic types—subnuclear, nuclear, and joint—qualified by the adjectives lineal, collateral, and supplemented, yield ten family types to which we assign numerals as identifying symbols to be used later in the analysis: (1) subnuclear; (2) supplemented subnuclear; (3) nuclear; (4) supplemented nuclear; (5) lineal joint; (6) supplemented lineal joint; (7) collateral joint; (8) supplemented collateral joint; (9) lineal-collateral joint; (10) supplemented lineal-collateral joint. Kolenda also recognizes single-person families and a residual category that she terms "other category." We did not require the "other" category, and as Shanti Nagar had only one single-person family in 1958-59 and none in 1977-78, we made no use of the single-person category, classifying the one such family as subnuclear.

Another set of family types can be formed in a similar fashion based on the polygynous family composed of a man and more than one wife. Thus, a supplemented polygynous family is a polygynous family with an unmarried relative who is not a child of the husband and one of his wives; and a polygynous lineal-collateral joint family is a lineal-collateral joint family in which at least one of the component families consists of a man and his two or more wives. Shanti Nagar had the following types of polygynous families at both the earlier and later periods: (11) polygynous; (I2) supplemented polygynous; (13) polygynous supplemented collateral joint; (14) polygynous lineal-collateral joint.

Kolenda has been criticized for using "family" and "household" interchangeably (Sinha 1977:64). This objection involves principally the failure to make a consistent distinction between the property-owning group or coparcenary family, and the residential unit or household. Kolenda has not ignored the problem, but points out that in practice it may not be particularly serious because the residential and coparcenary families probably often coincide, and moreover, the term joint family is used as frequently to refer to the residential group as to the group of coparceners (Kolenda 1968:348-349). Nonetheless, there is some confusion, principally because her procedures for including or excluding important classes of relatives are not specific enough. Our definition of the family is a compromise between the residential unit and the group of persons with specific joint interests in family property. Such an approach seems to us to be the best method for presenting the basic structure of an Indian family and/or household and the relationships of its members. The practical definition of the social unit that we call a family resolves problems that would be intractable if one were to insist on a rigid distinction between household (residential group) and coparcenary family.

We define a family as a group of kin who usually cook together when circumstances permit and who share at least their food supplies. Although this definition serves as a useful starting point for distinguishing one family from another yet, it must be qualified in a number of ways in order to deal with the variety of situations that develop concerning family structure. When a large family divides into two or more families, the critical step is the division of food supplies and cooking, at this point, the village as a whole recognizes the formation of independent families. Such recognition is manifest at specific ceremonial occasions when, for example, there is a distribution of one-rupee notes to heads of families. The family head of each newly created family receives a rupee. It must be emphasized that although the families have divided, the process of the division of family property has in all probability not been completed; there is often considerable undivided family property, such as land, buildings, and machinery, that will be divided in some cases during the course of a number of years. For example, when a son separates from his father he may receive only a part of the land to which he is entitled, or none at all. But when his father dies, the son receives his full share. Thus, the son heads an independent family while maintaining his coparcenary rights in undivided family property. Such a situation should cause no conceptual confusion concerning the independence of families, the ethnographer needs only accept the judgement of the families themselves, and of other villagers, concerning the status of the families in question.

The keeping of common accounts is probably more important as a criterion of family unity than is common cooking, because even when all the members of a family are living in Shanti Nagar, they may in some cases cook on two or more stoves (*chulha*) for convenience or by preference. However, the food so cooked is drawn from a common store. In a few of the larger joint families, it is difficult to prepare a meal if only one stove is in use. Just as family members may use more than one stove, so too they may occupy several buildings. Young married couples in joint families may have separate rooms or apartments. There is considerable variety in such matters, depending on the economic circumstances of families and the personalities of the involved individuals.

The problem of the distinction of residential group and family arises chiefly from three circumstances. First, family members might be living away from the village; for example, a family head in military service. Sometimes the absent family members form the equivalent of a family, for example, a man in urban employment who has his wife and children with him. We include absent family members as part of the family for purposes of defining family types. All such persons form a single family. They retain their share of common family property and contribute as much as possible to general family expenses. Although it is often necessary to accept the assertions of family members in Shanti Nagar that an absent couple and their children have not separated to form an independent family, supporting evidence could sometimes be uncovered; for example, the absent family members might send regular remittances to their family in Shanti Nagar or, at least, contribute to the expenses of major ceremonials. If they visit Shanti Nagar, they cook with others in the family, and on returning to the city they often take a supply of grain and, especially, *ghee* (clarified butter) from the common larder.

Second, wives are sometimes absent from the village. Young wives, especially, move back and forth between their parents' and their husband's villages (villages are exogamous); and in the early years of marriage, they spend a good deal of time with their parents. A wife is a member of her husband's family no matter where she resides. The wedding ceremony includes a ritual whereby she passes as property to her husband's family. Thus, a family consisting of a man, his wife, and a married 17-year-old son whose wife lives with her parents in another village, is classed as a joint family.

Third, relatives who are not members of a family sometimes reside with it for various reasons, such as to be near a particular school, because of affection, or because they have no close relatives in their own village. These relatives are often children; for example, sisters' or daughters' children who, because they belong to the families of their fathers, are not members of their families of residence. Such individuals are household members, and we therefore, recognize them in defining the family type of the unit in which they reside. Kin such as these are almost always unmarried or widowed and serve only to supplement the family in which they are resident.

In defining family types, we do not count servants from outside of Shanti Nagar (eight in 1958-59, five in 1977-78) who reside with various families. They are neither related to their employers nor members of their families, although their employers feed and shelter them. Because they live with their employers, they have not established families of their own. They receive their sustenance as payment rather than through the rights inherent in family membership. In short, they are not members of any of the families of Shanti Nagar. In the matter of servants, we differ from Kolenda, who includes them in defining family types.

Indian Domestic Cycle

Orenstein and Micklin (1966-67) and Gould (1968) propose similar versions of the Indian domestic cycle. The Orenstein-Micklin (1966-67:321) cycle, from the point of view of a male ego, begins with his marriage while he is a member of his father's family; hence, he is a member of a joint family. When his father dies, he becomes head of a nuclear family. Ego's son marries and the family becomes joint. Then ego dies to complete the cycle. Gould (1968:417-418) formulates a set of unique family types, but when they are translated into the customary terminology of joint and nuclear family, his domestic cycle is nuclear family to lineal joint family to collateral joint family when the family head dies, and then back to nuclear family, thus completing "the circular pathway of temporal changes in the domestic group." Gould's scheme has the considerable merit of being based on his own field data concerning 43 households situated in Sherupur, a village in eastern Uttar Pradesh, both at the beginning and end of a five-year period. A basic principle of the domestic cycle as outlined by Orenstein and Micklin and by Gould is that the joint family dissolves only upon the death of the family head. Gould (1968:416) notes that:

> Mitakshara succession makes provision for partition of the joint property whenever that is the desire of any legal coparcener who is of age. In practice, however, it is rare for a partition to be called for in the lifetime of the patriarch. Patriarchal authority is so absolute as to discourage sons from making such a demand while their father still lives.

The structural changes that the families of Shanti Nagar have undergone provide a substantial body of data for evaluating the domestic cycle as defined by Fortes and the specific cycles proposed by Orenstein and Micklin and by Gould. Of the 110 families in Shanti Nagar in 1958-59, 11 had died out or disappeared by 1977-78. The remaining 99 families were represented by 168 families in Shanti Nagar and 8 outside the village, a total of 176 families. Fifty-four of the original families had not divided and were represented by a single family 19 years later (see Table 1). A family that leaves only one descendant family is termed as an *unbranched family*. When a specific family develops into two or more families, we speak of a branched family or a cluster of families. There were 45 clusters in Shanti Nagar in 1977-78; that is, 45 of the families of 1958-59 had branched, yielding 114 families in Shanti Nagar and 8 outside the village, a total of 122 families (see Figure 1). The family in a cluster that contains the original family head and/or his wife is designated as the primary family; the other families in a cluster are called secondary families. The distinction between branched and unbranched families is convenient for the presentation and analysis of the data; however, this analytical convenience must not be interpreted to mean that some families never branch (although a few die out without branching) or that branching in a family is never preceded by a long period without branching. In general, branching represents one aspect of a family's history and lack of branching, another aspect.

Our analysis rests principally on detailed census information that we collected in Shanti Nagar in 1958-59 and 1977-78. Both censuses include, among other data, the name, age, sex, marital status, caste, clan, education, and employment of each family member. The relationships of family members are shown by a genealogical diagram. We made maps of the village that show the location of each building, its use, and the family that owns it. The relationships of families to one another were investigated, and we kept records of births, weddings, and deaths during our two periods of fieldwork. Individuals were interviewed about developments in their own and/or related families, which often helped to clarify critical points. These data made it possible to reconstruct family histories by comparing the earlier and later censuses of each family, noting the births, weddings, deaths, and family divisions, and then deducing the order of these events, thereby arriving at the sequence of types that a family had assumed during the 19-year period between our studies. Some family histories may be reconstructed with great certainty; others are problematic because, although we know that weddings, deaths, and family divisions have taken place, we do not know the sequence of these events. The order of such events determines the sequence of family types.

In view of the uncertainty of some inferred family histories, why deal with reconstructions at all, thus confounding firm census data with problematic creations? There are several important considerations that make it necessary to do so. In many cases, the form that a family displayed in 1977-78 could not have been derived from its form in 1958-59 without intervening steps. For example, a cluster of two nuclear families descended from one original nuclear family is impossible without at least one intervening stage, usually a lineal joint family. Even with their defects, reconstructed sequences generally are much more valid depictions of family histories than just the two stages represented in the census data. Moreover, if there is a typical domestic cycle that involves more than two stages, it could best be demonstrated by analyzing a number of families that had assumed at least three types during the 19-year period of study. We are dependent on one or more reconstructed types in any family sequence of more than two stages. The sequences of family types of the 54 unbranched families are presented in Table 1; the histories of the 45 branched families are depicted in Figure 1.

TABLE 1
Sequence of Family types of Unbranched Families of Shanti Nagar, 1958-59 to 1977-78.

	Family Types[a]				
Sl. No.	*1958-59*	*Intervening (Reconstruted)*	*1977-78*	*Sequence*	*Mortality Sequence Code[b]*
1.	2	4	2	2-4-2	5
2.	2	none	3	2-3	6
3.	3	none	3	3-3	1
4.	3	none	9	3-9	1
5.	3	none	9	3-9	1
6.	3	none	5	3-5	1
7.	3	none	5	3-5	1
8.	3	none	5	3-5	1
9.	3	none	9	3-9	1
10.	3	none	5	3-5	1
11.	3	4 or 5	6	3-4-6 or 3-5-6	1
12.	3	none	5	3-5	1
13.	3	none	7	3-7	1
14.	3	none	3	3-3	1
15.	3	5, 9	10	3-5-9-10	1
16.	3	1, 4, 8	4	3-1-4-8-4	3
17.	3	5, 9	8	3-5-9-8	4
18.	3	none	3	3-3	1

Sl. No.	Family Types[a] 1958-59	Intervening (Reconstruted)	1977-78	Sequence	Mortality Sequence Code[b]
19.	3	none	5	3-5	1
20.	3	none	4	3-4	1
21.	4	none	3	4-3	1
22.	4	several possibilities	4	uncertain	4
23.	4	none	6	4-6	1
24.	4	none	3	4-3	1
25.	4	6, 4, 6	5	4-6-4-6-5	1
26.	4	none	6	4-6	6
27.	4	3	5	4-3-5	5
28.	4	3	5	4-3-5	1
29.	4	3, 5, 9 or 3, 5, 4	8	4-3-5-9-8 or 4-3-5-4-8	4
30.	4	none	6	4-6	1
31.	4	2 or 6	4	4-2-4 or 4-6-4	4
32.	4	3	5	4-3-5	1
33.	4	3, 5, or 6, 5	9	4-3-5-9 or 4-6-5-9	5
34.	4	none	3	4-3	1
35.	4	6	10	4-6-10	1
36.	4	none	4	4-4	6
37.	4	3	5	4-3-5	1
38.	4	3	5	4-3-5	1
39.	4	none	3	4-3	1
40.	4	3	5	4-3-5	5
41.	4	2, 4	8	4-2-4-8	6
42.	5	4	10	5-4-10	3
43.	5	4, 3 or 4, 6	5	5-4-3-5 or 5-4-6-5	2
44.	5	none or 4	6	5-6 or 5-4-6	3
45.	5	9	8	5-9-8	2
46.	5	9	10	5-9-10	1
47.	5	4	6	5-4-6	4
48.	6	10	9	6-10-9	1
49	8	none	8	8-8	1
50.	9	none	10	9-10	4
51.	9	several possibilities	6	uncertain	4
52.	10	none	8	10-8	2
53.	10	9, 6, 5, 4, 3	5	10-9-6-5-4-3-5	2
54.	11	3	1	11-3-1	4

[a] The numbers represent the following family types: (1) subnuclear; (2) supplemented subnuclear; (3) nuclear; (4) supplemented nuclear; (5) lineal joint; (6) supplemented

lineal joint; (7) collateral joint; (8) supplemented collateral joint; (9) lineal-collateral joint; (10) supplemented lineal-collateral joint; (11) polygynous; (12) supplemented polygynous; (13) polygynous supplemented collateral joint; (14) Polygynous lineal-collateral joint.

[b] The mortality code concerns the survival of the family head and his or her spouse from 1958-59 to 1977-78. The numbers represent the following categories: (1) head and spouse both alive; (2) head and spouse both dead (or left the village, leaving family behind); (3) head and both spouse dead; (4) head dead, spouse alive; (5) head dead in 19-year interval, spouse already dead in 1958-59 (or head was celibate); (6) head alive, spouse already dead in 1958-59 (or head divorced or celibate). Note that most family heads were men, but 3 of 110 families were headed by women in 1958-59 and 7 of 170 families had female family heads in 1977-78.

Table 1 and Figure 1 reveal some noteworthy regularities concerning single changes of type. The nuclear family was frequently followed by the lineal joint family, due to the marriage of one of the sons of a family. The nuclear family was succeeded by the lineal-collateral joint family when two sons of a family were married on the same day. Such "double weddings" were popular because they cost less money than two weddings held at different times. The supplemented nuclear family was often succeeded by either the nuclear family or the supplemented lineal joint family. Although in unbranched families the various forms of the joint family changed relatively infrequently to nuclear or supplemented nuclear families, these family types often evolved from joint families as the result of branching. While it is generally assumed that the Indian joint family does not divide during the lifetime of the family head, family division in Shanti Nagar often occurred while both the head and the spouse were still alive.

There are three sequences involving two changes of family type that occur often enough to be noteworthy. The series of supplemented nuclear to lineal joint family (4-3-5) took place 12 times; the series of nuclear to lineal joint to lineal-collateral joint family (3-5-9) occurred 11 times; and the series of nuclear to lineal joint, which then divided into two nuclear families (3-5-3 and 3) had a frequency of 7. Only one sequence of three changes of family type occurred more than twice the series 3-5-9-5 and 3 took place 5 times. In evaluating the significance of series that occurred 12 (the maximum) or fewer times, one must bear in mind that they took place in the context of 99 original families that divided into 176 families 19 years later.

The sequence that Gould identifies as the domestic cycle is nuclear to lineal joint to collateral joint to nuclear (3-5-7-3).

Because a lineal joint family cannot be changed directly into a collateral joint family unless a second son marries and the parents die, all on the same day, a most improbable occurrence, our classification of types would logically require the addition of type 9 (lineal-collateral joint). Thus, Gould's domestic cycle, in our terms, becomes essentially 3-5-9-7-3. A number of alternative series could justifiably be considered tantamount to this basic cycle if the supplemented forms of the various family types in the cycle could be treated as equivalents of the unsupplemented forms. For example, the supplemented collateral joint family (8) could be taken as the equivalent of the collateral joint family (7); thus, the basic sequence could be 3-5-9-8-3 as well as 3-5-9-7-3. None of the possible forms of Gould's complete domestic cycle occur in Shanti Nagar during the 19-year period of study; however, the 3-5-9-8 sequence occurs twice, a frequency so inconsequential that this particular series could hardly be considered as the domestic cycle of Shanti Nagar. Because the families of Shanti Nagar manifest considerable diversity of sequences of family type, the comparison of the domestic cycle to a "circular pathway" appears to a large extent to be inappropriate. A more suitable analogy would be a lattice: at each intersection, or point of choice, a family may be changed into one of several forms; thus, two families starting from the same point (type) may become quite dissimilar as they pass through an intersection or two.

It seems clear that there is no domestic cycle in Shanti Nagar if one thinks in terms of a "single general form," or even in terms of two or three dominant cycles. Although there are important regularities involving a single change in type—for example, the evolution of nuclear families into lineal joint families—the frequency of regularities declines sharply in the case of sequences involving more than one change of type. Beginning with the second change in type, family histories show more diversity than regularity. This characteristic results from the general unpredictability of the sequence of the events (birth, death, marriage, divorce or separation, and family division) that produce change in family type. The largely random nature of the sequence of such events, and of the form that they take in specific families, means that similar sequences of family types involving as few as two changes will be relatively rare.

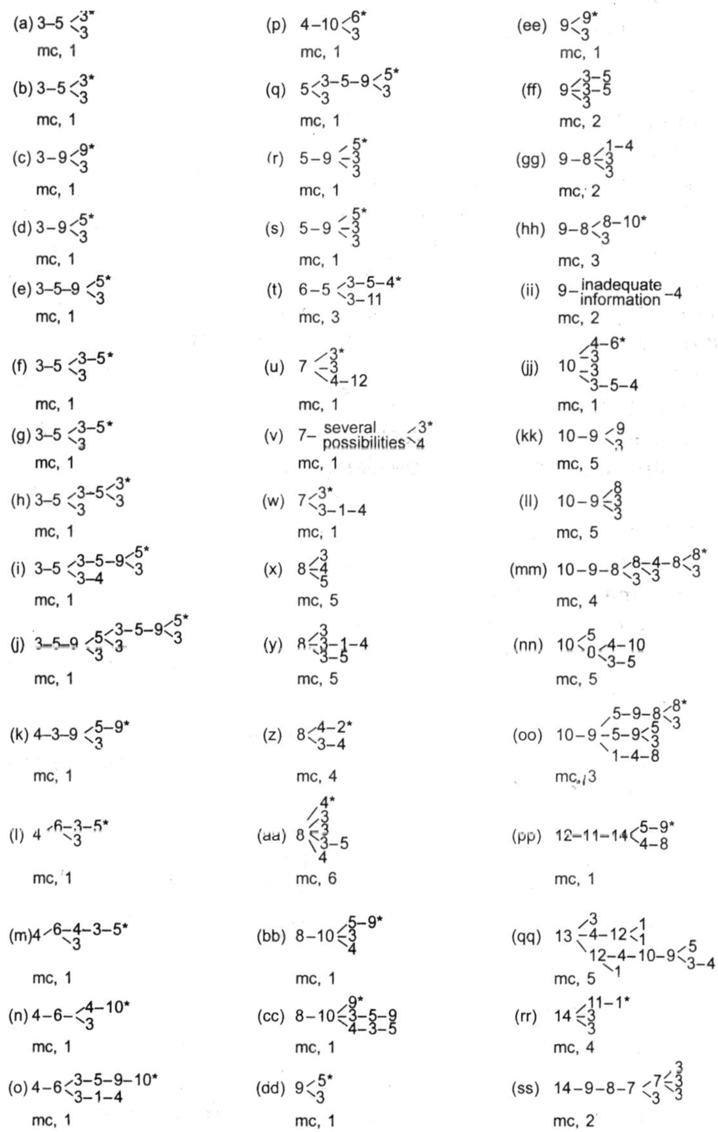

Figure 1. Sequence of family types of branched families of Shanti Nagar, 1958-59 to 1977-78. The diagrams are to be read from left to right The first number represents the family type in 1958-59; the numbers at the ends of the branches represent the family types in 1977-78 the intervening numbers represent reconstructed family types. An asterisk marks the primary family, defined as the descendant family containing the original family head and/or spouse. There are 122 descendant families represented in the diagrams. Of these families, 114 lived in Shanti Nagar and 8 lived outside the village. See Table 1, notes a and b for key to family types and mortality codes (denoted mc).

The histories of two families that pass through four changes of type illustrate the proposition that family histories are so diverse that repetitive sequences of two or more changes of type characterize only a small minority of the families of an Indian village. The two families were similar in many ways: the family heads were landowners of the same age, their wives were alive at the beginning of the sequence, and both had two sons. The head of one family, 42 years old in 1958-59, lived with his wife, mother, mother's brother, two sons, and five daughters. The family was supplemented nuclear. The mother's brother died, the elder son married and then died, the younger brother married his brother's widow, and finally the mother of the family head died. The sequence of family types was 4-6-4-6-5 (Table 1, number 25). The head of the other family, also 42 years of age, lived with his wife, two sons, and three daughters. His wife died, one son married, then the second son married, and finally the older son's wife died. The sequence of family types was 3-1-4-8-4 (Table 1, number 16). Since the elder son was engaged in 1978 and would soon remarry, the next probable stage in the sequence would be 8. Thus, different sequences of weddings and untimely deaths in these two families resulted in dissimilar sequences of family types, even without the additional complication of family division.

Not only is it a fruitless task to discover a single general form of the domestic cycle, but also the question of determining the beginning and end of the domestic cycle has proved to be somewhat perplexing when one attempts to reconcile definitions of the domestic cycle with ethnographic facts. In the Orenstein and Micklin formulation, a family cycle ends and a new one begins with the death of the old family head, the transfer of family leadership to his married son, and the formation of a nuclear family.[4] Gould's domestic cycle begins with the emergence of a nuclear family or families from a joint family after the death of the old family head, a process in which his married son (or sons) assumes the role of family head. In short, the end of one domestic cycle and the beginning of another, and by implication the formation of a new family, involve the death of the old family head and the formation of nuclear families headed by his married sons. For Orenstein and Micklin, the three events (death of family head, change of headship, and formation of nuclear family) occur simultaneously; Gould's more sophisticated model recognizes that the formation of nuclear families need not follow immediately after the old family head's death, but the intervening stage of a collateral joint family is assumed to be brief.

Because death of the old family head, transfer of headship to a married son, and emergence of nuclear family often do not occur together, it is difficult to define a "new" family or the "beginning stage" of a domestic cycle, especially in the case of unbranched families. We illustrate this point by reference to the 17 cases in which headship changed due to death in 16 unbranched families in the 19-year interval between studies. Change of headship usually involved the death of a family head, although transfer also took place when a family head became too old or too ill to function,or when the son of a widow came of age. In 11 cases a married son became head; there were two cases of grandfather to grandson succession, one of grandmother to grandson, one of son to mother, one of husband to wife, and one of brother to brother. The family types after the change of head (N = 15) were two sub-nuclear (women succeeded), two nuclear, six supplemented nuclear (generally because of a surviving widow), and five joint families of various types. If we ignore surviving widows and other relatives who supplement a family, and combine nuclear and supplemented nuclear families, then 8 of 15 families (53 per cent) were nuclear just after the transfer of headship. Thus, the change of leadership and the emergence of a form of the nuclear family do not occur together to an overwhelming degree, moreover, supplemented nuclear families often emerge without a change in leadership. In the two sequences described in detail above, for example, supplemented nuclear families occurred without a change of headship.

Examination of a few cases that illustrate the range of complexity of family histories gives an idea of why it is difficult to say what is meant by a "beginning stage" in the sequence of types of an unbranched family. A simple case concerns a widower, his son, the son's wife, and two grandsons. The widower died and his son became head of a nuclear family while in his early 30s. A similar case involved a man who, upon the death of his father, became head of a nuclear family while in his late 30s or early 40s, when he had seven children succession to headship in unbranched families generally took place when a man was in his

30s, but it could occur from the early 20s to the 50s. One man in this group of families was 62 years old when he became a family head. A more complicated case involved a man who had married three times; his first marriage was without issue, his second produced only daughters, and his third, at the age of 46 years to a woman about 30 years his junior, produced sons and daughters when he died, his eldest son, at 25 years of age, became head of a supplemented collateral joint family of 17 persons. A rather unusual history concerned a supplemented subnuclear family headed by a grandmother; when her grandson had married and was old enough, he became head of a supplemented nuclear family. Then both he and his grandmother died and his widowed mother became head of a supplemented subnuclear family with seven grandchildren and her late son's wife.

If we apply the Orenstein and Micklin formula of a beginning stage to the above family histories, the third case does not fit because the death of the family head did not create a nuclear family; moreover, the family became nuclear on two occasions by the remarriage of the widower and not by the death of the family head. The fourth case is not provided for in the Orenstein and Micklin scheme because the succession of family headship was from grandmother to grandson to mother. Gould's beginning stage of the domestic cycle also does not deal with such contingencies as widower remarriage, the emergence of a family type other than the collateral joint family after the death of the family head, or any succession to headship other than father to son. Furthermore, the implication of a relationship between the domestic cycle and the life cycle causes incongruities. How sensible is it to say that a family has just begun its domestic cycle when, as in the second case above, seven children had already been born to the founding couple? To try to resolve this problem by shifting the beginning of the domestic cycle to a man's marriage, rather than to his assumption of family leadership, is unsatisfactory because it is inconsistent with ethnographic fact; the new marital unit is not an independent family but part of a joint family headed by the father. Concerning the end of the domestic cycle, does it make sense to say that a family has completed its cycle because the old family head has died when, as in the third case above, a family unit of 17 persons, including the old family head's widow, continues to exist? The family has an existence independent of the fate of any specific member. To equate the individual life cycle with the history of a family confounds analysis.

Orenstein and Micklin ignore women in their formulations of the domestic cycle, probably because women were not coparceners under Mitakshara succession. However, there is no legal basis for widows and daughters to inherit land if they so choose, a development that lays the groundwork for a more assertive role of women in family life and lessens the justification for ignoring women in dealing with family structure and evolution. In Shanti Nagar, relatively few women headed families: three in 1958-59 (2.7 per cent) and seven in 1977-78 (4 per cent). Women with strong personalities have always appreciably influenced family life. In the future, supported by their improved legal and economic status, and by considerably more education, women may not only heighten their influence on husbands and sons but may also increasingly choose to head independent families.

It is easier to denote the beginning of a family for branched than for unbranched families. Sons frequently separated from their fathers to form independent families that were generally nuclear. Villagers took such families as new families. Because one can clearly mark the beginning of a new secondary family, and because its form is generally nuclear, it is tempting to take the nuclear family as the beginning stage of the domestic cycle. However, to equate the beginning stage and the nuclear family in the context of a domestic cycle like the life cycle of an organism results in the anomaly that the nuclear family may appear several times in the sequence of types that a family assumes under the tutelage of a single head. Consider some of the clusters in Figure 1, where the primary family changes type a number of times during the lifetime of the head (e.g., Figure 1, f to j). In these cases, the primary families repeatedly assume the nuclear, lineal joint, and lineal-collateral joint forms. The domestic cycle is obviously not like the life cycle of an organism, for an organism cannot retrace its steps and reassume an earlier form. Were one to define the beginning stage of the domestic cycle as the moment that two or more families separate, regardless of whether the descendant families are primary or secondary, then there is no necessary correspondence of family type and beginning stage, especially in clusters where the patriarch and his wife are dead. For example, the clusters illustrated in Figure 1, hh and ll to pp, have various kinds of joint families as well as nuclear families among the descendants of an ancestral joint family.

Finally, the implied correspondence of domestic cycle and life cycle, whereby a couple begins the domestic cycle rather close to the beginning of their marital life, is bedeviled by the same incongruities for clusters as for unbranched families. It appears that sons often separate from their fathers while in their late 20s or early 30s. However, many married men who were not family heads lived in joint families, although some had been married for years and had several children.[5] If and when their joint families divide, such men may "begin" their domestic cycles in middle age with several children. For example, the family diagrammed in Figure 1, ss, was in the process of dividing while we were in Shanti Nagar. The original family head had died 11 years previously, but the family continued as a joint family until all four sons had married. About three years after his marriage, the youngest son, at the age of 25, separated from his brothers. This succession triggered the breakup of the family, each of the remaining three brothers establishing his own nuclear household. The eldest brother was 41 years of age at the time and had four children, one of them a married daughter.

Conclusion

It may be argued that the diversity of the Shanti Nagar data is a function of an excessive number of family types and that a domestic cycle could be posited if the number of family types were substantially reduced. It is true that if the number of family types is reduced to two, nuclear and joint, then the domestic cycle becomes nuclear to joint to nuclear to joint. However, even this simplification does not solve the problems of determining the beginning of the domestic cycle, the implied relationship of the domestic cycle and the life cycle, the fact that in their lifetimes some individuals may skip one of the family types, and the possibility that in a given period of time, one family may undergo several changes of type and another may undergo none. If a third or fourth family type is added to the sequence, there will be many families that do not conform to the posited domestic cycle.

Kolenda's types are ethnographically descriptive and conform to established usage. The ten of her types that we use (and their polygynous variants) do not appear to be too many. "On the whole", comments Kolenda (1968:349), "past parsimony—too few types—has resulted in lack of clarity and incompleteness." We do not regard Kolenda's classification as the final word, any more than she herself does. The "supplemented" family types appear to be in need of reappraisal. However, it would appear that at the present time more progress in the study of the Indian family can be achieved if investigators would use a more or less standard typology, such as that of Kolenda. After accumulating a sufficient number of studies so that the major weaknesses of the classification become apparent, the typology can be revised.

The study of the Indian family by means of types is implicitly concerned with the validity of models in description and explanation. The domestic cycle is an ethnographic model. A full discussion of ethnographic models is beyond the scope of this essay, but one aspect of models needs to be mentioned in relation of a model to the ethnographic facts that it is intended to describe and explain. Models are constructed, Scholte (1973: 668) states, "to reduce the multiplicity of empirical observations to a small number of manageable variables..." Models can be appraised in terms of their internal consistency, from this perspective, the relation of model to ethnographic reality is irrelevant (Schneider 1965: 73). By contrast, one could reasonably take the position that the usefulness of a model varies directly with the degree to which it corresponds with ethnographic facts. As Schneider (1965: 60) sensibly remarks, the correspondence of models and real societies "is perhaps, for some of us, the ultimate concern and the ultimate test." As measured by this test, we submit that the concept of an Indian domestic cycle, as it is generally understood, falls short of the mark.

Although the ethnographic diversity of family histories in Shanti Nagar appears to preclude the existence of a single domestic cycle that comprehends a majority of families, there are nonetheless significant regularities. Nuclear families frequently evolve into lineal joint families, the nuclear family predominates among the family types that emerge from the division of a joint family; nuclear families often separate from joint families during the lifetime of the patriarch and his wife, nuclear families are relatively rarely formed from a lineal joint family due to the death of the patriarch and his wife; and a few three-step sequences are worthy of note. If one is content with these modest conclusions, one can avoid the problems of trying to force the ethnographic diversity into the inappropriate format of a single domestic cycle that is like the growth cycle of a living organism.

One should remember, however, that there is considerable cultural diversity in India and that the greatest caution should be exercised in trying to generalize conclusions based on a single village. Shanti Nagar and Sherupur, for example, are widely separated. The customs of Shanti Nagar are not necessarily typical of more than a small area, and Gould's suggestion that sons rarely separate from living fathers may indeed characterize Sherupur. If this is the case, the domestic cycle that he proposes could possibly be a noteworthy sequence of family types in Sherupur. In all likelihood, however, it would characterize only a small minority of families, just as we have identified a few sequences of three or more family types that occurred frequently enough in Shanti Nagar to attract attention, and yet appeared in only a small proportion of family histories. Although, a domestic cycle in the generally understood sense of the term is not present in Shanti Nagar and has not been shown to exist elsewhere in India yet there are, as yet, insufficient intensively analyzed data for drawing more than tentative conclusions for the country as a whole.

NOTES

Acknowledgments: Field research in India in 1977-78 was sponsored by the Indo-U.S. Subcommission of Education and Culture; the Indo-American Fellowship Program, which awarded a Senior Research Fellowship to R.S. Freed, and the American Institute of Indian Studies, which granted a Senior Research Fellowship to S.A. Freed. We thank those two organizations and also the Department of Anthropology, University of Delhi, with which we were affiliated while in India. We owe a special debt of gratitude for hospitality and invaluable assistance to many colleagues at the University of Delhi: Indera Pal Singh and his associates, Department of Anthropology; J.P.S. Uberoi and M.S.A. Rao, Department of Sociology; and T.N. Madan, Institute of Economic Growth. We greatly appreciate the guidance and unfailing assistance of

P.R. Mehendiratta, Director, American Institute of Indian Studies. We thank Laila Williamson for reading and criticizing the manuscript, and Nicholas Amorosi, who prepared the figure.

1. The various terms appear to be used more or less interchangeably. In their discussions of sequences of family types, Singer (1968:425) writes of the domestic cycle, Gould (1968) describes the developmental cycle, and Kolenda (1968 349) discusses the family cycle Fjellman (1977), who bases his study on the work of Hammel (1961), nonetheless uses domestic cycle, while Hammel uses family cycle. Foster (1978) uses domestic development cycle and family development cycle interchangeably Colever's (1963) analysis of the family cycle in India and the United States deals almost exclusively with demographic data, such as age of marriage, spacing of births, number of children, and mortality. He barely mentions family types, which suggests the possibility of reserving "family cycle" for studies that are largely demographic and "domestic cycle" for research that is oriented toward the sequence of family types. In view of the present diversity of nomenclature, however, any attempt at making terms more precise would probably be premature because of the absence of an emerging consensus.

2. *Mitakshara* law has been substantially modified by post-independence legislation, especially the Hindu Succession Act of 1956. The most noteworthy provision of this act is that mothers, widows, and daughters, as well as sons, may inherit the property of a male Hindu dying intestate (Derrett 1978:xi-xii; Luthra, Raj, and Mediratta 1961:65). This provision of the act has had little effect in Shanti Nagar. Although customary law based on the *Mitakshara* still prevails, the legal basis for substantial change in inheritance has been established. Were women to begin to assert their rights under the Hindu Succession Act of 1956, there would in all probability be substantial repercussions in family life.

3. Desai (1964) advances a noteworthy classification of family types in his admirable study of the Indian family in Mahuva. Because Desai's system is based partly on intensity of interaction among relatives, it involves subjective evaluation by the classifier to a greater extent than does Kolenda's classification. Moreover, Desai's criteria of jointness would not be in accordance with the judgment of the villagers of Shanti Nagar in all cases. For example, households that possess joint property give evidence, according to Desai (1964: 35), of a high degree of jointness. However, in Shanti Nagar some families recognized by everyone as being separate may own property in common, including land. To define family membership in terms of obligations, sentiment, or intensity

of interaction, without taking into account one or two relatively unambiguous criteria recognized by the villagers themselves as defining independent families, such as the use of a common hearth, has the disadvantage that, as noted by Goode (1963:243), "defined thus... almost all family systems... become 'joint families." By contrast, one must keep in mind that Indian nuclear families do not live in isolation and that they generally maintain extensive relations with kin outside the family (Ishwaran 1974:177). On balance, we prefer Kolenda's classification, while recognizing that other classifications have merit and may reflect the emotional ties and reciprocal obligations among relatives in India better than does a more mechanical classification.

4. We have modified the Orenstein and Micklin cycle to bring it into accord with that of Gould. In Orenstein and Micklin's scheme, the domestic cycle begins with a man's wedding while a member of his father's family, and not with his establishment of an independent nuclear family. In this regard, Orenstein and Micklin confuse the male life cycle and the domestic cycle. Since their domestic cycle consists of only two alternating types, the cycle itself is not affected by our shifting the initial point from the joint stage to the beginning of the nuclear stage. The sequence necessarily remains nuclear to joint, to nuclear to joint and so on.

5. In 1958-59 there were 65 married men, not family heads, who lived in joint families. Their mean and median ages were 26.1 and 23 years, respectively. Seven such men (10.8 percent) were older than 37 years. In 1977-78 the mean age of 116 married men, not family heads, who lived in joint families was 28.6 years and the median age was 25.7 years. Seventeen such men (14.7 per cent) were older than 37 years.

REFERENCES

Collver, Andrew: 1963: "The Family Cycle in India and the United States". *American Sociological Review* 28, pp. 86-96.

Derrett, J. Duncan M.: 1978: *The Death of a Marriage Law*. New Delhi: Vikas Publishing House.

Desai, I.P.: 1964: *Some Aspects of Family in Mahuva*. New York: Asia Publishing House.

Fjellman, Stephen M.: 1977: The Akamba Domestic Cycle as Markovian Process. *American Ethnologist* 4, pp. 699-13.

Fortes, Meyer: 1958: Introduction. In *The Developmental Cycle in Domestic Groups*. Jack Goody, ed. pp. 1-14. Cambridge: Cambridge University Press.

Foster, Brian L.: 1978: Domestic Development Cycles as a Link between Population Processes and Other Social Processes. *Journal of Anthropological Research* 34, pp. 415-41.

Freed, Ruth S., and Stanley A. Freed: 1979: "Shanti Nagar. The Effects of Urbanization in a Village in North India. 3. Sickness and Health." *Anthropological Papers of the American Museum of Natural History*. 55, pp. 285-54.

————: 1980: "Rites of Passage in Shanti Nagar." *Anthropological Papers of the American Museum of Natural History* 56, pp. 323-554.

————: 1981: "Enculturation and Education in Shanti Nagar." *Anthropological Papers of the American Museum of Natural History* 57, pp. 49-156.

Freed, Stanley A., and Ruth, S. Freed: 1976: "Shanti Nagar: The Effects of Urbanization in a Village in North India. 1. Social Organization." *Anthropological Papers of the American Museum of Natural History* 53, pp. 1-254.

————: 1978: "Shanti Nagar: The Effects of Urbanization in a Village in North India. 2. Aspects of Economy, Technology, and Ecology." *Anthropological Papers of the American Museum of Natural History* 55, pp. 1-153.

Goode, William J.: 1963: *World Revolution and Family Patterns*. New York: *The Free Press*.

Goody, Jack, ed., 1958: *The Developmental Cycle in Domestic Groups*. Cambridge: Cambridge University Press.

Gould, Harold A.:1968: "Time-Dimension and Structural Change in an Indian Kinship System: A Problem of Conceptual Refinement." In *Structure and Change in Indian Society*. Milton Singer and Bernard S. Cohn, eds. pp. 413-21. New York: Wenner-Gren Foundation for Anthropological Research.

Hammel, E. A.: 1961: The Family Cycle in a Coastal Peruvian Slum and Village. *American Anthropologist* 63, pp. 989-1005.

Ishwaran, K.: 1974: "The Interdependence of Elementary and Extended Family." In *The Family in India. A Regional View*. G. Kurian, ed. pp 163-77. The Hague Mouton.

Kolenda, Pauline M.: 1968: "Region, Caste, and Family Structure: A Comparative Study of the Indian "Joint" Family." *In Structure and Change in Indian Society*. Milton Singer and Bernard S. Cohn, eds. pp. 339-96. New York: Wenner-Gren Foundation for Anthropological Research.

Luthra, S. K.. Baldev Raj, and G. P. Mediratta: 1961: "A Socio-Economic Study of Village Jhatikra." *Census of India*, 1961, Vol. 19, Part 6, No. 8. New Delhi: Government of India Press.

Mandelbaum, David G.: 1970: *Society in India: Continuity and Change*. Vol. 1, Berkeley: University of California Press.

Orenstein, Henry, and Michael Micklin: 1966-67: The Hindu Joint Family: The Norms and the Numbers. *Pacific Affairs* 39, pp. 314-25.

Otterbein, Keith F.: 1970: "The Developmental Cycle of the Andros Household *A Diachronic Analysis.*" American Anthropologist 72, pp. 1412-19.

Scholte, Bob: 1973: "The Structural Anthropology of Claude Levi-Strauss." *In Handbook of Social and Cultural Anthropology*. John J. Honigmann, ed. pp. 637-16. Chicago: Rand McNally.

Schneider, David M.: 1965: "Some Muddles in the Models: Or, How the System Really Works." In *The Relevance of Models for Social Anthropology*. A.S.A. Monographs 1. pp. 25-85. London: Tavistock Publications.

Singer, Milton: 1968: "The Indian Joint Family in Modern Industry." *In Structure and Change in Indian Society*. Milton Singer and Bemard S. Cohn, eds. pp. 423-52. New York: Wenner-Gren Foundation for Anthropological Research.

Sinha, Ramesh P.: 1977: "Indian Joint Family: An Attempt toward Taxonomic Refinement." *Man in India* 57, pp. 60-68.

5

Changes in the Indian Family: An Examination of Some Assumptions

A.M. Shah

The belief that large and joint households were widely prevalent in pre-British India is probably false. The average size of the household in the early decades of the 19th century was more or less the same as it is now.

The assumption of large households in the past has been based on confusion between the household, as a residential unity of patri-kin and their wives, and the family, conceived as an ideal or a legal and emotional entity. Such residential unity was greater in towns than in villages, and in the higher and Sanskritised castes than among others.

It is possible that Sanskritisation of lower castes and Adivasi tribes tends to increase and Westernization to diminish the size of, and the number of relationships in, a household.

The author criticizes the assumption that there has been an inevitable trend from large and complex to small and simple households. There is need to have a fresh look at the problems of the impact of industrialization and urbanization on the household.

"From joint family to elementary (or nuclear or individual) family". This has been a slogan to summarise changes in the family in India during modern times. Recently, some sociologists have pointed out that the change implied by the slogan is not taking place. What is emerging, they say, is not the elementary family but a new form of the joint family. Even these sociologists, however, do not question the correctness of describing the traditional family system of India as the joint family system. This belief about the traditional Indian family subsumes a set of some other beliefs:

(a) traditional India was village India, and the joint family was therefore, a characteristic of village India;

(b) contrari-wise, urban areas are new and characterized by the elementary family;

(c) urbanization, therefore, leads to disintegration of the joint family.

Some sociologists have pointed out that urbanization does not lead to disintegration but only to transformation of the joint family. They do not, however, question the belief that the joint family was always a characteristic of village India. This paper attempts to examine these beliefs about the traditional Indian family because a proper understanding of social change requires a proper understanding of the past. It is concerned with the beliefs about the traditional family only insofar as they refer to its household aspect. It has now become commonplace in the sociology and social anthropology to distinguish between 'household' and 'family'. In common English parlance the word 'family' has several different meanings, including 'household'; the common Indian word for the family, viz., *kutumb*, has likewise several different meanings but, for the sake of technical analysis, 'household' should be distinguished from the other referents of 'family'. For example, two brothers and their wives and children may live in two separate households, but they may be bound by a number of relationships of many kinds. For the sake of clarity, it is necessary to consider such inter-household relationships as distinct from relationships within the household. Although the aim of the study of the family should be to study it in all its aspects, a beginning has to be made with the study of the household. An examination of ideas about the past of the Indian household is, therefore, crucial in a comprehensive study of changes in the Indian family.

II

If we take a census of households in any section of Indian society – a village, town, or caste—and examine their numerical and kinship composition we find a number of types of composition, ranging from the most simple single-member household to a very complex household of many members. A 'simple' household is composed of a complete elementary family or a part of an elementary family. A 'complex' or 'joint' household is composed of two or more elementary families, or of parts of two or more elementary families, or of one elementary family and parts of one or more other elementary families.[1]

Types of Composition

One of the first tasks in an analysis of households is to formulate the types of composition. The structure of the household becomes more complex as more categories of relatives are included. In a one-member household there is no relationship; in a two-member household there is one relationship; but beyond this the addition of one relative means an addition of more than one relationship. For example, the addition of a son's wife to a household of father, mother and son means the addition of relationships not only between the son and his wife but also between father-in-law and daughter-in-law and between mother-in-law and daughter-in-law. Addition of relationships tends to create conflict between roles. For example, the conflict between a man's loyalty to his wife and loyalty to his parents is proverbial. Each person in a household is involved in a complex pattern of behaviour with every other member. Everyone in a household has his own likes and dislikes, habits, tastes and idiosyncracies. Life in a household is marked by sentiments and emotions, and co-operation as well as conflict. Therefore, if our aim is to understand household life in its entirety, the formulation of types of household composition should take into account all the various members of a household. After the types have been formulated, it is necessary to examine the frequencies of households of various types.

Classification of households according to types of composition is not, however, an end in itself. The types are not discrete and haphazard but are interrelated in a developmental process. This process may be in progression or in regression. Progressive development of a household takes place due to increase in membership, mainly by birth and marriage, while regressive development takes place due to decrease in membership, mainly by marriage, death and partition. It may be mentioned in passing that there is always some pattern in the developmental process, but it is not cyclical in nature as considered by Fortes and his associates.[2]

Principles of Aggregation

One of the determinants of the developmental process is a set of explicitly stated rules or norms governing the formation of households. In most sections of Indian society, the bride after marriage leaves her parental home and goes to live in her conjugal home. A son and his wife are required not only to start their married life in his parental home but also to continue to live there afterwards. This norm has a number of implications. For instance, if a man has more than one son, each of the younger sons and his wife will have to live not only with his parents but also with his elder brothers and their wives and children. In fact, frequently people state that a man and his wife should live with his brothers and their wives. Furthermore, they say that brothers and their wives should live together not only during the lifetime of the (brothers') parents but also after their death, and the brothers' sons and their wives should also live in the same household. Sometimes the norm is extended still further.

Taking all these norms together, the central idea is that while female patrilineal descendants of a male ancestor go away to live with their husbands, the male patrilineal descendants and their wives should live together. The wives should be so completely incorporated into their husbands' kin-group that they should not be divorced and that even after their husbands' death they should stay on in the same household. Unmarried children should be with their parents; in the event of divorce or death of their mother, they should stay with their father or his male patri-kin. I would call the central idea behind these norms briefly the principle of residential unity of patri-kin and their wives. It is necessary to clarify that this principle is normative in nature, and that there are always deviations from it as in the case of all norms. The measurement of conformity to and deviation from the principle is therefore, an important problem of inquiry.

Variations from Norms

While the principle is common to almost the entire Hindu society, there are differences among different sections of the society in the extent to which it is observed. First of all, there are differences in the maximum extent to which the developmental process goes in progression along the path set by the principle. For example, in a Gujarat village I have studied, there is no case of two or more married brothers living in a single household after the death of their parents. In a nearby village, on the other hand, there is a considerable number of households of this type. Such differences in the maximum extent may also exist between villages and towns, between one caste and another caste, and between one region and another region.

Secondly, while the maximum extent of the developmental process may be the same in two sections of the society, there may be differences in the frequencies of the cases in which the norm is observed within this extent. For example, in the Gujarat village cited above, only 5 per cent of the total number of households are composed of one or both parents and two or more married sons and their wives and children, while 19 per cent of the households are composed of one or both parents and one married son. This is mainly due to the fact that married sons tend to live separately from parents even before the death of parents. Out of 41 cases of parents having two or more married sons, only 12 in cases (29.26 per cent) all the sons live with the parents in a single household, while 29 in cases (70.73 per cent) all or some of the sons live in separate households (in the village itself). And out of 50 cases of parents having one married son each, in 38 cases (76 per cent) the parents and the son form a joint household, while in 12 cases (24 per cent) the parents and the son live in separate households.

One of the factors affecting the degree of extension of the principle of residential unity of patri-kin and their wives appears to be the degree of Sanskritisation of a caste. This is due to the great emphasis which the Hindu scriptures lay on the high degree of observance of this principle. The ritually higher castes, who are under the greater impact of the scriptures, tend to have a higher degree of extension of the principle. Another factor affecting the degree of extension of the principle appears to be the institution of cross-cousin and uncle-niece marriages.

Family beyond Household

Whatever be the maximum extent to which the principle goes in progression in a particular section of the society, it is important to note that the processes of progressive and regressive developments go on simultaneously in the society taken as a whole. One household may be undergoing progression, another may be undergoing regression. As a result, there are always households in the society which are small and simple in composition, along with households which are large and complex in composition.

When a complex household, say, of two or more married brothers, is partitioned, two or more separate households come into existence, but at the same time a number of other relationships continue to operate. They would cooperate in economic pursuits, hold and manage propertv jointly, help each other on many occasions, celebrate festivals, rituals and ceremonies jointly and so on. This is also a normal process, which highlights the importance of technical distinction between 'household' and 'family' mentioned at the outset. Thus, two or more households may be separate but they may constitute one family.

III

For a long time, students of the Indian family have used ancient Indian literature for information about its past. This information is of two main kinds: (a) pertaining to the property aspect of the family, which is generally included in the study of Hindu Law, and (b) pertaining to certain family rituals, such as the Shraddha.[3]

Definition of Joint Family

The Hindu legal text *Mitakashara* first defines a coparcenary: it comprises only those males who are entitled by birth to an interest in the joint or coparcenary property, i.e., a person himself and his sons, son's sons, and son's grandsons. As each son acquires by birth an interest in coparcenary property, even a father and his unmarried son are sufficient to constitute a coparcenary. Under the Dayabhaga, there is no coparcenary between a man and his son(s), married or unmarried, even though they may be living in a single household. The legal definition of the joint family is based on that of the coparcenary: it consists of all males included in the coparcenary, plus their wives and unmarried daughters. The latter are not coparceners but have only a right to maintenance.

The main points here are two: (i) The legal definition of the joint family is a highly specialized one and has nothing to do with the sociological distinction between elementary family and joint family. A joint family of the legal conception can exist even within an elementary family of the sociological conception. For example, a father and an unmarried son, or a widow and her unmarried son are sufficient to constitute a joint family according to law. (ii) The law does not lay down the rule that the joint family of the legal conception should always be a joint household. A son may live separately from his father, and one brother from another, but they continue to be members of their respective joint property group. In brief, the law is concerned primarily with the rights of constituting a property-holding group and of maintenance therefrom, and not with the constitution of the household group.

In the sacred texts (Shastras), the question as to who should hold and inherit property is discussed usually in relation to the question as to who should perform the Shraddha ritual for whom. In other words, the legal definition of the constitution of the joint family tends to coincide with and is sanctioned by the definition of the circle of persons required to perform the Shraddha. This circle of persons need not live in a single household, just as the persons constituting the joint property group need not live in a single household. It seems to me that it was because of the coincidence of the legal and the ritual definitions of the joint family that the definition given in the Shastras came to be accepted as the general definition of the Hindu joint family. I shall call it the Indological definition. As most of the early studies were carried out by Indologists (including historians, Sanskritists, and Orientalists) on the basis of sacred literature, and as both Indologists and lawyers were dominant in the academic field in India, the Indological idea of the joint family carried a lot of weight and gained popularity.

The Indological-cum-legal material on the Indian family was used by Henry Maine in his general theory of the evolution of the family. He compared and contrasted the joint family of India with the individual family of the West, and considered the latter as later in evolution than the former. He, thus, laid the foundation of the sociological study of the Indian family, and through him the Indological view of the Indian family came to be accepted in sociology.

I have pointed out the fact that the Indological definition is not concerned primarily with the composition of the household. Insofar as it was concerned with the household, it laid down only the definition of the ideal household, or in my terms, only the maximum extent of progression of the developmental process of households. The Indological literature does not provide any information on the various types of households, nor on the frequency of households of each type. Obviously there was no census of households, in any section of Hindu society, at any period of time. Furthermore, the literature provides information more about the Brahmins and a few other higher castes whose property relations and rituals were governed by the sacred texts. With regard to the household also, the ideal that the texts emphasized was high–a household of four generations[4] – and it seems only the higher castes tried to emulate the ideal to a higher degree. The texts do not provide any idea of differences in the family life of different sections of the society.[5]

IV

We begin to get more precise data on the household only with the beginning of the British administration in India. The Office of the Census Commissioner of India has planned to publish a series of volumes on population estimates for the period from the 18th century to 1871 on the basis of censuses conducted in different parts of India during that period. The first volume in this series, dealing with the decade 1820-30, was published recently.[6] It seems to me that it will be extremely useful if attempts are made to find and then analyze the original schedules of all these censuses. My experience in Gujarat indicates that such attempts are likely to be fruitful. During my search for sources for the study of social history of villages in central Gujarat, I found in the taluka headquarters the original schedules of a census carried out by Captain Cruikshank and his associates,[7] the same schedules that he used in compiling general reports on different parts of Gujarat, which have in turn been used by the

Bhattacharyas in their volume on population estimates for 1820-30 mentioned above. In this census of Gujarat, a Census Register was prepared for every village, in which were listed the names of heads of households in the village according to their religion and caste, and against each name were given the following details: (i) houses and huts, (ii) men, (iii) women, (iv) servants and slaves, and (v) total number of persons.

Households in Gujarat

I have made a detailed analysis of the 1820-30 census data on the household composition in a Gujarat village.[8] It shows (a) that the average size of the household was 4.5, and (b) that progressive development of households rarely, if ever, went beyond the phase of co-residence of two or more married sons during the lifetime of their parents. It is significant that census data of a village in Maharashtra of the same period, which Professor Ghurye has presented in his book *After a Century and a Quarter,*[9] shows the same average size of the household as in the Gujarat village. The early nineteenth century data, thus, indicate that we cannot start the study of changes in the family in India with the assumption that villagers in traditional India always lived in large and complex households of three or four generations. We need a more realistic base line, and the early nineteenth century census data are a very useful source for reconstructing such a base line.

As regards differences in the family between rural and urban areas also, it is important to keep in view the position at the beginning of the nineteenth century. The early nineteenth century census data indicate that there was a higher proportion of the population of higher and more Sanskritised castes in towns than in villages. The bulk of the population in villages consisted of lower and less Sanskritised castes. If this point is related to my earlier point that the higher castes were under the greater impact of scriptures and there was, therefore, a higher degree of observance of the principle of residential unity of patri-kin and their wives among higher castes, it follows that there was a higher degree of observance of this principle in towns than in villages. The reality was, thus, quite the reverse of the widely prevalent belief that there was a greater emphasis on joint households, (i.e., on the principle of residential unity of patri-kin and their wives) in villages than in towns in traditional India.

V

Although the censuses upto 1871 had certain obvious drawbacks–they covered only small areas in the country, and even within a small area the census was not taken simultaneously in all the villages and towns–it is remarkable that they collected and recorded a great deal of information of demographic and sociological value. The later censuses covered wider areas and became uniform in techniques, terminology and classification, but there was retrogression in the case of information concerning the household. In all the censuses from 1867 upto 1941, the distinction between 'household', 'house' and 'building' was not followed uniformly in all the Provinces and States and sometimes not even in all parts of a single Province or State, and hardly any attempt was made to collect information either on the kinship or on the numerical composition of households. Nevertheless, even the meagre information they provided is highly suggestive.

False Belief

All of them show that the average size of the household was rather low, between 4.5 and 5. E.A. Gait, the Census Commissioner for 1911, stated the position very succinctly: "the average population per house is 4.9 or much the same as in European countries. In the British Isles it ranges from 4.8 in Scotland to 5.2 in England and Wales".[10] This suggests that the people in India lived mostly in small and simple households. It is noteworthy, however, that almost all the census officials interpreted their figures unrealistically. They assumed that Indians in pre-British days always lived in large households, and therefore, they concluded from their figures that the traditional household system was disintegrating due to modernization. The assumption about the past was a great obstacle in a realistic interpretation of the figures before them.

In a recent paper, Henry Orenstein[11] has used the census data to examine the usual general idea about changes in the Indian household. He has posed the problem as follows: If the widespread belief that the modern processes of industrialization, Westernization, etc., of traditional societies such as India lead to smaller households, then the increasing industrialization, Westernization, etc. should be reflected in a decreasing average size of the household. He presents figures to show that the average size of the household has not only not decreased from the 1867 to the 1951 census, but there has been on the contrary a slight tendency–very slight indeed–towards increase. This suggests that the modern processes of industrialization, Westernization, etc. have not brought about the so-called disintegration of large and joint households. Orenstein conjectures, I think quite rightly, that the belief about the wide prevalence of large and joint households in pre-British India is false.

VI

During the last thirty years or so, professional sociologists and social anthropologists have studied the problem of changes in the family in India. Some of these studies are concerned only with the household and some with the household as well as other aspects of the family. I would refrain from commenting here upon those studies which are not concerned with the household, as well as upon those studies of the household which are not concerned with the problem of change.[12] As far as the studies of changes in the household are concerned, I submit that most of them have suffered from the assumptions I have examined in this chapter. It seems to me that we need a more sophisticated framework for our study.

First of all, we have to distinguish the normal developmental process from change. This is a difficult task, but we have to face it. Studies of the early nineteenth century data on the household seem to me to be very necessary for this purpose.

Secondly, there is no point in postulating a single line of change for the entire Indian society. I suggest that it would be profitable to bring into the study of the household Srinivas's ideas on Sanskritisation and Westernization. In this context it is worthwhile to recall the slight increase in the average size of the household indicated by Orenstein. It is possible that this increase may be due to some demographic factor. Orenstein himself has suggested that it may be due to a rise in the average number of children or in the average number of adults per household. (If the latter is true, it strengthens the argument in favour of an increasing overall emphasis on large and joint household). Notwithstanding the influence of demographic factors, it seems worth inquiring whether the Sanskritisation of lower castes and Adivasi tribes that has been going on a massive scale in the country has contributed anything to an overall greater emphasis on the principle of residential unity of patri-kin and their wives. It cannot be denied that Westernization of the higher castes has contributed to a lesser emphasis on the principle, but the countervailing influence of Sanskritisation might have led to an overall tendency in favour of greater emphasis on it. What I plead is that let us not assume that there has been an inevitable trend from large and complex (or joint) to small and simple households.

Finally, we require to have a fresh look at the problem of the impact of industrialization and urbanization on the household. It has already been pointed out that the situation in the past was possibly quite the reverse of what we have been assuming it to be. That is to say, there was greater emphasis on large and joint households in towns than in villages. Migration of rural people to towns, therefore, does not necessarily mean migration from a social environment of large and joint households to that of small and simple households. It seems to me that the study of the long established population of older towns and cities is extremely important. I have in mind for example the walled cities of Delhi, Agra and Ahmedabad, certain sections of the population of even Mumbai, Calcutta and Chennai and the large number of small towns. We should also examine the extent to which migrants to a town tend to be its permanent residents, and whether they practise the old norms when they are permanently settled. The whole question of relation between migration and the household in India seems to be complicated. In any case, we begin to understand it better if we get rid of the old established assumptions.[13]

NOTES

1. The terms 'simple household' and 'complex household' are not discussed here in detail for want of space. However, it may be noted that (i) 'elementary family' is not the same as 'simple household'; actually, a household composed of a complete elementary family is only one of the several types of 'simple households'; and (ii) 'joint household' is only a convenient alternative of 'complex household'. The background for discarding the usual dichotomy of elementary and joint family is provided in my paper "Basic Terms and Concepts in the Study of Family in India", "Indian

Economic and Social History Review", Vol. 1, No. 3, January-March 1964, pp. 1-36. I have dealt with most of the points of this paper at length in my forthcoming book on the family in India.

2. See Jack Goody (ed.), "The Developmental Cycle in Domestic Groups", Cambridge University Press, Cambridge, 1958.
3. For a fuller discussion of this literature as well as for citations, see my paper, *op. cit.*, pp. 10-14.
4. The definition of the household composition on the basis of generations is also confusing. For a discussion of this point see my paper, *op. cit.*, pp. 5-6.
5. The Indological literature is wider than the literature I have considered here, but I doubt if the other literature also provides the kind of data the sociologist needs for the study of the household.
6. D. Bhattacharya and B. Bhattacharya (eds.), Census of India 1961, Report on the Population Estimates of India (1820-30), Office of Registrar General, Delhi, 1965.
7. For a detailed description of these records, see A.M. Shah, R.G. Shroff and A.R. Shah, Early Nineteenth Century Village Records in Gujarat", in Tapan Raychaudhuri (ed), "Contributions in Indian Economic History", Vol.II, Firma K L Mukhopadhyaya, Calcutta, 1963, pp. 89-100.
8. See my Ph.D. dissertation "Social Structure and Change in a Gujarat Village", in the library of the University of Baroda, Baroda, 1964, pp. 76-86.
9. Popular Book Depot, Bombay, 1960, p. 14.
10. "Census of India 1911", Vol.1 (India), Part I (Report), Government Printing, Calcutta, p. 47.
11. "The Recent History of the Extended Family in India", Social Problems", Vol. 8, No. 4, Spring 1961, pp. 41-50.
12. I have dealt with the terminological and conceptual aspects of some of the other studies in my paper, *op. cit.*, and my forthcoming book on the Indian family includes a rather lengthy review of the literature on the subject.
13. I thank all those who commented upon my paper at the seminar on "Trends of Socio-economic Change in India – 1871-1961", Indian Institute of Advanced Study, Simla; a seminar in the Department of Sociology, University of Delhi; and a panel discussion on "Industrialisation and Its Social Consequences: The Family", Conference of Indian Sociologists – 1967, Bombay. I thank Dr. R.D. Sanwal for his comments on the penultimate draft of the paper.

6

Changing Family Types in India[1]

Stanley A. Freed and Ruth S. Freed

Studies of the Indian family have strongly been affected by the common assumption of social science, based largely on Western experience, that industrialization, urbanization, and modernization lead inevitably to a transition from the extended family to the nuclear family. The Indian form of the extended family, commonly called the joint family, is usually patrilineal and patrilocal and/or virilocal. It emphasizes filial and fraternal solidarity and, based on the *Mitakshara*, a twelfth century legal text, each male family member is entitled to an equal share of the family property (Mandelbaum 1970: 35). Two general factors are commonly identified as stimulating the transition from joint to nuclear family. First, it is argued that the nuclear family is better adapted to modern economic conditions than the joint family (Goode 1963:10-18); for example, the nuclear family is said to be better suited to the modern labour market because its geographical and social mobility are relatively unhampered by ties of kinship. In this view, family type is directly influenced by economic factors; the employment practices and conditions of work in modern industrial enterprises favour small social units and promote the disintegration of larger ones. Second, there is an ideology of the nuclear family, Western in tone and origin, which is in accordance with the ideology and conditions of technological development and economic progress (Goode 1963:19). This ideology extols independence, equality, and the importance of the individual. It is potentially destructive of the traditional Indian joint family. When economic development increases employment opportunities, young men, supposedly chafing at living under the control of older kinsmen, presumably seize the opportunity to establish independent households.

Empirical research has not yet settled the question of whether the nuclear family is gaining ground at the expense of the joint family under the stimulus of economic development and modernization. Proponents of the two basic positions in the "joint family controversy" argue from different perspectives, a circumstance which makes it difficult to evaluate the relative validity of the two points of view. Those social scientists who hold that the incidence of the joint family has remained relatively unchanged frequently invoke the normal functioning of the domestic cycle as the variable that produces the illusion of change in a basically stable situation (e.g., Gould 1968; Kessinger 1974). Birth, marriage, and death eventually produce changes in the structure of all families and can result in a fair amount of variation in the proportions of various family types in a given community from year to year. Such variation is random and should not be interpreted as a unidirectional trend.

Studies that support the hypothesis of a transition from joint to nuclear family generally establish a correlation between a family type and a specific variable; if the variable has increase or will increase, as often seems likely, so will the proportion of the associated family type. For example, Yadava (1966: 27-28) presents data that demonstrate the family heads who hold non-traditional jobs that pay a cash income and provide relative economic independence are much more likely to head a nuclear family than those who follow traditional occupations. Converting the correlation to a causal relationship, Yadava (1966:29) sees a definite trend toward an increase in the proportion of nuclear families, for the number of non-traditional jobs is increasing (see also Bhadra 1977:46).

The trouble with the correlational approach to the joint family controversy is that it has proved difficult to establish a consistent relationship between a particular variable one and a family type.

For example, while Yadava (1966) observed a correlation between occupation and family type in one village in the Union Territory of Delhi, S. Freed and R. Freed (1969:352-353) present data from another village in Delhi Union Territory demonstrating that this apparent correlation is actually due to the age of a family head rather than to his occupation. Younger men were more likely to be employed in non-traditional occupations than older men and were also less likely to head a joint family because they would generally have no son old enough to be married. A test, controlled for age, of occupation and family type showed that these two variables were not correlated.[2]

The joint family controversy is further bedeviled by problems of definition and by a scarcity of studies that involve a significant time dimension. In her comparison of 26 studies of Indian family types, Kolenda (1968) notes that no two social scientists used the same definitions. The few studies that involve a time period of more than a decade are usually based on governmental records. Such studies tend to be inconclusive because of the problems of interpreting the census and other archival data in terms of family structure.

We offer an analysis of changing family types in the North Indian village that we call Shanti Nagar based on holistic ethnographic studies that we made in the village in 1958-59 and 1977-78. The approximately nineteen-year interval between the two studies, during which substantial social and economic change occurred, was long enough to permit the identification of any significant trend involving family types that might have taken place. The same set of definitions was used in both studies, which resolved the problem of dissimilar definitions that generally afflicts comparative studies. The fact that we have holistic ethnographic data for both studies permits us to analyze the effects of similar variables at both points in time, moreover, the earlier data could be reanalyzed in terms of variables that were seen to be critical only after the later data had been analyzed.

We do not deal with the domestic cycle in this essay. The analysis of the domestic cycle is a complex problem in its own right and will be treated in another essay (S. Freed and R. Freed n.d.). However, in our analysis of changing family types, we have taken into account the random effects of the domestic cycle and controlled them by routine statistical procedures.

We define a family as a group of kin who usually cook together when circumstances permit and share at least their food supplies. In our earlier analysis of the families of Shanti Nagar (S. Freed and R. Freed 1969), we used Kolenda's (1968) classification of family types, for it identifies a sufficient number of types to do justice to the ethnographic situation and yet is not overly elaborated; it fits the Shanti Nagar data very well; and the descriptive names used for each category make it easy to visualize the structure of a family with considerable precision from its type. Kolenda's system has proved to be a significant advance in the study of the Indian family and appears to be coming gradually into general use. She defines the nuclear family as a married couple with or without unmarried children, the subnuclear family as a fragment of a former nuclear family (for example, a widow or widower and unmarried children), and a joint family as consisting of at least two married couples related either lineally (for example, a father, mother, and their married son) or collaterally (for example, two married brothers). The unmarried family members who are not children of any of the married couples of a family supplement the family. The three basic types, subnuclear, nuclear, and joint, qualified by the adjectives, lineal, collateral, and supplemented, yield ten family types: nuclear, supplemented nuclear, subnuclear, supplemented subnuclear, collateral joint, supplemented collateral Joint, lineal joint, supplemented lineal joint, lineal-collateral joint, and supplemented lineal-collateral joint families. Kolenda also recognizes single-person families and a residual category that she terms "other." We did not require the "other" category, and, as Shanti Nagar had only one single person family in 1958-59 and none in I977-78, we made no use of the single-person category, classifying the one such family as subnuclear.

Another set of family types can be formed in a similar fashion based upon the polygynous family composed of a man and more than one wife. Thus, a supplemented polygynous family is a polygynous family with an unmarried relative who is not a child of the husband and one of the wives; and a polygynous lineal-collateral joint family is a lineal-collateral joint family in which at least one of the component families is composed of a man and his two or more wives. Shanti Nagar had a few polygynous families of various types in both the earlier and later periods (see Table 2).

Because of the small number of many types of families in Shanti Nagar, it is sometimes necessary for purposes of discussion and analysis to combine them into a smaller number of categories. These combined family types are as follows: "nuclear" includes nuclear families, all types of subnuclear families, and polygynous families; "supplemented nuclear" includes supplemented nuclear families and supplemented polygynous families; "joint" includes all forms of joint and polygynous joint familles.[3]

Shanti Nagar

Shanti Nagar is located in the Union Territory of Delhi northwest of the City of Delhi. As is typical of the region, the village consists of a compact habitation site surrounded by, cultivated fields. Although agriculture was the principal occupation, many men had salaried urban jobs. Men often practiced more than one occupation; the combination of farming and urban employment was common. Most women also had two principal occupations: agricultural work and housework. A detailed description of the village as it was in 1958-59 may be found in a series of monographs that have appeared in the last several years (S. Freed and R. Freed 1976, 1978; R. Freed and S. Freed 1979, 1980, 1981).

In the interval between our two periods of research in Shanti Nagar, a number of social and economic trends had become established: the educational level had risen dramatically, there had been a substantial increase in salaried urban occupations, the technological level of agriculture was considerably higher, and the villagers were more deeply involved in markets outside Shanti Nagar, owing largely, to the construction of the immense Delhi Vegetable Market in north Delhi and within easy reach of the farmers of Shanti Nagar. Some of these trends are often said to favour an increasing proportion of nuclear families and a decreasing proportion of joint families (e.g., Kolenda 1968: 340-341).

Changing Family Types

Our earlier study of family types in Shanti Nagar (S. Freed and R. Freed 1969) focused on the traditional joint family problem; we attempted to find significant correlations between family types and social variables that would, perhaps, suggest a trend toward an increasing proportion of nuclear families in the village and a breaking apart of joint families. Our roster of social variables included the urban experience, education, age, and type of current employment of the family head and the caste, type of house (mud or fired brick), and landholding status of the family. We found only two variables that seemed to correlate significantly with family type: the ownership of land and age of family head. Families that owned land (almost all such families were cultivators also) and those with heads aged 40 years or older were significantly more likely to be joint than were landless families and those with younger family heads. The correlation of family type and age of family head was strong ($P < .001$); the correlation of landholding status and family type was considerably weaker ($P < .02$). Neither of these correlations suggested a trend toward an increasing proportion of nuclear families.

Although one may cautiously infer the presence or absence of trends from an analysis of synchronic data, the question of change is better studied with data from at least two points in time. We can now make such an analysis for Shanti Nagar because data from 1977-78 are available for comparison with those from 1958-59.The combined family types of Shanti Nagar at those two points in time are presented in Table 1. The most impressive features of these data are the absence of a trend towards nuclear families and an increase in the proportion of joint families, chiefly at the expense of supplemented nuclear families. These differences may be identified more precisely from the full list of family types which is presented in Table 2. Here we see that there has been a considerable increase in the proportion of lineal and supplemented lineal joint families to the detriment of the proportion of supplemented nuclear families. Are these observed differences significant or are they no more than random fluctuations owing to the normal functioning of the domestic cycle? Statistical analysis is the best way to deal with this question. We may rephrase the question as follows: how well does the distribution of family types in 1977-78 conform to the distribution of 1958-59? To answer this question, we calculated a value of chi-square (see Thomas 1976:284-291 for a discussion of the procedure) which showed that the differences in the two sets of data are too large to be due to random variation (Table 3). A factor or factors other than chance appear to have been involved. This conclusion is not affected when the family types of table 3 are collapsed into combined family types in order to eliminate cells with fewer than five cases; the probability that the later data represent the same distribution of family types as the earlier data is less than .001 (Table 4).

Most of the growth in the proportion of joint families took place among landless villagers, as can be seen from the data presented in Table 5. This change in the proportion of joint families has been of such magnitude that, by 1977-78, landless families had attained a proportion of joint families quite similar to that of landowning families and there remained no hint of the correlation between differences in landholding status and family type that could be observed in the data from 1958-59 (S. Freed and R. Freed 1969:354-356). In searching for social factors that could be the correlation of this development among landless families, we focused on two variables that appeared to be promising. The first was the fact that many landless people in 1977-78 were participating in agriculture as cultivators rather than chiefly as labourers as had previously been the case. Bose (1978: 159-163) and Sen (1965:15-16) report that cultivating families are more likely to be joint than non-cultivators. Second, the increase in the proportion of joint families involved almost entirely lineal and supplemented lineal joint families, which suggested that an increase in the average age of landless family heads might be involved because older men would generally be more likely to have married sons than younger men.

TABLE 1
Combined Family Types in Shanti Nagar by Time Period

Period	*Nuclear*	*Supplemental Nuclear*	*Joint*	*Total*
1958-59	41 (37.3)	28 (25.4)	41 (37.3)	110
1977-78	67 (38.1)	22 (12.5)	87 (49.4)	176

(The figures in parentheses are row percentages).

TABLE 2

Family Types in Shanti Nagar by time Period

Family type	*Period* 1958-59	1977-78
Subnuclear	3 (2.7)	4 (2.3)
Supplemented subnuclear	2 (1.8)	2 (1.1)
Nuclear	34 (30.9)	60 (34.1)
Supplemented nuclear	27 (24.5)	21 (11.9)
Lineal joint	9 (8.2)	38 (21.6)
Supplemented lineal joint	2 (1.8)	9 (5.1)
Collateral joint	3 (2.7)	3 (1.7)
Supplemented collateral joint	8 (7.3)	11 (6.2)
Lineal-collateral joint	8 (7.3)	16 (9.1)
Supplemented lineal-collateral joint	8 (7.3)	10 (5.7)
Polygynous	2 (1.8)	1 (0.6)
Supplemented polygynous	1 (0.9)	1 (0.6)
Polygynous supplemented collateral joint	1 (0.9)	0
Polygynous lineal-collateral joint	2 (1.8)	0
Total	110	176

(The figures in parentheses are column percentages).

TABLE 3

Chi-Square Test of the Significance of the Different Distributions of Family Types in Shanti Nagar, 1958-59 and 1977-78

Family types	*Observed (O) in 1977-78*	*Estimated (E) for 1977-78 from Data of 1958-59*	*$(O-E)^2/E$*
Subnuclear	4	4.8	.1333
Supplemented subnuclear	2	3.2	.4500
Nuclear	60	54.4	.5764
Supplemented nuclear	21	43.2	11.4083
Lineal joint	38	14.4	38.6777
Supplemented lineal joint	9	3.2	10.5125
Collateral joint	3	4.8	.6750

Family types	*Observed (O) in 1977-78*	*Estimated (E) for 1977-78 from Data of 1958-59*	*(O–E)²/E*
Supplemented collateral joint	11	12.8	.2531
Lineal-collateral joint	16	12.8	.8000
Supplemented lineal-collateral joint	10	12.8	.6125
Polygynous	1	3.2	1.5125
Supplemented polygynous	1	1.6	.2250
Polygynous supplemented collateral joint	0	1.6	1.6000
Polygynous lineal-collateral joint	0	3.2	3.2000
Total	176	176	70.6363

(Chi-square = 70.6363; degrees of freedom = 13; $p < .001$)

In our report concerning the family types of 1958-59, we surmised that cultivation may have had a significant relationship with the joint family because "the greater resources of the joint family, especially the larger number of persons available for farm labour, make it a more efficient farming unit under the present conditions of village agriculture" (S. Freed and R. Freed 1969:356). However, we were not able to demonstrate the existence of a connection apart from the possible effects of landownership because almost all landowners were cultivators and only a few landless persons were tenant-cultivators. A noteworthy economic development that characterized the 1977-78 period was that twenty landless families were leasing land and participating in agriculture as cultivators. Leasing agreements varied in their details but generally involved the leasing of from one to three acres of land for the cultivation of tomatoes. The cultivation and marketing of tomatoes involved considerable family labour and appeared to be well suited to joint families or large nuclear families.

The presence of so many landless cultivators permitted a chi-square test of the correlation of family type and cultivating status that was to some extent independent of landholding status, although most cultivators were still landowners. While there was a higher proportion of joint families among cultivators than those among non-cultivators (55 per cent and 40 per cent respectively), the difference was not statistically significant (P < .1 5). Moreover, it is much more likely that the leasing of land for a tomato crop depended upon the form and size of a family and not *vice versa*. That family type is the independent variable seems evident because a given family may lease land intermittently from year to year but does not change its structure every, time it enters into or terminates a leasing agreement. Families generally search for economic opportunities that fit their personnel and structure rather than making fundamental changes in family structure to suit economic circumstances. Families do, however, adjust to the economic situation in many ways; for example, family members may live away from home because of employment opportunities.

TABLE 4
CHI-SQUARE TEST OF THE SIGNIFICANCE OF THE DIFFERENT DISTRIBUTIONS OF COMBINED FAMILY TYPES IN SHANTI NAGAR, 1958-59 AND 1977-78

Combined Family types	*Observed (O) in 1977-78*	*Estimated (E) for 1977-78 from Data of 1958-59*	*(O–E)²/E*
Nuclear	67	65.6	.0299
Supplemented Nuclear	22	44.8	11.6036
Joint	87	65.6	6.9811
Total	176	176	18.6146

(Chi-square = 18.6146; Degrees of freedom = 2; p< .001)

TABLE 5
COMBINED FAMILY TYPES IN SHANTI NAGAR BY OWNERSHIP OF LAND AND TIME PERIOD

Landownership	*Nuclear*	*Supplemented Nuclear*	*Joint*	*Total*
Owns land				
1958-59	15 (25.4)	16 (27.1)	28 (47.5)	59
1977-78	34 (35.1)	14 (14.4)	49 (50.5)	97
Landless				
1958-59	26 (51.0)	12 (23.5)	13 (25.5)	51
1977-78	33 (41.8)	8 (10.1)	38 (48.1)	79

(The figures in parentheses are row percentages).

Because the change in patterns of cultivation was not significantly correlated with the increase in the proportion of landless joint families, we turned to a detailed analysis of census data from both periods. The analysis showed that a rise in the average age of landless family heads had taken place; this increase in age appears to be the principal factor associated with the growth in the proportion of landless joint families. In simplified form, the argument is that older family heads will, in general, more often have sons old enough to marry than younger family heads. The marriage of a son transforms a family from a nuclear family to a lineal joint family. Therefore, a rise in the average age of family heads will hypothetically be correlated with an increase in the proportion of joint families.

This hypothesis involves nuances which will become clear from the analysis of the relevant population parameters, several of which must be calculated in order to test the hypothesis. They are: the mean age of fathers with a son or sons (A), mean age of oldest living son (B), most probable age of marriage for a male (C), and mean age of male family heads (D).[4] The age of the average father at the wedding of his eldest son is the critical, or threshold, value (T); once a father's age approximately equals or exceeds the threshold level, his son would be old enough to marry at which time the family would be transformed into a lineal joint family. The threshold value is calculated as follows: T = A – B + C. In this equation, A – B yields the mean age of fathers at the birth of their eldest living sons. These data are presented in Table 6.

An appraisal of the potential proportion of lineal joint families can be made by comparing T and D, as given in Table 6. When D is significantly lower than T, we would expect relatively few lineal joint families. When D is as great or greater than T, we would anticipate a relatively greater proportion of lineal joint families, for the mean age of fathers at the wedding of their eldest sons (T) acts as a threshold. A slight rise in the average age of family heads in the vicinity of T significantly augments the anticipated transformation from nuclear to lineal joint family. Because so much (84.5 per cent) of the growth of the proportion of landless joint families (as a combined family type) in comparison with other family types has been due to a rise in the proportions of lineal and supplemented lineal joint families, we regard an

TABLE 6

Selected Ages of Males (in Years) and Proportion of Joint Families by Landownership and time Period*

Landownership	Mean Age Fathers with Sons (A)		Mean Age Eldest Living Son (B)		Most Probable Age of Male Marriage (C)	Threshold Age (T)†	Mean Age Male Family Heads (D)		Proportion of Joint Families Male Heads	
Time Period	*Number*	*Mean*	*Number*	*Mean*			*Number ‡*	*Mean*	*Number*	*Per cent*
Owns Land										
1958-59	69	44.5	69	17.2	19	46.3	58	47.2	58	48.3
1977-78	121	45.6	121	19.2	22.5	48.9	92	50.3	92	53.3
Landless										
1958-59	41	40.1	41	13.3	15.5	42.3	48	41.0	49	26.5
1977-78	86	41.2	86	15.7	20	45.5	76	45.2	77	49.4

* The population of Shanti Nagar in 1958-59 was 799 persons of whom 407 were males and 392 were females. Of the 110 families, 107 families had male heads. In 1977-78, the population was 1324 persons of whom 695 were males and 629 were females. Males headed 169 of the 176 families.

† Threshold age is the mean age of fathers at the wedding of their eldest sons. It is calculated by the formula, T = A – B + C.

‡ No age was recorded for one family head for each time period.

explanation of the latter phenomenon as sufficient explanation for the general increase in the proportion of joint families.

The ages needed for the calculation of the threshold age were all mean ages except for the most probable age at which a male gets married. Our census data do not contain the ages at which individuals marry; therefore, it was not possible to calculate the mean age of marriage. However, this age could be estimated because the data contain the age and marital status of each individual. To estimate the age at which the average male married, we prepared a frequency distribution by age of ever-married and never-married males broken down by landholding status for both time periods. We looked for the age in each of the four arrays at which there appeared to be a division between ever-married and never-married males, that is, few males younger than the age in question were married and few males older than that age were unmarried. The typical, or most probable, age of marriage for the 1958-59 landowning males (N=238) was 19 years; for the 1958-59 landless males (N = 161), 15.5 years; for the 1977-78 landowning males (N = 395), 22.5 years; for the 1977-78 landless males (N = 295), 20 years.[5]

Although we have set the most probable age of marriage at a point rather than an interval, inspection of the frequency distributions indicates that these probable ages are best understood as rather narrow intervals of two or three years during which almost all men married. Before the interval, very few males were married; after it almost all of them were married. The intervals for landless males appeared to be from I4 to 16 years of age in 1958-59 and from 19 to 21 years of age in 1977-78; the intervals for landowning males were from 17 to 19 or 20 years of age in 1958-59 and from 21 to 24 years of age in 1977-78.

The significance for changing family types of the increase in the mean age of male landless family heads is apparent by an inspection of the data in Table 6. In 1958-59, the mean age of landless family heads was 1.3 years below the threshold age. In 1977-78, it was only .3 year below the threshold age. Therefore, the proportion of landless fathers whose sons were old enough to marry had presumably increased considerably during the period between the two studies. Mostly, it is not the rise in the mean age of family heads that produces an increase in the proportion of lineal and supplemented lineal joint families as it is a rise of age in the vicinity of the threshold age. Note that the age of landowning family heads and the proportion of landowning joint families also increased, but the increase of joint families was considerably less among landowning than among landless families. This difference is due to the fact that in 1958-59, the average age of landowning male family heads already exceeded the threshold age, which meant that most of their eldest sons had already married. The increase of the average age of landowning male family heads between 1958-59 and 1977-78 (which raised the difference between the mean age of family heads and the threshold age by .5 year) would produce less of an effect on family types than a similar increase occurring at or just before the threshold age.

Although the foregoing analysis is reasonable and suggestive, it should be viewed with considerable caution. First, the ages that we collected in our census interviews were sometimes inexact (S. Freed and R. Freed 1971: 275-276). If the errors were randomly distributed, their effect upon the analysis is probably negligible; however, undiscerned systematic bias is a possibility. Second, the analysis is so detailed that there may be only a few individuals at significant positions in the frequency distributions from which the probable ages of marriage were deduced. Small numbers increase the potential for sampling error in estimating probable ages of marriage.

Researchers concerned with historical demography have called attention to the influence of demographic factors on the proportion of various family types in a society (Levy 1965:50 ff.; Hammel and Wachter 1977). Wachter, Hammel, and Laslett (1978:1, 5) state that "The demography of a population imposes constraints upon its household composition. The demographic circumstances filter out households producible by some rules and let others through. We talk of passing an hypothesis through the demographic filter to yield a pattern of occurring household types." The concept of a demographic filter that intervenes between the decisions and wishes of individuals regarding family composition and the actual distribution of family types in a society vividly draws analytical attention to an important phenomenon. We would, however, suggest that in societies of any complexity there may be a number of demographic filters characterizing various population components, as, for example, in Shanti Nagar where the parameters of the demographic filters of landless and landowning families had different values.

Demographic change in Shanti Nagar, specifically the increasingly close approach of the mean age of male landless family heads to the threshold age, establishes a necessary condition for a rise in the proportion of landless joint families; that a significant increase actually takes place, however, requires an additional factor or factors that support the joint family, thereby stimulating its growing frequency under favourable demographic conditions. Without such factors, married sons might choose to separate from their natal families a few months after marriage. The additional elements involved in this trend toward the joint family are apparently not the social variables, such as landownership or degree of urbanization, that we have investigated, for they seem to have little influence on family type. Rather, this trend appears to reflect general attitudes toward the family that are based partly on economic considerations, partly on emotional needs. The trend also seems to derive, in some measure, from a few of the fundamental religious beliefs that are part of Hindu ethos and shape the basic Hindu personality.

The attitudes of our respondents toward the family strongly favoured its joint form, as indicated by the responses of 123 individuals to a questionnaire that included questions about the preferred type of family, joint or nuclear, and the reasons for the preference (S. Freed and R. Freed 1976: 235-236; see also Ishwaran 1974: 169). A large majority of respondents preferred the joint family, "if you can make it work," as a few people commented. Those respondents who chose the joint family cited reasons related to economics and mutual aid, e.g., assistance in case of illness or misfortune, lower costs, greater financial strength, and strength in a fight and emotional reasons, e.g., one is not lonesome, greater family prestige, plenty of love. Almost all the respondents who preferred the nuclear family mentioned the quarrels that arose in the joint family, often among wives, as the reason for their preference. In short, the joint family was chosen for its positive qualities; the nuclear family was considered to be a kind of refuge from an unpleasant feature of joint family life but was generally not valued for its own qualities. Several respondents used the analogy of a broom—a bundle of straws and a single straw to illustrate the advantages of the joint family. "A broom can move a heavy weight; one straw can't do anything and breaks quickly." The villagers' appraisal of the advantages of the joint family was generally perceptive and in agreement with our observations and impressions. The joint family was well adapted both to agriculture and to the common economic arrangement, whereby some family members farmed while others had urban employment.

The importance of Hindu ethos and basic Hindu personality traits is best appreciated by contrasting them with corresponding Western ideals of the family and the self. The ideal adult Westerner, both male and female, is independent, concerned to a large extent with self-development and personal satisfaction. Independence from parents is sought as early in life as possible. The mature adult ideally lives alone or with mate and/or children in an economically independent social unit. Independence is emotional as well as economic. Typical Westerners guard themselves from interactions that would lead to an extensive network of close emotional and economic dependency relations. There would be onerous obligations; personal satisfactions and independence would be compromised.

The Hindu adult is quite different. The mature Hindu is able to manage skilfully a large complex hierarchy of dependency relations. No special value is placed on independence. Indians must have many people around them in order to feel at ease. *Dharma* (duty), defined as ethical, proper and religious behaviour is a concept that strongly influences every Hindu. An adult acts according to a set of objective codes appropriate to a specific time, place, and social status; obligation takes precedence over conscience and personal satisfaction (cf. Surya 1969:390; Ramu 1972: 221-222). Analyzing family relationships from the perspective of psychology, Kakar (1978:120) writes, "The psychological identification with the extended family group is so strong that even the loosening of the family bond, not to mention an actual break, may be a source of psychic stress and heightened inner conflict." In some cases, the division of a joint family implies a kind of failure on the part of its adult members.

Attitudes that strongly favour the joint form of the family and an ethos that extols family life, emphasizes *dharma* and the reciprocal obligations of father and son, and sees no particular merit in individual economic and social independence will tend to produce lineal joint families under favourable demographic conditions. Not everyone finds joint family life congenial and many sons separate from their fathers. Villagers regard nuclear families as a normal development; they come into existence because of a variety of demographic, psychological, social, and economic reasons. However, the joint family is still preferred. Technological progress and economic change have not been inimical to it; rather they seem to have created demographic conditions that favour it. Greater prosperity and improved medical facilities are probably involved in the increased longevity of family head[6] which, in combination with basic attitudes and Hindu ethos, have enhanced the proportion of joint families in Shanti Nagar.

The foregoing model of changing family types differs from the standard model that has so strongly affected the study of family types in India. In our model, economic and technological development does not directly affect either family type, attitudes, or ethos. It does, however, change population parameters. The effect of attitudes and ethos, which currently support the joint form of the family, is then enhanced when population parameters are altered to create a more favourable environment for the joint family. The result is an increase in the proportion of joint families. It is worthy of note that our model is based on indigenous concepts. Hindu ethos is at the heart of it. Modernization is an important element in the equation because it is capable of modifying population parameters. However, it affects only the peripheral aspects of cognition and behaviour.

In the standard model, modern economic development is thought to affect family type directly. Modern industrial enterprises are believed to favour small social units at the expense of larger traditional units, such as the joint family. In addition, industrialization, urbanization, and modernization are assumed to lead to the replacement of traditional ethos by a new ideology, largely derived from the West, that regards the nuclear family as desirable, inevitable, and even natural, for it extols the Western values of personal independence, equality, as opposed to hierarchy, and the wishes of the individual in contrast to the welfare of the family. With the new ideology in place, the joint family is assumed to be under assault from a modern economy that acts directly on the family through its presumed compatibility with small social units and indirectly through the new ideology that displaces the traditional ethos.

The results of our research in Shanti Nagar suggest that, at least in a rural context, the standard model is invalid.[7] Contrary to the standard model, the joint family is more frequent in Shanti Nagar than formerly, the new ideology has yet to make a significant appearance, traditional Hindu ethos is unchallenged, we could discern no change in attitudes toward the family, and the alleged incompatibility of a modern economy and the joint family has not yet been demonstrated.

This essay is only a tentative step in the resolution of the joint family problem. Even on the miniscule scene offered by the village of Shanti Nagar, our model may require modification in future decades. The current trend toward the joint family may prove to be temporary and in any case, the proportion of joint families must inevitably reach a ceiling (the data suggest that a proportion of about 50 per cent may be the maximum for Joint families), for demographic processes inevitably produce nuclear families whatever may be the wishes of family members. It is quite likely that investigations elsewhere in India will show trends other than the one that currently characterizes Shanti Nagar and will suggest the influence of presently unsuspected variables.In such an event, the Shanti Nagar data could possibly be reanalyzed to take account of other variables.

NOTES

1. Field research in India in 1977-78 was sponsored by the Indo-U.S. Subcommission of Education and Culture, the Indo-American Fellowship Program, which awarded a Senior Research Fellowship to R. S. Freed, and the American Institute of Indian Studies, which granted a Senior Research Fellowship to S. A. Freed. We thank those two organizations and also the Department of Anthropology, University of Delhi, with which we were affiliated while in India.

   We owe a special debt of gratitude for hospitality and invaluable assistance to many colleagues at the University of Delhi: Indera Pal Singh and his associates in the Department of Anthropology; J. P. S. Uberoi and M. S. A. Rao, Department of Sociology; and

T. N. Madan, Institute of Economic Growth. We greatly appreciate the guidance and unfailing assistance of P. R. Mehendirattra, Director, American Institute of Indian Studies.

We thank Jeffrey P. Bonner, Celia Orgel, Charlotte Revilia, David Hurst Thomas, Baidya Nath Varma, and Laila Williamson who read and criticized the manuscript, and Etienne van de Walle for bibliographic suggestions. Menachem Petrushka provided programming assistance.

2. Ghosh's (1974) demonstration, based on historical data, that in another Delhi village there has been drastic shift from the joint family to the nuclear family during the period from 1910 to 1966 must be disregarded because of a methodological flaw: the data that were selected to support the hypothesis were strongly biased in its favour. Ghosh (l974: Table 2) presents distributions of household types for the years 1910, 1927, 1947, and 1966 which list not a single nuclear family for the first three years and only two families that were anything but joint. Such distributions are highly improbable; they), reflect Ghosh's methodology rather than the actual distributions of family types in those three years. Ghosh interviewed 57 individuals, apparently all men, about the form of their families at the time of their weddings. Since this ceremony was sufficient to convert nuclear families into joint families, it is not surprising that almost all the informants' families were joint. On the other hand, the distribution of family types in 1966 was based largely on a survey which, in all probability, gives a generally valid picture of the actual frequency distribution. Nuclear families were relatively numerous. It is meaningless to compare the data for the first three years with those from the survey of 1966.

3. The problems involved in the definitions of family types and in decisions concerning the independence or jointness of specific families are discussed in greater detail in S. Freed and R. Freed (n.d.).

4. Orenstein and Micklin (1966:322) developed a model to predict the percentage of nuclear families in an Indian population which uses three ages: average age of marriage for men, average age at which a man's first son is born, and average life expectancy of adult men. A man often lives in a nuclear family between two critical ages; his age at the death of his father and his age at the marriage of his first son.

5. Servants are not included in these figures. There were eight servants in 1958-59 and five in 1977-78.

6. Statistics for all of India show that the expectation of life for twenty-year-old males was 33 years in the 1940s, 37 years in the 1950s,

and 40.2 years in the 1960s (India 1978:table 1.5). The comparable ages for females were 32.9, 35.8, and 39.7 years.

7. In fact, the standard model may be invalid for Northern and Western Europe, the areas which are thought to furnish the historical data upon which the model is based. Laslett (1973:93-94,103) notes that in preindustrial England the average family was small, the family group was not composed of two or more married couples, and the multigenerational household was not characteristic of society. Laslett (1973:94) says, "our English ancestors had the same rule as we have, or would like to have, no two married couples in one family." However, he notes that economic development has modified population parameters, especially life expectancy, possibly with resultant changes in family organization. In support of this hypothesis, Laslett (1973:95) observes, "In the eastern part of the Netherlands, peasant farming still survives. During the early 1950s, no less than 25 per cent of farms there were being worked by married couples living with their in-laws. This compares as we have seen with the quite low percentage in those seventeenth-century English communities we have so far examined.... An obvious cause is the lengthening of life."

REFERENCES

Bhadra, R. K.: 1977: "Some Observations on the Study of Family Change in India." *Man in India* 57, pp. 44-59.

Bose, P. K.: 1978: "Family Structure and Classes in Four Villages." *Man in India* 58, pp. 151-70.

Freed, R.S., and S.A.: 1979: Shanti Nagar: The Effects of Urbanization in a Village in North India 3. Sickness and Health. *Anthropological Papers of the American Museum of Natural History* 55, pp. 285-54.

————: 1980: "Rites of Passage in Shanti Nagar." *Anthropological Papers of the American Museum of Natural History* 56, pp. 323-554.

————: 1981: "Enculturation and Education in Shanti Nagar." *Anthropological Papers of the American Museum of Natural History* 57, pp. 49-156.

Freed, S.A., and R.S.: 1969: "Urbanization and Family Types in a North Indian Village." *Southwestern Journal of Anthropology* 25, pp. 342-59.

————: 1971: The Relationship of Fertility and Selected Social Factors in a North Indian Village. *Man in India* 51, 274-89.

———: 1976: "Shanti Nagar: The Effects of Urbanization in a Village in North India. 1. Social Organization." *Anthropological Papers of the American Museum of Natural History* 53, pp. 1-254.

———: 1978: "Shanti Nagar: The Effects of Urbanization in a Village in North India. 2. Aspects of Economy, Technology, and Ecology." *Anthropological Papers of the American Museum of Natural History* 55, pp. 1-153.

———: 1983: "The Domestic Cycle in India: Natural History of a Will-o'-the Wisp." *American Ethnologist* 10, pp. 312-24.

Ghosh, B.R.: 1974: "Changes in the Size and Composition of the Household Brought about by Urbanization in Delhi Area." *The Family in India–A Regional View,* ed. G. Kurian, pp. 249-61. The Hague.

Goode, W.J.: 1963: *World Revolution and Family Patterns,* New York.

Gould, H.A.: 1968: Time-Dimension and Structural Change in an Indian Kinship System. *A Problem of Conceptual Refinement: Structure and Change in Indian Society,* eds. M. Singer and B. S. Cohn, pp. 413-21. New York.

Hammel, E.A., and K.W. Wachter: 1977: Primonuptiality and Ultimonuptiality: Their Effects on Stem-Family-Household Frequencies. *Population Patterns in the Past,* ed. R.D. Lee in collaboration with R.A. Easterlin, P.H. Lindert, and E. van de Walle, pp. 113-34. New York.

India. A Reference Annual: 1977 and 1978, 1978: *Publications Division, Ministry of Information and Broadcasting,* Government of India.

Ishwaran, K.: 1974: "The interdependence of Elementary and Extended Family." *The Family in India–A Regional View,* ed. G. Kurian, pp. 163-77. The Hague.

Kakar, S.: 1978: *The Inner World, A Psycho-Analytic Study of Childhood and Society in India*: Delhi.

Kessinger, T. G.: 1974: *Vilyatpur, 1848-1968, Social and Economic Change in a North Indian Village.* Berkeley.

Kolenda, P.M.: 1968: "Region, Caste, and Family Structure: A Comparative Study of the Indian "Joint" Family." *Structure and Change in Indian Society,* eds. M. Singer and B.S. Cohn. pp. 339-96. New York.

Laslett, P.: 1973: *The World We Have Lost.* New York.

Levy, Jr. M.J.: 1965: "Aspects of the Analysis of Family Structure." *Aspects of the Analysis of the Family Structure,* A.J. Coale, L.A. Fallers, M.J. Levy, Jr., D.M. Schneider, and S.S. Tomkins, pp. 1-63. Princeton.

Mandelbaum, D.G.: 1970: *Society in India. Volume One. Continuity and Change.* Berkeley.

Orenstein, H., and M. Micklin: 1966-67: "The Hindu Joint Family: The Norms and the Numbers." *Pacific Affairs* 39, pp. 314-325.

Ramu, G.N.: 1972: "Researches on the Family in India." *Man in India* 52, pp. 212-27.

Sen, L.K.: 1965: "Family in Four Indian Villages." *Man in India* 45, pp. 1-16.

Surya, N.C.: 1969: "Ego Structure in the Hindu Joint Family: Some Considerations." *Conference on Mental Health Research in Asia and the Pacific,* eds. W. Caudill and T. Lin, pp. 381-92. Honolulu.

Thomas, D.H.: 1976: "Figuring Anthropology," *First Principles of Probability and Statistics*. New York.

Wachter, K.W., E.A. Hammel, and P. Laslert: 1978: "Demographic Rates and Complexity of Households: Rationale for Experiments." *Statistical Studies of Historical Social Structure,* eds. K. Wachter with E.A. Hammel and P. Laslett, pp. 1-12. New York.

Yadava, J.S.: 1966: "Changing Family Structure in a Delhi Village." *The Anthropologist* 13, pp. 21-29.

PART - II

FAMILY COHESION AND KIN NETWORKS

7

The Extended Family as an Independent Factor in Social Change: A Case From India*

George H. Conklin

This essay tackles the assumption that as a country with a joint family system modernizes, the result will be the decline of the joint family in terms of the property relations among fathers, sons and brothers. There are two important aspects of a joint family in India: household composition and property held in common. Urbanization and education have not yet resulted in decreasing levels of joint household participation in India. Legally, though, the joint family is defined as those holding property in common. It was found that urbanization and education (a) have not increased the proportion of sons who separate their property from their fathers before his death, but (b) are associated with a significant increase in shared property among brothers. Neglecting the property aspect of joint family life in survey literature may have falsely led to the conclusion that education and urbanization will preclude the cooperation of brothers and other relatives in using family property to its full economic potential.

One of the recurring issues in the study of the family and social change is the way in which contact with kin is modified by the pressures of education and urbanization. This is especially true in the areas of the world where a joint family system exists.

In India, the family is defined not only by, those who live together, but by law also as those kin who are entitled to share property in common. Karve's well-known definition of the family in India notes both its household and property dimensions as follows: "A joint family is a group of people who generally live under one roof, who eat food cooked in one kitchen, who hold property in common ...and are related..." (Karve 1965:8). The father is the head of household, and his sons are supposed to bring their wives home and live jointly. Under traditional Mitakshara law, in force in most of India until recently, fathers and sons each own a share of the land. To keep the family from becoming too big separations were permitted by the sons after the death of their father. Orenstein has neatly summarized the literatures as follows:

> The norm requires that Hindus accept paternal authority so long as the father remains capable. They anticipate remaining in a joint family while he is alive. Brothers believe they may, if they wish, continue to live jointly after their father dies, but while it may be thought to be ideal to do this in some parts of India, it is not usually the norm, and most do not (Orenstein 1966:314).

The ancient lawgiver Manu laid down the rule that brothers might even be encouraged to separate after the death of the father. As Manu put it, "Either let them live together or, (get) apart if each desire (to gain) spiritual merit" (Quoted in Kapadia, 1966:221).

Recent research on the response of the family in India to urbanization and economic development by Collver (1963), Goode (1963,1968), Orenstein (1961,1966), Dandekar and Unde (1967), and Gould (1968) has reached a general conclusion that there has probably been very little modification of at least the household aspect of the joint family in India in recent years. A minority of all households, urban or rural, are joint, but this reflects the fact that fathers do not live very long after their sons are married, given current demographic conditions. Yet Goode, especially, feels that there will be very strong pressures in the future which will affect the solidarity of the kin as economic development takes place. He argues that the nuclear (or conjugal) family is more flexible than the joint "...since couples are free to set up their households independently, they may move physically to wherever the demands of the industrial system call them" (Goode 1968:

65). Logically, therefore, frequent movement of one brother or son away from the native village or city due to an industrial job would weaken the tie of kinship, and lead to a partition of the family property. Since the joint family system in India is in theory based on cooperation of fathers and sons (and brothers), pressures for change might arise with urbanization, education and industrialization. For now, however, Goode argues that education has begun to cause the emergence of the conjugal family in India. Education, stressing the ideology of individualism and equality, has made itself felt even before industrialization. Comments Goode, "Although no procedures exist for quantifying with precision the contributions from industrialization, as against those of new ideological elements, the modest amount of change in Indian family patterns seems far greater than could be imputed to industrialization and urbanization alone" (Goode, 1963:204).

Although household and land are usually a common unit in India, yet, legally speaking the joint family is defined only as those who share property in common, or, alternately, those who could share property if there were any. Neither under ancient Mitakshara law, nor under current definitions of the joint family in law, is it assumed that a family need live together in a common household in order to own property in common and thus, be legally a joint family (Gopal 1964:526). However, as education begins to allow job mobility and sons and brothers begin to move away from home, it is still possible to argue that any social pressure to cooperate on a common family venture would sharply diminish. Education, especially if it stressed Western values, could well be a force in causing brothers and sons to end not only joint residence, but also the jointly owned property. Goode seems to note this when he says that the conjugal family system in "industrial decisions can be made without interference by the larger kin structure" (Goode, 1968: 65). Thus, the forces of modernization can be seen to be a theoretical threat not only to the household aspect of the joint family, but also to the legal or property holdings of a family.

This chapter addresses itself to the ways in which education and urbanization have affected the property and household functions of joint families in urban and rural Dharwar, in Mysore State, India. Using data from other areas of India, it is suggested that the adaptation of the urban joint family to new situations is more complex than previously argued.

Source of Data

The sample for this study was collected in Dharwar District. Dharwar city (population 77,000 in 1961), is the site of a government sponsored Demographic Institute, and through the institue population information on many district villages which were representative of the district in terms of size. Each village was enumerated by a team of workers, and detailed questionnaires were administered to household heads in every sixth household. A household was defined as in the Census of India, as those living under one roof, taking food cooked from one hearth. 766 rural household heads completed the questionnaire. Dharwar city was sampled using a sampling base supplied by the Demographic Centre in Dharwar and compared closely with samples previously collected in the area (Jorapur, 1968). 382 schedules were completed in the city. In neither section of the sample was refusals more than one per cent. Interviews were conducted in the local language.

Because the traditional residence norms of India apply to fathers and sons living together, with females joining the family of their husband, each male household head was asked where his brothers and sons lived to give an indication of the "availability" of close relatives with whom the head of household could live and thus, also the effects of death upon household structure. Note was made of the ownership of immovable property, who owned property at present, and how the head of household came to own either the land or the house in which he lived. For all currently-married male household heads, questions relating to whether or not the man felt the joint family best as an ideal were asked to check on the degree to which traditional 'ideal type' residence rules were agreed to by the people themselves.

Household types were tabulated in terms of the relationship of each member to the head of household. After exhaustive examination of actually observed household types, households containing a father and two or more married sons were classified as simply lineal father-son joint, since the rule of not separating from a living father had been observed. Brothers who continued living together were classified separately, however (see Table 1).

No effort was made to trace the various types of households the head had lived in his lifetime, since pretesting revealed that most heads of households were unable to specify the dates and times that various members of the household died or moved away with an accuracy.

Kin, Household and Social Change

Table 1 presents the observed household types for the urban and rural samples. There was no significant difference between the city and the villages in households made up of only parents and their unmarried children. Two-couple joint households comprised less than 20 per cent of each sample, with over 40 per cent of each sample simple nuclear households. It should be noted that brother-brother joint families are also very few, representing approximately five per cent of the household types in each sample. Brothers simply do not in practice continue to live on together after the death of the father. As the laws of Manu previously quoted allowed, they do break up joint living arrangements after the death of the father. Large joint households made up of brothers living together are neither the norm for India nor the practice in Dharwar.

TABLE 1
Household Composition of Urban and Rural Sample: Male Household Heads Only*

	Rural Per cent	*Urban Per cent*
1. Sub-Nuclear–2 or more single relatives living together	7.7	5.3
2. Nuclear—parents and any unmarried children only	47.7	45.7
3. Transitional—couple plus one or more unmarried relatives	24.8	27.7
4. Lineal Father-Son Joint—Including any married brothers under headship of father and any other single relatives	12.4	10.0
5. Fraternal Joint Families—including any other single relatives	5.1	6.5
6. Othe Joint Families—any two or more married couples living together	2.4	4.7
Chi^2 = 85, N.S.	N=703	N=339

* There is also no urban-rural difference when all heads of household are included

Few sons were found to be living away from home. A total of 397 rural families headed by males have sons 15 or older, and 43 or 10.8 per cent have one or more sons living away, while in the city 209 families have sons aged 15 or up and 28 or 13.4 per cent have one or more sons living elsewhere. This difference is not statistically significant. Household composition in urban and rural Dharwar are thus similar. In terms of values, over 90 per cent of both urban and rural samples reported that after marriage sons and fathers should live together. Response was similar in all economic and caste groupings, and represents virtual complete agreement that joint family living is the norm in all sectors of society.

But while household structure remains constant in both the city and the villages, the property aspect of the family reveals that urbanities are starting to use traditional laws in new and unpredicted ways. We asked each male head of household how he had obtained the property he owned, and when the family property had been divided in the previous generation (Table 2). About 30 per cent of the heads of household had inherited their property because they were the only surviving son, while the most common pattern was that brothers divided the property following the death of the father (Table 2), both in the cities and the villages, as the traditional norm specifies.

There is, however, a significant difference between the division of the property in the city as against the villages. Among brothers, there is a highly significant greater proportion in the cities which have kept their property undivided following the death of the father (Table 2, category 3). Only 7.6 per cent of the village heads of household kept property but not household in common, but nearly 20 per cent of the urbanities did so. Within the city, therefore, there would seem to be a pattern different from the villages, a pattern where brothers tend to keep property in common after the death of their father. Thus, while the villages would appear to be more "traditional" on this point than would the urbanites, it is of interest to note that urban brothers would seem, to be increasing contacts with their kin through the keeping of property jointly.

TABLE 2

Inheritance and Ownership of Property by Male Head of Household (not including those Heads of Household who inherited no Land)

	Rural Per cent	*Urban Per cent*
1. Only one son alive at father's death	29.4	23.6
2. Undivided property: more than one brother living together now	11.8	10.8
3. Undivided property: more than one brother living separately now	7.6	19.6
4. Undivided property but head away from home	1.0	8.0
5. Property divided before father's death	8.7	7.2
6. Property divided after father's death	40.6	30.8
7. Father in household	0.8	—
	N=608	N=250

$Chi^2 = 61.4$, df = 6; P = .001

Does urbanization increase the amount of property separation between fathers and sons before the death of the father? This practice, while technically possible under Mitakshara Law, is simply not very common in either the cities or the villages, nor has urban living increased the predilection for sons to demand their property before the death of the father. Urban living has, however, altered the relationship of brothers. In that system brothers in the city separate their property less readily than do villagers. Thus in the village, household and property are more often a single common unit than they are in the city.

Analysis of the correlates of an increase in participation in joint family property among brothers reveals that the increase is significantly correlated with two other variables besides urbanization: education of the head of household and his wife (Table 3). Increased education and urbanization, it would appear, are not barriers to contact with kin as far as property is concerned; on the contrary, they seem clearly to increase such contacts. Using the three variables—education of head of household, his wife, and urbanization, as predictors, the multiple *r* is .40, and is statistically significant at the .001 level.

TABLE 3
Correlates of Increased Property Sharing among Brothers*

Element Added	Multiple *r*
1. Education of wife of household head	0.36
2. Urbanization	0.39
3. Education of household head	0.40
4. All other SES	0.41

*Using only those male heads of household who have family property and one or more living brothers

P = 0.001

While some heads of household had separated their property from their fathers' before their deaths, in the present survey no son had yet separated his property from a head of household, either in the cities or in the villages. It would thus appear that while a small percentage of sons lived away from their fathers, they were part of the family as far as the property aspect was concerned. Though at first glance this could be taken as evidence that more property is now being held in common than previously, it is possible that the longer sons live away, the more likely they are to demand seperation of property. However, it is quite clear that sons living away from their fathers are not in a hurry to divide the property.

Discussion and Case Studies

In conformity with previous research on household change in modern India, a sample from urban and rural Dharwar showed no urban-rural difference in household structure. However, contact with kin through the formal mechanism of property kept in common after separations of the household showed an important urban-rural difference, for urban heads of household who were living in households separate from their brothers were much more likely than villagers to keep any property in common.

Non-Western sociologists from India have often pointed out that it is far too easy to assume that urbanization itself means a decline in the joint family, and point out that such assumptions on the part of many writers tend to be simplistic and often ignore the spirit and the legal base of the joint family-shared property (Srinivas, 1967; Desai, 1964). The term "joint family" is a Western term, for in Indian languages the concept of "family" quite clearly does not refer primarily to household, but concentrates on the duties and obligations which groups of persons owe other persons. Duties are expressed in terms of legal relationships between those males who own property in common, called coparceners. The family may have a joint or nuclear household; this, however, is not the legal focus. Rather, traditional laws define the family purely in terms of who inherits what, with sons having a claim at birth on family property under Mitakshara law. Widowed mothers, for example, are protected and are owed maintenance from the sons until her death. Thus, legally a joint family exists as a set of duties and responsibilities which may or may not be carried out through the common pattern of joint household living.

The act of sharing property among brothers or fathers and sons in India is highly symbolic. Even Westernized Indians living far from their homes will make a point of keeping ties with kin in the home city or village. The word used for this purpose is "native place," a concept which denotes in India a place to which one can always return. One man in the present survey had taken back his brother, a man with a responsible government job who had gone insane and then returned to live at his brother's house with his wife and children. It certainly is not dysfunctional to the needs of industrialization therefore, to find that urbanization correlates with increased use of kinship among brothers, a pattern optional under traditional law.

Two case studies perhaps can illustrate the differences found between the urban and rural samples in respect to use of kinship. The following case is typical of the way in which rural brothers divide the property at the death of the father irrespective of the economics of land partition:

> Ram is 42 and literate. He lives with his wife, 16-year old unmarried son and three younger daughters. When his father died, Ram, an only son, inherited land and a modest house. As a child, Ram remembers clearly that when his grandfather died, his father and uncles split the property as soon as possible after a very violent fight over land use. This dispute, in fact, led Ram to sell his land to strangers and leave the village to find a better life. In commenting on his new home Ram said, "I am happy here. Before, I was afraid of my uncles and their sons." [Case 595]

Ram's case is a typical in that family fighting caused him to leave the village, but is typical in that it shows how brothers tend to separate land as quickly as possible the death of the father. Fighting is usually always given as the reason. Fragmentation of the family holding was the result.

In the city, however, more brothers are choosing to cooperate on any land held in common.

> Bal, 57, is a retired clerk, living in a middle-income section of the city on a modest pension. His family jointly owns ample land, which one of his brothers actively manages in the village from which Bal migrated after finishing school. Bal speaks of his children with warmth. One son, a B.A. from a local college, is working as a clerk in another city, and sends home a substantial amount of his paycheck each month. Bal returns to the family farm in the village often. Bal volunteered the information that it was his mother who was successful in keeping the brothers friends, and praised his mother for selecting him a good bride. Now, the jointly held farm supplies Bal with food at harvest time, enabling him to live in the city without purchasing much basic foodgrains. [Case 1074]

While the great deal of cooperation among brothers seen in Bal's case is not the pattern of the majority of urban families owning land. Bal is typical of a growing proportion of educated, urban families which have consciously tried to keep their land unfragmented, be the holding large or small.[1] The economic benefits of the new pattern are that one or more brothers has a viable economic unit; and, in Bal's case, the urban part of the family gets its food supply guaranteed each year as its share of the operation. Further, it is of interest to note that Bal's son returns a good proportion of his income to the family, even though he is a college graduate in another city.

Even though Dharwar is a smaller city, evidence from other surveys in India supports the findings concerning joint family participation. Srinivas (1967), for example, feels that middle-class status leads to the notion that kin should "get along" well together, and believes that often pressures for what are felt to be traditional patterns may even be greater among the educated than among the villagers. Among industrialists who keep nuclear households in Madras, Singer has found that joint property is still held in common. The brothers manage their business as one unit: "all major... decisions are discussed at informal meetings of the brothers, which take place at least once a month. These decisions require complete consensus..." (Singer, 1968:441-442). Ames (1970), in studying workers in a modern steel mill, found that nearly all male heads of household kept joint property in common with those living outside the steel city. Lastly, Vatuk (1972) has documented the detailed ways in which white-collar urban residents maintain close contact with kin in the village. Thus while surveys on joint family participation and urbanization or industrialization are very few, there is little existing evidence to support the notion that urbanization in fact leads to less participation in joint family life, at least as far as the property aspect of the joint family is concerned.

As the case of Ram has shown, brothers in the villages around Dharwar would routinely separate household and divide the property even if the result was uneconomic, while in the city, effort was made to use property not as a social factor but more as an economic unit. As one respondent whose brother kept the small joint farm in the village said, it was better for all to share the three acres which could be economically farmed than to split up the land according to village practice. These particular brothers got together every three months for joint decision-making on the common property. Their goal for these meetings was to keep down conflict so income could be maximized from the land.

Even though urbanization does not lead to less contact with kin as far as the legal base of the joint family is concerned, it does significantly modify rural practices. The new extended family is non-traditional in that it does not imply domination of one brother over another, nor does it imply a return to traditional law, for either the urban or rural practice is permitted traditionally. Instead, it implies a new relationship based more on equality and economic rationality. The urban practice does not discard the institution of the joint family, but, as far as the economic aspect of the family is concerned, modifies the institution to meet new circumstances and desires.

Goode (1963, 1968) is correct in stressing that education and urbanization will bring with them new goals, but it cannot be inferred from this conclusion that new goals may not include increased cooperation with kin to meet those new expectations. Brothers are not taking up new joint households in the city (Table 1), but they are cooperating with each other on an apparently new basis. Litwak found a similar pattern in the United States and commented that a modified extended family does "not demand geographical propinquity, occupational involvement.... nor does it have a hierarchial authority structure. On the other hand, it differs from the isolated nuclear family structure in that it does provide significant and continuing aid to the nuclear family" (Litwak 1960: 10).

It is proposed, therefore, that Goode's summary of the literature on family change is incomplete. Education and urbanization do lead to new, stronger emphasis on the economic goals of life. However, it cannot be concluded that these new goals are mutually exclusive of increased use of kin to achieve the new goals. Nor can it be concluded that in the urban areas common joint property will decline as a special case of the predicted decline of joint families in general in face of the demands of economic development. In fact, the new use of kin found in the present survey is strongly associated with education and urbanization, and the new goals supplied by education. Straus (1969, 1970) has proposed that contact with kin would be a barrier to change only if the kin were conservative. The present findings support the view that as education and urbanization increase, kin will adopt old customs to new uses, uses which are not contrary either to kin contact or to the purposes of economic development.

Goode is completely correct in stressing the fact that new situations arise with economic advancement and education. But, given the economic situation in India, economic rationality demands greater, not less, cooperation among brothers, fathers and sons to maximize return. Joint residence is not essential according to ancient law to maintain a joint family, and this technicality is being used by urban educated to adjust the traditional system to the needs of industrialization. Among the urban educated, a son will leave home if he must to obtain a good job, but he will carefully refrain from breaking up the joint family. Brothers will continue to live separately, but some, unlike most villagers, will refrain from splitting the land and will cooperate in maximizing the economic return from the joint family.

In conclusion, for the educated people of Dharwar, economic rationality requires more, not less, contact with kin to meet the needs of economic development. Kin contact has not only strong emotional appeal to the educated urbanite, but a strong economic functionality as well. This paper does not hold that brothers keeping property, in common is a return to tradition, for, as it was mentioned earlier, traditional law allows either pattern. Rather, it is concluded that even within traditional institutions there is a flexibility, which enables existing institutions to meet new circumstances without great difficulty. Goode is correct in believing that economic rationality will increase with education and urbanization. But economic rationality and contact with kin through increased use of the legal basis of the joint family are not mutually exclusive factors.

NOTES

* The research for this paper was conducted with the help from the National Science Foundation and the American Institute of Indian Studies. The author wishes to thank the Institute of Economic Research, Dharwar, for its help in the Survey work.

1. The case studies reported here were collected after reinterviewing for additional detail 50 households selected in the original sample. Brothers born and raised in the city also tended to keep a greater proportion of any urban properties jointly. For example, a house might be rented rather than sold and the money divided among two or more brothers following the death of the father.

REFERENCES

Ames, Michael M.: 1970: "Structural dimensions of family life in the steel city of Jamshedpur, India." *Unpublished paper presented at the Conference on Occupational Cultures in Changing South Asia*, University of Chicago, May 15-16, 1970.

Collver, Andrew: 1963: "The family cycle in India and the United States." *American Sociological Review* 28 (February), pp. 86-96.

Dandekar, K., and D.B. Unde: 1967: "Inter-state and intra-state differentials in household formation rates." In Ashish Bose (ed.). *Patterns of Population Change in India,* 1951-1961. Bombay: Allied Publishers.

Desai, I.P.: 1964: *Some Aspects of Family in Mahuva.* Bombay: Asia Publishing House.

Goode, William J.: 1963: *World Revolution and Family Patterns.* New York: The Free Press.

————: 1968: "The role of the family in industrialization." Adapted from *Social Problems of Development, Vol. 7 of the United States papers* prepared for the United Nations Conference in 1963 on the application of science and technology for the benefit of less developed areas. United States Government Printing Office. n.d. In Robert F. Winch and Louis Wolfe Goodman, Selected Studies in Marriage and Family. 3rd ed. New York: Holt, Rinehart and Winston.

Gopal, Shiva: 1964: *The Hindu Code.* Allahabad:Central Law Agency.

Gould, Harold A.: 1968: "Time-dimension and structural change in an Indian kinship system: a problem of conceptual refinement." In Milton Singer and Bernard 5, Cohn (eds.), *Structure and Change in Indian Society,* Chicago:Aldine Publishing Company.

Jorapur, P.B.:1968: *Demographic Survey of Dharwar.* Dharwar:Institute of Economic Research.

Kapadia, K.M.: 1966: Marriage and Family in India. London:Oxford University Press.

Karve, I.: 1965: *Kinship Organization in India.* Bombay: Asia Publishing House.

Litwak, Eugene: 1960: "Occupational mobility and extended family cohesion." *American Sociological Review* 25 (February), pp. 9-21.

Orenstein, Henry: 1961: "The recent history of the extended family in India." *Social Problems* 8 (Spring), pp. 141-50.

————: 1966: "The Hindu joint family: the norms and the numbers." *Pacific Affairs 39* (Fall-Winter), pp. 314-25.

Singer, Milton: 1968: "The Indian joint family in modern industry." In Milton Singer and Bernard S. Cohn, (eds.). *Structure and Change in Indian Sceiety.* Chicago:Aldine Publishing Company.

Straus, Murray: 1969: "Social class and farm-city differences in interaction with kin in relation to societal modernization." *Rural Sociology 34* (December), pp. 476-95.

———: 1970: "Family organization and problem solving ability in relation to societal modernization." Kolner Zeitschrift fur Soziologie Supplement 14. *Author's reprint PS-1* referred to.

Srinivas, M. N.: 1967: *Social Change in Modern India.* Berkeley: University of California Press.

Vatuk, Sylvia: 1972: *Kinship and Urbanization.* Berkeley:University of California Press.

8

Industrialization and the Indian Joint Family

Raymond Owens

Studies of industrialization have generally shown that, from a narrow economic point of view, development everywhere and always takes the same general form; that is, it consists of a progressively more rational application of scarce resources towards the achievement of specific material ends. General theories, such as that of Parsons (I951: 182-191) suggest that with increasing economic rationality come changes in the social system, including an increasing percentage of nuclear families. Studies of the family in the pre-industrial West and a recent international survey of the family in relation to industrialization also seem to suggest either that nuclear families are an important precondition to industrialization (Fursterburg 1960: 337) or that they develop rapidly as industrialization occurs (Goode 1963: 239).

However, studies of the family and industrialization in India have not consistently shown the same correlation between industrialization and an increasing incidence of nuclear families. In fact, Indian studies present a confusing array of apparently contradictory results. This may in part be due to the fact that a wide variety of different, imprecise, and even contradictory definitions of "family" and "industrialization" are employed in them, as Ames (1969), Singer (1968), and Kolenda (1968) have suggested in recent reviews of the literature. My own work in the industrial city of Howrah, West Bengal,[1] suggests that much of the confusion may also result from the presumption that industrialization is a uniform process which affects all individuals and groups in society in the same way. I found that, within the same industrial context, individual and group "self-interest" i.e., what was economically rational varied widely. As a result, the economic value to an individual of living within a joint family[2] or of making use of the authority structure and role relationships of a joint family as the basis for a business, for example also varied widely.

My study compared families of entrepreneurs, i.e., persons who had founded, owned, and operated engineering workshops for five years at the time of the study, with families of non-entrepreneurs, or persons who were not self-employed. These same families were also compared on the basis of caste background; Mahisyas, members of a formerly low placed agricultural caste, were contrasted with Brahmins, Baidyas, and Kayasthas, castes which jointly occupy the top of the hierarchy in Bengal. I also compared family types according to the kinds and quantities of rural and urban property which family members control. Concepts of the ideal family type were contrasted with actual living arrangements. Finally, I tried to examine changes in authority patterns and role relationships within the family. By analysing the values lost and gained by particular actors in varying industrial contexts in Howrah, I have attempted to arrive at a somewhat conditional or "middle range" level of generalization about the relationship between industrialization and Indian family organization.

Definitions

Industrialization

Howrah District (including Howrah City), an area of 560 square miles, is one of the most industrially advanced areas in India. Its growth is centered in Howrah City, but the work force has been drawn primarily from the villages of Howrah District. Howrah City is located just across the Hooghly River from Calcutta, the administrative headquarters of the British in India from 1690 to 1910 and also the major port of India from 1690 to the present time. In 1850, when the Indian railways began to be built, no technically feasible plan for bridging the Hooghly River (1/3 mile wide) had yet been devised and the Eastern Railway terminus, which later became the busiest in India, was located in Howrah. To assist in construction and to service both the railways and the markets, which later sprang up beside them, a wide range of industries, most important of which was to be the engineering industry, sprang up in Howrah. During the first half of the twentieth century, for which fairly reliable statistics are available, the industrial growth in Howarh District occurred at unusually rapid degrees, while India as a whole remained relatively stagnant.[3] By 1961 over 41 per cent of the earning population of Howrah District was engaged in manufacturing, and only 25 per cent in agriculture and mining. By contrast, in India as a whole, only 11.6 per cent of the 1961 population was engaged in manufacturing; 72.3 per cent in agriculture and mining (Census of India 1961).

Within Howrah District and West Bengal the single most important industry is now engineering. In the 26 months between October 1960, and December 1962, 60 per cent of the "gross value added in industries" came from engineering, and 63 per cent of all wages within all industrial groups was paid by the engineering industry. (Calcutta Metropolitan Planning District 1967, pp. 37-45).

The research discussed below was conducted within an urban ward of Howrah City, an area approximately one-quarter mile square. Within this ward is found the densest concentration of small-scale engineering workshops in Howrah City, numbering some 500 in all out of more than 3,000 in the city as a whole. Most of these factories are quite small. Over 60 per cent have fewer than 10 workers; 90 per cent have fewer than 25; and 97 per cent have fewer than 100. Nonetheless, the founding of an engineering workshop can be a very profitable enterprise; for an industrial worker it can mean an almost immediate tripling of income. For the more successful it means levels of income not matched by the most highly trained professionals. In Howrah City as a whole, during the last 30 years more than 125 men who started with nothing but savings from their wages have become millionaires. Several of the most successful of these have factories in the ward I studied. Today the richest men in the ward are all entrepreneurs in the engineering industry, as were three out of four politicians who ran for ward commissioner in the election held while I was there (Owens 1970b). The son of one of the most successful entrepreneurs in the ward was also elected to Parliament in the 1967 general election. Everyone in the community is powerfully affected by the community's industrialization; and it has toppled a high-caste, well-educated aristocracy, from power and put in its place a group of lower-caste self-made industrialists. It, therefore, seems appropriate to call the industrialization of Howrah "dynamic" and "catalytic for change." The present process of industrialization for Howrah seems clearly to contrast with the more stable form of industrialization which Ames observed in Jamshedpur and which he asserts (Ames 1968: 7)[4] represents "more the results of a particular and earlier process of industrialization than the process itself."

Family Types

(a) Commensal Family: The most usual meaning attached to the term "family" is that of the "hearth group," i.e, the group which budgets and eats together, or the commensal family (Kolenda 1968). In categorizing the ways in which the members of a commensal family may be related to each other I have made use of the following definitions, which have been adapted from Kolenda:

(1) A family, which contains only one married couple and their unmarried children is a nuclear family.

(2) A family which contains at least two married couples related to each other is joint. In a lineal joint family, the husbands are usually related as father and son; in a collateral joint family, the couples are usually related through a brother-brother tie; and lineal-collateral joint families contain at least three couples, related as father-son and brother-brother.

(3) Any family which does not contain married couple is subnuclear.

Unmarried, including widowed and divorced, relatives may supplement any of the above family types, but their presence does not alter the classification. In the tables presented here only the above three distinctions have been made.

(b) Coparcenary Family: A second kind of family, in which the members are coparceners or owners of joint property, may also be distinguished. A coparcenary family may in some cases be identical with a commensal family, and particular attention will be given below to instances in which commensal and coparcenary families are indeed the same groups. However, the coparcenary unit often includes a larger group of relatives than a single commensal family. Frequently, even after a commensal family has divided into smaller units, rights to common property are still maintained by those relatives who comprised or would have comprised the larger unit.

As in a commensal family, there is also agreement between coparceners as to who is the *karta* or head of the group, and certain role relationships are expected among coparceners. A coparcenary family frequently runs a business, whether or not its members live together as a commensal family; in such instances the coparcenary family frequently assumes more importance than the commensal family. In fact, commensal relations often appear to be deliberately arranged to promote harmony within the coparcenary group. Studies, which focus exclusively on the commensal joint family therefore, run the risk of missing the extremely important coparcenary aspect of the Indian family.

Like commensal joint families, coparcenary families can be classified as nuclear, subnuclear, or joint, according to the generational relationships between coparceners. However, no effort will be made to do so here, since our main concern will be to explore the effects which coparcenary relationships, especially in family businesses, have on the organization of commensal families.

Relation of Coparsenary and Commensal Families

The controlling authority of the Indian joint family, whether commensal or coparcenary, resides in a family head, or *karta*, who is usually the eldest male in the family. Sometimes the same *karta* serves both commensal and coparcenary families (when they overlap), but often different *kartas* direct a family in its commensal and coparsenary dimensions. It is upon the wisdom of the *karta* that the success and harmony of the family depends, whether his primary task is to stretch a small income for the maintenance of a large family or to train and co-ordinate family members in a large business. Often very complex judgements, which do not lend themselves readily to summation in tables are required of him. To help illustrate the kinds of decisions a karta makes, therefore, and to provide a concrete point of reference for later discussion, I shall begin with three examples:

Family 1[5]

When I first began research in South Bentra I noticed that a new and very elaborate three-storeyed house, glistening with pink acrylic paint and surrounded by a large "compound" with wrought-iron gates, was standing empty. I was told that it had never been occupied in the three years since it had been completed. It was further explained to me that the house had been built by the eldest son of one of the richest Mahisya entrepreneurs in Howrah. This son, an entrepreneur in his own right, had made a considerable fortune as an order supplier. However, before the pink house had been finished, the father had died; and the eldest son had decided that he should remain in his father's house, where his three younger married brothers also lived and thereby hold the family together. Few persons in the community were ready to attribute noble motives to this decision. It was generally agreed that the eldest son had realized that by moving into his own new house he would encourage each of his three brothers to press for a house of his own, thereby leading to the dissipation of capital needed to run the family engineering factory (one of the largest in the area) and the family cotton mill. Moreover, the family's considerable wealth would then become obvious, and the government tax collectors would become more of a problem. During the time I was in Howrah the four married brothers and their families all continued to live and eat together as a commensal joint family in the large three-storeyed mansion built by the father. The four brothers were also coparceners in the engineering factory and cotton mill, as well as in the revenue from a considerable amount of urban property. The elder brother was *karta* in both the commensal and the coparcenary joint families.

Family 2

The Mahisya founder of one of the most successful engineering firms in Howrah had two sons whom he sought to educate in ways that would be beneficial to the family business.

The elder and more academically promising son completed an engineering degree in India and was then sent to England for first-hand experience working in English and Scottish engineering factories and foundries. The second son meanwhile completed a Bachelor of Cornmerce course in India. When he had completed his studies, his father, who was then well over 65 years of age, wrote and asked the elder son to return from England. As an inducement the father also built the elder son a very modern house within the walled enclosure ("compound") surrounding the family house but clearly separate (with separate kitchen, servants, etc.). The father knew that the elder son's well educated (B.A.), sophisticated, and "modern" wife would not be happy working under her mother-in-law and took pains to make it unnecessary. This was done even though the very large house of the father could comfortably have accommodated the entire family, including the elder son's two children. At present the father's house stands almost empty and is only occasionally used because the father spends a great deal of his time at a retirement home in the mountains of Bihar. The younger brother now lives with his elder brother. However, though the sons seem to live peaceably together, the father sensed that they would not be happy running the family business together. He, therefore, divided the latter into two parts: a large engineering firm and a foundry. The elder son was put in charge of the engineering firm, and the younger son took over the foundry. Each brother owns a 50 per cent share of the other brother's firm but has direct control only of the management in his own firm. The engineer-elder brother gives technical advice to his younger brother and has helped to make the foundry one of the most advanced and modern in the area. The engineering factory has also been modernized by the elder brother, but somehow it has not thrived as much as the foundry. It is said by some that the younger brother is more serious minded and a better manager. Whatever the reason, the elder brother seems to be kept on his toes under the pressure of his brother's success and suppresses some of his numerous intellectual side interests to look after the engineering factory. It is clear from talking to the elder brother that had it not been for his respect for his father's wishes he would have stayed in England or joined a giant Indian firm, as did many of his engineering school classmates. He said that his salary at a large Indian firm would have been considerably greater than the income he received from the family firms during the first few years after his return from England and that he would also have had to work far fewer hours per week. However, he now earns much more than he ever would have earned on salary. Moreover, he has come to value very highly his independence in running his own firm and would not now want to work for someone else. Because of his loyalty to his father and because of his father's very considerable understanding of his elder son, the son is now providing modern technical guidance not only for his own and his brother's firms but also indirectly to the other, more alert entrepreneurs in Howrah.

Family 3

In the late nineteenth century a well-educated (B.A.) Mahisya married the only daughter of a successful Mahisya entrepreneur from outside South Bantra and subsequently inherited his father-in-law's factory, which he ran until the time of his death in 1930. Unfortunately, all of his four sons were still minors at that time, and in her efforts to educate them the widow found it necessary to sell the factory and much of the family property. However, the large family house was retained, and the widow headed the family (serving as *karta*) until she died about ten years ago. During the life of the mother and until about 1965, the families of the four married brothers continued to live together (commensally joint) in the large family house. The two elder brothers managed to complete their education through tenth grade (matric) and obtained moderately good jobs in service. However, the third brother had to quit school before he was far enough along to qualify for a service job, and went to work in a factory. He was thus able to help the youngest brother complete an education through the tenth grade. The fourth brother worked for several years in government service, and then he and the third brother started a factory, using the savings of the third brother and some capital supplied by their mother. Eventually all four brothers came into the firm as partners, and after their deaths their sons or widows were made partners. When the mother died, the youngest brother became head of the family. (The brother with whom he had founded the firm had died, as had the eldest brother.) For some time the family continued to eat together, but friction began to develop over budgeting and management. As the conflicts grew, more and more money was being spent. At last the family head decided to put each of the four partners in the firm on salary and have them feed and clothe their families separately. He observed: "When the joint family was in existence Rs. 30.00 per day was spent for the dependents of each of the partners; but now after introducing the salary system only Rs.16.00 per day is spent for each unit because the heads have become economical." The four partners and their families continue to live together in the family house, but they do not eat together.

Although Families 1 and 3 live together in a single house, only Family 1 satisfies the criteria of commensal jointness (Ames, 1970: 3; Kolenda, 1968). Yet all three families are intimately bound together by the joint ownership and operation of a business (i.e., they are coparceners). In Families 2 and 3, commensal jointness has been dispensed with in order to increase harmony and efficiency in running the business or to cut expenses. In all three cases economic factors seem to have determined the commensal arrangement. The operating procedures in each family were determined by agreements reached within the family, particularly between the recognized head of the family and other married male family members. These agreements were not completely permanent, although certain of them (such as the distribution of company shares) may have been placed in legally binding public documents. Before such documents ever came into existence, however, and to keep them viable, many informal agreements had to be worked out.

Careful preparation of family members for the roles they are to play in future (e.g., the education of the elder son in Family 2) and appeals to kin loyalty often bring about the submergence of the short-run desires of individuals for the long-run benefit of the family as a whole. In Family 2, the father adjusted his own desire to have the family live together, and his wife's probable desire to have a daughter-in-law to "help her," in order to keep his eldest son in the family firm. The elder brother in Family 1 sacrified his own desire to live in an ultra-modern house so that he could require the same sacrifice from his brothers. In Family 3 the family head intelligently realized that tensions within the family, which he had attempted to resolve by spending increasing amounts of money, could better be managed by establishing a salary system and giving more autonomy to individual nuclear and subnuclear units. A similar objective was achieved by the decisions illustrated in the other two examples. Even the building of an "unnecessary" house for the elder son in Family 2 was a sound economic investment, because it helped return the latter's technical skills to the service of the family business.

Not only in the above three examples, but also in over one hundred other families which I studied, I was struck by the great skill required of the *karta* in resolving disputes within the family and in building relationships of trust and loyalty between family members. Similar skills are required of the head of a business. In fact, the whole authority structure of the joint family can provide an extremely viable basis for a business. Similar conclusions have been reached by Singer (1968) as a result of his study of family business in Madras, by Cohen (1967) in his administrative study of Indian family businesses, by Benedict (1968) in his work on family businesses in East Africa, and by Morton (1968) in his history of the Rothschild family. Not only has a careful play on family loyalties often ensured the support of more highly skilled employees than a moderate-size firm would be able to hire on the open market (as in Family 2), but family members with whom relations of trust have been established over a long period of time are more loyal than "outsiders." No doubt an important part of such loyalty derives from the knowledge of family members that they will receive a fair share of the return of the business.

Family businesses in which a relationship of trust is lacking usually get divided. One of my respondents explained to me why he and his elder brother had decided to divide their business, which had been inherited, from their father:

He was my partner. Legally I had the same right as my elder brother, but my elder brother would insist that he would make all the decisions. He used to consult me sometimes, but the final decision was always with him. He handled the money; especially the banking was done in his name. After the war I began to get uneasy. I thought, after all if he dies or I die, then I or my children won't have any legal document. My elder brother thought me foolish. Finally, I got angry, and I insisted upon my share. Unfortunately, I did not know the total amount of our assets, so

I had to be satisfied with what he gave me. He did not cheat me that I know of. Yet he thought I was breaking up the joint family, and that I ought to be punished. What really happened was that he saw it from a different point of view.

In this instance it appears that the elder brother was insensitive to the younger brother's feeling of insecurity. Had the elder brother been willing to draft a legal document, the family and the business would probably have held together.

I found that the kind of heavy-handedness, which characterized the elder brother in the above instance, was rare among entrepreneurs, i.e., persons who had founded their own businesses. In fact, the most successful entrepreneurs seem also to have been persons who were very skilled in human relations and applied this skill both to their families and to their businesses.

Entrepreneurs within my sample who were living in commensally joint families, even when not all the earners in the family were partners in their businesses, were also usually the largest earners in the family. As a result, other family members were unusually dependent upon the entrepreneur's contribution to joint family expenses; and it was in the interest of other family members to conform to his wishes in order not to alienate him from the family. As a result most entrepreneurs wielded considerable influence, whether or not they were in fact the designated heads of their families.

Family Income and Commensal Jointness

If one divides the 104 families which I studied into those which included entrepreneurs and those, which did not, the resulting comparison presents a striking economic contrast. Most entrepreneurial families have much higher incomes than families which do not include entrepreneurs as is indicated in Table 1. Just under 80 per cent of all commensal families which include entrepreneurs have incomes of Rs. 700 per month or more, as compared to only 14.3 per cent of the Mahisya families without entrepreneurs, and 21 per cent of the upper caste families without entrepreneurs. Moreover, none of the non-entrepreneurial commensal families has a total income of more than Rs. 1500 per month, whereas 50 per cent of the entrepreneurial families have incomes above this figure. Twenty per cent of the commensal families of upper caste entrepreneurs and nearly 27 per cent of the commensal families of Mahisya entrepreneurs have incomes exceeding Rs. 4000 per month.

TABLE 1

Monthly Incomes of Commensal Families

Income per month in rupees	HIT[1] study	South Bantra Study (Percentage of families) Upper caste non-entre-pre-neurs	Upper caste entre-preneurs	Mahisya non-entre-preneurs	Mahisya entre-preneurs
50 or less	4.6				
51 to 100	27.1			14.3	
101 to 200	28.7	5.3		28.3	
201 to 350	16.2	10.5	3.3	23.8	5.9
351 to 700	6.6	63.2	16.7	19.1	14.7
700 and above	4.2	21.1	80.0	14.3	79.4
unknown	12.6				
Total number of households	285	19	30	21	34

1. The Howrah Improvement Trust (HIT) Study was a survey of those families within the ward I studied whose homes would fall in the path of a new expressway (yet to be built). It was conducted in 1963. See discussion in the text.

Also included in Table 1 are 1963 family income figures for 285 families whose homes fall in the path of an expressway which is to built be diagonally across my research area. (The figures are from a Howrah Improvement Trust survey). A resurvey of over 10 per cent of these families[6] indicated that HIT income figures for non-entrepreneurs were fairly accurate, though the income figures for entrepreneurs had been underestimated in many cases by 50 per cent or more. No doubt some of the difference is accounted for by increases in income during the three to four years separating our studies. It may also be supposed, however, that people would be less likely to be candid about income when surveyed by a government body, which might be expected to disclose that information to taxing authorities, than when interviewed by a foreign researcher. Despite these limitations, the HIT survey gives some rough idea of the income ranges within an undifferentiated cross-section of the community.

The HIT study appears to show that both Mahisyas and upper castes considered separately have higher income ranges than a cross-section of the whole community, which includes a much wider range of castes.[7] The average income of upper castes as a group and of Mahisyas as a group is fairly high for the community as a whole. However, the really high incomes belong to entrepreneurs; and there are four or five times more Mahisya entrepreneurs in the community than upper caste entrepreneurs. The Mahisyas dominate the community economically.

In Table 2, I have made two types of comparison, on the basis of family type, between families from four groups in my study. In the first comparison (Part A of Table 2) the usual practice of family surveys has been followed, i.e., men whose wives and children are living separately from them and outside metropolitan Howrah-Calcutta have been classed as "subnuclear" families.[8] Part A of the chart shows that the percentage of entrepreneur families which are joint is more than twice the percentage of joint families among non-entrepreneurs.

TABLE 2-A

Percentages of Family types in the four subsamples of the South Bantra study which live in Howrah city, and Calcutta only and families surveyed by the Howrah Improvement Trust in South Bantra

Sample	*Subnuclear*	*Nuclear*	*Commensal joint*	*Number in sample*
Total	10.58 (per cent)	59.62 (per cent)	29.80 (per cent)	104
Upper caste non-entrepreneurs	36.84	45.37	15.79	19
Upper caste entrepreneurs	6.66	56.68	36.66	30
Mahisya non-entrepreneurs	4.76	80.95	14.29	21
Mahisya entrepreneurs	2.94	55.88	41.18	34
HIT study	19.53	59.10	21.37	379

In Part B of Table 2, separated husbands whose wives and children live with families outside the Howrah-Calcutta metropolitan area have been included in the column for joint families if the addition of the separated husbands would make these families joint. Although most of the time such a husband does not live and eat with his wife and the other family members with whom she may be living, and even though he may only see his wife and family on week ends or perhaps no more than once a month, yet supports his wife by regular contributions of money. In this sense he shares a common budget with his wife and with the other family members with whom she may be living.

When the families of this "separated joint" type are added to the other joint families, as in Part B of Table 2, the families with entrepreneurs still appear to be more frequently joint than those without them, but the contrast becomes, less dramatic.

TABLE 2-B

Percentages of Family types when Separated husbands are included with the families with whom they Share Common Budgets

Sample	*Subnuclear*	*Nuclear*	*Commensal joint*	*Number in sample*
Total	3.85 (per cent)	57.69 (per cent)	38.46 (per cent)	104
Upper caste non-entrepreneurs	10.52	52.63	36.84	19
Upper caste entrepreneurs	3.33	50.00	46.67	30
Mahisya non-entrepreneurs	—	76.19	23.81	21
Mahisya entrepreneurs	2.94	52.94	44.12	34

An additional row of figures in Table 2-A shows the composition of 379 families in South Bantra surveyed by the Howrah Improvement Trust in 1963.[9] Unfortunately, the HIT figures do not parallel my own. If a direct correlation indeed existed between percentages of jointness and levels of income, one would expect to find fewer joint families in the HIT sample than among the non-entrepreneurs in my study (the average income in the HIT sample was lower than the average for non-entrepreneurs; see Table 1). However, there appear to be more. No doubt this may be accounted for in part by different family patterns among castes other than Mahisya or "upper" (Brahmin, Kayastha, and Vaidya) castes, as well as by the above-mentioned underestimation of income in the HIT study. (Unfortunately, I did not study these possible differences in family patterns.) At face value, the comparison with HIT figures implies that there is less jointness than average among the non-entrepreneurs in my sample and more jointness than average on the part of entrepreneurs. If this is indeed the case, level of income does not correlate directly with a tendency towards jointness. Thus, the jointness of entrepreneur families must be based on more than wealth alone. In the following sections we will consider some of the variables other than income which may be related to jointness.

Commensal Jointness in Relation to Kinds of Property Owned

An analysis of the kinds of property controlled by the 104 families in my sample suggests that joint control of some kinds of property is likely to reinforce or lead to commensal jointness, but that ownership of other types of property, is much less likely to do so. As many respondents in my sample are recent migrants from villages (where they may still own property), and as some still commute daily from nearby villages, property can be either rural or urban, or both. The principal kinds of property owned by respondents in my sample are at least six in number:

1. Rural house
2. Rural agricultural land
3. Rural business other than agriculture
4. Urban house
5. Urban rental property
6. Urban business, i.e., engineering factory

An individual may have an interest in one or several (or more) of the above kinds of property. There are also wide variations in the quantity of property of each type which may be owned by an individual. A house, either rural or urban, may be large enough for a joint family or allow only the room enough for a small nuclear family. Similarly, rural agricultural land holdings may range from quantities sufficient to support all the members of a large joint family to considerably smaller amounts.

In a study of two West Bengal villages, Nicholas (1961: 1057) reports a very direct correlation between family size and the amount of rural land owned by families. He indicates that nuclear families have almost twice as much land as subnuclear families, that lineal joint families have nearly three times as much land as nuclear families, and that collateral joint families have over four times as much land as nuclear families. Nicholas (1961: 1058) concludes that if fair amounts of land are jointly owned, as a rule a married son remains in a lineal joint family "in order to preserve his patrimony". The frictions within joint households of brothers are likely to be much more intense than in lineal joint families and only if the family "is of above average wealth is cooperation among household members likely to be an important unifying factor" (Nicholas 1961: 1060). Nicholas also stresses that the joint family is a more economic unit for moderately large holdings, especially if these holdings are planted with labour-intensive cash crops, such as betel. If the family is joint, some women can be freed from the cooking to water the betel, thereby expanding the labour force.

However, an urban factory which is jointly owned and utilizes the services of several family members has different requirements than rural land. While it is true that a jointly owned engineering factory can often provide greater income to co-sharers than would be possible for most of them on their own, a factory does not necessarily require the services of all potential members of the joint family. The labour of women, for instance, is not required, so there is no special economy to be realized by a joint household, which could free some women from the cooking for other work. "Dull" male members of the family also need not be taken on.

In early stages of a business, when capital is scarce and profits are low, there appears to be a real economy in living jointly. However, on a higher level of income, when the basic necessities are all easily within reach and competition for luxuries between branches of the family becomes a problem, commensal jointness can become more expensive (as in the case of Family 3) than maintenance of separate households. Still, the decision to maintain a commensally joint household in Family 1 and the decision not to do so in Family 2 were both made to achieve greater rationality in business operations rather than to reduce household expenses. Such freedom from worry about the relative costs of living jointly or singly was a luxury granted to very few of the entrepreneurs whom I studied, perhaps only to the 20 per cent or so who earned over Rs. 4000 per month. For most of the entrepreneurs interviewed, the liquid capital needed to run and expand their businesses was in sufficiently short supply that the clear economies that could come from commensal jointness were attractive.

In a high percentage of both the large, rural, landowning families described by Nicholas and in the entrepreneurial families in my study, the property-sharing or coparcenary family completely includes the commensal family. In both settings, skills of family members are needed within the joint enterprise though the skills differ in each case. Since female labour is not used in an urban business, commensal groups are often divided though businesses remain joint. In families whose businesses are too small to supply employment for all male members, or in families with no business, there is even less pressure for commensal jointness. It is also my impression that if family members are employed at different outside jobs, each earner is likely to leave the commensally joint family as soon as the advantages of keeping his income to himself outweigh the advantages he receives as part of the commensally joint family (free rent etc.).

Cohn observed a similar exodus of wage earners with few dependants from Chamar joint families owning very modest amounts of common property. Most of the wage earners worked near the village as agricultural labourers, and the earnings of all working family members were about the same. Needs, however, varied with the size of the family sub-units, resulting in much discontent. Among brothers the most frequent cause for separation was "squabbling over food." In the words of Cohn, (1961: 1053) "A brother with one small child does not see why he should share his meagre earnings with a brother who has three small children and hence gets a larger share of the household food supply."

However, for rural landowners who find employment in the city, such as the workers in my sample (who worked in Howrah and only visited their wives and families on weekends), a joint family can render a considerable service. If a worker must be away from his wife and children for long periods of time, the joint family can provide the latter with shelter and food at lower prices than would be possible in the city.[10] Such village joint families are therefore, much more stable than the families of the Chamar agricultural labourers described by Cohn. For a man to take his wife and children out of such a family, and move them to the city would require sufficient income to rent an urban house and to afford the higher quality of urban food and maintenance costs. At the time of my research, the cost of food alone in Howrah city was nearly double what it was in the countryside. Moreover, the rural cost of living was even less if a family could raise part or all of its own food items. Only some of my respondents whose wives and children lived in a rural joint family owned enough land to meet all the food needs of the joint family there (which is why many had migrated to the city for employment in the first place). One suspects, however, that their holdings could have been profitable to them even though smaller than the size necessary to hold rural families together in Nicholas's village, because the land of urban employed workers would not have to produce all of the family's income.

Respondents in my sample who earned enough to have separated their wives and children from rural agricultural joint families were for the most part either very well educated or earning high urban salaries or were entrepreneurs. A Mahisya non-entrepreneur from one huge rural joint family, which in the "old days" had had income from fifteen to twenty villages and their surrounding lands, described the breakup of his family as follows:

> The family got a Jaigir from the Moghul Court, and for more than 250 years it was a joint family, which grew to over 200 members. All the family expenses were met from the zamindari, and food was supplied for the family from the same source. Then intelligent boys began to be sent to college, and this led to bickering, especially after some moved to the city and kept their personal incomes to themselves. There was quarrelling, especially among the women, over this. It led to civil and criminal cases which broke up the family.[11]

This respondent's father had been one of those who left the joint family to come to Howrah, although he had maintained a small amount of property in the village, to which he later retired.[12]

For entrepreneurs the break with the rural joint family is often more gradual than for highly educated professionals, because entrepreneurs often work for fifteen to twenty years as skilled labour at a much more modest salary than professionals receive before starting their own businesses. During both the period of employment as labourers and the early stages of business development, the need to economize is very great. In order to free as much capital as possible for investment in business, they often do not sever ties with rural joint families for several years after becoming entrepreneurs. However, once an entrepreneur becomes fairly successful, he finds that he is contributing far more to his rural joint family than he is receiving. He may also prefer to set up a household in Howrah to be closer to his work. At this point, unless other members of the family have joined him as partners in the business, the entrepreneur usually separates from the joint family.

After separation many entrepreneurs continue to hold some interest in rural lands or in a rural house as insurance against a severe business reversal or a breakdown in health, in which event there is still an inexpensive place to which to retreat until business picks up or health improves. A number of entrepreneurs have also retired to their native villages, often buying large village estates for themselves where none (or only a very small one) existed before. Some have built village schools, hospitals, impressive new houses for themselves, and shrines for their parents, establishing themselves as country squires on the basis of their urban earnings and showing off their wealth among those who knew them when they were poor.

However, such entrepreneurs are a minority of the very successful. Like the aged Henry Ford, who restored his boyhood home, they want to preserve or recreate the past. For most rising entrepreneurs, ties with the village seem to drop fairly quickly when security of income is guaranteed either by the steady growth of a factory or the acquisition of urban property.

Most individuals who move to Howrah from the countryside purchase urban property and build a house on it as soon as they can afford to do so. Usually the new house is also large enough to contain the joint family of the founder and his sons and their families; and this group usually remains joint during the lifetime of the founder. Such jointness is most assured if the founder is also an entrepreneur. If not, the family may be subject to the same sort of divisive pressures as the rural families of wage earners described by Cohn.

In Table 3, I have attempted to list in isolation as many as possible of the above-mentioned economic factors which influence the maintenance, and breakup of joint families in Howrah. In relation to these factors I compared those 42 families which were joint and an additional 44 families which had sufficient married couples to be joint but which chose to live separately. The remaining 20 families did not contain married couples related as brother-brother or father-son.

Some interesting contrasts can be seen between parts A and B of Table 3. For example, seven entrepreneurs who have very high incomes gave their migration to Howrah for work (line 6) as their reason for having separated from a commensal joint family. On the other hand seven non-entrepreneurs, who earn much less than the entrepreneurs, have found it advantageous to maintain joint households with families in the village even though they work in Howrah. The chart also shows that the most stable of commensal joint arrangements is the lineal joint family; among the upper caste all potential lineal joint families (10) actually exist, and among Mahisyas two-thirds of them (12 out of a possible 18) exist.

Fully 85 per cent of the potentially joint families which have chosen to live as separate units have been collateral joint, rather than lineal joint. Behind this lies the fact that under the *Dayabhaga* legal system, which applies in Bengal and Assam, a son does not acquire an interest in his father's property at birth. His rights arise for the first time at his father's death. Moreover, under this legal system a father can dispose of both ancestral property and his self-acquired property, such as a factory which he has founded,[13] as he likes. It, therefore, is in the interest of a son who is in a position to inherit a substantial amount of property from his father to remain on the best possible terms with his father; this often means continuing to live within a lineal joint family, at least until his father's death. Once the property rights of the children have been clearly established, there is less incentive

TABLE 3-A
Economic Factors Influencing the Maintenance or Break-up of Joint Families in Howrah

Economic Circumstances	*Number of Joint Families in the Sample*							
	Lineal or Lineal-Collateral				*Collateral*			
	Upper caste non-entre	*Upper caste entre*	*Mahisya non-entre*	*Mahisya entre*	*Upper Caste non-entre*	*Upper Caste entire*	*Mahisya non-entre*	*Mahisya entre*
1. Jointly owned agricultural land in village; family income supplemented by someworkers working in Howrah (usually remaining there during the work week) for moderately law wages	3		2		1		1	
2. Jointly owned and operated business		2		6		3		5
3. One or two brothers or sons work with the entrepreneur in the family business; other members work outside; joint family financed the start of the business		5		3		4		2
4. Large house in Howrah, skilled family head			1		3		1	

TABLE 3-B

Circumstances Conducive to the Separation of Potentially Joint Families	Number of Joint Families in the Sample							
	Lineal or Lineal-Collateral				Collateral			
	Upper caste non-entre	Upper caste entre	Mahisya non-entre	Mahisya entre	Upper Caste non-entire	Upper Caste entire	Mahisya non-entre	Mahisya entre
5. Quarrels over differences in income or income allocation within joint family; no joint business			3		4	6	7	3
6. Migration from ancestral place for work; high income						3		4
7. Increase in family size beyond house capacity; or loss of house to road construction					1	2		
8. Participation in jointly owned business by sons or brothers of wealthiest entreprencurs; separate residences maintai-ned by preference				1				3
9. Brothers orphanced as children, raised separately						2		
10. Insufficiently large family house; brothers, partners in a very large joint business separated as they wed						1		
11. Son earlier left a lineal joint famly (several married brothers working in service and a retired father, now dec.) iin order to go into business						1		
12. Entrepreneur, whose married sons work outisde the business, remarried; business and house divided; one son (who fell in sample) went into business				2				
13. Insufficient information to judge			1					

for continuing to live jointly unless, as indicated above, a business is involved. When no urban business is included, the inheritance can easily be sub-divided by heirs as soon as disagreements arise; and quarrels also arise rapidly in households in which brothers do not jointly run a business.

Fully 79 per cent of the potentially joint families in the sample appear to have broken up in disputes over the allocation of income. In Table 3 it is interesting to note that jointly owned and operated businesses (#2) or businesses in which at least two members of the family work and for the founding of which economic assistance is given by the joint family (#3) give rise to almost equal numbers (16 and 14 respectively) of lineal and collateral joint families. For non-entrepreneurial families, possession of a large urban house under the guidance of a particularly wise *karta* can be an incentive for remaining joint (#4); loss of a house can also apparently break up a family (#7). Line 8 represents Families 2 and 3 presented at the beginning of this paper. Lines 9 and 12 list unusual circumstances which are fairly self-explanatory. Circumstance 10 is functionally similar to the situation described under Family 2. Line 11 represents a case in which a son had to leave a lineal joint family in order to go into business against his father's wishes. Line 12 represents a situation in which the wives of sons feared they might be deprived of their inheritance by the father's second wife and insisted that they receive their share while the father was alive. Line 13 represents the most successful entrepreneur in Howrah, of whose family situation I simply do not know enough to be sure why his eldest son separated. It appears, however, that the circumstances could be similar to those described in Family 2 above.

Commensal Jointness in Relation to the Possession of Rural Property

In Table 4, I have attempted to correlate types of individual respondents and types of families from my sample with four degrees of attachment to the village and village property (house and/or land). It was not possible for me to acquire very accurate figures on the amounts of village land owned by respondents, nor was it always clear exactly which other relatives shared rights to the rural property. It appears, however, that there is a rough correlation between the frequency of visits to the village and the

TABLE 4
Degree of Connection with the village

Type of Respondent	*Number of Respondents*			
	Full-time urban resident, does not visit ancestral village or own rural property	*Infrequently visits an ancestral village, owns no rural property*	*Infrequently visits an ancestral village, owns some rural property*	*Frequently visits village home of wife and family, owns village property, lives in Howrah temporarily*
	1	*2*	*3*	*4**
Upper caste non-entrepreneur	4	2	4	8
Upper caste entrepreneur	17	2	4	8
Mahisya non-entrepreneur	4	13	1	3
Mahisya entrepreneur	12	4	8	9
Types of Upper Caste Families	(percentages of upper caste families)			
Subnuclear	4.8 per cent	—	12.5 per cent	6.3 per cent
Nuclear	57.1	75.0 per cent	62.5	31.2
Joint	38.1	25.0	25.0	62.5
Types of Mahisya Families	(percentages of Mahisya families)			
Subnuclear	—	6.3 per cent	—	—
Nuclear	62.5 per cent	88.2	66.7 per cent	16.7 per cent
Joint	37.5	6.3	33.3	83.3

* Percentages indicated for families in column 4 are based upon the composition of the rural family which results when the respondent is at home with his wife in the village.

amount of land owned there. Individuals and families in Table 4, column 4 own the most land (with the exception of a number of well-to-do entrepreneurs who have purchased rural estates) and return every weekend, or at least once a month. Most of those in columns 2 and 3 return less frequently than once a year, though one or two visit somewhat more often. Those in column 2 return to visit relatives; those in column 3, to attend to repairs in the ancestral house or in a few cases to take part in *pujas* which their family has run in the village for generations. Apart from ties of sentiment, most respondents felt that keeping in touch with property or relatives in the village was good insurance against a tragedy or illness, which might befall them in the city.

Those respondents represented in column 1 have lost all connections with the village. A few had had village homes in the part of Bengal which became East Pakistan at the time of partition in 1947, and for that reason they had lost control over their property. Most of the families represented in column 1, however, have simply been residents in Howrah or Calcutta for three or more generations and do not consider themselves to have a village home.

In contrast to the families of industrial workers in Jamshedpur, in which 87 per cent owned rural property, only 42 per cent of my sample, less than half as many, have any claim to rural property. On this basis one might say that the sample which I studied is much more "urban" than that studied by Ames. It is interesting that the highest amount of jointness occurs among the families in column 4, in which the husbands have been separated from families by work. These families are not representatives of the amount of jointness in rural families in West Bengal as a whole, however. For instance, only 28.3 per cent of the predominantly Mahisya families in the two villages studied by Nicholas in the adjacent district of Midnapur were joint.

The high degree of jointness of the families in column 4, as I have suggested above, is better explained by the particular economic situation in Howrah District rather than by the location of the families in a rural area. Similarly, the fairly high percentage of joint families among those who have no village homes is probably best explained by the fact that 78 per cent of them are entrepreneurs.

The foregoing exercise should demonstrate that it is not easy to generalize about the effects on family structure of the impact of either urbanization or industrialization. Clearly, what happens depends upon the relative advantages to individuals in particular circumstances.[14]

The Real and the Ideal

The foregoing focus on the economic factors involved in the survival or breakup of joint families was not intended to exclude consideration of non-economic factors. Although I believe that an understanding of economic features best elucidates most cases, we must also consider the important relationships between widely held ideals about family structure and family structure as an actuality.

While interviewing respondents, instead of directly eliciting attitudes towards the joint family, I asked questions about the time of breakup. The first question was: "Do you think that a son should separate from his father when he marries?" If the respondent answered yes, he was assumed to be expressing sentiment against the lineal joint family. The second question was: "Do you think brothers should separate after the father's death?" If the respondent agreed with this question, he was assumed to oppose a collateral joint family (but not a lineal or lineal-collateral joint family). In Table 5 below, responses to these questions have been correlated with actual living arrangements of families in which there are sufficient married couples to create each of these family types.

Among all respondents answering question 1, 82 per cent were in favour of the married son remaining with the father. Yet for only 28 per cent of those answering was a lineal or lineal-collateral joint family possible, i.e., only that percentage belonged to families in which there were married couples related as father-son. Among those for whom lineal or lineal-collateral joint families would have been possible, however, 75 per cent were in existence. Clearly, the sentiment for lineal or lineal-collateral joint families is very strong, and practice follows closely the sentiment expressed. The seven cases which did not follow the ideal were all Mahisyas

TABLE 5
Attitudes Toward Jointness Versus Actual Practice

	Q-1: Do you think a son should separate from his father when he marries?				*Q-2: Should brothers separate after the father's death?*			
	All respondents		*Families with sufficient married couples for lineal or lineal-collateral joint families*		*All respondents*		*Families with sufficient married couples for couples for collateral joint families only*	
	Yes	*No*	*Non-joint*	*Joint*	*Yes*	*No*	*Non-joint*	*Joint*
Upper caste non-entrencur	2	14	0	3	7	9	6	4
Upper caste entreprencur	5	25	0	6	12	18	16	7
Mahisya non-entreprencur	2	18	3	3	5	14	7	2
Mahisya entrepreneur	9	24	4	9	14	19	8	7
Total	18	81	7	21	38	60	37	20

The table represents only those respondents from whom answers were obtained. Responses from 99 out of 104 respondents were obtained for question 1: 98 out of 104 for question 2. For only 28 of 104 respondents was a lineal (or lineal-colleteral) joint family possible, and for only 57 respondents was collateral (but not lineal or lineral-collateral) joint family possible. It seemed more meaningful to consider only the situation of these families, since of otherwise the non-joint column would simply be inflated by families for whom joint families were biologically impossible.

which suggests that sentiment for lineal joint families among Mahisyas may not be quite as strong, even though the percentage of Mahisyas actually answering "no" to question 1 (79 per cent) is close to the average for all respondents. It appears that Mahiyas may be taking on a value which they have not yet fully been able to realize, although the richer Mahisya entrepreneurs have been more successful in doing so than have the Mahisya non-entrepreneurs. In the past, fewer Mahisyas have had family property to inherit. Hence, they have been less subject than upper castes to the influence of the above-mentioned inheritance law, which encourages lineal jointness in families with substantial inheritance property.

Among all respondents 61 per cent were against the separation of brothers at the death of the father (and hence favoured collateral joint families), although only 37 per cent of the families which could have been collateral joint were actually found to be living jointly. In this case the ratio of actual to possible (9:15) is higher among Mahisyas than among upper castes (1:2).

Table 5 shows that Mahisya entrepreneurs are responsible for the greater percentage of collateral joint families among Mahisyas. If a Mahisya becomes an entrepreneur, his brother is much more likely to join him as a partner than would be the case among upper castes. When this happens, as was indicated in the description above, the possibility is very high that a commensally joint family will result. Among entrepreneurs considered separately only 7 out of a possible 22 collateral joint families were realized among upper castes; but 7 out of 15 were realized among Mahisyas. As in the case of lineal jointness, collateral jointness is a reflection of broader cultural changes, which are taking place within the two groups here compared.

Such broader changes were reflected in remarks which respondents made while answering the two questions listed in Table 5. The tensions, which the comments reveal between the real and the ideal, are difficult to quantify. The statements, however, do represent the somewhat amorphous, perhaps principally emotional, notions, which influence decisions within the family. As indicated in Table 5, a much higher percentage of respondents favour the joint family, lineal or collateral, than find it possible or tolerable to live in one. Their comments reveal how they adjust their ideals to reality.

Especially strong feelings are attached to the concept of the lineal joint family, and it is often stated that it is the duty of a son to care for his parents. This is emphasized most in families in which the parents could not be expected to have much in the way of savings or a pension to live on in their old age. It is not stressed by sons whose parents have sufficient means to live comfortably. In fact, one of the strongest and most consistently voiced arguments for the joint family is that the joint family is, in a country which lacks social insurance, the least expensive means of caring for the aged, unmarried or widowed sisters, orphans, and disabled or sick persons. One of my respondents was orphaned at the age of six and raised by an uncle. Recently, the uncle died, and the respondent is now taking care of the uncle's dependents. When unusual dependency is not involved, such as between married brothers who are both earning, enthusiasm for jointness is not usually great. The "potential economy" of jointness, the value of a "common pool of resources" or "more facilities" is then no longer stressed by informants (except as it applies to business).

The separation of eating and living arrangements is explained in many ways by the respondents. It is said that "girls nowadays are not taught to be under anyone," or that "the other women in the household take advantage of the girl who marries in." It is said that quarrels start in the women's quarters and spread to the whole house. Some people say it is thus better to break up a commensal joint family at the first sign of trouble than to have family members facing each other with bitterness. Others become extremely incensed at any suggestion of division and say "partition looks bad" or "to divide a family is to go to Hell." One young politician, who has separated from his father, declared to me, "We should make all of mankind into an extended family."

Obviously one has to tie values down to specific contexts. What does "separation" mean? Is it separation of all property, or only of food and housing or both? It is important to note that the general sentiment for the unspecified "joint family" is still generally strong; it may be that this will provide the energy to adjust the ideal to the new context of industralization.

Internal Change in the Family

Much of the adjustment of the ideal to reality takes place within the family and in ways, which would never show up in a survey of family types.

Among respondents from my sample, it was generally agreed that the family has been changing very much internally, especially the way in which authority is exercised. Almost all reported a great loosening of the authority of the *karta*, or family head. It was the almost universal recollection of respondents that in their own childhood the *karia* "used to be respected without question." The karta had chosen clothing for the family and brides as well without even consulting the family members for whom they were intended. In contrast, it is now usually the custom for family members to accompany the *karta* to select clothing or to select their own.

No doubt some of the difference in practice may be accounted for by changes in clothing styles. In the "old days," most men wore a *dhoti* wrapped from a single piece of cloth. One size would fit everyone. Today young men wear tightly-fitting "stove pipe" slacks, which leave almost no room for guesswork as to fit. "Trim line" shirts present the same kind of problem, unlike the old loose-fitting *jamas*. Most young men still wear sandals, but the wealthier and the college boys usually have at least one pair of western shoes which require careful fitting. Despite these facts, the selection of clothes by individual family members, rather than by the *karta* alone, seems to be a reflection of a general decentralization of authority within the family.

Many respondents said that they had never seen their brides until their wedding day. In contrast, it is now customary for a boy to see a prospective bride, often in the company of his friends rather than family members, in order to give his approval. It is recognized by the fathers of sons that their sons might possibly choose their own brides. Many respondents who were *kartas* seemed to express the hope that they would be able to choose brides for their sons rather than the belief that it was the father's right. One Brahmin entrepreneur said, "I would like to choose and get my sons' consent on brides. If they marry without my consent, it will hurt me, though I will receive them because they are my children."

The loosening of authority within the family is most obvious when an entrepreneur or another major contributor to the family coffers is not family head. A Kayastha entrepreneur whose brothers are all salaried directors of an engineering factory, observed:

> The head does not have much control over the family. There is a difference of personality. Few dependents are in the family, so the head does not command. All are self-sufficient, so they argue and have their own way.

This respondent, although the biggest earner in his joint family, is not the *karta*. Another entrepreneur, who is also the major financial contributor in his family, reports: "Although my elder brother is *karta*, I buy my own clothes and send my wife to her father's place when I like. In most cases I do not seek my elder brother's permission for what I do." It is recognized by families that big earners must be given special consideration so that they will not separate, as many within the sample have done. Despite the presence of a *karta*, an earning member's authority in the family is proportional to his income. One respondent even said, "If the *karta* does not have the highest income, he will not be obeyed." It is also recognized that in the past the unusual authority, which the *karta* exercised, was often rooted in his control over large landed estates. One respondent observed that the ideal *karta* should be the eldest, the smartest, and the richest. It was clear that relative wealth was the most important factor; it was apparent also that the big earner need not be the *karta* in order to exercise great influence.

To get a notion of the ideal view of the *karta*, I presented the following four alternatives and asked respondents to indicate which they preferred:

(1) In the first family all live and work together, and all go their own ways. (In Bengali this expression conveys the lack of dominant head.)

(2) In the second family all work together, and they select an intelligent man, not necessarily the eldest, as *karta*.

(3) In the third the eldest is the head of the family.

(4) In the fourth the man who earns the most is head.

Within the whole sample (98 answering), over a half selected the second alternative (the most intelligent = *karta*); 39 per cent selected the eldest; 4 per cent chose the first alternative; and 7 per cent the fourth (the one who earns the most = *karta*). Among the wealthiest upper-caste entrepreneurs (earning over Rs. 4000 per month), "the eldest" was selected twice as frequently as any other choice. Among Mahisya entrepreneurs in the same income category the choice was predominantly for the "most intelligent." All but one of the votes for the "richest" came from the poorest Mahisya non-entrepreneurs, several of whom had been "abandoned" by brothers who earned more. I sought to compare the ideal with actual practice among the joint families in the sample and found the results indicated in Table 6.

TABLE 6

Ideal and Actual Bases for Selection of Karta

	Actual Situation					
Preferred Situation	*(1) No real family head*	*(2) Smartest is karta*	*(3) Eldest is karta*	*(4) Biggest earner is karta*	*(5) Leader-ship is shared*	*Total*
(1) No real family head	1		2			3
(2) Smartest is *karta*	1		14		7	22
(3) Eldest is *karta*			10		3	13
(4) Biggest earner is *karta*						
Total	2		26		10	38

The apparent characteristics of (2) "the smartest" and (4) "the biggest earner" have been omitted from Table 6. In 20 of 26 cases in which the karta is eldest he is the biggest earner; in 19 of 26 cases he is an entrepreneur; in three cases he is an elder brother who has become a partner of the entrepreneur. In one case an entrepreneur's elder brother, who is not active in the younger brother's firm, provided the capital with which his younger brother got started. In twelve cases in which the biggest earner is not the head there is either a conspicuous sharing of leadership (column 5) and reduction of authority of the karta or real authority among earning members of the household (column 1). In five cases of families which have "separated men" working in Howrah, authority is also shared between several individuals. I did not interview every family member, so it is not possible to give an independent judgment of the intelligence of *kartas* in relation to other members of the family. However, it was my subjective impression that the brightest member of most families was also the entrepreneur. In 19 out of 38 cases the entrepreneur was also both the eldest and the *karta*. It seems very probable that in close to 50 per cent of the cases the ideal of a *karta* who is "smartest, richest, and eldest" was met.

The difficulty of making meaningful generalizations from statements about such abstract characteristics as "smartest", "richest", or "eldest" is made clear from some of the remarks which respondents made about these categories:

"The intelligent man may be a cheat."

"The *karta* should not only be intelligent but liberal, too."

"The man who earns most may become a dictator."

"A big earner may be more lucky than intelligent."

One *karta*, whose particularly wise leadership I had occasion to observe, remarked: "The family is like a miniature nation; the ruler should be able and intelligent." As yet another respondent put it, "He should be intelligent. The intelligent person has tact enough to give good advice after the angry man cools off. He can compromise with two points of view without annoying either party." Such skill as this in interpersonal relationships is also one of the more salient characteristics of the most successful entrepreneurs. It is small wonder that individuals possessing this skill are frequently entrepreneurs as well as heads of joint families. Perhaps these qualities of character should be taken as the extra, independent variable, which brings about the strong correlation between entrepreneurship and commensal joint families.

Summary and Conclusion

So far, I have argued that economic self-interest is a principal cause for the maintenance or breakup of commensal joint families, and that what is economically rational differs from individual to individual and from group to group. It has been asserted that industrialization is not a homogeneous process but rather one which creates a variety of opportunities which may be exploited by diverse strategies. Consequently, life in the joint family, either in the sense of a coparcenary family, comprised of those who share joint property, or a commensal family, one which budgets and eats together, also has variable economic advantages or disadvantages for particular individuals within particular economic contexts.

The fact that the coparcenary joint family provides a viable basis for a business was stressed. It was also noted that in a majority of the cases in which coparceners run a business, they also live as commensal joint families. However, these families all contain entrepreneurs (those who originally started the business). A limited number of cases suggests that when businesses are inherited, they tend to be run by joint coparcenary families whose members live in non-joint commensal families. It was suggested that in such instances in particular a focus upon the commensal family unit alone would be misleading.

Similarly, research which looks only at urban households may be misleading because many migratory workers live temporarily separated from joint families (containing their wives and children) in villages. In fact, the percentage of rural joint families (over 60 per cent) among such migratory workers was the highest of any group studied. The economic advantage to an urban, migrant worker of keeping his wife and children in a rural joint family is reinforced by the economic advantage to the rural joint family of receiving regular financial contributions from the worker.

It was found that unless family members became partners or coparceners in a business, entrepreneurs, whose incomes rapidly increased, tend to separate from rural joint families, because the amount of income they put into such families rapidly outpaces the economic advantages which they receive in return. Similarly, highly trained professionals, who can command high salaries, tend to separate from rural joint families; while industrial workers, whose income is much less, tend to remain within rural joint commensal families, or at least to continue to share in the coparcenary joint family.

A contrast was made between joint ownership of an urban business and shared ownership of an urban house. An urban house in most instances does not produce income and unlike a jointly owned business (or jointly owned rural agricultural land), provides no greater economic advantages to its owners in an undivided estate. Consequently, disparities in income and expenses in such a house can easily lead to quarrels. The result may be a separation of the commensal joint family and perhaps partition of the house.

Attention was focused upon the *karta* or family head and the crucial role which he (in a few cases she) plays in maintaining harmony and working out agreements within both commensal and coparcenary families. It was indicated that the same wisdom and judgment, which can result in, a harmonious commensal family contributes greatly to entrepreneurial success and the running of a family firm. Respondents in almost all families in the sample reported that the *karta* has become less authoritarian than he was in their childhood; commensal family members now often choose their own clothes; bridegrooms give their approval of prospective brides, etc. In families in which the largest earner is not the *karta*, his wishes are given especially careful consideration so that he will not be alienated from the family. It was found in a majority of cases that although respondents indicated that the wisest or most intelligent man should be the head of the family, the *karta* is in most cases (20 out of 26) the eldest and the biggest earner. Thus, it is certainly in the economic interest of family members to "go along with" such as *karta*. If the *karta* is also an entrepreneur with an expanding business, it is in his Interest to provide generously for the education of members of the commensal family and later, on the basis of trust and obligation built up in this and other ways, to bring them into his firm as partners (or coparceners). In just this way many of the most successful engineering firms which I studied have expanded and modernized. If such firms are regarded as one of the most dynamic expressions of industrialization, then they also most dramatically belie the general expectation that industrialization is inimical to the joint family.

NOTES

1. The study took place between September, 1966, and September, 1968. The first year was financed by a Junior Fellowship of the American Institute of Indian Studies; the second was supported by a fellowship and research grant from the National Institutes of Health. The Committee for the Study of Economic Development

and Cultural Change of the University of Chicago (Dr. Bert Hoselitz, Chairman) also provided funds for the purchase of equipment and to pay additional expenses resulting from a collaboration that was arranged in India with Ashis Nandy, a psychologist from the Center for the Study of Developing Societies in Delhi. Also cited in Tables 1 and 2–A of this paper is information from a study of families conducted in the same ward by the Howrah Improvement Trust (HIT) in 1963.

2. In the section below I deal in detail with definitions of types; I generally follow those of Kolenda (1968).
3. In another paper (Owens 1970a) I have dealt with the economic setting of Howrah in greater detail.
4. The sample of families studied by Ames also differs from the Howrah sample discussed below. The Jamshedpur respondents were all unskilled workers, skilled workers, or supervisors, while over 50 per cent of my sample was comprised of entrepreneurs.
5. Because this family is not headed by the original entrepreneur, it has not been included among the 104 families on whom data are presented later in this paper.
6. I used the families surveyed by the Howrah Improvement Trust as a universe from which to draw the samples of non-entrepreneurs whom I interviewed.
7. Caste affiliation was not elicited by the HIT study (as is customery in government sponsored research). However, judging by the wide range of castes identifiable from names on community voters' lists, it may be presumed that a fairly wide range of castes was also represented in the HIT study.
8. All non-entrepreneurs were residents within the urban ward which I studied, although some entrepreneurs had homes in Howrah city outside the ward. A few entrepreneurs also lived in Calcutta. A larger number of non entrepreneurs lived separated from their families, and these were designated in the comparison as living in subnuclear families.
9. The total number of families from the HIT study has been increased by adding to the 285 families whose homes are directly in the path of the expressway (as indicated in Table 1) 94 families whose property will be "improved" by the expressway, for a total of 379 families.
10. The percentages of "single men" who are actually members of joint households in their villages is quite high (as can be seen from Table 2-A). There were in my sample a number of government

servants (especially among upper castes) who left their wives and children in Howrah City while they worked in other cities. However, the majority of "separated" husbands were living in Howrah while their wives stayed in a village.

11. These disputes occurred prior to the Gains of Learning Act of 1930 which stipulated that an individual, though educated with the aid of his family, has the right to keep all income acquired through his education (O'Malley, 1941:44-49, 53-60).

12. The respondent had retained part ownership of this property along with his brother; but he says that while he was serving in the army during World War II, his brother sold the property and kept all the money with himself. The respondent and his brother now live separately.

13. By contrast, under the *Mitakshara* system, which applies to the rest of India, a son acquires a right to ancestral property at birth and the right of the father to dispose of such property is limited (see Gulati and Gulati, 1962:1-6).

14. The overall percentage of joint families reported in the HIT study of my research area (21 per cent) would be considered somewhere between "medium" and "low" by Kolenda (1968:375) in relation to an all-India average. However, one would like to know how many of the 19.5 per cent of the families reported by HIT as subnuclear households were families with wives living in joint families in villages (see Table 2).

References

Ames, M.M.: 1970: "Structural Dimensions of Family Life in the Steel City of Jamshedpur, India." *Economic Development and Cultural Change* (in press).

Benedict, B.: 1968: "Family Firms and Economic Dvelopment." *Southwestern Journal of Anthropology,* 24, 1-19.

Calcutta Metropolitan Planning Organization: 1967: *Survey of Manufacturing Industry-1962*, Calcutta Metropolitan District, V. 2. Calcutta.

Census of India: 1961: I, Part II-A, *Union Primary Census Abstract,* pp. 4-7; 16, Part II-B, 60-61.

Cohen, A.R.: 1967: Tradition, Values and Inter-Role Conflict in Indian Business. Unpublished Ph.D. dissertation, Harvard University.

Cohen, B.S.: 1961: Chamar Family in a North Indian Village; a Structural Contingent. *Economic Weekly,* 13, pp. 1051-55.

Fursterburg, F.E.: 1960: "Industrialization and the American Family: A Look Backward." *American Sociological Review,* 31, pp. 326-337.

Goode, W.J.: 1963: *World Revolution and Family Patterns.* Glencoe.

Gulati, I.S. and K.S. Gulati: 1962: *The Undivided Hindu Family: A Study of its Tax Privileges.* Bombay.

Kolenda, P.M.: 1968: "Religion, Caste, and Family Structure: A Comparative Study of the Indian Joint Family." *Structure and Change in Indian Society,* ed. M.B. Singer and B.S. Cohn, pp. 339-96. Chicago.

Morton, F.: 1961: *The Rothschilds, A Family Portrait.* New York.

Nicholas, R.: 1961: "Economics of Family Types in Two West Bengal Villages." *Economic Weekly,* 13, pp. 1057-60.

O'Malley, L.S.S.: 1941: *Modern India and the West.* London.

Owens, R.: 1970a: "Peasant Entrepreneurs in a North Indian Industrial City." *Economic Development and Cultural Change* (in press).

————: 1970b: "Preliminary Reflections on Small-scale Entrepreneurs and Politics in a North Indian Industrial City." *Unpublished paper presented at the 1970 Meeting of the Association for Asian Studies.*

Parsons, T.: 1951: *The Social System.* Glencoe.

Singer, M.B.: 1968: "The Indian Joint Family in Modern Industry." *Structure and Change in Indian Society,* ed. M.B. Singer and B.S. Cohn, pp. 423-52. Chicago.

9

The Adaptive Extended Family in India

A.A. Khatri

This essay critically examines hypothesized trends towards the conjugal family in India. The author offers empirical evidence on the involvement of family members and outside kin in decision-making in nuclear, joint, and extended households, as well as upon attitudes towards the joint family on the part of a sample of 118 adult respondents from families of children from two schools in Ahmedabad, India. Among the nuclear households, in about half the cases, non-residential family members were involved with decisions of respondents, family members. It was also found that the overwhelming majority of respondents from nuclear, extended and joint households and from various socio-economic strata (upper and middle class) were in favour of the joint family. Other trends which have been interpreted as supporting movements towards the Western model of the conjugal family have been critically examined. These trends are also consistent with another model of the family, tentatively titled "The Adaptive Extended Family".

Goode (1963) has hypothesized that the family organizations all over the world are gravitating gradually, but inevitably towards the ideal typical Western model of the conjugal family. Among the determinants of this inevitable march, postulated by a number of sociologists, are industrialization, industrial urbanization, exposure to Western ideology and democratization. The role of humanism and scientific rationalism are not adequately emphasized in these attempts to search for the determinants of family change. As India is increasingly exposed to these determinants, the Indian family is bound to move towards the conjugal family, according to these sociologists.

In order to understand the realistic or mythical character of this march, it is necessary to present here the ideal types of the Indian joint family and the Western conjugal family. The following are among the core characteristics of the ideal typical joint family in India:[1] Marriage as a sacrament, and as a religious and social duty; familial responsibility for arrangement of marriage in the context of sex segregation; caste endogamy and other family-oriented considerations; indissolubility of marriage; patrilocal residence; domination of parent-child over husband-wife relations; young husband-wife relations characterized by various constraints and restricted interaction; premium placed on reproduction of sons; familial responsibility for survival and socialization of children; common residence of patrilineally-related males, their spouses and children; common property; common purse; dominance of seniority and male sex in the hierarchy of intrafamilial relations; final authority of decision-making vested in the family head (usually the eldest living male); and identity of the joint family as a social unit in their caste and the community. Description of characteristics of the ideal type of the Indian joint family, and accounts of interpersonal relations within the joint family, their caste, class and regional variations, etc., have received attention from many investigators of the Indian family.[2]

Among core characteristics of the ideal type of the Western (particularly American) conjugal family are the following: autonomous mate selection based on heterosexual love; marriage as a contract; domination of spousal over parent-child relations; establishment of a self-sufficient social and economic unit as a pair (to the exclusion of the kin) and acceptance of the identity of the conjugal dyad in the community; fulfillment of sexual, companionate and affectional needs from each other; reproduction on a voluntary basis; responsibility for survival and socialization of children; and the conjugal dyad as a decision-making unit without kin involvement or interference. A vast volume of literature is available on the Western family—ideal typical and reality-based—and its diverse variation (Aldous and Hill, 1966).

Considerable evidence about changes in the Indian family has been presented by many investigators. This evidence, along with changes in Indian law, has been interpreted to provide a basis for the conclusion by Goode and others that the Indian family is moving towards the Western conjugal family. It is submitted here that (1) this evidence is at times conflicting; (2) just as this evidence can be interpreted to provide indices of moves towards the conjugal family, it can be also construed to fit in with a form of family organization different from the Western conjugal family; and (3) much of this evidence does not negate the current expression of the core characteristics of the ideal type of joint family as described above.

It is proposed here to present evidence based on partial analysis of the data secured as part of the author's efforts to quantify dimensions of the ideal type of the joint family in India (Khatri, 1971). This evidence sheds some light on (i) involvement of family members and outside kin in decision-making in nuclear, joint, and extended households,[3] and (ii) attitudes towards the joint family.

Evidence concerning specific propositions derived from the ideal type of the conjugal family and that of the joint family would be presented and discussed, and would be followed by a critical examination of the presumed trends towards the conjugal family in India. The specific propositions are as follows: (1) In the conjugal family, decisions concerning the important family affairs would be made by the conjugal dyad and would not involve kin. (2) In the joint family, decisions would be made by the family head. In cases where the joint family is split up in separate households on residential level, decisions concerning important family matters would be taken in joint consultation among family members of these households.

Certain key concepts are now briefly described. A respondent's family is called his/her residential family, while family units residing separately are called his non-residential families. These are residential and non-residential stems of a potentital joint family. The potential joint family consists of those patrilineally related males with/without their spouses and children who would have stayed together under one roof as one family unit bound by ties of common residence, common kitchen, common property, common purse managed by *pater familias* (the eldest active living male usually who has authority to decide about important family matters) but who do not reside together.

Sample and Procedure

The sample consisted of 118 adult respondents from families of children studying in (a) Balghar, a nursery-kindergarten and primary school and (b) Sharada, a school for the retarded operated by B.M. Institute, Ahmedabad. One respondent from each of these families was interviewed.[4] The respondent was usually the father or mother of the child studying in each of these schools. For the purpose of determining reliability, one additional member, usually the other parent, was interviewed. In the present analysis, protocols for fathers were used when two protocols of one family were available. Twenty-nine (93.55 per cent) of 31 families of Sharada were interviewed and included in the sample. Ninety-one (96.81 per cent) of 96 families of Balghar were interviewed. However, only 89 families (94.68 per cent) were included in the sample. Two families who had been interviewed were not included because the children's parents were residing in different towns. The children ranged in age from 2 years to 14 years and 8 months. The mean age of the sample was seven years. Socio-economic status as measured by Kuppuswami's scale (Kuppuswami, 1962) was predominantly upper class (I) and upper-middle class (II) in the case of Balghar families while upper-middle (II) and lower-middle class (III) for Sharada families. The sample is small and slanted towards upper socio-economic status. Again the sample consists of families of young school children. Thus, it is not representative of the population of families of Ahmedebad. Hence, its generalizability is grossly limited.

Findings

The following findings deserve mention:

(1) In nuclear households, in about half the cases (46.1 per cent) non-residential family members are consulted by respondents' family members in important matters like selection of a mate, career, etc. (decision-making Mode I, Table 1). With about the same frequency (50.1 per cent), decisions are made

within the nuclear household (Modes II-VII). (2) In the joint households, consultation with non-residential kin has taken place in 21.9 per cent of cases. (3) The conjugal dyad is involved in decision-making in 44.3 per cent of cases in nuclear households while only in 15.7 per cent in joint households (Mode VI). (4) In only 1.8 per cent of the cases, the individual whom a given decision primarily affected (decision-making Mode V, the party concerned) has decided on his own without consulting other family members (Table 1).

An attempt was also made to investigate the role of types of households and socio-economic status on attitudes towards the joint family. The overwhelming majority of respondents from nuclear, extended and joint households and from various socio-economic strata (upper and middle class) are in favour of the joint family (Tables 2 and 3).

Discussion

In the present study, we have considered evidence concerning decision-making in nuclear and joint households and expression of attitudes towards the joint family. Analysis of different sectors of data from the same study reported elsewhere (Khatri, 1973) revealed involvement of the residential family in decision-making in 37 per cent of 392 kin households. Again, the possibility of consultation among non-residential stems themselves is not contraindicated. Thus, kin involvement stands out conspicuously in a significant number of households.

TABLE 1

Family Types* and Decision-making**

	Decision-making patterns	Family Types			
		Nuclear Family (N=52) Per cent	*Joint Family (N=32) Per cent*	*Extended Family (N=26) Per cent*	*Total (N=110) Per cent*
I	The sole mode***	36.5	18.8	23.1	28.2
I	One of the modes	9.6	3.1	11.5	8.2
II	The sole mode	1.9	6.3	7.7	4.5
II	One of the modes	3.9	0.0	7.7	3.6
III	The sole mode	0.0	0.0	0.0	0.0

	Decision-making patterns	Family Types			
		Nuclear Family (N=52) Per cent	*Joint Family (N=32) Per cent*	*Extended Family (N=26) Per cent*	*Total (N=110) Per cent*
III	One of the modes	0.0	6.3	0.0	1.8
IV	The sole mode	0.0	25.0	15.4	10.9
IV	One of the modes	0.0	3.1	0.0	0.9
V	The sole mode	0.0	3.1	0.0	0.9
V	One of the modes	0.0	3.1	0.0	0.9
VI	The sole mode	38.5	6.3	7.7	21.8
VI	One of the modes	5.8	9.4	15.4	9.1
VII	The sole mode	0.0	21.9	11.5	9.1
VII	One of the modes	0.0	0.0	7.7	1.8
VIII	The sole mode	13.5	3.1	11.5	10.0
VIII	One of the modes	0.0	6.3	3.8	2.7
Totals :	The sole mode N	47	27	20	94
	Per cent	90.4	84.4	76.9	85.5
	One of the modes N	10	10	12	32
	Per cent	19.2	31.3	46.2	29.1

* Three cases of broken family and five other cases were omitted for smallness of sample and other reasons. Nuclear Family = one couple; Joint Family = at least two couples; Extended Family = one couple plus one or more relatives without spouse/s.

** Decision-making patterns were classified into the following modes: I. Joint consultation between residential and non-residential family members. II. Residential family head only. III. Family head and party concerned about whom decision in made. IV. Residential family head consults other residential members. V. The party concerned on his own. VI. Consultation by mother and father. ("Mother" and "Father" of the child studying in a school from whose family an adult member was interviewed.) VII. Family head and one or more residential family members excluding mother. VIII. Any other; total.

*** When any one of several decision-making patterns was the only mode adopted, it is referred to as the sole mode.

**** Percentages do not add up to 100 as in 16 families out of 110 more than one mode of decision-making are reported, thus contributing 32 modes rather than 16 modes. Two modes are adopted by each of remaining 5 MF, 5 JF and 6 EF types.

TABLE 2

Attitudes Towards the Joint Family According to Three Family types

	Attitude Towards the Joint Family	*Nuclear Family (N=46) Per cent*	*Extended Family (N=19) Per cent*	*Joint Family (N=29) Per cent*	*Total (N=94*) Per cent*
A	Strongly Approve	43.5	42.1	37.9	41.5
B	Mildly Approve	32.6	42.1	51.7	40.4
C	Do not care about it one way or the other	6.5	10.5	0.0	5.3
D	Mildly Disapprove	8.7	5.3	6.9	7.5
E	Strongly Disapprove	8.7	0.0	3.5	5.3

*Data on this section "Attitudes toward Jointness" were also analyzed according to socio-economic class reported in Table 3. On 24 out of 118 interviewees, data pertaining to socio-economic status and attitudes towards the joint family were not available.

TABLE 3

Socio-Economic Status and Attitudes Towards the Joint Family

	Attitudes Towards the Joint Family	*Socio-economic Status Levels*			
		Level Number I (N=56) Per cent	*Level Number II (N=28) Per cent*	*Level Number III (N=9) Per cent*	*Total (N=93*) Per cent*
A	Strongly approve	33.9	53.6	44.4	40.9
B	Mildly approve	44.6	35.7	33.3	40.9
C	Do not care about it one way or the other	5.4	7.1	0.0	5.4
D	Mildly Disapprove	12.5	0.0	0.0	7.5
E	Strongly Disapprove	3.6	3.6	22.3	5.4

* On 24 out of 118 intervieweers, data pertaining to S.E.S. and attitudes towards the joint family were not available. There was only one case belonging to socio-economic status level IV. This has been omitted.

Though the conjugal dyad is involved in decision-making to an appreciable extent in nuclear households (44.3 per cent), it plays a rather insignificant role (15.7 per cent) in decision-making in the joint households (Table 1, Decision-making Mode VI). Most of the respondents who are either mothers or fathers of children in the schools studied, express positive attitude towards the joint family while they play an insignificant role in decision-making as referred to above. This is all the more noteworthy because the sample is predominantly middle and upper socio-economic status with many educated respondents. Furthermore, autonomy in decision-making on important matters is a rare phenomenon (1.8 per cent). The above findings are corroborated in Gore's study of Aggarwal families in and around Delhi. In the joint family, primary decisions were made by parents in 12 per cent of the rural and 19 per cent of the urban samples while in 81 to 88 per cent of instances, parents made decisions in nuclear families. The party concerned made decisions in "only a small minority" of cases (Goode, 1963: 249).

This study has pointed out the current expression of only one dimension, (i.e., decision-making) of ideal types of the conjugal and joint families in a small sample of contemporary families in an industrial town in India.

Here this author's attempt to explore the concept of jointness held by respondents by means of an open-ended question may be mentioned. Analysis of their spontaneous responses reveals that common residence is mentioned by 66.1 per cent of the respondents as either the sole or one of the characteristics of the joint family while pooling of income and jointness in property altogether are mentioned by 16.8 per cent. Thus, a large number of respondents (66.1 per cent) consider common residence as the core dimension of jointness.

As the focus of this essay is consideration of trends towards the conjugal family in India, we would briefly deal with the evidence on the trends which have been interpreted as supporting movement towards the Western model of the conjugal family.

Reference has been made to increasing involvement of Indian boys and girls in the mate selection process. However, there is hardly any evidence of emergence of the core characteristics of the Western conjugal family, such as (1) heterosexual love with concomitant idealization of the mate as a prelude to mate selection and (2) after marriage, the emergence of the conjugal dyad as an intensely involved identity recognized as such by each other, by kin, by primary and other groups. In the early phase of conjugal relationship, emotional involvement of Indian spouses remains predominantly in their family of orientation.

Changes in other areas–increase in age at marriage, expansion of educational opportunities for both boys and girls, reduced hold of caste endogamy and dowry, preference for nuclear households, lessened restrictions on heterosexual relations, widow remarriage and divorce, expression of attitudes in their favour–these are the changes which have been reported to have taken place (Ghurye, 1952, 1954; Goode, 1963; Gore, 1968; Kapadia, 1954-55, 1956, 1957, 1959, 1966; Khatri, 1964; 1970a, 1970b; Kuppuswami, 1957; Merchant, 1935; Ross, 1961). Findings of a number of these studies are conflicting. There is no firm evidence of increase in incidence of nuclear family households. Findings of incidence of nuclear and joint households are conflicting due to diversity of samples drawn, methods used and definitions adopted (Desai, 1964; Goode, 1963; and Khatri, 1972). Shifts in family types are inevitable and a part of the Indian cultural pattern (Goode, 1963; Karve, 1963; Khatri, 1972; Kolenda, 1968; Mandelbaum, 1970; A. M. Shah, 1974). Again these changes are not necessarily moves towards the conjugal family. They are also consistent with another model of the family radically different from the ideal type of the conjugal family. The model is tentatively titled the "Adaptive Extended Family", abbreviated as AEF.

Its main features are as follows: (1) Though common residence of patrilineally related kin – particularly ego, his brothers, married and unmarried, their spouses and children, and parents of ego–is valued, AEF permits the possibility of formation of separate households in the event of migration, restricted space, etc. If a nuclear household is formed, members of this household would continue to hold allegiance to the AEF household from which it became separated. Very significant relationships would be maintained with the AEF in the context of a network of rights and obligations. In her study of 135 Khatri households, Kapoor (1965) found a number of interhousehold relationships among the separated households, Khatri (1963) found likewise in his study of a smaple of Gujarati families. Agarwala (1955), Desai (1955, 1956, 1964), Kapadia (1959, 1966), Dube (1955), Ross (1961) and Prabhu (1956) have provided substantial evidence for various involvements of "trunk" and "stem" families. (2) The AEF still considers that it is its responsibility to arrange for selection of marriage partners for its unmarried boys and girls. Almost all marriages in India are negotiated by family elders. However, needs of the young, usually of educated wards, for some degree of involvement on their part – specifically a preview of prospective mates and perhaps even limited interaction between them – are felt and to some extent fulfilled by the AEF (Ghurye, 1952, 1954; Kannan, 1963; Kapadia 1966; Khatri, 1964; Ross, 1961; B.V. Shah, 1964). Even professional young men working in Western countries fly to India to get married through the aid of their families. (3) The AEF does not act as a barrier in the process of industrialization and industrial urbanization. Christian (1973) found a fit between the family organization of three castes of silk weavers in South India and modern demands of business and industry. Agarwala (1955, 1962) found that his Marwari community owning a significant sector of industry in India utilized the traditional pattern of joint family management admirably to fulfil the needs of industrial management.

Kapadia (1956) found no conflict between industrialized urbanization and extended family organization. Desai (1964) has referred to economic benefits from joint family ownership and management of a string of shops. Further corroborative evidence has been presented by Lambert (1963), Orenstein (1961), Rao (1968) and Singer (1968). Mukherjee (1965) found emphasis on the extended family increasing with passage from villages through small towns to big cities. (4) In the AEF a rigid hierarchy of family relations with formal distance and awe may be reduced as "emancipation" and "democratization" limelight the role of formal education in addition to sex and age as criteria of rank. Strict observance of "Rules of Avoidance" and such sex-segregating practices are not an integral part of the AEF. However, respect for persons higher in the family hierarchy can continue to be fostered without throttling the uniqueness of the individual and the fulfilment of personality needs which need not be diametrically opposed to family welfare in the AEF. Some evidence for an ideological gap between generations, respect for family elders, and adjustment of the elderly to the needs and demands of the young is present in a number of studies (Kapadia, 1966; Madan, 1965; Mandelbaum, 1970; Ross, 1959, 1961).

Residentially any family type (nuclear, extended, joint, even broken as described earlier) can be AEF if it remains emotionally, economically, and socially involved with various stems of the potential joint family. The model presented above is neither the prototype of the ideal type of the joint family, though it retains some of its salient dimensions; nor is it an accurate reflection of any specific contemporary Indian family pattern, though diverse family types in various parts of India may approximate this model in varying degrees. This model of the AEF is more likely to fulfil the economic and emotional needs of family members in a developing country like India and also to support the cultural mores deep-seated in its ethos. The model excludes the core characteristics of the ideal type of the conjugal family; i.e., heterosexual love with its concomitant idealization of the mate, neolocal residence immediately following marriage, identity of the conjugal dyad as an exclusively emotionally involved pair and a social unit with decision-making primarily confined within its four walls.

FIGURE 1

Indicating Possible Trends of the Family Organization in the United States and India

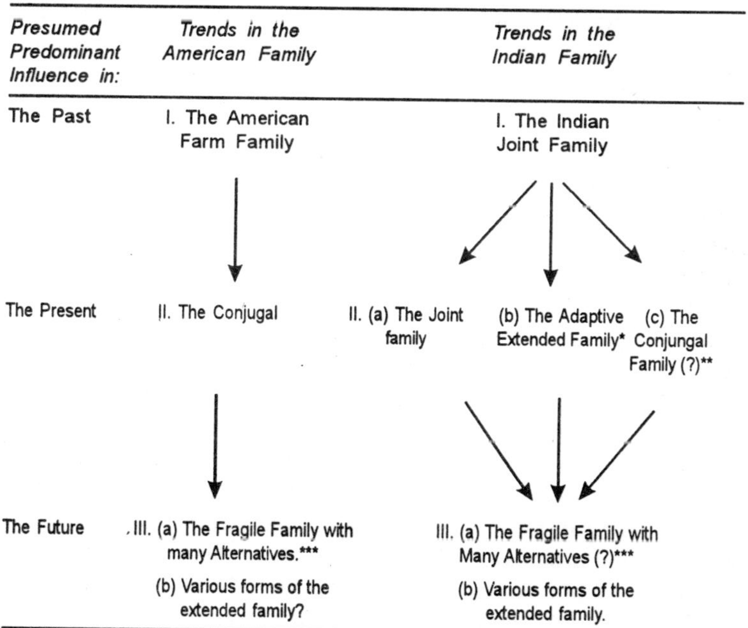

* The Adaptive Extended Family is an emergent model that has evolved out of the ideal type of the joint family.

** The symbol (?) means that though theoretically possible, serious doubts exist concerning the transformation of the family into the model in question in the foreseeable future.

*** The fragile family with many alternatives is also an emergent American model which reflects high divorce rate, social acceptance and increasing incidence of live togethers, of spouse swapping, group sex, communal living, group marriage, lesbian and homosexual relationships.

It is necessary at this stage to distinguish between the conjugal family as prevalent in the United States, and the nuclear household as found in India. Even though both are residentially nuclear, attitudes and expectations towards and from each spouse and their non-residential relatives are radically different. Similarly, if parents of the male spouse stay with the conjugal dyad in the United States, this fact of common residence does not convert the conjugal family into the joint family. Here, at any rate, psychological attributes are more significant than structural properties of the family. Psychological dimensions of the ideal type of the conjugal family need not flow from prolonged residence of an Indian couple in a nuclear household as has been assumed by some sociologists. Slight changes in the overt behaviour of the Indian spouses moving about in pairs, etc. should not be considered as expressions of conjugal dyadic identity in the Western sense. In the cultural context characterized by sex segregation, familial arrangement of marriage, constraints and restricted interaction governing the husband-wife relations in the patrilocal Indian family, connotative significance of "closeness" as tapped by Gore (1961, 1968) and of "egalitarianism of conjugal role patterns" as found by Conklin (1973) are not likely to approximate emotional intimacy and identity of the conjugal dyad in the cultural context characterized by spontaneous heterosexual relationships, autonomous mate selection, and the romantic complex governing the spousal relations in the neolocal Western family. There is growing dissatisfaction with the Western conjugal family in its ability to fulfil sexual, affectional, security and personality needs of emancipated, freedom-loving, "variety" and "stimulating-seeking" individuals. The emergence of communes, the increasing number of singles and one-parent families, wife-swapping and group sex are among the phenomena which appear to reflect doubts concerning the validity of the ideal type of conjugal family for increasing numbers of persons involved in these alternative life styles".[5]

Figure 1 describes the author's perception of trends in the American and Indian family organizations. It is essential that family researchers in different parts of the world critically examine the hypothesized trends towards the conjugal family and conduct investigations aimed at a detailed understanding of changes in their specific family patterns. So far as India is concerned, perceptions of trends of the Indian family towards the ideal type of the conjugal family may be myths, imposed from a Western perspective rather than verified aspects of Indian reality.

Notes

1. As Hindus constitute the majority to the extent of about 85 per cent of the population in India, the general term "Indian" is used in the title in accordance with the English usage of a figure of speech of synecdoche ("whole" for "a part"). Again, most of the Muslims and Christians in India have been converted from Hinduism. The ideal-typical joint family derived from Hindu scriptures has a profound influence on family organization, familial behaviour and attitudes of the non-Hindu population in the opinion of the present author. At the same time, it should be emphasized that in a very heterogeneous Indian society with religious, regional, caste, social class and other subcultural variations, generalizations should be drawn with extreme caution from the limited data in the study.

2. Agarwala, 1955, 1962; Carstairs, 1957; Conklin, 1973; Cormack, 1961; Desai, 1955, 1956, 1964; Devanandan and Thomas, 1966; Dube, 1955, 1958; Dumont, 1964; Dumont and Pocock, 1957; Goode, 1963; Ghurye, 1952, 1954-55; Gore, 1962, 1965, 1968; Kaldate, 1962; Kannan, 1963; Kapadia, 1947, 1954-55, 1956, 1957, 1959, 1966; Kapoor, 1965; Karve, 1968; Khatri, 1962, 1963, 1966, 1970a, 1970b, 1971, 1972, 1973, 1974; Khatri and Sutaria, 1973; Kolenda, 1968; Madan, 1965; Mandelbaum, 1970; Minturn and Hitchcock, 1963; Morrison, 1959; Prabhu, 1963; Ross, 1961; Sarma, 1951, 1964; A.M. Shah, 1964, 1974; B.V. Shah, 1964; Srinivas, 1942, 1966; Straus and Winkelmann, 1969.

3. In this section of the essay where the author's empirical study is reported, only the household size dimension has been considered to distinguish "nuclear family" (one couple), "joint family" (at least two couples), and "extended family" (one couple plus one or more relatives without spouse/s). However, the term "joint family" has been used by different investigators to designate various combinations of characteristics of Indian family organization, such as common residence of patrilineally related males, their wives, and their offspring; common kitchen, common property, common

purse and authority of decision-making vested in the family head–usually the eldest living male. Due to the controversial nature of what constitutes "The Joint Family", and also due to the adaptive character of the family organization in contemporary India, the present author has termed the latter model as "The Adaptive Extended Family" and described it in some detail later in the essay.

4. A number of training sessions were held before interviewing was conducted. The author offers thanks to Chinubhai Patel, Madhuben Shroff, Pragnaben Bhachech, Junjabale Majmuder, Mrudulaben Vyas – Balghar teachers; Hansaben Patwa, Harishbhai Upadhyay–Sharada teachers; Devi Mangaldas, Rupande Sutaria, Urvashi Shah, and Gargi Munshi – research workers. The author is also indebted to Smt. Kamalini Sarabhoy, Director, B.M. Institute, Ahmedabad (India), for releasing school and other personnel and providing needed facilities.

5. Adams, 1974; Bartell, 1972; Constantine and Constantine, 1972; Cadwaller, 1975; Davidson, 1972; Denfeld and Gordon, 1972; Delora and Delora, 1972; Durham, 1973; Farson, 1974; Glenn, 1972; Gordon, 1972; Haughey, 1972; Hunt, 1975; Kanter, 1973, 1974; Krippner and Fersh, 1972; Lyness et al. 1975; Moran, 1972; Neubeck, 1969; Otto, 1975; Perrucci and Targ, 1974; Roy and Rustum, 1970; Skolnick and Skolnick, 1974; Toffler, 1972; G.J. Wells, 1975; T. Wells and Christie, 1972.

REFERENCES

Adams, M.: 1974: "The single woman in today's society: a reappraisal". In A. Skolnick and J.H. Skolnick (eds.). *Intimacy, Family, and Society.* Boston: Little Brown.

Agarwala, B.R. 1955. "In a mobile commercial community". "In symposium: caste and joint family". Sociological Bulletin 4, pp. 138-146.

————: 1962: "Nature and extent of social change in a mobile commercial community". *Sociological Bulletin* 11, pp. 141-45.

Aldous, J. and R. Hill: 1966: *International Bibliography of Research in Marriage and the Family.* 1900-64. Minneapolis: University of Minnesota Press.

Bartell, G.D.: 1972: "Group Sex Among the Mid-Americans." *Intimate Life Styles.* J.S. Delora and J.R. Delora (eds.), Palisaders, Cal.: Goodyear.

Cadwaller, M.: 1975: "Marriage as a wretched institution". In G.J. Wells (ed.). *Current Issues in Marriage and the Family.* New York: Macmillan.

Carstairs, G.M.: 1957: *The Twice Born: A Study of a Community of High Caste Hindus.* London: The Hogarth Press.

Christian, J.: 1973: "Structure of communication: acquisition among Hindi and Telugu learning children of India." Ph.D. dissertation. University of Texas, Austin.

Constantine, L.L. and J.M. Constantine: 1972: "The group marriage". In M. Gordon (eds.). *The Nuclear Family in Crisis.* New York: Harper and Row.

Cormack, M.: 1961: *She Who Rides a Peacock.* Bombay: Asia Publishing House.

Conklin, G.H.: 1973: "Emerging conjugal role patterns in a joint family system: correlates of social change in Dharwar, India". *Journal of Marriage and the Family* 35, pp. 742-48.

Davidson, S.: 1972. "Open land: getting back to the communal garden". In G.B. Carr (ed.). *Marriage and Family in a Decade of Change.* Reading, Mass.: Addison-Wesley.

Delora, J.S. and J.R. Delora (eds.): 1972: *Intimate Life Styles: Marriage and its Alternatives. Palisades:* Goodyear.

Denfeld, D. and M. Gordon: 1972: "The Sociology of Mate Swapping". In J.S. Delora and J.R. Delora (eds.), *Intimate Life Styles.* Palisades: Goodyear.

Desai, I. P.: 1955: "An Analysis". "In Symposium: Caste and Joint Family". *Sociological Bulletin* 4: pp. 97-117.

————: 1956: "The joint family in India: an analysis". *Sociological Bulletin* 5, pp. 144-56.

————: 1964: *Some Aspects of Family In Mahuva*, New York, Asia Publishing House.

Devanandan, P.D. and M.M. Thomas: 1966: "The changing pattern of family in India". Bangalore: *Christian Institute of Study of Religion and Society.*

Dube, S.C.: 1955: *Indian Village. Ithaca,* N.Y.: Cornell University Press.

Dumont, Louis: 1964: "Marriage in India: the present state of the question; postscript to part one," *Contributions to Indian Sociology* 7, pp. 77-98.

Dumont, Louis and D. Pocock: 1957: "Kinship". Contributions to *Indian Sociology* 1, pp. 43-64.

Durham, M.: "Experiments in marriage". In A.A. Khatri and E. Porterfield (eds.). *Perspectives on Marriage and the Family: A Reader,* Lexington, Mass.: Xerox.

Farson, R.: 1974: "Why good marriages fail". In S. Friedman (ed.) *Readings in Marriage and Family.* Guildford, Conn.: Dushkin.

Ghurye, G.S.: 1952 and 1954: "Social change in Maharashtra". *Sociological Bulletin,* 1.1. and 3.1.

———: 1955: Family and Kin in Indo-European Culture. Bombay: Oxford University Press.

Glenn, M.: 1972: "Intimacy and oppression". In G.B. Carr (ed.). *Marriage and Family in a Decade of Change,* Reading, Mass.: Addison-Wesley.

Goode, William, J.: 1963: *World Revolution and Family Patterns,* New York, The Free Press of Glencoe.

Gordon, M. (ed.): 1972: *The Nuclear Family in Crisis: The Search for an Alternate,* New York: Harper and Row.

Gore, M.S.: 1962: "The husband-wife and the mother-son relationships." *Sociological Bulletin,* 11, pp. 91-102.

———: 1965: "The traditional Indian family", pp. 209-31 in M.F. Nimkoff (ed.), Comparative Family Systems, Boston: Houghton Mifflin.

———: 1968: *Urbanization and Family Change.* Bombay: Popular Prakashan.

Haughey, J.C.: 1972: "The commune-child of the 1970s". In J.S. Delora and J.R. Delora (eds.) *Intimate Life Styles: Marriage and its Alternatives.* Palisades: Goodyear.

Hunt, Morton: 1975: "The future of marriage". In G.J. Wells (ed.). *Current Issues in Marriage and the Family.* New York: Macmillan.

Kaldate, S.: 1962: "Urbanization and disintegration of rural joint family". *Sociological Bulletin* 11, pp. 103-11

Kannan, C.T.: 1963: *Intercaste and Intercommunity Marriage in India.* Bombay: Allied Publishers.

Kanter, R.M.: 1973a: "Communes", In A.A. Khatri and E. Potterfield (eds.). *Perspectives on Marriage and the Family. Lexington, Mass.: Xerox.*

———: 1973b: "Communes for all reasons", In S. Friedman (ed.). *Readings in Marriage and Family.* Guilford. Conn.: Dushkin.

Kapadia, K.M.: 1947: *Hindu Kinship: An Important Chapter in Hindu Social History.* Bombay: The Popular Book Depot.

———: 1954-55: "Changing pattern of Hindu marriage and family". *Sociological Bulletin* 3(1, 2) and 4(2).

———: 1956: "Rural family patterns: A study in urban-rural relations," *Sociological Bulletin* 5, pp. 111-26.

———: 1957: "A perspective necessary for the study of social change in India," *Sociological Bulletin* 6, pp. 43-60.

———: 1959: "The family in transition", *Sociological Bulletin* 8, pp. 68-99.

———: 1966: *Marriage and Family in India,* 3rd ed. Bombay: Oxford University Press.

Kapoor, S.: 1965: "Family and kinship groups among the Khatris in Delhi", *Sociological Bulletin* 14, pp. 54-63.

Karve, I.: 1963: "The individual case study and the statistical method in social investigation". *The Economic Weekly* 15(7), pp. 1-6.

———: 1968: *Kinship Organization in India*, 3rd ed. Bombay, Asia Publishing House.

Khatri A.A.: 1962: "Social change in the Hindu family and its possible impact on personality and mental health". *Sociological Bulletin* 11, pp. 146-65.

———: 1963: "Rationale for a scale to measure jointness-nuclearity of families". *A paper presented before Anthropology Section,* Indian Science Congress, Delhi.

———: 1964: "Heterosexual friendships and involvement in the mate selection process of secondary and primary teacher trainees in Ahmedabad." To be published as a chapter in George Kurian (ed.). *The Family in India: A modern regional view.* Mouton: The Hague.

———: 1966: "Marriage and family in India: an overview of researchers." *Researchers in Child Development, Marriage and Family Relations Done in Indian Institutions of Teaching and Research.* Baroda: Department of Child Development, Faculty of Home Science, University of Baroda.

———: 1970a: "Personality and mental health of Indians (Hindus) in the context of their changing family organisation". In E.J. Anthony and C. Koupernik (eds.). *The Child in His Family*. New York: John Wiley.

———: 1970b: "Marriage and family relationships inGujarati fiction". Ph.D. thesis, University of London.

———: 1971: *Manual of the Scale to Measure Jointness of Families in India.* Ahmedabad, India: B.M. Institute.

———: 1972: "The Indian family: an empirically derived analysis of shifts in size and types". *Journal of Marriage and the Family* 34(3), pp. 725-34.

———: 1973: "Decision-making and mutual consultation among patrilineally related families in India." *Mimeographed.*

———: 1974: "Understanding changes in the family in contemporary India: a few hypotheses." *Presented before a meeting of the Family Research Committee of the International Sociological Association during the VII World Congress of Sociology,* Toronto, Canada, during August, 1974.

Khatri, A.A. and E. Porterfield (eds.): 1973: *Perspectives on Marriage and the Family.* Lexington, Mass.: Xerox.

Khatri, A.A. and R.R. Sutaria: 1973: "Family types and lineality-collaterality in families in India–glimpses into their jointness". *Mimeographed.*

Kolenda, Pauline Mahar: 1968: *Region, Caste and Family Structure: A Comparative Study of the Indian Society,* M. Singer and B.S. Cohn (eds). Chicago:Aldine Publishing Company.

Krippner, S. and D. Fersh: 1972: "Spontaneous paranormal experience among members of intentional communities." In G. B. Carr (ed.). *Marriage and Family in a Decade of Change.* Reading, Mass.: Addison-Wesley.

Kuppuswami, B.: 1957: *Study of Opinion Regarding Marriage and Divorce.* Bombay, Asia Publishing House.

———: 1962: *Manual of Socioeconomic Status Scale (Urban).* Delhi: Manasayan.

Lambert, R.D: 1963: *Workers, Factories and Social Change in India.* Princeton: Princeton University Press.

Lyness, J.L. *et al*: 1970: "Living together: an alternative to marriage." In G.P Carr (ed.). *Marriage and Family in a Decade of Change.* Reading. Mass. Adison-Wesley.

Madan, T.N.: 1965: *Family and Kinship: A Study of the Pandits of Rural Kashmir.* New York: Asia Publishing House.

Mandelbaum, D.G.: 1970: *Society in India.* Berkeley-University of California Press.

Mead, M.: 1974: "Too many divorces, too soon." In S. Friedman (ed.). *Readings in Marriage and Family.* Guilford, Conn: Dushkin.

Merchant, K.T.: 1935: Changing Views on Marriage and Family. Madras: B.G. Paul.

Minturn, L. and J. Hichcock: 1963: "The Rajputs of Khalapur, India". pp. 203-61 in B.B. Whiting (ed)., *Six Culture: Studies of Child Rearing*, New York and London: John Wiley and Sons.

Moran, R.: 1972: "The singles in the Seventies." In J.S. Delora and J.R. Delora (eds). *Intimate Life Styles.* Palisades: Goodyear.

Morrison, W.A.: 1959: "Family types in Badlapur: an analysis of a changing institution in a Maharastrian village." *Sociological Bulletin* 8, pp. 45-67.

Mukherjee, R.K.: 1965: *The Sociologist and Social Change in India Today.* Delhi: Prentice-Hall.

Neubeck, G.: 1969: "Extra-marital Relations". Englewood-Cliffs, N.J.: Prentice-Hall.

Orenstein, H.: 1961: *The Recent History of the Extended Family in India.* Social Problems 8, pp. 341-50.

Otto, Herbert A.: 1975: "Has monogamy failed". In G.J. Wells (ed.). *Current Issues in Marriage and the Family.* New York: Macmillan.

Perrucci, C. and D.B. Targ: 1974: *Marriage and the Family: A Critical Analysis and Proposals for Change.* New York: David McKay.

Prabhu, P.N.: 1956: "Bombay: a study on the social effects of urbanization". In UNESCO: *The Social Implications of Industrialization and Urbanization South of Sahara.* Paris: The International African Institute.

————: 1963: *Hindu Social Organization–A Study in Social Psychological and Ideological Foundations.* 4th ed. Bombay: Popular Book Depot.

Rao, M.S.A.: 1968: "Occupational diversification and joint household organisation." *Contributions to Indian Sociology,* New Series, 2, pp. 98-111.

Ross, A.D.: 1959: "Education and family change." *Sociological Bulletin* 8, pp. 39-44.

————: 1961: *The Hindu Family in its Urban Setting.* Toronto: University of Toronto Press.

Roy D. and Rustum: 1975: "Is monogamy outdated?" In G.J. Wells (ed.) *Current Issues in Marriage and the Family.* New York: Macmillan.

Sarma, J.: 1951: "Formal and informal relations in the Hindu joint household of Bengal." *Man in India* 31, pp. 51-71.

————: 1964: "The nuclearization of joint family households in West Bengal." *Man In India* 44, pp. 193-206.

Sennett, R.: 1970: "Brutality of modern families." In G.B. Carr (ed.). *Marriage and Family in a Decade of Change.* Reading, Mass.: Adison-Wesley.

Shah, A.M.: 1964: "Basic terms and concepts in the study of family in India". *Indian Economic and Social History Review* 1, pp. 1-36.

———: 1974. *The household dimension of the family in India.* Berkeley: University of California Press.

Shah, B.V.: 1964: *Social Change and College Students of Gujarat.* Baroda, University of Baroda.

Singer, M.: 1968: "The Indian joint family in modern industry." pp. 423-52 in Milton Singer and B.S. Cohn (eds.). *Structure and Change in Indian Society.* Chicago: Aldine Publishing Company.

Skolnick, A. and J. Skolnick: 1974: *Intimacy, Family and Society.* Boston: Little Brown.

Srinivas, M.N.: 1942: *Marriage and Family in Mysore.* Bombay: New Book Company.

———: 1966: *Social Change in Modern India.* Berkeley and Los Angeles: University of California Press.

Straus, M.A. and D. Winkelmann: 1969: "Social class, fertility and authority in nuclear and joint households in Bombay," *Journal of Asian and African Studies* 9, pp. 61-74.

Toffler, A.: 1972: "The fractured family". In J.R. Delora and J.S. Delora (eds.). *Intimate Life Styles,* Palisades: Goodyear.

Wells, Gipson J. (ed.): 1975: *Current Issues in Marriages and the Family.* New York: Macmillan

Wells, T. and S.L. Christie: 1972: "Living together: an alterative to marriage." In J.S. Delora and J.R. Delora (eds.). *Intimate Life Styles.* Palisades: Goodyear.

10

Urban Kinship Ties in South India: A Case Study

G.N. Ramu

Sociological analysis of the Indian family organisation deals mainly with change in the composition of the joint family. The major hypotheses and data are usually focused on one issue—whether or not the joint family is giving way to the nuclear family under the pressure of urbanization and industrialization.

The preoccupation with the "joint family controversy" has reduced research efforts related to other important aspects of family life in India. For example, what of the interactional dimensions of family life? At present such questions as the following remain unanswered: What is the nature of the kinship organization in urban-industrial settings? What is the structure of kin interaction? Are extended kin relationships in urban contexts functional to the individual and the family? Are there differences in kinship ties that occur when controlling for caste and class?

Joint-family oriented research tends to ignore these questions while traditional anthropological research on kinship concerns itself mainly with the principles of descent and alliance. Therefore, it is necessary for current research to recognise the significance of ego-based kinship behaviour for, in urban contexts, kinship does not operate at corporate or group levels but rather operates instead at interactional levels among only selected groups of persons.

The nonselectivity of kin characteristic of the traditional kinship organization, is not likely to operate (as will be shown later) in urban areas because here the organization of kinship ties tends to be based not on social expectations but on personal preferences.

The present essay is an attempt to pursue this line of inquiry focusing on ego-based kin behaviour in an urban context. Its major objectives are (1) to provide a general descriptive analysis of urban kin networks; (2) to point out that, in urban areas, kin relations are structured in terms of ego's likes and dislikes, and therefore, that kin interaction is a selective process; and (3) to suggest that there is a relationship between mutual aid and such social characteristics of the interactors as class and caste.

In the following analysis the first objective—the nature of kinship ties—will not be specifically treated because the whole analysis is addressed to this issue. The other objectives will be discussed in relation to relevant data. First, however, a brief account of the research setting and methods is in order.

The Data

The data presented here were collected as part of a larger project conducted in Kolar Gold Fields (hereafter KGF), an industrial city in Mysore State.[1] Two federal industrial establishments—gold mines and a heavy earthmoving factory—are situated in KGF. In aggregate these establishments employ more than 16,500 persons. Located also in KGF are a small-scale steel furniture industry, a starch factory, a granite materials industry and other business concerns dealing with consumer goods. Provincial government agencies in KGF employ over 1,800 persons (1961 Census figures). According to the 1961 Census, about 20,000 KGF persons follow non-agricultural pursuits.

KGF's 1971 population was 123,123. About 50 per cent of the KGF adults were born in KGF, the rest migrated to KGF from other villages and towns. In 1971 there were about 160 primary schools, 13 high schools, and 2 junior colleges in KGF, and the percentage of literacy in the population was about 65.9. About 70 per cent of the KGF people are Hindus, about 22 percent Christians, the remainder are Jains, Buddhists, and Muslims. KGF, according to the Census definitions, is the fifth largest city in Mysore State.

The findings of this essay are based on data collected from a subsample (N=388) of a probability sample of all KGF male household heads (N=414). The materials from 26 Muslim and Anglo-Indian cases were excluded from analysis because the kinship and family organizations of these groups are quite different from those for which materials are included: their inclusion would have needlessly complicated the analysis.

Of the 388, then, 281 are Hindus and 107 are Christians. Social organization within Hindu society can be understood in terms of caste (*varna*) and subcaste (*jati*). While *jati* refers to an endogamous, hereditary social group that has a name and a combination of attributes (Mandelbaum, 1970: 15), *varna* refers to the more general classification in terms of the five traditionally defined hierarchic divisions in Indian society (for more on *jati* and *varna* models of Indian society see Srinivas, 1962). The respondent's *jati* status was determined during interviews, and 27 *jatis* were thus identified. Although a comparative analysis of the kinship ties among all of these *jatis* would be interesting, it would also be cumbersome in view of the numerous *jatis* involved. Hence, for analytical reasons, our KGF jatis here have been classified in terms of the more general varna categories. By number and per cent, our sample includes 52 Brahmins (13.4 per cent), 12 Kshatriyas (3.1 per cent), 25 Vaisyas (6.4 per cent), 58 Shudras (15 per cent), 134 Hindu Harijans (34.5 percent).

In a separate analysis (Wiebe and Ramu, 1973) we found that Christian respondents in KGF do have *jati* identities and that they tend to identify themselves as Harijans. In general, they have comparable family and kinship and other socio-economic characteristics with the other KGF Harijans. Therefore, for analytic purposes, the Christian Harijans are treated along with Hindu Harijans here. The 107 Christian Harijans constitute 27.6 per cent of our 388 respondents.

Using occupation, education and income as crucial class variables, our respondents could be roughly classified into three general classes – lower, middle and upper (for details, see Ramu, 1972a). In turn, controlling for class and varna, we found a rough correlation between varna and class among our respondents (see Table 1).

As can be seen in Table 1, it is clear that most Brahmin respondents belong to the upper and middle classes, most Panchama respondents to the lower classes. At the intermediary levels, the correlations are not so clear. It is assumed here that these social status indices enable an analysis of kin interaction across class and caste lines.

TABLE 1
Percentage Distribution of Respondents by their Class and Caste (*Varna*)

Varna			*Lower class*		*Middle Class*		*Upper Class*	
	N	*Per cent*	*N*	*Per cent*	*N*	*Per cent*	*N*	*Per cent*
Brahmin	52	13.4	4	7.7	28	53.8	20	38.5
Kshatriya	12	3.1	10	83.2	2	16.7	—	—
Vaisya	25	6.4	15	60.0	7	28.0	3	12.0
Shudra	58	15.0	31	53.5	22	37.9	5	8.6
Hindu Harijans	134	34.5	115	85.8	18	13.4	1	0.8
Christian Harijans	107	27.6						2.8
Total	388	100.0	90	84.1	14	13.1	3	

Selectivity and Significant Kin

In general, the ascriptive nature of kinship allows for a set of expected patterns of kinship relations. For example, the dyadic relationship between ego and his father, siblings, or other consanguinal and affinal kin is generally institutionalized. An individual is obligated to conform to the expected patterns regardless of his personal feelings toward the kin in question. Further, if the kinship organization is local in character, as it is in the countryside, the expectations must be fulfilled. Failure will invoke appropriate sanctions

However, as R. Firth (1956, 1970) has pointed out, the nature of family life in urban areas allows a person a certain degree of freedom in the choice of relatives for regular interaction. Because kinship is less effective as the basis of urban social organisation, social sanctions here cannot be easily invoked in relation to the breach of kinship expectations. Therefore, kin interaction becomes not only voluntary in many cases but also occurs only among a group of selected kin. Such a selection of kin, according to our data, is a result of two factors: (1) size of one's kinship universe and (2) geographic distribution.

Size of One's Kinship Universe

Contrary to the "structural isolation" hypothesis (Parsons, 1943), urban dwellers in KGF have demonstrated an unusual degree of kin knowledge. Kin knowledge is understood as an ability to recognise the presence of kin and some relevant biographical information. The amount of kin knowledge varies across societies and class lines. Raymond Firth (1956: 38), for example, in his study of kinship in a London suburb found the total number of relatives reckoned by an individual *vis-a-vis* his kin universe to average 146. Phillippe Garigue (1962) in his study of French Canadian kinship in Montreal found the number to be around 200. Contrariwise, kin knowledge is considerably lower in Adam's (1968) study of urban kinship in the US. He reports a mean of 38.3 and a median of 27.6. In our KGF study, on an average, the respondents were found to recognise roughly 240 relatives.

Geographic Distribution of Kin

The nature of economic life in urban areas in India does not usually encourage clusters of kin to converge in any one given city (for example, Ramu, 1972b). Nevertheless, this does not rule out the possibility of a few relatives residing in the same city or the formation of a geographical area containing a few extended families. As a principle, though, localized kinship organization here remains impractical and norms governing kin interaction now tend to become flexible enough to accommodate individual preferences.

In essence, the magnitude of the kin universe and the nature of urban life, in general, make selection of kin inevitable. In turn, such a selection naturally will be based on the importance of a given kin to ego. The key factors involved in the choice are personal knowledge, personal compatibility, mutual likes and dislikes, age, performance of desired services, and affective attitudes. The kin so chosen are conceptualized here as "significant kin."[2]

Attempts were made to examine the notion of "significant kin" in relation to KGF the respondents. At the pretest stage of the study approximately five per cent of the estimated sample of the respondents (30 in number) were interviewed in detail regarding kin knowledge and interaction. Every respondent, thus interviewed came up with a long list of living relatives and demonstrated a good biographical knowledge of each of these kin. However, in relation to the pattern of interaction the list dwindled from over 240 to, at the most, 15 relatives who were designated as "significant kin". The statuses of kin who were thus chosen fell into a pattern reflecting similarities in age, kinship distance, respect and avoidance criteria and geographic propinquity. Encouraged by these cues, we decided to probe into the selective patterns in kin interaction in our final interviews and in our final questionnaire, a battery of questions seeking behavioural data on preferred kin and interactional patterns with such kin were included. From our respondents, information concerning their kin only were sought after. As our focus was ego-based kin behaviour and our research design enabled only one interview per household only the head of the household was Interviewed. We did not obtain data on significant kin from other members of the households.

In response to the question, "Who are the important kin with whom you have regular contacts by way of correspondence, exchange of gifts, visits, or aid?" the respondents listed the following kin: grandfather, father, brother, sister, son, daughter, father's brother, father's sister, mother's brother, mother's sister, father-in-law, brother-in-law, son-in-law. In essence, each respondent listed on an average 15 persons as his "significant kin". A large proportion of these 15 are consanguinal kin who at one time or another had been the members of the respondent's family of orientation or who have had very close associations with it.

When asked for the rationale for their choice most respondents drew the line between "kith and kin" and "dinner relatives" (this is a rough translation of phrases used by the respondents). The kith and kin are mostly blood relatives who have mutual concern, respect, and helping attitudes. Statements such as the following were frequently expressed: "We get along fine", "We care about each other," "I can depend on these relatives when I am in trouble", or "We grew up together sharing everything, feeling like we are one, and this feeling continues even now". In short, strong affective attitudes characterize the respondent's reasons for selectivity.

On the other hand, "dinner relatives" are general kin, those with whom the respondents' relations do not matter as much. These are so labelled because most general kin are expected to be present during events marking phases of the life cycle such as marriage or death, occasions usually followed by ceremonial dinners. In most cases such kin are seen only at such dinners.

In order to find out the closest of all kin the following question was asked: "Every person has a relative with whom he consults regarding important family matters and with whom he shares the joys and sorrows of his life. Among the relatives which you stated earlier as important, which two would you say are the most important given such a count?" Table 2 provides the distribution of the responses.

TABLE 2

The Percentage Distribution for Respondents Indicating their Choice of two of the Most Important Relatives

Category of Kin	*First Important Kin*		*Second Important Kin*	
	N	*Per cent*	*N*	*Per cent*
Brother	135	34.8	87	22.4
Mother	55	14.2	28	7.2
Brother-in-law	41	10.6	91	23.5
Father	21	5.4	27	7.0
Mother's brother	19	4.0	39	10.1
Father-in-law	15	4.9	18	4.6
Sister	7	1.8	16	4.1
Father's brother	6	1.6	2	.5
Cousin (mainly paternal)	6	1.6	9	2.3
Grandfather	5	1.3	2	.5
Son	4	1.0	2	.5
Daughter	4	1.0	3	.8
Other	18	4.8	12	3.1
None	52	13.5	52	13.5
Total	388	100.0	388	100.0

TABLE 3

Percentage Distribution of the Respondents who have a Relative Living in a Separate Household in KGF (N = 388)

Relative who Resides Separatly	*Percentage of the Respondents Who have Kin Mentioned in Column 1*	
	N	*Per cent*
Brother	360	92.8
Sister	27	7.0
Mother's brother	19	4.8
Father's brother	7	1.8
Father's sister	13	3.3
Father-in-law	38	9.7
Other kin	13	3.3

According to the data in Table 2, the most significant kin (in order of preference) are brother, brother-in-law, mother, mother's brother, father, and father-in-law. In order to explain such a preferential order we further analysed our data. The following relationships were conspicuous:

First, age is an important factor in the choice of such kin. The brother and the brother-in-law, cited as the most important kin, had an age difference of only about two to five years.[3] Nearly all involved in these two categories of kin belong to the same generation. Therefore, "significant kin" ties tend to occur at intragenerational levels.

Second, residential propinquity strongly influences the choice of two of our "significant kin". Table 3 indicates those who live in separate households in KGF. We found that such "significant kin" as brother, mother, mother's brother, sister, father's brother were drawn from kin resident in KGF. However, significant differences regarding the generalizations occurred with respect to our data concerning the father-in-law, father's sister, and father categories.

The exclusion of father-in-law and father's sister can be explained in terms of their relative kinship distance. They are farther than brothers who are, perhaps, the closest consanguinal kin. However, the most conspicuous exclusion is that of fathers and this will be explained later in this essay.

Third, respondents tend to make distinctions between "in-town and out-of-town significant kin." The in-town "significant kin" are usually consanguinal relatives, the out-of-town "significant kin" are generally affinal relatives. All of the brothers-in-law and nearly all of the father-in-law who were mentioned as "significant kin" were out-of-town residents. Most respondents conform to patrilineal and patrilateral kinship traditions. Any conspicuous demonstration in KGF of matrilateral behaviour is subjected to gossip and social criticism. For example, relatives living with a married couple commonly are kinsmen of the husband rather than of the wife. This is consistent with the patrilateral emphasis of the local expectations of the kinship system. If and when a wife's relative joins a couple, the husband often explains the presence apologetically. On the other hand, the presence of his own kinsmen is usually accepted without explainations.

However, the freedom of choice of kin for interaction in KGF has enabled a definite but subdued swing toward matrilaterality, especially when the selected kin are not residents of KGF. Certain unobtrusive indicators support this observation. For example, it is common for KGF residents to have their pictures taken with "significant kin" and to display these pictures in their living rooms. While the pictures of consanguinal kin are conspicuously displayed, pictures taken with affinal kin are hung in corners or in sleeping areas.

Fourth, co-residents are generally not viewed as kin with whom "significant" interaction can occur. Table 4 provides data on the composition of the respondents' households.

As an example, the case of the father may be discussed. Among the 388 respondents, 129 (33.2 per cent) have fathers alive. Among these 64 have their fathers residing with them in KGF and in the rest of the cases their fathers live elsewhere. However, in our analysis we found that those respondents who chose fathers as their most "significant kin" are generally the ones whose fathers live elsewhere.

Although in kinship terms the father is the closest relative to the respondents, at interactional levels there occurs a sense of respect and avoidance. Also, the interaction between the father and the son is structured in terms of dominance-submission patterns. Hence, many respondents have found it difficult to treat the father on such friendly and egalitarian terms as, for example, a brother. But the ties of the respondents with their mothers occur in a permissive atmosphere where authority is absent. Therefore, many respondents have chosen "mother" as the most important kin.

Fifth, when we controlled for class, there were no significant differences. The only exception was that middle-class respondents tended to choose brother-in-law as their most "significant kin" in larger proportions than did the rest. In some of these cases, our qualitative data show that there were conflicting relationships with parents because of differences of opinion on matters pertaining to financial assistance and marital choice.

TABLE 4
Classification of the KGF sample Households in Terms of Membership Composition

Type	*Name*		*N*	*Per cent*
IA	Lineal Joint	Respondent, his wife, unmarried children, his parent(s), and grandparent(s)	7	1.8
IB	Lineal Joint	Respondent, his wife, unmarried children, and his parent(s)	57	14.7
IC	Lineal Joint	Respondent, his wife, unmarried children, and married children with or without their offspring	52	13.4
II	Collateral Joint	Respondent, his wife, unmarried children, married brother(s) with his (their) wife (wives) and children	12	3.1
III	Supplemented nuclear	Respondent, his wife, unmarried children, unmarried brothers, and/ or sisters	120	30.9
IV	Other types	Respondent, his wife, unmarried children, and other kin (father-in-law, FaBr, MoBr, or mother's sister and so on)	7	1.8
V	Nuclear	Respondent, his wife, and unmarried children	103	26.7
VI	Conjugal	Respondent, his wife	30	7.7
	Total		388	100.00

TABLE 5

A Description of the Giving and or Taking of Monetary Aid Among the KGF Respondents

Aid giving person	*Aid receiving person*	*N*	*Por cent*	*Lower Class N*	*Lower Class Por cent*	*Middle Class N*	*Middle Class Per cent*	*Upper Class N*	*Upper Class Per cent*
Respondent	Respondent's son	18	7.1			4	22.2	14	77.8
Respondent's son	Respondent	35	13.9	25	71.1	10	28.6		
Respondent	Respondent's parent(s)	33	13.1	18	54.5	12	36.4	3	9.1
Respondent	Resondent's brother	105	41.7	65	61.9	30	28.6	10	9.5
Respondent's brothers	Respondent	49	19.4	35	71.4	14	28.6		
Respondent	Others	12	4.8			4	33.3	8	66.7
Total		252	100.0						

(Total N = 388, Upper Class = 35, Middle Class = 105, Lower Class = 248)

Patterns of Kin Interaction

The selection of a smaller group of "significant kin" can enable persons to maintain more intimate ties than would otherwise be possible. Of the various media used in this respect, aid, visiting and correspondence are crucial. An examination of each of these follows.

Mutual Aid

Table 5 presents information on reciprocal monetary aid patterns. Monetary aid is exchanged mostly between consanguinal kin and especially between brothers or between sons and parents. The data in Table 5 refer only to regular monthly or bimonthly remittances. The actual amount transacted varied according to the class of the aid-giver and aid recipient. In general, however, the amount involved is about one-third of the net earnings of the giver or receiver.

The respondents who were involved in one or another way in monetary aid were asked during informal discussions to indicate the reasons for the support, especially if the remittance was proportionately large. In general, two basic motivations tend to operate here: moral obligations and reciprocal expectations. For example, helping parents is looked upon as an inescapable moral responsibility, just as fathers are morally obligated to assist their sons until the son is occupationally settled. What underlies this reciprocal arrangement is not only moral expectations but also mutual regard. At least ideally the father likes to help his son as much as his son likes to provide for his father.

In view of this, mutual help patterns between father and son are very strongly institutionalized. This view is supported by the following kinds of statements: A KGF college lecturer, "My parents brought me up in relation to all kinds of trials and tribulations. They sent me to college. What I am today is because of their kindness. How can I be comfortable without returning their help? It is my duty!" A clerk in the gold mines said, "I have not forgotten how my parents toiled to educate me. Now if I don't help them they will starve ... that is not *dharma* (righteousness)".

Attitudes are different when it comes to the giving of help among brothers. And it is usually the elder brother who helps his younger brothers. Here the elder brother often serves as a surrogate parent and, in turn, a moral right or obligation, a sense of compassion tend to operate. This becomes obvious in the following statements: a lower-class worker, "We came into being by sharing blood, now if I don't share my earnings, he will be ruined ..."; a foreman, "My brother is too young to be left to himself, he is like my son ... he is too helpless ... someone should help him all right. I suppose I am the right one."

The sense of moral obligation is buttressed by kinship norms and expectations. Among the consanguinal kin, brothers, parents and children are expected to assist each other and the failure to do so often subjects them to social criticism. Also, the sense of reciprocity built into such transactions tends to compel kin not to ignore their obligations.

However, such a reciprocity is noncontractual. In this regard, Blood (1970: 89) observes "... there are seldom written promises to repay... Return is simply taken for granted as an implicit assumption in ongoing social systems. The terms of repayment extend to an extraordinary long period of time ... the frame of reference in kin exchanges often extends over decades." Because of the non-contractual nature of the exchange pattern among KGF kin, normative checks and balances operate, taking the form of social criticism, the intervention of neighbours, friends, other kin and caste leaders. If one fails to fulfil an obligation, he is understood to have broken a trust and is subjected to pressures to conform.

Although mutual aid patterns usually exist primarily between parents and children, or among siblings, several respondents also indicated that they could also look for help, on unusual occasions, from others in a position to extend help. A brother-in-law and a mother's brother are generally the most dependable kin at such times. The brother-in-law has a respected place in one's life and it is common for an individual to seek help from a brother-in-law in monetary as well as other terms.

One middle-class respondent spoke about the help rendered by his brother-in-law, as follows:

> I was admitted to the Kolar sanatorium and stayed there for four months. I did not have much savings to depend on. My brother-in-law came to my rescue. He paid the hospital bills and provided my family for four long months. If it had not been for him, I would have been dead and gone by now and my family would have been begging in the streets of Robertsonpet.

Not every respondent expects such help to come from his brother-in-law. Further, if a brother-in-law does not extend help, he is seldom criticized by most of the KGF people.

In general, then, few persons expect help from either brothers-in-law or from a father-in-law. Criticism for not helping when necessary is levelled primarily against consanguinal kin such as brothers and uncles. And for such persons not to extend help is considered a dereliction of their responsibilities.

In addition to money, help patterns involve the giving of "soft goods" in terms of companionship, care in times of illness, pregnancy and childbirth, consultation on matters related to marriage, and advice in property buying and selling.

Help by way of service is not demanded and is not offered on a regular basis. But what is important is that that, which is required by individual families are often offered instantly. And this quick reaction can lead to more firmly established kinship ties. In situations such as marriage or childbirth, help must usually be on a voluntary basis, not in relation to formal requests.

A careful review of the data presented in Table 5 suggests a relationship between the direction in which aid flows and class background. Of our 388 respondents, only 252 (64.9 per cent) are involved in aid-giving or taking. If we examine the direction of the aid and class background of the giver and recipients we find that all respondents of the upper classes are at the giving end. These people assist children many of whom are in professional schools outside KGF. Education towards a professional degree is expensive and beyond the reach of most lower and many middle-class respondents. Few lower-class respondents and a few middle-class respondents support their children in such activities.

However, here too the aid process is reciprocally defined, as we can see in examining our data on just the middle and lower-class respondents. For example, the giving and taking of aid occurs between brothers, and parents and children. Considering the fact that brothers are "most preferred kin" that is not surprising. But what is surprising is that very little monetary relationship occurs in relation to such affinal kin as brothers-in-law or fathers-in-law. It may be that mutual aid among consanguinal kin is not only based upon affective ties but also on institutionalised expectations while relations with affinal kin are based on just affection.

TABLE 6
A Description of the Kin Visiting Pattern among the Respondents

Relatives visited by the respondents	*No. of these relatives reported living*	*No. of these relatives residing in KGF*	*No. of respondents who visit these relatives*	*Frequency of visits*
Brothers	1263	360	298	Once or twice a month
Mother's sister	216	3	172	Once a year
Mother's brother	219	19	170	Once a year
Father's brother	176	7	159	Once a year

Relatives visited by the respondents	*No. of these relatives reported living*	*No. of these relatives residing in KGF*	*No. of respondents who visit these relatives*	*Frequency of visits*
Father's sister	151	131	140	Once a year
Father-in-law	202	38	141	Once a year
Father	129	64	62	Once a month
Son-in-law	59	4	54	Several times a year
Son	49		43	Several times a year
Brother-in-law	50	5	42	Several times a year

TABLE 7
A Description of the Patterns and Frequency of Letter Writing by the Respondents to their relatives who are living outside KGF

Letter to	*No. of the Kin Reported Alive*	*No. of Relatives Residing in KGF*	*No. of Respondents Who Write Letters*	*Frequency of letter Writing*
Brother	1263	360	295	Once a week
Mother's sister	216	3	173	Occasional
Mother's brother	219	19	148	Occasional
Father's brother	176	7	151	Occasional
Father's sister	151	13	149	Occasional
Father-in-law	202	38	139	Occasional
Father	129	64	63	Once a week
Son-in-law	59	4	44	Once a month
Son	49		44	Once a week
Brother-in-law	50	5	43	Once a week

Kin Visiting and Exchange of Letters

The data in Table 6 show that the respondents in general have chosen to visit some relatives more frequently than others. These relatives are the ones who were chosen as their most "significant kin"–brother, brother-in-law, son, son-in-law and father. A smaller group of "significant kin" enables more frequent visits among all of those involved. However, the frequency of visits is also determined to a large extent by distance, accessibility and availability of time. Most of these relatives live in places at an average distance of 200 miles from KGF and are accessible by bus or railway. Furthermore, the respondents and their significant kin who visit each other frequently do so individually, not in family groups. Usually, the entire family goes out visiting common kin in summer. It is also true, in general, that during summer holidays, most marriages are arranged and most feasts, fasts and other special family rituals are scheduled. The latent reason behind these summer activities is to enable more families to interact in a leisurely atmosphere. There are no significant differences across class groups so far as visiting patterns are concerned.

The exchange of letters occurs in high frequency between the respondents and their significant kin. Other kin have contacts only on an occasional basis. The average frequency of letter writing is a letter once every two or three months. No difference in this can be noted across class lines.

Summary and Conclusions

The main object of this essay was to describe the nature of urban kinship ties in a South Indian setting. It was also aimed at finding differences in kinship ties across class and caste lines.

First, it was found that although the respondent in general could remember and narrate the biological details of over 200 relatives, their regular interaction was confined only to a selected group of about 15 kin.

Second, this group of selected kin was conceptualized as "significant kin".

Third, it was found that the respondent further narrows down this range of likeable kin. The two most preferred kin are "brother" and "brother-in-law". The next most preferred are "mother" and mother's brother".

Fourth, father was not viewed as one of the "significant kin".

Fifth, mutual aid occurs regularly between brothers, and between parents and children.

Some variations across class were noticed. Upper-class respondents tend to give out aid, less frequently receiving it. Middle and lower-class respondents tend to give aid more frequently than they receive it. A reciprocity in monetary aid is more conspicuous among the lower and the middle classes than among the upper class.

Sixth, kin visiting and exchange of letters occur most frequently between the respondent and his "most significant kin". Among the rest, annual visits tend to suffice.

Kinship ties tend to be based on ego's personal preferences and likes and dislikes. In urban areas such as KGF, there is no institutional compulsion to maintain close ties with certain relatives. This is evident from the fact that many respondents do not view "father" as the most important kin. This does not mean they do not respect or care for him. It means, on the other hand, that traditional expectations in this regard are weakening. It seems that more and more kinship ties are being established only with those kin who bring certain amounts of gratification to ego. Visits and exchange of letters serve as reinforcing factors.

We are not suggesting that the selection by ego of kin significant to ego is entirely a new phenomenon. It is possible such a practice existed in the past. We are now suggesting that it is important here to recognize that urban living, a monetized economy, industrial labour, and housing in urban areas are more suited to small families where selection of kin occurs more commonly. When kinship organization ceases to be local in character, as it is in KGF, sanctions cannot be easily invoked against an individual for his ego-oriented choice of kin. The emerging matrilateral tendencies among the KGF respondents are illustrations of ego-based kinship behaviour which is free of negative sanctions. In the countryside such a tendency will be curbed by social criticisms and pressure.

NOTES

1. The research was funded by the following sources at the University of Illinois, Urbana, USA: Geisert Fellowship in honour of Hiller from the Illinois Foundation, Center for International Comparative Studies, Research Board and the Department of Sociology. The author is indebted to these agencies.
2. For similar and related concepts see Firth (1956, 1970), Bott (1957) and Piddington (1970).
3. The median age of the respondent is 39 years and the median ages of his most significant kin are brother 42 years, brother-in-law 35 years.

REFERENCES

Adams, Bert N.: 1968: *Kinship in an Urban Setting.* Chicago-Markham.

Blood, R.O.: 1970: "Social change and kinship pattern". In R. Hill and R. Koenig (eds.). *Families in East and West.* Paris: The Mouton.

Farber, B.: 1971: *Kinship and Class: A Midwestern Case.* New York: Basic Books.

Firth, Raymond: 1956: *Two Studies of Kinship in London.* London: Athlone Press.

Firth, Raymond et.al.: 1970: *Families and Their Relatives.* New York: Humanities Press.

Mandelbaum, David: 1972: *Society in India*–1. Berkeley: University of California Press.

Parsons, T.: 1943: "Kinship system of contemporary United States". *American Anthropologist,* 45.

Piddington, Ralph: 1965: "A study of French-Canadian kinship", *International Journal of Comparative Sociology.* Reprinted in C.C. Harris (ed.). Readings in Kinship in Urban Society. 1970, Oxford-Pergman Press.

Ramu, G.N.: 1972a: "Family and Caste in Urban India". *Unpublished Ph.D. dissertation,* University of Illinois, Urbana.

————: 1972b: "Geographic mobility, kinship and the family in South India," *Journal of Marriage and the Family* 34, pp. 147-52.

Srinivas, M.N.: 1962: *Caste in Modern India and Other Essays.* New York: Asia Publishing House.

Wiebe, Paul, D. and G.N. Ramu: 1973: "Hindu and Christian Harijans: Effects of Christian Programs in India". *Under editorial review.*

11

Trends in North Indian Urban Kinship: The "Matrilateral Asymmetry" Hypothesis*

Sylvia J. Vatuk

Studies of family life in various Western societies have revealed a tendency toward "matrilateral asymmetry" in interaction between members of the nuclear family and extended kin of the two spouses. It has been suggested that such a tendency might also be found to be emerging in those newly industrializing societies which are traditionally patrilineal and patrilocal. This essay examines data from a study of kinship in an urban neighbourhood in India and shows that while "matrilateral asymmetry" cannot be said to characterize the present kinship system, certain trends in this direction can be noted. These trends are on the behavioural rather than the ideological level; they involve increased interaction between a married woman and her sisters in the urban setting and a broadening of the range of permissible roles for a wife's kin as against those formerly considered appropriate only for the kin of the husband.

A number of investigators of urban family life in American society, in England, and in several European countries, have noted a tendency for closer ties to be maintained between the nuclear family and kin of the wife/mother than with kin of the husband/father (e.g., Habenstein and Coult 1965; Ishwaran 1959;

Poggie and Pelto 1969; Sussman 1965; Sweetser 1963, 1964a, 1966, 1968, 1970; Townsend 1957; Young and Willmott 1957). Despite bilateral kinship norms in Western society generally, "there is nevertheless a behavioural regularity ... which favours the wife's side rather than the husband's" in varying degrees in most of the western urban communities studied by sociologists and anthropologists (Sweetser 1968:236). This "matrilateral asymmetry," as it has been called, characterizing both intergenerational and sibling relationships, has been noted in residence patterns, in patterns of aid, in frequency of interaction, and in feelings of affective closeness. Sweetser has suggested that matrilateral asymmetry in industrial societies is associated with the separation of men's instrumental roles from their kin relationships. Where men do not need to cooperate economically with their fathers and brothers in a joint enterprise, the solidarity of mother and daughter and of sisters, buttressed by their common interests and needs in household tasks, is permitted expression in the maintenance of close "matrilateral" ties outside of the nuclear family (Sweetser 1963, 1964a, 1966, 1968, 1970).

A test of this hypothesis has been suggested by Sweetser (1966) in the study of agricultural societies in which a system of patrilineal inheritance and succession, with patrilocal residence, undergoes the impact of urbanization and industrialization. In such a case, the separation of sons from the patrimonial estate and their close agnates as they take up urban wage employment should lead to increasing emphasis on relations with the wife's kin. Studies by Sweetser (1964a, 1964b) of Finnish and Swedish families in both rural and urban areas appear to support her hypothesis. She (Sweetser 1966: 160-161) has also quoted passages from Dore (1958) on changing patterns of kinship in urban Japan which suggest a possible tendency towards matrilateral asymmetry in that traditionally patrilineal agrarian society.

I

This essay considers the usefulness of Sweetser's hypothesis for the analysis of changing kinship patterns in urban North India, specifically among middle-class residents in a city of western Uttar Pradesh. But first it is useful to provide background on the kinship system of the rural villagers of this part of India, since the majority of these urban residents are recent migrants from rural areas. Descent and inheritance is patrilineal and residence patrilocal. Sons share equally in their father's estate, which is normally held jointly and undivided by the males of the patrilocal extended family at least until the father's death; often the estate remains undivided through three or more generations of agnates. Ideally, the property-sharing agnatic unit comprises a common household. However, simple nuclear households and nuclear households supplemented by the addition of unmarried or widowed relatives are in fact common as a result of extended household fission and the normal cycle of births, marriages and deaths. However, most married couples spend at least the early years of marriage within the husband's parental household. Even if a separate household is established in later years, they typically remain close by, perhaps within the original home courtyard. The husband often continues to cooperate economically with his father and/or brothers and cousins on the jointly-owned land or in a common business enterprise.

Strict village exogamy in this part of India, combined with patrilocal residence, means that the local village community typically consists of a core of real and fictive agnates with their in-married wives. Occasional instances of matrilocal or avunculocal residence, brought about in the absence of male heirs, are responsible for the presence of a rare sister's son or daughter's husband. A man, thus, normally lives in the village of his birth throughout his life in close and intimate contact with his own agnatic kin. A woman, on the other hand, spends the better part of her adult life separated from the kin among whom she was raised in her natal village (*pihar*). A married woman must rely for companionship on affinally-related women: her mother-in-law, the wives of her husband's brothers, and other women who have married into her conjugal village (*sasural*). The ritual and residential incorporation of a woman into the agnatic extended family of her husband is supported by norms stipulating that a married woman's primary identification and loyalty, her most binding obligations, are to her conjugal rather than her natal family.

It is well recognized that sentiment and the difficulties of adjustment to a new family tend to interfere with a woman's easy adherence to these norms. The practice of early marriage for women and the preference for arranging marriages between young people whose villages are at a considerable distance from one another are explicitly recognized as mechanisms aiding in the socialization of a new bride to her conjugal home. While the adjustment period is gradual, providing in the early years of marriage for lengthy visits to the *pihar*, the worlds of *pihar* and *sasural* are never permitted to overlap. They remain structurally as well as spatially separate.

One aspect of this structural separation is the double standard of behaviour expected of a woman in her natal village (a "village daughter," *gaon ki beti*) and that expected of a woman in her conjugal village (a "village bride," *gaon ki bahu*). The former role is one of considerable freedom of movement, both within and outside of the home. After marriage—and even before marriage if a brother's wife is co-resident—a woman in her natal home has little domestic responsibility. If she has brought her children with her, their care is taken over as much as possible by her mother, unmarried sisters and brother's wives. A "village bride", on the other hand, is virtually secluded within the home during the early years of her marriage, at least in families economically capable of dispensing with her labour in the fields or in the family trade. Within the household she must avoid all males older than her husband and avoid him also when others are present.[1] She is subservient to the senior women of the household and to her husband's adult sisters, expressing her status in various symbolic gestures of deference and in the performance of personal services for them. After the first weeks of residence in her conjugal home, the young bride is also responsible for the bulk of the domestic tasks, although this work is shared with the other women of the extended household. It is perhaps to be expected that, whatever the individual circumstances and relationships may be, the *pihar* symbolizes for a woman the locale of a pleasant and carefree existence, and relationships with consanguineal kin mean warmth, ease and absence of tension and strain. To an important extent this perception of the *pihar* contrasts with that of the *sasural*, although in reality women become fully accustomed to their conjugal home as the years go by and they form intimate and satisfying ties there to replace those of the natal home which time and distance have attenuated.

The structural separation of *pihar* and *sasural* is also ensured by the fact that there is normally no overlap in personnel between the two,[2] and by the fact that contact between the kindreds of husband and wife is minimized and formalized to a considerable degree. A woman normally visits her *pihar* alone or with her children—possibly with other young members of her conjugal extended family as well—but rarely accompanied by her husband or elder affines. Such visits are not casually arranged by the woman herself. With the exception of certain ceremonial occasions, a woman returns to her natal home only when invited and called for by a male kinsman—a brother, cousin or brother's son in most cases.

The inherent structural tension between bride-giving and bride-taking kin groups is handled by the maintenance of strict asymmetry in their relationship, in which bride-takers are perpetual recipients of hospitality and of the balance of gift exchanges. Bride-givers, on the other hand, avoid accepting food, services or material goods from those to whom they have given a daughter in marriage and do not allow themselves to be placed in the position of indebtedness to them. With the exception of her brother or male cousin, no elder member of a woman's kindred, nor anyone of senior generation, should visit her in her conjugal home. This bar applies most strictly to her mother. Close kin who are older than a married woman even avoid her conjugal village altogether if possible. When led there by business or other necessity they go to the home of her parents-in-law only briefly, to pay their respects, being careful not to accept food, drink or lodging. On departure, they present their kinswoman and other wives of the household with a token cash gift.

In the same way, women of a man's household do not visit his wife's natal home. This prohibition of mutual visiting by women whose offspring or other close kin of the junior generation have married is further buttressed by the prescribed avoidance (*parda*) by a woman of any man of her generation to whom she is related through this marriage, specifically the daughter's husband's father and the son's wife's father (termed *samdhi*).

Men of the husband's kindred may visit the natal home of the wife, and they are entertained there with conscientious hospitality. But the nature of the relationship militates against lengthy, frequent, or casual visits. Only the husband's younger brother, who stands in a joking relationship to his brother's wife and to her sisters, may maintain a less formal relationship with her family.

The husband himself, though the "welcome guest" *par excellence*,[3] is expected to visit his wife's kin seldom and to remain no longer than two or three days at a time. Usually the occasion for visits by the daughter's husband is when he comes to call for his wife after she has spent some weeks or months in her natal home. While he is there, his wife must strictly avoid him. She must cover her face—just as she does before him in her conjugal home when others are present. Husband and wife may neither sit together nor speak to one another in her natal home, and it is particularly disapproved for them to sleep together there.

From the point of view of the child, the patrilateral kin are omnipresent, while the matrilateral kin are normally seen only on periodic visits to the mother's *pihar* (the child's *nanihal*). These visits, during which the child usually comes to expect special attention and indulgence, provide a welcome diversion from the day-to-day activities of the home village. Only the mother's brother, among the matrilateral kin, may be encountered more frequently. On his periodic visits to a child's home village he provides for the child, as well as for the child's mother, a continuing link to her natal home. Despite the important role of the mother's brother in providing contact with matrilateral kin in general and in providing gifts on ceremonial and non-ceremonial occasions for the child and his mother, the male child is very early made aware that his future is bound up in his membership in the agnatic group. The female child, on the other hand, is prepared for the day on which she will, inevitably, go away to her "own home" (*apna ghar*).

A son has a prime responsibility for the care of his parents in their old age, a responsibility which he may be fortunate enough to share with several brothers. But a daughter is never expected to have to care for her aging parents by taking them into her home or contributing financially to their support. Indeed, for them, to accept such help from a daughter—which would in fact mean becoming dependent upon a daughter's husband and his kin—would be considered shameful in the extreme. Any other alternative is preferred by a man or woman without living sons.

They may depend upon the support of the man's brothers' sons, adopt a close male relative as an heir, or arrange for a son-in-law to live matrilocally, turning over to him the management of land or business and providing that his sons will eventually inherit it. In all of these arrangements the assumption is implicit that an elderly person or a couple still posses a share of the estate upon which they are to be supported. Therefore, the practice of taking in a son-in-law does not reflect adversely on the father-in-law's prestige or honour, but places the son-in-law in an anomalous "outsider" position, which is reflected in the term for a matrilocally resident male, *ghar jamai* ("son-in-law of the house").

From this background summary of the rural North Indian kinship system, it is clear that a patrilateral emphasis, both structurally and normatively, is one of its most obvious features. Men are expected to have their most intimate and lasting ties with agnates. Their most important rights and duties are linked with membership in the agnatic group. Economic cooperation, between father and son, between brothers, and even between patrilateral parallel cousins is fundamental. Women, on the other hand, are expected to interact most frequently and intensively with affinal kin and to regard their obligations to them as the most significant and binding. Although the strength of a woman's sentimental bonds to her natal kin is recognized, the system makes these bonds secondary and relegates their expression to limited and specified contexts. Particularly, bonds between women of the natal family tend to be allowed little interactional support. Those between a woman and her mother may only be activated in the context of occasional visits to the natal home, and that between sisters is made tenuous by their dispersal in marriage. Only the brother-sister tie significantly bridges the gulf between *pihar* and *sasural* and carries over into the succeeding generation in a special relationship of the man and his sister's children.

II

The study upon which the following discussion is based was carried out in 1966-1967 in two multi-caste neighbourhoods (*mohallas*) in the city of Meerut, Uttar Pradesh. The population of Meerut is approximately 300,000. The city is the administrative headquarters of the larger District and Division of the same name and is an important educational centre for the region as well as being the site of a large army base. The neighbourhoods studied include approximately 400 households or 2000 persons. They adjoin one another and are located near the edge of the city in an area that has become settled gradually over the past 40 years. Most of the population is upper caste and can be considered middle class on the basis of income and occupation.[4] Educationally the residents of these *mohallas* are a select group by an all-India as well as the regional standards; the predominance of employment in white-collar occupations is a reflection of this fact.[5] But the majority of the population is nevertheless of recent rural origin. Many of them are not only first generation urbanites, but are also of the first generation in their families to have significant formal education or to acquire salaried employment.[6]

In view of the occupational situation of the men in these neighbourhoods, it is clear that in their work they are in most cases independent of any cooperation with male agnates. There are, of course, cases in which employment was secured through the efforts of agnatic kinsmen, and occasionally father and son or two brothers are found to be employed in the same office or government department. But personal histories reveal that a wife's kinsman or a matrilateral relative is as likely to have provided this kind of aid.

On the other hand, almost half of the male household heads in the neighborhood surveyed report owning property (other than their present residence) jointly with a father, brother, or more distant agnate.[7] In the majority of cases this property is agricultural land in the village of origin. While joint ownership of such land is typically retained, and a share of the produce may be taken for consumption in the urban household, the property rarely provides a substantial proportion of the city resident's subsistence needs. Generally it is worked by those members of the agnatic extended family who remain in the village as agriculturalists.

Support for the "matrilateral asymmetry" hypothesis in Western urban societies in the sociological literature has been found primarily in quantitative data on household sharing, residential proximity, help patterns, frequency and quality of interaction, and expressions of sentiment or affect (for example, Cumming and Schneider 1961; Habenstein and Coult 1965; Komarovsky 1956; Leichter and Mitchell 1967; Mogey 1956; Poggie and Pelto 1969; Sussman 1965; Sweetser 1964a, 1964b, 1966, 1968, 1970; Townsend 1957; Willmott and Young 1960; Young and Willmott 1957). In view of the fact that the present study was not undertaken with the test of this hypothesis in mind, and that participant observation was the primary research technique, comparable quantitative data on all of these subjects cannot be presented here. In any case, my qualitative data leads me to doubt seriously that quantitative information would support the hypothesis that Indian urban kinship in now characterized by "matrilateral asymmetry". The reverse seems clearly to be the case; very strongly on the normative level, but also at the level of actual behaviour. But what I wish to describe here is the presence of some incipient trends on the behavioural level towards accordingly increasing "equality" to matrilateral kin (or from the point of view of the married couple, to kin of the wife) in residential proximity, help, and interaction patterns. To put it another way, there is to be observed an increasing tendency to blur the traditionally sharp lines of role differentiation for "matrilateral" and "patrilateral" kin. This gives tentative support for that aspect of the hypothesis which suggests the direction of change for patrilateral societies under urbanization.

With respect to the intergenerational sharing of households, and taking the junior couple as a reference point, data from these neighbourhoods indicate that a minority of couples share a household with parents or grandparents of either spouse.[8] Of a total of 179 households in the *mohalla* surveyed, 44 (slightly less than 25 per cent) include a married couple plus one or both parents of either spouse. Thirty of these have only one parent present, usually a widow or widower. In one of these 44 cases, three generations of patrilineally related married couples share a common household. In three other cases, two married brothers share a household with parents. The remaining households contain only one couple with a single parent, or two couples in which the men are related as father and son. In only three cases is the wife's mother present in the household of her daughter and son-in-law.

We may add to these cases of intergenerational household sharing others in which a widowed, divorced, or separated person shares a household with parents or parents-in-law. Three such women reside with their own fathers or mothers. Another woman resides in the household of her husband's maternal grandparents (her husband having been brought up in this household by his widowed mother). Two formerly married men share a household with their own mothers.[9]

It is also relevant to consider the extent to which married couples share a household with kinsmen of their own generation. In this milieu such sharing is usually a result of the practice of taking in young or adolescent siblings from their rural homes in order to provide them an opportunity to gain quality education. In a few cases the additional kinsman is a widowed, divorced or separated adult sister or brother. Sometimes, collaterally-linked married couples may share a household with or without their parents. Table 1 indicates the relationship of kinsmen of own generation sharing the household of a married couple. Where there are two married couples, the senior couple, or the one in whose house both are living, is taken as the reference point.

Some couples share their households with collaterals of a junior generation or with grandchildren when the latter's parents are not present in the household. In such cases, we find that six couples have children of sons present in their household, while one couple shares their household with the children of a daughter. Three couples have co-resident children of a husband's brother, while one widow with children of her own has taken her own brother's daughter into her home in order that she may attend school in Meerut.

When this information on the sharing of households with kin outside of the nuclear family is classified according to the "patrilateral"/"matrilateral" dichotomy, it is quite clear that in most cases co-residence involves "patrilateral" kin, whether they be of a senior, equivalent, or junior generation (considering in the latter case grandchildren as "patrilateral" if they are the offspring of sons, "matrilateral" if the offspring of daughters). Whether a married couple has joined the household of parents, or parents have joined the neolocal household of one of their children (information on this is not available for every case), the parents involved are almost exclusively those of the husband. There are no cases of true matrilocal residence, in the sense of a married couple joining the pre-existing household of the wife's parents. In those cases where a couple shares the household with the wife's mother, the latter has joined the neolocal household of her daughter some time after the latter's marriage, and has done so because she is aged and has no living sons with whom she can live. When kinsmen of the same generation or junior collaterals share the household of a married couple, they are in an overwhelming number of cases kin of the husband. Couples who take grandchildren into their home (or retain them after the departure of their child, usually for employment elsewhere) do so with the children of a son rather than a daughter.

TABLE 1
Sharing of Households by Married Couples with One or More Kinsmen of Own Generation

Relationship of Kinsman Sharing the Household	*Number of Households*
"Patrilateral"	
1. Husband's brother/sister	20
2. Husband's brother and brother's wife	3
3. Husband's father's brother's son	1
4. Husband's brother's wife*	1
Total	25
"Matrilateral"	
1. Wife's brother/sister	2
2. Wife's father's brother's son	1
3. Wife's mother's brother's and mother's brother's son's wife	1
Total	4

* This individual is both the husband's brother's widow and the wife's sister—one of the unusual cases in which two sisters are married to two brothers.

The only somewhat unexpected finding here—and because of the small numbers it is an undramatic one—relates to the residence of widows. According to the norms of the kinship system, a widow should remain in the extended household—or at least within the village—of her late husband. There she has an incontrovertible right to support on his share of the family estate, and there her children, if any, belong unequivocally. Even if for sentimental reasons she would prefer to return to her natal home, the facts that she would probably not be allowed to remove her children from her late husbands house and that, if she did, her sons might lose by default active rights in the family estate would strongly motivate her to remain. Her opportunities for remarriage are slight, at least in middle and upper castes of the region, because of the strict disapproval of the marriage of widows. Remarriage is virtually out of the question for a woman with children. While she may return to her natal home and claim support from her natal kin, it is generally felt that, at least after the death of her parents, the position of a woman living by sufferance in the household of her brother and his wife is a difficult one. The principal fear is that the brother's wife may resent her presence and the economic burden she represents.

While no quantitative data are available in literature regarding the extent to which rural women in this region remain in the conjugal home upon widowhood, the impression one gains is that they generally conform to normative expectations in this regard (see, for example, Wiser 1965; Lewis 1965). Very probably differences in age and the presence or absence of children are significant variables. It is interesting to note that in the *mohalla* surveyed, four widows reside with natal kin and only one remains in her late husband's home. This is the childless woman cited in Table 1 who is also the sister of her co-resident husband's brother's wife. The majority of widows reside in the household of their sons, but four live with daughters. One of these resides with a widowed daughter. In these cases it is difficult to ascertain without extensive personal history data whether the majority remained with conjugal kin or returned to natal kin after their husband's death. In most cases, as far as information is available, the husband's death occurred while the couple was residing neolocally in a nuclear household or after their children had married. A number of widows thus reside neolocally with their unmarried children as they did before the husband's death. In some cases they live near or even in the same dwelling with the husband's parents or brother, but in no case do they share a common household with them.

The broader question of residential proximity is more difficult to deal with quantitatively in terms of the available data. Information was sought on the census schedule concerning the presence and the identity of relatives (consanguineal and affinal) living in the same *mohalla*. In addition to this, knowledge of the extent of other kinship links not only within the mohalla, but with adjoining *mohallas* and other parts of the city was gradually obtained during the course of the year's participant observation. This latter information greatly supplements that provided by the interview schedules, although it has little quantitative value because it does not cover the sample universe systematically.

With respect to replies on the census schedule, 34 respondents indicated that kin of the husband or son live in the same *mohalla*, but in a separate household. Such kin are classified as "patrilaterally" related. But 26 reported that kin of the wife or daughter live there. A number of the former actually share a residence with the respondent, but maintain a separate household. One of the "matrilateral" kinsmen does so. These figures include both consanguineally and affinally related persons and include such "distant" kin as a sister-in-law's son, aunt's son and a cousin's father-in-law with "close" kin like a brother-in-law or father-in-law. These figures do not include persons who report having relatives in an adjoining *mohalla* (who in terms of distance may be as close as some relatives in the same mohalla) or those who were discovered later to have relatives living nearby who had not been mentioned.

Even, these limited data provide evidence of a "patrilateral" emphasis that is surprisingly slight in view of normative residence patterns and those actually practiced in the rural area, whence, most respondents have come. An emergent pattern of "bilocal" residence seems to exist here, if the *mohalla* is taken as the residence unit. The existence of such a pattern would be further substantiated if we reconsidered the classification as "patrilateral" of those kin who are related to the husband through his grandmother, mother, sister and so on. The proximity of such kin actually indicates the strength of "matrilateral" ties in the previous generation. It must be realized in interpreting the data that where a tie with a cross-sex pair is concerned, the relationship is "matrilateral" from the point of view of one party and "patrilateral" from the point of view of the other. Considering the fact that in most cases both parties have reported the relationship—the two lists overlap. Similarly, each list includes within itself overlapping pairs and triads where kin of the same sex report the proximity of one another.

An important aspect of residence patterns in these neighbourhoods is that the vast majority of married couples reside neolocally. This is partially a function of the recency of settlement of the *mohallas* studied. The oldest homes are no more than 40 years old, while the majority have been built within the past 15 years; building still continues on the peripheries of both neighbourhoods. In the *mohalla* surveyed, only two households have occupied a home there for more than 35 years, 33 have lived there for 20 years or more, while 124 households have done so for less than 15 years. Taking these facts into consideration, we do not find that the greatest possible prevalence of patrilocality has been realized in these *mohallas*. Instead, a pattern is found in which the adult sons of *mohalla* residents move out of the neighbourhood for employment and establish neolocal residence in other cities and towns, while new couples from elsewhere move in as tenants in order for the husband to take up salaried employment in Meerut.

The result is that very few couples are in fact residents in the place they consider to be the husband's "real home," his *khas ghar*, i.e., his village of origin (or, in the case of third or fourth generation urban residents, his *mohalla* of origin). Most locate the *khas ghar* within the rural districts surrounding Meerut; a few do so in one of the older *mohallas* of Meerut or in some other North Indian cities. They say of their present residence, "We are living 'in service' (*naukari par*)" or "We are living 'outside' (*bahar*)". As long as a man has not been brought up in the mohalla, and as long as his parents or other senior consanguines do not live there, the *mohalla* is not regarded as the "conjugal home" (*sasural*) of his wife. Therefore, the usual standards of behaviour for a woman in her conjugal village do not apply. She need not observe parda avoidances in the neighbourhood except when receiving visits by affines or male friends—not neighbours—of her husband, nor need she treat neighbourhood women with the deference appropriate to female affines. In fictive kin relationships she frequently uses consanguineal rather than affinal terms for address and reference (Vatuk 1969). On the other hand, in cases where a man's parents or other senior kinsmen reside in the *mohalla*—

even in a separate household, and even if the man has come to the *mohalla* as an adult—the standards of the *sasural* do apply to his wife. Specifically, she must observe *parda* in front of his kinsmen and all older male neighbours (except those to whom she may actually be related consanguineally) and remain secluded in the home as much as possible. If visits are made to the husband's home village from time to time, that is her "real" *sasural* and the constraints, of course, still apply.

There are some women for whom the *mohalla* in which they live—or an adjoining mohalla—is considered their natal home because they were brought up there or at least moved there before marriage. In most such cases the wife's parents located or arranged for the couple's accommodations, but in no case do they share a common household or even live in the same dwelling. None of the couples are economically dependent upon the wife's family. Men living in the natal *mohalla* of their wife in their own *sasural* are not accorded the term used for matrilocal males in the village milieu and are not regarded as being at a disadvange *vis-à-vis* other *mohalla* residents. An obvious reason for this is that the mohalla as a group of primarily neolocal families does not present a solid agnatic front against the intrusive "sister's husband". Married women whose parents live or have previously lived in the *mohalla* consider themselves to be living in the *pihar* even though their "real" *pihar* may be elsewhere, and behave accordingly in relationships with neighbours.

These residence patterns, and particularly the predominance of nuclear and neolocal households, have an obvious impact on kin interaction. In the context of the present hypothesis, certain changes are to be noted in the relationship of a married couple to the parents and other kin of the wife. However, the changes are generally not in evidence for that minority of couples who reside in close proximity to the husband's parents or other close consanguineal kin.

A woman who lives in her natal *mohalla*, particularly if her parents or other close consanguines continue to reside there, cannot sharply separate and compartmentalize her statuses as "daughter" and as "bride". As long as she does not also live with her husband's parents,[10] she can be in and out of her natal home, or those of other natal kin, almost daily, rather than spending periodic extended visits with her natal family. Furthermore, her siblings and even her parents may feel free to visit frequently in her home. Her mother and siblings can help her in childcare and other household tasks, while she can be available reciprocally to aid them when necessary. In fact, my data show considerable visiting and mutual aid between parents and daughters when the latter reside nearby and in nuclear households.

Most visiting is in fact undertaken by the daughter to her parents. Visits by parents particularly by a woman's mother, tend to take place during the day while the son-in-law is at work. But parents also on occasion come to their daughter's home when the son-in-law is present, and he visits his parents-in-law more frequently and casually than he would do if they lived at a distance. Inevitably, then, the formal respect relationship between parents-in-law and son-in-law is modified. The practice of avoiding the husband in the natal home tends to be abandoned, making it possible for the couple to sit together and converse informally with her parents. Abandonment of *parda* in the natal home can only be accomplished with the cooperation of a woman's parents. Public opinion generally—particularly among the older generation—continues to disapprove of this "modern" innovation and to criticize parents who allow it. But a number of *mohalla* families have ceased to observe this practice in their homes, despite their awareness of others' disapproval.

The kind of accommodations made to urban matrilocal residence are illustrated by the case of a young woman, childless, who lives with her husband in a rented room near the home of her parents. She spends most of every day with her mother and invalid father while her husband is at work. The two old people live alone in a house they own themselves. The mother rarely comes to her daughter's room, but does so on occasion, usually when her son-in-law is not present. The daughter explains that she is lonely with her husband away at work whole day, despite the company of her landlady, with whom she and her husband share a common courtyard. To a question about her husband's attitude toward these daily visits to her parents, she replies, "There is nothing to do here, and he doesn't mind as long as I get my work done."

In another young family the wife's mother spends the greater part of each day at the home of her neolocally resident daughter. The elderly woman lives in an extended household with her husband, youngest son, and daughter-in-law in an adjoining *mohalla*, not more than five minutes walk. She does not get along well with her daughter-in-law, who married her son for love rather than the arrangement by her parents. An asthmatic condition prevents her from doing any household work. Her son-in-law's parents are deceased; he has no senior consanguineal kin residing in the neighbourhood, but a cousin and his wife live nearby. Although he is at home most of the time, being self-employed, he generally keeps out of his mother-in-law's way and she treats him deferentially. She never accepts food at her daughter's house, nor does she sleep there, but almost every day she may be found sitting in her daughter's courtyard in the congenial company of her daughter and the wives of her tenants. When the older woman is not there, very often the daughter is at her home with her three children.

The restraining effect of the presence of a daughter's parents-in-law on this kind of visiting cannot be overemphasized and is illustrated by an example from this same family. The old woman's daughter-in-law has parents who live in a third adjacent *mohalla*. Her parents have never been inside their daughter's conjugal home and see her rarely, because she is not free to visit them without the permission of her mother-in-law. When she does visit her parents it is usually for a period of several weeks, rather than for the daily "dropping in" that her husband's sister is accustomed to with her parents. She does not observe *parda* before her husband in her natal home; her husband visits her parents more often than she does and has an informal relationship with them. It is relevant to note, however, that in this case the wife's parents had been well acquainted with their son-in-law before the marriage, as they were former tenants in his sister's home.

Thus, when a couple lives in the same *mohalla* or in the same vicinity of both sets of parents, the traditional prescriptions for interaction with the wife's kin tend to be upheld. Residence of the couple is almost always with the husband's parent or parents. The wife's parents never visit her in her conjugal home, except perhaps when she or a member of her husband's family is seriously ill; on such occasions they do not accept food or drink at their daughter's natal home. Junior members of the wife's natal family and her brothers may visit her freely, however, and generally do so unless relations between the two families are strained. The wife typically makes frequent, though not daily, visits to her parents' home, but only with the express consent of her husband and parents-in-law. However, as we have seen in the previous case, she maybe prevented from making casual visits at all. She may, with permission, take her children to visit their maternal grandparents often and leave them there periodically for an extended visit.

When the parents of neither couple reside in the same city, interaction with the wife's and husband's families tends to diverge also from the traditional pattern. Perhaps the most radical divergence occurs in the incidence of overnight visits by older women to the homes of their married daughters, when the latter live neolocally "in service" in another city or town. This was noted for couples in the *mohallas* studied who welcomed a visit by the wife's mother sometimes with the father, sometimes alone, and for women in the *mohallas* who went out of town to visit a married daughter during the research period. As I have shown, such visits would be out of the question when a married daughter lives with her husband's kin. For urban residents also, the conviction that mothers should not visit their married daughters remains strong. In practice this attitude is modified when the daughter lives nearby in a nuclear household. It is being increasingly modified to permit lengthier visits to a married daughter who lives at a distance. The real motives behind such visits lie, of course, in the sentimental mother-daughter bond, but a mother's love for her daughter and the desire to see and be with her is not considered sufficient justification for such a breach of custom. A mother's love for and intimacy with her daughter is axiomatic, but the situation must also be defined in such a way that some other compelling reason leaves no alternative but for the mother to undertake a visit. Obviously then, visits by a mother to her married daughter are not casually planned or frequent; they always coincide with some crisis in the daughter's household, some difficulty in which the daughter "needs" her mother.

Such a need must be balanced against the rights of the married woman's affines to attend her and her children in times of trouble or when her domestic burdens become unmanageable. Instances were observed in which a woman came from another city to help a daughter with housework and childcare while she studied for a college examination. One woman in the neighbourhood spent over a week in another city helping her daughter to nurse her sick husband. Another travelled over 300 miles when she received the news that her young grandchild had burned his hand badly. One woman, whose daughter and grandchildren regularly spent two months of the year (the school vacation) with her in Meerut, has over the past seven years gone to her daughter's home in another province three times to help in childbirth. For crises of these kinds it would have been proper to ask some woman of the husband's kindred—his mother, sister, brother's wife, cousin, or aunt—to take over the household responsibilities. In similar situations most couples in the neighbourhood studied did indeed call on husband's kin and thus, acknowledged the latter's right to care for their "bride" in adversity. This right is particularly compelling at the time of the birth of a new addition to the man's descent group, who ideally should be born in his own home, among his own people. When the wife's mother takes over the helping role she must, therefore, not only justify her daughter's need for help, but also show the inability of her son-in-law's kin to provide it. Thus, in the instances cited, it was explained that "no one in his family would come," or "he doesn't have anyone who can help at this time," or "she doesn't have a mother-in-law, unfortunately, and his sisters are all living 'in service,' so what could I do?" Young women and sometimes even their husbands, are often willing to cooperate in not finding help in the conjugal kindred because they feel more at ease with their natal kin, particularly if they have lived neolocally since their marriage.Even though such justifications are made by the women involved, they do not fully silence the criticism. Normatively, the ban on such visits persists

Whatever the rationale for a woman's visit to her married daughter, it is expected as a matter of course that she will pay for her food and lodging while there, for it is shameful to accept the hospitality of a son-in-law. The alternatives—to order ready-cooked meals from a nearby restaurant or to buy raw ingredients and cook separately—may be resorted to instead. When payment is given, the exact amount is not reckoned. However, the daughter or her husband are given a sum on departure which is clearly well in excess of what could have been spent on the mother's behalf.

The traditional periodic and lengthy visits of a woman to her natal home are not as easy to reconcile with her domestic responsibilities if she lives with her husband in a nuclear household, particularly if other kinsmen do not live nearby. Arrangements must be made for one of the husband's kinswomen to take over the cooking and other household tasks, or the husband must be left to fend for himself while his wife and children are away. In the conjugal village such a husband is easily absorbed into the larger extended household unit for his meals, even if his wife normally maintains a separate hearth. The husband in an urban nuclear household is very often reluctant to permit his wife to spend weeks or months with her natal kin while he is left alone in the city. Once their children begin to go to school, trips interfere with their educational progress as well. Normally, then, the urban couples living away from both sets of parents plan to fit in visits to them during yearly holidays, usually taken during school vacations. If they live close enough they may also visit their parents on the major festivals when a few days' leave from the job is available. While both sets of parents have the right to expect a visit at such times, the scale is tipped by the society in favour of the husband's kin. All of them recognize that it is his and his parents' prerogative to permit or disallow the wife's home visit and, if they permit it, to determine its length.

On the other hand, wives—and their parents—try to prolong their natal visit as long as possible and consequently to spend a minimum time at the home of their in-laws. The couple may first visit the home of the husband and wait for the wife's brother or other kinsman to come to "invite" her to her natal home, as is the rural custom. But commonly the urban husband will himself deliver the wife to her natal home for a brief visit, and return to his own home for the greater part of his vacation. He will call for his wife again when he or his parents decide that she should return. He will rarely if ever spend the night in his wife's home if his own is within the same city, and in any case will not remain longer than two or three days.

I have stressed residence patterns as they affect interaction with "matrilateral" and "patrilateral" kin for Indian urban couples, but there are other factors as well which support the trends outlined. The traditional segregation of conjugal roles in Indian society may in one sense facilitate any tendency toward increasing an equivalent interaction with the wife's kin when this is combined with neolocal residence or residence near the kin of the wife. Husbands and wives in the urban setting tend to have their own social networks, overlapping but not coinciding. While husbands are at work the whole day, outside of the neighbourhood, cultivating their own circles of male friends and possibly meeting their relatives as well, wives remain behind to interact with women whom the husband rarely sees. And even in a man's free time the pattern of companionship of husband and wife is generally so little accepted that in most cases he will socialize with his own male friends, talking in their homes, and going to restaurants and tea shops and to the movies. Couples rarely participate together in leisure-time recreation. A man in the evening or on his day off typically spends his time in activities with other men, while his wife participates in women's gatherings with her own group of neighbours and kinswomen. As long as his parents or other senior kin are not present, and as long as his wife fulfills what he sees as her obligations to him and his relatives, a man generally does not object to her associating primarily with her own kin.

Increasing literacy is also important, for it allows young urban women to keep up regular contact with natal kin whom they may rarely have the opportunity to meet. Letters become a means of direct and frequent communication between mother and daughter and between married sisters, who traditionally would not only be spatially dispersed at marriage, but would be unable to maintain frequent contact except indirectly through news or messages brought by others.

Recent changes in Hindu family law are consistent with the trends noted here, in so far as provisions were made in the Hindu Succession Act of 1956 for inheritance by daughters equally with sons and for inheritance by a widow of an absolute share in the estate of her husband, rather than merely maintenance for life. However, there is little evidence that these provisions, particularly the former, are taken advantage of in practice. Women are extremely reluctant to claim a share of the patrimonial estate, even when they are aware that they have this legal right. The feeling of both men and women in this region is that a woman's share of her father's property is given in the form of dowry and later in the form of gifts from her brother at childbirth and on the marriage of her children. A woman who takes an equal share of the property on her father's death cannot expect the continued support of her brothers in the form of ritual presentations, nor can she rely on them for emotional support or emergency aid in the future; by her act she has shown disregard for the ideally close brother-sister bond.

III

In summary, I have tried to approach the study of changing kinship practices in urban India from the viewpoint of the "matrilateral asymmetry hypothesis" which developed in the study of the Western urban kinship system. Neither quantitative nor qualitative data from a North Indian urban neighbourhood support the notion that "matrilateral asymmetry" presently characterizes its kinship system on either the normative or behavioural level. But both kinds of data do indicate that the direction of change in this patrilineal and traditionally strong "patrilaterally asymmetric" system is toward increasing emphasis on matrilateral kin. From the point of view of the married couple, which has been taken here, there is increasing recognition and expression of the bonds that tie a couple to kin of the wife. The importance of the wife's kin in social interaction and in providing help and support to the neolocally resident couple is clearly greater than in the traditional rural setting. The wife's kin are increasingly allowed to "trespass" into areas of interaction formerly reserved for kin of the husband. The principal barriers to a full acceptance of the legitimacy of a balanced and equivalent role for the wife's kin and the kin of the husband lie in the persistence of norms which define the relationship of kin groups linked by marriage as a strictly asymmetrical one and which regard the primary ties of a married couple to be those which link them to the husband's kin, specifically to his agnates. It seems apparent that these barriers are beginning to be lowered among the urban middle-class people considered in this study, as kinship behaviour which conflicts with the traditional normative prescriptions becomes increasingly common and gradually acceptable.

NOTES

* Research for this paper was carried out from September 1966 to August, 1967, under a Junior Fellowship from the American Institute of Indian Studies. A shorter version was presented at the annual meeting of the American Anthropological Association in San Diego in November 1970. I am indebted to my husband, Ved Prakash Vatuk, for his helpful comments and suggestions during the writing and revision of this paper. I also wish to thank Subhashini Khullar for research assistance in the field. Because of typographic limitations, length and nasalization are not indicated in the Hindu forms cited.

1. The practice of avoidance (*parda*) involves covering the face with the shawl or the end of the *sari* and refraining from speech in the presence of the man being avoided.

2. In addition to local exogamy, marriage rules proscribe marriage between known consanguines of any degree, between members of the same clan (*gotra*), and, in some castes, with a person belonging to the mother's natal *gotra*, the father's mother's natal *gotra*, or that of the mother's mother. Furthermore, most castes proscribe marriages which involve the exchange of women between kin groups (marriage to the brother's wife's brother or sister's husband's sister). Marriage of two sisters or female cousins to two brothers or male cousins is permissible but uncommon.

3. A frequently-used term for "daughter's husband" is *pahuna*, literally "guest".

4. A census survey of one the *mohallas*, containing 950 persons in 179 households, revealed a caste composition by household of 41 per cent Brahman, 36 per cent Bania and 5 per cent Kayastha, with lesser representation of Rajput, Gujar, Jat, Sunar and eight other castes. Incomes vary between Rs. 80 and Rs.1000 per month, with an average of about Rs.200. Of 189 employed or retired males whose occupation was reported, 163 may be classified as white-collar workers. The majority of them are salaried employees at various levels of city, provincial, or military administration. Teachers and professionals are included in this category, as are also independent businessmen.

5. Among men over 40 literacy is 94 per cent; for men under 40 per cent, literacy is almost 100 per cent, and the mean years of education completed is 12. Even among women literacy is over 80 per cent for those under 40 and 62 per cent for the older age group.

6. In the *mohalla* surveyed, approximately 15 per cent of household heads and wives were born in Meerut city and are thus second or third generation urbanites. A small number of others were born in other urban centres in North India. Most of the remaining household heads and wives were born in rural Meerut District or in the adjacent Districts.

7. Forty-four per cent of respondents acknowledged such ownership, but this figure is probably an underestimate as many respondents proved reluctant to answer queries pertaining to financial matters or to their assets.

8. The concept of household as used here refers to the group of persons who share a common kitchen, the commensal unit or "hearth group", as it is has sometimes been called in the literature on Indian social structure. In my data all households are composed of persons consanguineally or affinally related, with the exception of one household which includes a friend of the husband and several households which include a live-in male servant. Furthermore, all persons sharing a household as defined also share a common residence. In a number of instances related persons share a common residence (usually owned in common), but maintain separate kitchens. They usually also have separate income and independent budgets. Each commensal unit in such cases is considered a separate household.

9. Three of these households with widowed, divorced, or separated persons are also included in the figures for couples sharing a household with parents, since they contain the single partner's brother and brother's wife as well.

10. There is no formal rule forbidding marriage within the *mohalla* analogous to the rule of local exogamy enforced in the rural area. However, in practice, marriages do not appear to be arranged between residents of the same *mohalla*. I found no such cases in my investigations. It is nevertheless possible for both sets of parents of a couple to reside in the same *mohalla* when the marriage is a love match or if one or both sets of parents moved thereafter the couple's marriage; a few such cases were observed. More common are instances in which residents of adjoining *mohallas* arrange a marriage between their respective offspring and the couple continues to live in the home of the husband's parents.

REFERENCES

Cumming, E. and D. Schneider: 1961: Sibling Solidarity: a Property of American Kinship, *American Anthropologist* 63, pp. 498-507.

Dore, R.: 1958: *City Life in Japan,* Berkeley: University of California Press.

Habenstein, R. and A. Coult: 1965: *The Function of Extended Kinship in Urban Society,* Kansas City: Community Studies.

Ishwaran, K.: 1959: *Family Life in the Netherland.* The Hague: Van Keulen.

Komarovsky, M.: 1956: Continuities in Family Research: a Case Study. *American Journal of Sociology* 62, pp. 42-47.

Leishter, H. and W. Mitchell: 1967: *Kinship and Casework.* New York: Russell Sage Foundation.

Lewis, O.: 1965: *Village Life in Northern India.* New York: Vintage Books.

Mogey, J.: 1956: *Family and Neighbourhood: Two Studies in Oxford.* London: Oxford University Press.

Poggie, J. and P. Pelto: 1969: Matrilateral Asymmetry in the American Kinship System. *Anthropological Quarterly* 42, pp. 1-15.

Sussman, M.: 1965: "Relationships of Adult Children with their Parents in the United States," in *Social Structure and the Family* (ed. by E. Shanas and G. Streib), pp. 62-92. Englewood Cliffs: Prentice Hall, Inc.

Sweetser, D.: 1963: Asymmetry in Intergenerational Family Relationships. *Social Forces* 41, pp. 346-52

————: 1964a: Mother-Daughter Ties between Generations in Industrial Societies. *Family Process* 3, pp. 332-43.

————: 1964b: Urbanization and the Patrilineal Transmission of Farms in Finland. *Acta Sociologica* 7, pp. 215-24.

————: 1966: The Effect of Industrialization on Inter-Generational Solidarity. *Rural Sociology* 31, pp. 156-70.

————: 1968: Intergenrational Ties in Finnish Urban Families. *American Sociological Review* 33, pp. 236-46.

————: 1970: The Structure of Sibling Relationships. *American Journal of Sociology* 76, pp. 47-58.

Townsend, P.: 1957: *The Family Life of Old People.* London: Routledge and Kegan Paul.

Vatuk, Sylvia J.: 1969: Reference, Address, and Fictive Kinship in Urban North India. *Ethnology* 8, pp. 255-72.

Willmott, P. and M. Young: 1960: *Family and Class in a London Suburb.* London: Routledge and Kegan Paul.

Wiser, W. and C.: 1965: *Behind Mud Walls,* 1930-1960. Berkeley: University of California Press.

Young, M. and P. Willmott: 1957: *Family and Kinship in East London.* Baltimore: Penguin Books.

PART - III

VARIATIONS IN FAMILY STRUCTURE AND RELATIONS

12

The Hindu Family and Development*

T.N. MADAN

The Problem

There is a well-established viewpoint which alleges that Hindu social institutions have had a blighting effect on India's social and economic development. The so-called joint family is one such notable institution. Many Western observers, and under their influence many Indian scholars and social critics have also, written that India was almost completely a stagnant country, without any true history, till she came into life-giving contact with Western civilization in the eighteenth century. They contend that the economy and society in this country, and indeed the Indian mind, had remained frozen for about two thousand years till the British conquest of India introduced a vital element of dynamism into the "native" society.

Karl Marx was a passionate believer in this view of India's history, or lack of history (see Marx and Engels, 1959), but it perhaps found its most deliberate expression in the writings of Henry Sumner Maine. Maine's interest in India was professional–as a jurist and as a member of the Viceroy's Executive Council–and his contacts with the country were first hand and personal. He viewed Hindu society from the vantage point of classical evolutionism and, inevitably, found it wanting in progressive social forces and indeed in the moral qualities so essential to social development. Just as Marx had pointed to the stagnant mode of production underlying the village communities, Maine drew attention to caste and the rigid contractual basis of social life, to the family and the related institutions of customary law, and to the crippling restrictions under which women had traditionally been forced to live in Hindu society. He compared the individual family of the West with the Hindu joint family to bring out the contrast between "true" civilization and the lack of it (see Maine, 1917).

These scholars and their followers tried to identify what they regarded as the characteristics of economic, social and moral backwardness and traced the same to Hindu religious beliefs and attitudes and traditional socio-cultural institutions. Some of them suggested that India was in the grip of a vicious circle inasmuch as poverty and social backwardness on the one hand, and socio-cultural institutions sanctified by religion on the other, mutually reinforced one another.

As may well have been expected, the ethnocentric European view of India entailed a belief about the civilizing role of Western civilization in India. Rammohun Roy had expressed the hope, in the mid-nineteenth century, that Europeans would settle down in this country to help Indians get rid of superstitious beliefs and iniquitous institutions. Later Karl Marx, Max Weber and many others saw in British rule the hidden hand of destiny—the unconscious tool of history which would start Indian society on the path to historical development.

In course of time, as nationalist forces gained ground and imperialism came under attack, the modernizing influence of the impact of the West was dissociated from British rule and instead linked to such processes as urbanization, industrialization and Westernization. This is the viewpoint that has now been in ascendance for more than half a century. Though the obstructive role of Hindu social institutions is reiterated, the superior power of the processes of modernization is invoked to hold out the hope that traditional beliefs and attitudes, caste, the joint family, etc. will all be sooner or later swept away.

In assessing the role of the joint family in retarding social and economic development, the argument has generally been developed deductively: since family institutions in India are different from and in some respects even the very opposite of those in the West, it follows that the former is an obstacle to development and the latter a prerequisite of it. Thus, the allegedly intimate relationship between the nuclear family and modernization on the one hand, and between the joint family and socio-economic backwardness on the other, is stressed. This, I hope to show, is an example of the structuralist fallacy of viewing modernization everywhere in the world today as essentially a replication of what happened in the eighteenth and nineteenth centuries in Western Europe, Britain and North America. Enough has already happened in India, and in other countries too—most notably in Japan—to discredit this view.

As for the assertion that industrialization and urbanization will specifically change the traditional family institutions, and this too is based on what are believed to have been the consequences of these processes in the West. The writings of certain scholars, notably Louis Wirth (see, for example Wirth, 1938), have long dominated studies of urbanization and urbanizm and resulted in a perpetuation of the assumption that these phenomena are essentially the same everywhere and entail identical, or at least very similar, structural changes. What is more, empirical evidence is said to indicate that the family in all modernizing societies is changing in the direction of the nuclear family (see Goode, 1963). An examination of the materials on India clearly shows that the nature of changes that are taking place is complex and hasty conclusions must not be drawn on the basis of a partial examination of the data, stressing size and structure to the exclusion of functional aspects.

It is my intention in this essay to examine both the deductive argument and the empirical evidence, particularly the latter. It will be shown that comparisons with the West are misleading and that the empirical evidence in respect of the Western countries themselves is already being reinterpreted. So far as the Indian data on the nature of change in the family are concerned, these are seemingly contradictory. These contradictions can be readily resolved if we cleanse our concepts and attempt to evaluate the empirical evidence without theoretical preconceptions. The first and the most important of the concepts that needs to be defined is that of the joint family itself.

Terminological Clarification

The bewilderment that the Hindu joint family has caused among social scientists is the result of the incomprehension of the European scholars of an institution which is significantly different from what seems to be its counterpart in Western societies. A number of essays by Indian scholars, published in the recent past, have largely succeeded in clearing the terminological confusion (see, for example, Madan, 1962a and 1962b; Shah, 1964 and 1968). An attempt is made to sum up here what seem to be the definite conclusions in this regard reached so far.

It is clear that a basic distinction that needs to be drawn in India although it may be redundant to do so in respect of contemporary Western societies, is that between the family and the household. Most discussions about the family in India, whether of its structure or of changes affecting at, are in fact about households. It is these discrete units that the census enumerators focus on and the fieldworker readily identifies as the smallest observable units of Hindu society. The notion of the family in India is generally of the kind which is identified as the extended family in sociological literature. It is not the family, however, but the household which is functionally the more important group.

The household also may be structurally similar to the family, or it may be different. This has led to the household itself being designated as a joint or extended or as a nuclear family. To avoid this confusion, Shah (1973) has suggested that households should be characterized as 'simple' or 'complex', complexity or its absence being strictly defined in terms of the structure of kinship composition. A further distinction that must be made in this regard is between complexity and largeness, between simplicity and smallness. Desai (1955) was perhaps the first Indian sociologist to point out that numerical size gives us no clue to the relational structure of the household group.

If these two points are kept in mind—the difference between the family and household and between the structure and the size of a household—a dense fog which has enveloped the studies of the family in India will lift. This fog has been spread by census reports and by much spurious sociology ever since 1911 when the bogey about "a growing tendency" of the 'disintegration' of the joint family was first raised by Census Commissioner E. A. Gait (see Goode, 1963, p. 238). To drive home this point, he drew attention to the fact that the average number of persons in India at 4.9 was "much the same as in European countries" (see Shah, 1973, p 126).

Besides size and structure, there is the functional aspect which must be taken into consideration if a proper evaluation of on-going changes is to be made. This entails the making of some further distinctions between different levels or dimensions of kin groups. The family commonly known in North India by such terms as *parivar*, *kutumba* and *khandan*, is a grouping of households of agnatically related men, their wives and unmarried sisters and daughters. The property rights of the men and the women differ. Women enjoy the privilege of having to be maintained by they men, but the have only limited and provisional rights of ownership and inheritance. The component of males within a family constitutes a coparcenary and this has been confusingly referred to as the joint family by many jurists (such as Mayne, 1953, p. 323) and sociologists (such as Karve, 1953, p. 10). One of the most outstanding authorities on Hindu Law, P.V. Kane (1946, pp. 590-91) has, however, explicitly stated that the coparcenary is a narrower group than the joint family. Coparceners are the male descendants of a common third ascendant generation ancestor. Incidentally, the three lineal ancestors for whom an upper caste Hindu performs the *shraddha* (ritual offering of food to manes) are his father, father's father, and father's father's father. As Shah (1973, p. 125) has pointed out, the lawyers' and the indologists' conceptions of the joint family have tended to converge and the former have often sought justification for their own viewpoint in indological literature.

The coparcenary defines the limits within which ancestral property devolves through survivorship on death. Particular coparceners may, however, break away from the coparcenary, taking away their individual shares with them. We, therefore, need to distinguish between the coparcenary and the actual property-group. The latter may embrace several households yet not all the members of the coparcenary. The break-up through partition of a coparcenary which results in the setting up of additional property groups and households, does not, however, affect ritual ties between the kinsfolk; thus, birth and death pollution and the obligation to perform *shraddha* are unaffected by such events.

In other words, the Hindu family generally operates at four different levels: (1) as a household; (2) as a grouping of households constituting a property-group; (3) as a still wider grouping of households incorporating the coparcenary which defines the outer limits for allodial and obligatory ritual purposes; (4) as an all-encompassing dispersed grouping defined genealogically rather than in terms of active interaction. In practice there is much overlap between the four levels, but it is important for analytical purpose that these distinctions should be borne in mind, when we are examining data on socio-economic change affecting the family life.

Only the household, often designated as the hearth-group in North India (*chulah* or *chulla*), emerges as the commensal group. Two or more households may reside together in a house or in different houses but in the same locality (village, neighbourhood in a town). Property rights exist as between members of the household and often spill over household boundaries to include households of brothers and perhaps the closer (first and second) cousins. Ritual obligations embrace all those who perform the *shraddha* for a common paternal great-grandfather.

Finally, mutual expectations of support and amity, and the associated affective dimension of kinship, which are most intensely experienced and explicitly acknowledged among primary kin, whether residing in the same household or not, become gradually diluted with the stretching of degrees of kinship; but they never cease at the boundaries of the household. The cultural ideal of the large multi-generation joint family is more related to this pattern of affective ties than to any actually existent groups now or in the past. Not to speak of cousins, brothers and their wives and children, all living together till they are parted by death, belong, as Shah (1973, p. 83) rightly points out, more to folklore and mythology than to real life. It has been wrongly suggested by some observers that the Hindu family does not break up in terms of any principle but only under the compulsion of circumstances. The Manusmriti itself (Chapter 17, verse 23) exhorts brothers who find living together problematic to divide and set up separate households and thereby earn spiritual merit. The partition of a complex household with two or more brothers in the senior generation is as much a fact of Hindu society as the existence of the cultural ideal of the so-called large joint family (see Madan, 1965, pp 164-80).

The foregoing terminological excursion has one clear and important implication for any discussion of the nature and significance of familial change: we must be careful to precisely identify which particular level or what particular dimension is supposed to be affected by the processes of change under consideration.

The Deductive Argument

The question of the relationship between the Hindu family and economic development may now be discussed. As stated above, the earlier argument used to be that the family was an obstacle to development. It is obvious that the family that these writers had in mind was that of legal treaties and indological works rather than of ethnographical reality.

One of the earliest statements on this problem was made by Raja Rammohun Roy in a tract on "the condition of India" published in London in 1831 (see Ganguli, 1972, pp. 281-307). Exploring the causes of India's unsatisfactory social and economic conditions, he referred among other factors to two institutions associated with the Hindu family. Firstly, he held early marriage and the stay-at-home males responsible for rapid population increase, though he, a contemporary of Malthus, seemed to repose some trust in the corrective mechanism of "natural checks". Secondly, he drew pointed attention to the "disincentive effects" of the Mitakshara Law of ownership and inheritance. As is well-known, under this law, a man may not dispose of any ancestral real property without the consent of other coparceners, including his own sons and grandsons. It not only curbed individual property rights but also made expansion and accumulation of assets difficult. Roy regarded the expansion of credit beyond individual savings from personal income as essential for economic expansion through domestic and foreign commerce.

Now, the base of credit in Bengal had been in land mortgage transactions since the Dayabhaga Law of ownership and inheritance, prevalent there, allowed a man the full right of mortgage and sale in respect of all his property without any difference being made between ancestral and self-acquired assets. Roy complained that British judicial authorities introduced into Bengal the Mitakshara notion of inalienability of ancestral property by any individual coparcener, even if he was the manager (*karta*). Roy foresaw "legal contests", "confusion and misery", a decline in the process of capital formation and in the growth of capitalist enterprise. From having been a mobile capital asset, real property was being frozen in the joint control of the property group.

Later scholars have often held a view of British judicial decisions which is the very opposite of Roy's position. Radhakamal Mukerjee, for example, writing almost a century after Roy, complained that "our courts of justice, imbued with the spirit of individual proprietary right of free alienation of properties could not tolerate the strict anti-alienation rule of the Mitakshara" (1922, p. 24). Other writers, too, have held similar views (see, for example, Kapadia, 1959, pp. 250-51). In any case, it is quite clear that the principle of division into equal shares *per stirpes* has not only favoured accumulation of capital but has also resulted, in the long run, in much fragmentation of land. Since increase in the area of cultivable land has not been proportionate to the growth of population, the harmful effects of the inheritance laws have been particularly marked in the present century. The examples of nineteenth century Japan and Europe are cited to drive home the advantages of single-heir family systems which prevent fragmentation, induce occupational mobility and restrict population growth (see, particularly Habakkuk, 1955, pp. 1-12).

There are other elements in the old thesis regarding the inimical role of family institutions in the context of development which do not carry the same conviction. Thus, it is said that the pooling of resources and individual earnings within the household or the family, and their placement under the control of one decision-maker, the *karta*, kills individual initiative. A member's extraordinary efforts or better skills go unrewarded, if not unrecognized also. The incentive to achieve more and do one's work better and more efficiently fails to be reinforced by the system. Conversely, the security which joint living affords makes some members irresponsible and lazy drones. Earnings are limited but the mouths to be fed and the bodies to be clothed are many. Consequently, accumulation of capital does not occur, precluding investment and enterprise.

It has also been asserted that the authority-structure of the Hindu household discourages collective decision-making on rational grounds. The head expects and usually receives obedience from the other members, even if only grudgingly at times. On his own part, he is often guided in his decision-making regarding resource and work-allocation, for instance primarily by tradition. Innovativeness does not flourish in such a situation, for risk-taking may result in failure, and consequently in dissensions, within the group.

The emphasis upon hereditary occupation, a corollary of the foregoing argument, also is deleterious to economic development because it discourages the acquisition of new skills and the entry into new occupations and enterprises. The skills of one's trade and craft are learnt at home from one's elders, through a kind of apprenticeship system, reinforcing tradition and parental authority. In such a situation spatial mobility also is discouraged.

Moreover, physical and mental development of children particularly female children—is neglected. The pre-occupation of women with child-bearing and child-rearing throughout their adult lives results not only in over population but also precludes their participation in productive activity. Finally, wasteful expenditure on weddings, funerals, festivals and religious ceremonies is said to limit the accumulation of savings and even compel borrowing from money-lenders and eventually the sale of land, a process which, once it begins, is hardly ever reversed (see Bailey, 1957, pp. 47-93).

Scholars such as Anstey (1952, pp. 50, 55-56), Davis (1955, pp. 312-14), Mishra (1962, p. 204), Kapp (1963, p. 56), Gore (1963, pp. 201-3), and many others, have put forward the views summarized above. The question that arises here is: What is the empirical basis for these conclusions? Since most of the authors do not mention any, at any rate, not for all the points they make, it would seem permissible to suggest that such of the above views in respect of which one may reasonably question the underlying assumptions are at best hypotheses calling for research rather than definitive conclusions. Some of these assumptions are examined below:

1. Individualism, (individual decision-making, recognition of individual contribution as the only just basis of reward, importance of individual reward to the continuation of productive effort, etc.) is regarded as essential to initiative and enterprise everywhere and ought to be a value in India as it has been in the West. That this may not be so is no longer a heresy, considering what Japan has been able to achieve with her highly conformist culture which recognizes the individual even less than does the Hindu society (see Nakane, 1970). Moreover, an economist has recently suggested that if we acknowledge that a man may derive utility from the welfare of his own children, "so the member of an extended family may well identify in welfare with that of all members of him extended family" (Bhagwati, 1966, p. 94). Erikson remarks more assertively: "I am inclined to indulge in the generalization that Indians want to give and get by fusing—actively and passively ... The fusion enforced and, no doubt, often enjoyed in the joint family and in crowded life in general results in a polarity. There is, no doubt, a deep recurring need to escape the multitude, and there is a remarkable capacity for being alone... But aloneness, too, is often dominated by a deep nostalgia for fusing with another, and this is an exclusive and everlasting fashion ..." (1969, p. 40). One may also ask why it is supposed that decisions taken by an individual on behalf of a group are to be regarded as being invariably inferior in quality to decisions taken by an individual on his own behalf? Smelser (1959) has shown how authority in the English families involved in cotton cloth production in the late eighteenth and early twentieth centuries, representing a transitional stage between home consumption and the factory system, continued to be vested in the father as among agricultural families.

2. The traditional household has an authoritarian structure and dissensions in it are, therefore, said to be rare: the head is believed to enjoy absolute authority. This seems to be more an expression of a cultural ideal and a legal fiction based on what the people say they do rather than on observation of what they in fact do. Ethnographical literature brings out quite clearly the conflicts and consultations, the bargaining and the compromises,

which characterize decision-making within a household; and it is not only men who participate in it but also women, directly or through the influence they exert on their husbands and sons. In this connection, it must also be affirmed that the non-participation of women in productive activity is a characteristic of upper castes and the upper middle-classes rather than that of the whole of Hindu society. In any case there is no evidence to suggest that shortage of man-power, except in the highly skilled categories, has been a problem in India's recent economic history. On the contrary, unemployment and underemployment are the chronic ills afflicting the labour force.

3. Then, there is the dichotomy between traditional and rational decisions. Here the author would like to argue that, whereas unquestioning adherence to traditional may result in irrational decisions, it is hardly defensible to maintain, implicitly or explicitly, that decisions based on tradition are *ipso facto* irrational. Thus, a farmer's action when he rotates crops to maintain or increase productivity does not become irrational simply because his ancestors did likewise. An appeal to Max Weber on this score can be misleading unless we take care to note his distinction between customary behaviour and rational usage.

4. While the deleterious effects of high fertility on the average level of living may not be denied, the desire for children, particularly sons, is not totally irrational, for, the poor regard children as an investment in the form of addition to the supply of farm labour. This is the point of the much repeated statement of Mamdani (1972) that it is not over-population which produces poverty which generates relative over-population.

5. The arguments regarding the crippling effects of the laws of inheritance, the absence of occupational mobility, and improvident expenditure are more readily acceptable; but these too lose force if they are indiscriminately applied to all levels of economic development.

Having examined some of the underlying assumptions of what the author has called the deductive argument, he would now like to consider the empirical evidence regarding the relationship between the Hindu family and large complex households on the one hand and industrialization and urbanization on the other.

The Empirical Evidence

An argument has been developed in Western sociology regarding "the 'fit' between conjugal family and the modern industrial system" (Goode, 1963, pp. 10-26). Industrialization, urbanism, occupational and spatial mobility, a relatively open system of social stratification, narrow effective kin-groups, and an emphasis on the individual as against the group and on the emotional-affective nature of wife-husband relationship—all are seen as a cluster. Goode is concerned with the feasibility of the argument as such, independent of the empirical support that may be found for it in different places and times. It is important to note, however, that Goode does not causally relate the conjugal family and the modern industrial system; he only draws pointed attention to their compatibility. Indeed, he speaks of "the independence of the two sets of variables, the familial and the industrial, as well as the presence of some 'disharmonies' between the two" (1963, p. 15).

That the conjugal or nuclear family may not always be the result of industrialization is borne out by the fact that it is found among many so-called primitive societies, too numerous to be mentioned here. What is more important, new historical evidence accumulated of late, points to the prevalence of the nuclear family as the residential unit in England and in the United States before the industrial revolution. Members of the Cambridge Population Group have carried out a detailed examination of town records, parish registers and similar documents of the sixteenth and seventeenth centuries to conclude that for the past four centuries, and perhaps longer, the predominant type of household in England has been the small nuclear family rather than the large extended family see, for example, Laslett and Wall, 1972. Similar conclusions have been reported in respect of the United States by scholars like Demos (1970) and Greven, Jr. (1970). What is more, Laslett has suggested that, in England, the size of the household grew larger rather than shrank with the coming of industrialization. Urbanization, mechanical communication, the growth of wealth and the increase in expectation of life may actually have strengthened the familial tie in some ways and widened the network of kinship (1959, p. 589). The general situation in respect of Western Europe had earlier been summed up by Greenfield: "... the specific social system that grew up around machine technology in Western civilization may result from the fact that the small nuclear family existed in Europe and the United States before the industrial revolution" (1961, p. 312). The conclusion drawn by Nimkoff and Middleton (1960, pp. 215-29), on the basis of their examination of 549 cultures, that the family in most industrial societies is organized along independent and not extended lines, may now be seen to yield a different kind of understanding than its authors intended (also see Litwak and Figueria, 1970; Sussman, 1970). It is in the light of this reinterpretation of the data from the industrialized countries of the West that our own examination of the empirical evidence from India should be undertaken.

It is of interest to note that while the deductive argument centred round the obstructive role of the family and other social institutions in the social and economic development of India, recent (post-1950) empirical studies have concentrated on the impact of economic change generally, and or urbanization and industrialization in particular, on social structure. Some of these studies begin with the assumption that this impact is bound to be disruptive of traditional institutions. Thus, Epstein (1962) asserts that the conversion from subsistence to a cash economy had led to the breakdown of complex households among the Mysore peasants, she studied; and this was bound to happen, for "economic development will almost invariably result in the breaking up of joint family ties" (1962, p. 322). Her evidence is meagre and her conclusions are vitiated by a reconstruction of family life in the past which is methodologically suspect and also very sketchy. Nevertheless, she boldly proclaims her conclusion citing in support an earlier authority, Ralph Linton, who regarded it generally true of most societies than an increase in opportunities for profit weakens the ties of extended kinship.

Ross (1961) also takes it for granted that large complex households were typical of Hindu society in past and that they are breaking up now under the impact of urbanization. She identifies geographical mobility and neolocal residence as the principal factors responsible for accelerating change. Ross writes at considerable length about what she thinks will happen to different aspects of family life; these predictions flow not so much from the data she has as from what are regarded as axiomatic truths by her and by others of similar persuasion. Besides theoretical preconceptions, terminological inexactitude also mars the work of both Epstein and Ross.

The cumulative effect of socio-economic change on the Hindu family has most often been said to be in the direction of a reduction in the size of the household. The single most important source of social statistics in India is, of course, the decennial census. Ever since 1911, successive Census Commissioners have written about the "disintegration" of "the joint family" (by which they mean the complex household). The 1951 Census Commissioners wrote: "Such a large proportion of small households [33 per cent in rural areas and 38 per cent in urban centres] is a prima facie indication that families do not continue to be 'joint' according to the traditional custom of the country and the habit of breaking away from the joint family and setting up separate households is quite strong."

The conclusion is not, however, as obvious as the census commissioners make it out to be. Apart from the confusion between the family and the household which need not pose any problem since we know that the census data are on households, there are two questions to settle. First, what are the data on size over time? Second, what light do they throw on household types?

The variation in the average size of the household, as recorded in the censuses, turns out to be negligible. It was 4.6 in 1911, 4.6 in 1921, 4.8 in 1931, 5.0 in 1941, 5.0 in 1951, and 5.2 in 1961. Just over a hundred years ago, in 1868, it was 4.3. The trend is upwards. It must be noted, however, that the foregoing data are for all communities, and not for Hindus alone. Similarly, the many city surveys that have been conducted since 1950 contain materials on households in urban areas. Data from ten cities (namely, Baroda, Mumbai, Gorakhpur, Hubli, Hyderabad-Secunderabad, Jamshedpur, Kanpur, Lucknow, Poona and Surat) show that households with four to six members each form the highest percentage of the total, ranging from 36.3 per cent in Bombay to 42 per cent in Baroda. Besides, the number of households with seven to nine and even ten members is quite considerable (Bulsara, 1964, p. 15). In short, differences in household size over time and as between rural and urban areas do not warrant any assured conclusions regarding the decline in the incidence of large households.

Some writers would like to emphasize the stability in household size or, for that matter, the upward trend. Orenstein (1961) does so on the basis of census data and Kolenda (1970) on the basis of detailed data on a Maharashtra village spread over a century and a half. This itself is, however, a risky undertaking and that for two reasons. First, a mere breakdown of households into large or small, or into complex or simple, by itself provides only a partial insight into the phenomena under consideration. This information, as Shah (1973, p. 87) rightly points out, must be supplemented by data on what percentage of the total population lives in which type of household. Moreover, in so far as interpretation of the variation, or lack of variation, in household size is concerned, it is very important to find out whether a household is simple in composition by choice or under the compulsion of demographic factors. As Kessinger (1974) has demonstrated out, many households in past were of the simple type because people did not live as long they do now. "And since the population increased substantially after 1920 and percentage of life expectancy has continued to rise, the percentage of families nuclear 'of necessity' has continually declined. The technique of studying domestic and family group structure through percentages of each type does not take this change into consideration" (Kessinger 1974, pp. 83-84).

Regarding the relationship between size and structure, this is dubious and hard to establish considering that the average size of households in India is around five. A kin group of five could turn out to be a simple household consisting of a couple and their three unmarried children, or a complex household of two brothers, their wives and a child of one of the couples, or a complex household composed of a man, his wife, son, daughter-in-law and grandchild. Needless to add, other possibilities also exist. In view of the foregoing discussion, it should be clear that the preoccupation with numbers has failed to yield much understanding of the processes of familial change in the absence of other qualitative data.

Now, several research workers have concerned themselves directly with the problem of structure of the household in the context of rural-urban differences. They provide us with guarded conclusions which do not lend much support to the thesis of the breakdown of complex households in urban areas and their displacement by simple households. An early study by Mukherjee (1965) compared data from the cities of Calcutta and Howrah, four West Bengal towns, and 20 villages of the State to conclude: "the prevalence of the extended (non-nuclear) family type is of equal order for the cities, towns and villages" (p. 25). What is more, he found the nuclear family type or simple household more frequent in villages than in towns and cities in that order.

Kinship composition of a particular kind becomes socially significant in terms of the interrelationships and activities that go with it. Desai (1964) defines jointness in terms of joint activities– in respect of property relations, mutual obligations between kin, residence, etc. He maintains that traditionally there was a high degree of congruence between these different dimensions of family life. His study of the town of Mahuva in Gujarat revealed that as many as 95 per cent of the 423 households examined by him fell into the category of joint family (that is, complex household) though only 21 per cent were joint in the traditional sense (Desai, 1964, p. 145). What is more significant is the fact that those families which have been living longer in the town also show the higher degree of jointness. The belief that urban residence does not favour joint living is thus not confirmed. Other writers also have reported from their research that complex households are perhaps more characteristic of town-dwelling upper castes than of the rural population (see, for example, Shah, 1973, p. 100). Whether rural migrants come from complex or simple households, it seems that the fact of migration itself, or of occupational change, does not result in any drastic change in the kind of residential kin group in which they live and in the relationships that they maintain with other relatives (see Gould, 1965, p. 46).

In the best available study of the impact of urbanization on kinship, Vatuk (1972) maintains that her data do not support assumptions about "The rapid or radical change in the traditional Indian family system." She adds: "The changes in kinship organization [for example, the growth of bilateral kinship connexions] in .... middle class neighbourhoods .... do not result primarily from their being city neighbourhoods, but rather from an underlying chain of forces which begins with education and permits occupational mobility, consequent geographical mobility and neolocal residence patterns. Urban residence is intermediate in the causal chain leading towards changed kinship organization" (Vatuk, 1972, pp. 190-91).

In an earlier study Gore (1968) also had suggested that education and entry into new occupations and professions, rather than urban residence itself, produce a lack of satisfaction with old-style living in complex households. Households which maintain their traditional calling as businessmen uphold "joint family living in behaviour, role perception and attitudes" (Gore, 1968, p. 232). One perhaps would like to add a word of caution here. Some studies have questioned whether even entry into new occupations is by itself sufficient to bring about a change in familial organization (see, for example, Gould, 1965; Rao, 1968). The danger, as the author sees it, lies in judging the consequences of new occupations, or of migration, too soon after the event.

Besides urbanization, and perhaps more than it, industrialization has been seen as a solvent of the traditional family and household ties. Once again, empirical evidence supports neither this view nor the thesis that traditional kinship organization is an obstacle to industrial development. Several studies of the behaviour of entrepreneurs, as also of industrial workers, have been published and their conclusions point in the same direction. While the impact of industrialization on family life is far from uniform, it does generally seem to be much less disruptive than has been expected.

In his excellent study of factory workers in Pune, Lambert (1963) writes: "In much of the discussion of the impact of industrialization on countries such as India, the most common assumption seems to be that one of the earliest influences of industrialism upon the traditional society is the disorganization of the traditional family. Many of the changes predicted are qualitative changes not easily subject to measurement, but in so far as enumerative data are indicative of change, the factory population in Pune does not seem to differ radically or in the predicted direction from the general Pune population" (p. 39). He adds: "The primary test of an hypothesis that the factory is producing fragmented families should be the occurrence of a high proportion of factory workers who live away from their kin. We do not find this." It has been suggested by Sheth (1968) that industrialism has not dissolved traditional institutions in India because, contrary to what is generally believed, it has been a natural growth rather than an implantation from outside. Be that as it may, the fact remains—and there is a lot more evidence than what I have cited—that industrialization has not drastically altered the family life of the working class.

The evidence in respect of entrepreneurs is even more clear. Writing of industrial entrepreneurs of Okhla (Delhi), Srinivas *et al.* (1966) observe: "Kinship links play an important part at every stage and in every aspect of entrepreneurial activity. They represent one of the most important sources of financial aid in starting an industry. Entrepreneurs tend to work in close association with near kinsmen, sharing responsibilities, power and income. It is usual for a man to recruit his partners, managers and technical experts from among his close kindred" (p. 83). The support that entrepreneurs derive from undivided family assets and from their close kinsmen has been discussed in many published works (see, for example, Gulati and Gulati, 1962; Hazari, 1966; Ramu, 1973). In an authoritative statement, Singer (1972) writes about industrial leaders in Madras city: "While there have been striking changes within three generations in residential, occupational, educational and social mobility, as well as in patterns of ritual observances, the changes have not transformed the traditional joint family structure into isolated nuclear families. On the contrary, the urban and industrial members of a family maintain numerous ties and obligations with the members of the family who have remained in the ancestral village or town or have moved elsewhere. And within the urban and industrial setting, modified joint family organization is emerging" (p. 296). So impressed is Singer by the compatibility between the traditional family organization and industrial management that he wonders how the idea of the incompatibility between the two ever got started.

Having looked at the urban-industrial scene, it may be worthwhile to return to the rural setting for a quick look at the evidence emanating from there. Once again the over-all picture is similar. A study conducted in a village near Delhi revealed that the fact that an urban-oriented rather than a rural-oriented man is the head makes no difference to the type of household he and his family live in; caste and economic status would seem more important (Freed and Freed, 1969). Further north, in a Punjabi village, study of familial change over a period of more than a hundred years shows that the joint family continues to be the norm but the range of kinship within it has narrowed. New households in the 1960s came into existence oftener as a result of partition than of succession as in the past; but these households are not necessarily of the nuclear family type. A new type of joint family organization seems to be emerging (Kessinger, 1974, pp. 178-201). This is precisely what Singer notes about the Chennai industrial leaders.

There is a contradiction between the expected and the actual relationship between economic development, urbanization and industrialisation on the one hand and the Hindu family on the other. The empirical evidence is, on the whole, clear and remarkably consistent if only it is properly interpreted. There are unmistakable signs of change, but this is not uniform. The relationship between the family and the so-called determining variables can usually be explained in terms of rational calculation rather than by any general theory of change. Moreover, different aspects of the family that were outlined earlier in this paper respond in different ways to the same changes.

Thus, the type of household in terms of kinship structure that people live in is often the result of their calculation of economic advantage; but what is judged to be economically rational differs from individual to individual and group to group. And, "industrialization is not a homogenous process but rather one which creates a variety of opportunities which may be exploited by diverse strategies" (Owens, 1971, p. 247). Economic advantage is not, however, equally relevant in the context of aspects of family life other than household type and size. Mutual expectations of amity, and aid, ritual obligations, verbal expressions of adherence to the cultural ideal of joint living may seem impervious to the compulsions of economic interests. It has been observed through attitude surveys conducted over many years, and in several different parts of the country, that the sentiment for joint family living has remained generally undiminished irrespective of the kind of household the respondents themselves lived in.

Given the existence of compartmentalized aspects of the family, the response of the institution to external forces impinging upon it turns out to be complex. Depending on what particular aspect one focuses on—domestic arrangements, property ownership, expectations of support, ritual obligations, cultural values, sentiments, etc. the conclusions one draws regarding the role or state of the family differ (see Ames, 1973). It is due to our failure to distinguish between these differential responses that we detect contradictions in evidence where, in fact, there are not any. This is also why terminological clarification to which the author drew attention earlier in this paper is important. The effort to seek simple solutions to complex problems is bound to create confusion.

The conclusion that the above necessarily brief examination of the relevant literature leads to, then, is this: There is no substitute for empirical research in assessing the nature of on-going social change and the interplay between economic and non-economic forces in India. The experience of other countries may suggest areas of inquiry but cannot legitimately provide us with ready-made answers. For our own research and making it meaningful it is imperative that we operate with carefully chosen and refined conceptual tools. The need for vigilance against the distortion of research by preconceived notions and illegitimate comparisons is great. And, finally, our search for the institutional factors that impinge upon economic development should be released from a century-old preoccupation with Hinduism, caste and the joint family and also related to modes of production, patterns of ownership, governmental policy, etc. Then alone may we expect to obtain a rounded perspective on the nature and problems of development.

NOTE

* This paper is an extended version of part of a lecture which the author delivered at the SNDT University, Bombay, and at the University of Udaipur during 1975-76 under the University Grants Commission National Lectures Programme. It is based on a survey of sociological and social anthropological literature on contemporary Indian which the author was first able to undertake following the receipt of a research assistance grant from the Wenner-Gren Foundation for Anthropological Research, Inc. Later, the author was able to continue this work, thanks to the facilities for research

at the Institute of Economic Growth. The author is grateful to all three organizations.

REFERENCES

Ames, M.M.: 1973: Structural Dimensions of Family Life in the Steel City of Jamshedpur. In Milton Singer, ed., *Entrepreneurship and Modernization of Occupational Cultures in South Asia*. Duke University, Durham, N.C.

Anstey, Vera: 1952: *The Economic Development of India*. Longmans, Green & Co., London.

Bailey, F.G.: 1957: *Caste and the Economic Frontier*. Manchester, Manchester University Press.

Bhagwati, J.: 1966: *The Economics of Underdeveloped Countries*. Weidenfeld and Nicholson, London.

Bulsara, J.F.: 1964: *Problems of Rapid Urbanization in India*. Allied Publishers, Bombay.

Changes in the Indian Family: An Examination of Some Assumptions. *Economic and Political Weekly*, III, pp. 127-34.

Davis, K.: 1955: Social and Demographic Aspects of Economic Development in India. In Simon Kuznets *et al*. *Economic Growth: Brazil, India, Japan*. Duke University Press, Durham, N. C.

Demos, J.: 1970: *A Little Commonwealth*. Oxford University Press, New York.

Desai, I. P. 1955 An Analysis 'of the joint family'. *Sociological Bulletin*, IV, pp 97-117.

———: 1964: *Some Aspects of Family in Mahuva*. New York, Asia Publishing House, Bombay.

Epstein, T.S.: 1962: *Economic Development and Social Change in South India*. Manchester, Manchester University Press.

Erikson, E.: 1969: *Gandhi's Truth: On the Origins of Militant Non-violence*. Norton, New York.

Freed, S.A. and Freed, R.S.: 1969: Urbanization and Family Types in a North Indian Village. *Southwestern Journal of Anthropology*, 25, 4, pp. 342-59.

Ganguli, B.N.: 1972: Rammohun Roy on India's Contemporary Economic Problems. In S.L.N. Simha (ed.), *Economic and Social Development, Essays in Honour of C.D. Deshmukh*. Vora, Bombay, pp 281-307.

Goode, W.J.: 1963: *World Revolution and Family Patterns*. Free Press, Glencoe.

Gore, M.S.: 1963: Kinship Structure and Attitudes to Wealth. In R.D. Lambert and B.F. Hoselitz (eds.), *The Role of Savings and Wealth in Southern Asia and the West*. UNESCO, Paris.

Gould, H.A.: 1965: Lucknow Rickshawallas: the Social Organization of an Occupational Category. International *Journal of Comparative Sociology*, VI, 1, pp. 24-47.

Greenfield, S.M.: 1961: Industrialization and the Family in Sociological Theory. *American Journal of Sociology*, 67, 3, pp. 312-22.

Greven, Jr. P.: 1970: *Four Generations*. Cornell University Press, Ithaca, New York.

Gulati, I.S. and Gulati, K.S.: 1962: *The Undivided Hindu Family: A Study of its Tax Privileges*. Asia Publishing House, Bombay.

Habakkuk, H.J.: 1955: Family Structure and Economic Change in Nineteenth Century Europe. *The Journal of Economic History*, XV, 1, pp. 1-12.

Hazari, R.K.: 1966: *The Structure of the Corporate Private Sector: A Study of Concentration, Ownership and Control*. Asia Publishing House, Bombay.

Kane, P.V.: 1946: *History of Dharmashastra*. Vol III, Bhandarkar Oriental Research Institute, Poona.

Kapadia, K.M.: 1959: *Marriage and Family in India*. Oxford University Press, Bombay.

————: 1969: *Hindu Culture, Economic Development and Economic Planning in India*. Asia Publishing House, Bombay.

Karve, Irawati: 1953: *Kinship Organization in India*. Bombay, Asia Publishing House.

Kessinger, T.: 1974: *Vilyatpur: 1848-1968*. University of California Press, Berkeley.

Kolenda, P.: 1970: Family Structure in Village Lonikand, India: 1819, 1958, and 1967. *Contributions to Indian Sociology*, 4, pp. 50-72.

Lambert, R.D.: 1963: *Workers, Factories and Social Change in India*. Asia Publishing House, Bombay.

Laslett, P.: 1965: The History of Population and Social Structure. *International Social Science Journal*, 17, 7, pp. 582-93.

Laslett, P. and Wall, R.: 1972: *Household and Family in Past Time*. Cambridge University Press, Cambridge.

Litwak, E. and Figueria, J.: 1970: Technological Innovations and Idea: Forms of Family Structure in an Industrial Democratic Society. In Reuben Hill and Rene Koening, (eds). *Families, East and West*. Mouton, Paris.

Madan, T.N.: 1962a: The Joint Family: a Terminological Clarification. *International Journal of Comparative Sociology*, 3, 1, pp. 7-16.

————: 1962b: The Hindu Joint Family. *Man* (London), LXII, pp. 88-89.

Maine, H.S.: 1917: *Ancient Law*. J.M. Dent and Sons, London.

Mamdani, M.: 1972: *The Myth of Population Control: Family Caste and Class in an Indian Village*. Monthly Review Press, New York.

Marx, K., and Engels, F.: 1959: *The First Indian War of Independence, 1857-59*. Progess Publishers, Moscow.

Mayne, J.D.: 1953: *A Treatise on Hindu Law and Usage*. Eleventh edition by N. Chandrashekhara Aiyar. Higginbothams, Madras.

Mishra, N.: 1962: *Hinduism and Economic Growth*. Oxford University Press, Bombay.

Mukerjee, Radhakamal: 1922: *Principles of Comparative Economics*. Vol. II, P.S. King & Son Ltd., London.

Mukherjee, Ramkrishna: 1965: *The Sociologist and Social Change in India Today*. Prentice-Hall, New Delhi.

Nakane, C.: 1970: *Japanese Society*. University of California Press, Berkeley.

Nimkoff, M.F. and Middleton, R.: 1960: Types of Family and Types of Economy. *American Journal of Sociology*, 66, 3, pp. 215-25.

Orenstein, Henry: 1961: The Recent History of the Extended Family in India. *Social Problems*, 8, VIII, 4, pp. 341-53.

Owens, R.: 1971: Industrialization and the Joint Family. *Ethnology*, X, 2, pp. 223-50.

Ramu, G.N.: 1973: Family Structure and Entrepreneurship: An Indian Case. *Journal of Comparative Family Studies*, IV, 2, pp. 239-56.

Rao, M.S.A.: 1968: Occupational Diversification and Joint Household Organization. *Contributions to Indian Sociology* (ns) 2, pp. 98-112.

Ross, A.D.: 1961: *The Hindu Family in its Urban Setting*. Oxford University Press, Toronto.

Shah, A.M.: 1964: Basic Terms and Concepts in the Study of Family Life in India. *Indian Economic and Social History Review*, I, pp. 1-36.

————: 1968: Changes in the Indian Family: An Examination of some Assumptions. Economic and Political Weekly, III, p. 127-34.

————: 1973: *The Household Dimensions of the Family in India*. Orient Longman, New Delhi.

Sheth, N.R.: 1968: *The Social Framework of an Indian Factory*. Manchester University Press, Manchester.

Singer, M.: 1972: *When a Great Tradition Modernizes: An Anthropological Approach in Indian Civilization*. Praeger, New York.

Smelser, N.J.: 1959: *Social Change in the Industrial Revolution: An Application of Theory to the Lancashire Cotton Industry*. Routledge and Kegan Paul, London.

Srinivas, M.N. *et al.*: 1966: *A Sociological Study of Okhla Industrial Estate. In Small Industries and Social Change*. UNESCO Research Centre, Delhi.

Sussman, M.B.: 1970: The Urban Kin Networks in the Formulation of Family Theory. In Reuben Hill and Rene Koenig, (eds), *Families, East and West*. Mouton, Paris.

Vatuk, Sylvia: 1972: *Kinship and Urbanisation: White-Collar Migrants in North India*. California University Press, Berkeley.

Wirth, Louis: 1938: Urbanizm as a Way of Life. *American Journal of Sociology*, 44, pp. 124.

13

Urbanization and Family Types in a North Indian Village[1]

Stanley A. Freed and Ruth S. Freed

This essay based on data collected in a north Indian village, is an analysis of the relationship of family types to a number of variables: caste, type of house, ownership of land, and the urbanization, type of employment, age, and education of the family head. There is no statistically significant difference in family types between families headed by urban-oriented men and those headed by village-oriented men. Type of house, education, and type of employment also prove to be non-significant. Family type is correlated with high and low-caste status, landownership, and the age of the family head. High-caste landowning families are more likely to be joint than low-caste Landless ones. Also, older men are more likely to head joint families than younger ones.

A well-entrenched hypothesis holds that urbanization and industrialization result in the breakdown of the joint (or extended) family and its replacement by the nuclear family. This hypothesis has been challenged both as to its general validity and, relatively recently, its validity for India, a country which is undergoing urbanization and industrialization and in which the joint family is a quite common, if not the predominant, family type (see the discussions by Goode 1963, chapter 5; Gould 1968; Kolenda 1968; and Singer 1968). With regard to India, the relationship of urbanization and industrialization to family type is as yet unclear, as are the relationships to family type of other possibly relevant variables, such as education, wealth, landholdings, caste, type of employment, technological changes in agriculture, and legislative changes. This essay presents data on urbanization and type of family from Shanti Nagar, a north Indian village. In addition to investigating the relationship of family type and urbanization, we also studied the relation of family type to age, type of employment, type of house, caste, education, and the ownership of land.

Shanti Nagar is located about 11 miles from the city of Delhi, well within commuting distance by bus, train, and bicycle. Forty-nine per cent of the adult males defined as men 20 years of age or older, or those in their late teens who are married and have completed school, have lived or worked in urban areas, principally Delhi. Such experience is much more common among the younger men than among the older. Only 17 of 50 men (34 per cent) 50 years of age and older have had urban experience; but 67 of 121 men (55 per cent) younger than 50 years of age have had such experience. Sixty-four per cent of the adult men 25 years of age or younger (N=45) have had urban experience. These figures can reasonably be interpreted as indicating a trend. In the near future, adult men who have not lived or worked in cities will be a decided minority. However, at the time of our fieldwork, the adult males of Shanti Nagar were almost equally divided between those who had worked and/or lived in cities and those who had not.

Based upon the criterion of urban experience, we have classified the adult men of Shanti Nagar into two groups. One, which we categorize as urban-oriented, is composed of men who have lived and/or worked in urban areas; the other, which we class as village-oriented, is composed of men who lack such urban experiences. A random sample of 28 urban-oriented men showed that the average length of urban employment or residence was 7.8 years. Most urban-oriented men have been employed for wages or salaries in modern urban occupations. They have, on the average, more education than village-oriented men. Only 33 per cent of the urban-oriented adult men (N=79) are illiterate; 42 per cent are at least literate but have not studied to the level of matriculate (10 grades completed plus an examination); and 25 per cent have studied to the level of matriculate or beyond. Seventy-two per cent of the village-oriented adult men (N=79) are illiterate; 23 per cent are at least literate but have not reached the level of matriculate; and only 5 per cent have studied to the level of matriculate or beyond.[2] Urban-oriented men have been exposed to a somewhat greater degree than village-oriented men to motion pictures, newspapers, and other urban institutions. When 29 urban-oriented men, randomly selected, were asked if they attended the cinema, 9 (31 per cent) replied that they did; but only 4 of 20 (20 per cent) randomly selected village-oriented men said that they attended the cinema. When 29 urban-oriented men, randomly selected, were asked if they had read a magazine or newspaper in the last 2 or 3 weeks, 10 (34 per cent) replied that they had; but only one of 20 (5 per cent) randomly selected village-oriented men said that he had recently read a magazine or newspaper. The latter figures reflect, of course, differences in education between village-oriented and urban-oriented men as well as differing exposure to magazines and newspapers.

The experiences associated with urban employment and residence are to be distinguished from a number of other kinds of contact between villagers and the city, which occur constantly throughout the year and affect both village-oriented and urban-oriented people. Among the latter contacts are the trips that villagers make to Delhi for ritual bathing in the Yamuna River, for appearances in the courts, for medical treatment, and for selling various agricultural products in the markets of Delhi. A variety of urbanites come to Shanti Nagar: buyers of brown sugar who, during the season for crushing sugar cane, make 2 trips daily between Delhi and Shanti Nagar; buyers of raw hides who visit the leatherworker caste; a commission agent from the Delhi vegetable market who occasionally comes to Shanti Nagar to cultivate his steady clients and to gain new ones; the village school teachers who commute from Delhi; and occasionally, health officials, politicians, police, and development workers. By such means, most of the people of Shanti Nagar have at least some contact with the urban world. We have assumed, however, that employment and residence in the city are urban experiences considerably more intensive and intimate than the ephemeral contacts with visitors from the city and that they will have more pronounced effects upon the villagers exposed to them. Therefore, whatever may be the effects of urban experience upon individual behaviour, they will presumably be manifest among the urban-oriented to a greater extent than among the village-oriented. Thus, the village of Shanti Nagar provides us with an opportunity to investigate the relationship of urban experiences and family types by comparing the types of families headed by urban-oriented men with those headed by village-oriented men.

Our emphasis on men in this essay should not be taken to indicate that we ignored women in our field work, for we did not. One of the advantages of a husband and wife team in conducting field work is that they can give roughly equal attention to both men and women. The reason that we analyze urbanization and family type from the point of view of men is that relatively few women have had the urban experiences, especially employment, that are common for men. This, and the fact that heads of families are almost always men, led us to our method of comparing family types according to the urban experiences of the heads of families. The behaviour of women traditionally has a good deal to do with family type. A reason often given for dividing a joint family into its component nuclear families is that the wives of the family quarrel and fight. However, the decision about whether or not to divide a family rests principally with the adult males, whose authority in family matters derives in part from patrilineal descent and the equal inheritance of property by male family members. Of these, the family head is the most influential. Thus, we feel that comparing the proportions of the various types of families in the group of families headed by urban-oriented men with those headed by village-oriented men is the best way to gain some insight into the relationship of family type and urbanization in Shanti Nagar.

For classifying families as to type, we have used Kolenda's categories (1968: 346-348, 356). She defines the nuclear family as a married couple with or without unmarried children, the subnuclear family as a fragment of a former nuclear family for example, a widow and her unmarried children, and a joint family as consisting of at least 2 married couples related either lineally for example, a father, mother, and their married son, or collaterally for example, two married brothers. Any unmarried family members who are not children of any of the married couples of a family supplement the family. The three basic types, subnuclear, nuclear, and joint, qualified by the adjectives, lineal, collateral, and supplemented, yield 10 family types. The 110 families of Shanti Nagar are distributed among these types and the 4 types of polygynous families described below as follows: nuclear families 34 (31 per cent), supplemented nuclear families 27 (24 per cent), subnuclear families 3 (3 per cent), supplemented subnuclear families 2 (2 per cent), collateral joint families 3 (3 per cent), supplemented collateral joint families 8 (7 per cent), lineal joint families 9 (8 per cent), supplemented lineal joint families 2 (2 per cent), lineal-collateral joint families 8 (7 per cent), and supplemented lineal-collateral joint families 8 (7 per cent). Kolenda also recognizes single-person families and a residual category that she terms "other." We did not require the "other" category, and, as Shanti Nagar has only one single-person family, we made no use of the single-person category, classifying the one such family (a widow) as subnuclear.

Another set of family types can be formed in a similar fashion based upon the polygynous family composed of a man and more than one wife. Thus, a supplemented polygynous family is a polygynous family with an unmarried relative who is not a child of the husband and one of his wives; and a polygymous lineal-collateral joint famdy is a lineal-collateral joint family in which at least one of the component families is composed of a man and his two or more wives. Shanti Nagar has a few polygynous families. They are as follows: polygynous families 2 (2 per cent), supplemented polygynous 1 (1 per cent); polygynous supplemented collateral joint 1 (1 per cent), and polygynous lineal-collateral joint 2 (2 per cent).

We term a family as being joint if the component nuclear families share at least their food supplies and, when living in the same house, their cooking. If the component nuclear families are separated, as when one lives in Shanti Nagar and the other in Delhi, they naturally cook separately but they are still one family. Their cohesiveness can be observed on the occasions when the city dwellers visit the village. They cook with the others in the family and upon returning to the city often take a supply of grain and ghee from the common larder.

Wives are sometimes absent from the village. Young wives, especially, move back and forth between their parents' and their husbands' villages—villages are exogamous, and marriage is virilocal and patrilocal; and, in the early years of marriage, they spend a good deal of time with their parents. We considered an absent wife to be a member of her husband's family for the purpose of defining family types. Thus, a family consisting of a man, his wife, and a married teen-age son whose wife lives with her parents in another village is classed as a joint family. An absent husband is also considered a family member for purposes of classification, as in the case of a man, his wife, and a married son who lives in a city, the son's wife living with his parents in Shanti Nagar: this is a joint family.

Eight servants from outside Shanti Nagar who reside with various families of Shanti Nagar were not counted in defining family types. They are unrelated to their employers and are not members of their families although their employers feed them and give them shelter; and because they live with their employers, they have not established families of their own. They receive their sustenance as payment rather than through the rights inherent in family membership. In short, they are not members of any of the families of Shanti Nagar, and we have disregarded them in the analysis that follows.

In the classification presented above, the 110 families of Shanti Nagar are categorised among 14 family types. Because of the small number of many types of' families, it was necessary for purposes of analysis to combine these 14 types into a smaller number of categories. These combined family types are as follows: "nuclear" includes nuclear families, all types of subnuclear families, and polygynous families; "supplemented nuclear" includes supplemented nuclear families and supplemented polygynous families; and "joint" includes all forms of joint and polygynous joint families.

The families of Shanti Nagar by combined types and caste are given in Table 1. Thirty-seven per cent of the families are joint; the rest are nuclear (37 per cent) and supplemented nuclear (26 per cent). Although only 37 per cent of the families of Shanti Nagar are joint, 52 per cent of the population lives in joint families. This is possible because joint families are, on the average, larger than nuclear families. These figures can be used to support those who argue on either side of the question of whether or not the joint family is typical of India. In Shanti Nagar, at least, there are more nuclear and supplemented nuclear families than joint families, but more people live in joint families than in nuclear families.

If, instead of considering actual family types, we turn our attention to ideal types, we find that a large majority of people favour joint family living. Eighty-two percent of a stratified random sample of 82 adult villagers (47 men and 35 women), when asked whether they preferred to live in joint or nuclear households, replied that they preferred joint family living. Thus, the joint family appears to be the ideal type in Shanti Nagar although its incidence is less than it presumably would be if people could have their expressed preferences realized.

TABLE 1
Families by Combined type and Caste*

Caste	*Nuclear*	*Supplemented Nuclear*	*Joint*	*Total*
Bairagi Beggar	2 (40)	2 (40)	1 (20)	5
Baniya Merchant	0	1 (100)	0	1
Brahmin Priest	7 (32)	6 (27)	9 (41)	22
Chamar Leatherworker	3 (23)	5 (38)	5 (38)	13
Chhipi Dyer	1 (100)	0	0	1
Chuhra Sweeper	12 (70)	2 (12)	3 (18)	17
Gola Potter	8 (67)	3 (25)	1 (8)	12
Jat Farmer	7 (23)	6 (19)	18 (58)	31
Jhinvar Waterman	0	1 (50)	1 (50)	2
Lohar Blacksmith	0	0	1 (100)	1
Mahar Poter	0	0	1 (100)	1
Mali Gardener	0	1 (100)	0	1
Nai Barber	1 (33)	1 (33)	1 (33)	3
Total	41 (37)	28 (26)	41 (37)	110

*In this and subsequent tables, the figures in parentheses are row percentages.

If we consider families over a fairly long period of time, we note that often a family changes in type from nuclear to joint and back again. A young couple with their unmarried children form a nuclear family. Then their son marries and the family becomes joint. When one of the parents dies, the family becomes supplemented nuclear. The daughters then marry and go to their husbands' houses, the other parent dies, and the family is once again nuclear. Or, in another case, a couple has two married sons. Then the parents die. The family is still joint; but the death of the father is often the signal for brothers to separate into nuclear families. Thus, from the point of view of family structure, we may speak of a cyclical effect. There is no single cycle of family types through which all families pass but rather a number of possible cycles involving combinations of various kinds of joint and nuclear families.

While cycles of the formation and dissolution of joint families are general features of family life in Shanti Nagar, the amount of time that families spend in various stages of the cycles may vary according to a number of factors, such as urbanization, caste, and the other variables that we deal with in this essay. This situation can lead to different proportions of family types at a particular time among groups of families defined by any criterion, such as caste or differences in urbanization, for the probability of a family exhibiting a certain structure at the moment that it is observed depends upon the length of time that it maintains that structure. Thus, differences between groups of families as to proportions of various family types at a particular time can be viewed in historical perspective as reflecting to some extent differing lengths of time that families remain at one or another stage of a cycle.

A test of the relationship between urban experiences and family types can be made by comparing the types headed by urban-oriented men with those headed by village-oriented men. In a similar fashion, we can investigate the relationships of age, type of employment, type of house, education, caste, and landownership to family type. For purposes of comparison, we have calculated chi-square to test the null hypothesis that a set of observed frequencies differs no more from a set of expected frequencies than would be expected by chance. The expected frequencies are those calculated on the hypothesis that family type is independent of the foregoing variables. Thus, the calculations given in the tables test the null hypothesis of independence, that is, whether or not family type is independent of caste, landownership, type of house, and the age, type of employment, urban experience, and education of the family head. Such inferences are appropriately made from samples to larger populations. Our Shanti Nagar data include the entire population of Shanti Nagar. However, since the situation with regard to family types and the other variables constantly changes, we regard our data as a sample of conditions in Shanti Nagar over a period of, say, two decades beginning about 1950. Our Shanti Nagar data can also be regarded as a sample drawn from a population composed of similar villages of the Union Territory of Delhi.[3]

Table 2 compares the types of families headed by urban-oriented men with those headed by village-oriented men. Although joint families are slightly more frequent among families headed by village-oriented men, the differences in family type are not statistically significant. In this essay, we have adopted a level of significance of 0.05. Thus, the data presented in Table 2 show no evidence of a significant relationship between family type and the urban experience of the family head.[4]

TABLE 2
Families by Combined type and Urban Experience of Family Head*

Family Head	*Nuclear*	*Supplemented Nuclear*	*Joint*	*Total*
Village-oriented	16 (30)	15 (28)	22 (42)	53
Urban-oriented	22 (41)	13 (24)	19 (35)	54
Total	38 (36)	28 (26)	41 (38)	107

Chi-square, 1.30

Degrees of freedom, 2

Probability, $0.50<p<0.70$

*Three families headed by women whose urban experience is unknown have been omitted from this table.

The possibility that an urban effect might exist but be masked by other variables can be explored by investigating the relationship of urban experience and family type while holding other variables constant. Caste is one such variable. We have divided the castes of Shanti Nagar into two categories: high and low. The high castes are the Brahmin Priest, Jat Farmer, Bairagi Beggar, Baniya Merchant, Chhipi Dyer, Jhinvar Waterman, Lohar Blacksmith and

Mali Gardener. The low castes are the Mahar Potter, Gola Potter, Nai Barber, Chamar Leatherworker, and Chuhra Sweeper. This distinction rests on several considerations. First, it is based on village opinion, which ranks the castes classified here with a high degree of consensus (Freed 1963). Also, an examination of ritual interaction, that is, interaction that carries the potential for ritual pollution, reveals a sharp distinction between high and low castes. For example, the Jat Farmers, an undeniably high caste, will smoke the *hookah* with castes somewhat lower than they, the Lohar Blacksmith, Mali Gardener, and Jhinvar Waterman, but not with the Gola Potter, Mahar Potter, Nai Barber, Chamar Leatherworker or Chuhra Sweeper. It is noteworthy that Marriott (1968: 162, 164) makes a comparable high-low distinction in the caste hierarchy of Kishan Garhi, a village in western Uttar Pradesh with representatives of many of the castes found in Shanti Nagar.

All the castes of Kishan Garhi comparable to high castes of Shanti Nagar are also high; and the same is true of comparable low castes with the exception of the Barbers, who are low in Shanti Nagar but high in Kishan Garhi.

By dividing the families of Shanti Nagar into high and low-caste groups and comparing the families headed by urban-oriented men with those headed by village-oriented within each caste-group, one can investigate the relationship of urban influences and of family with caste position held relatively constant. Tables 3 and 4 present these comparisons.

TABLE 3
High Caste Families by Combined type and Urban Experience of Family Head*

Family Head	*Nuclear*	*Supplemented Nuclear*	*Joint*	*Total*
Village-oriented	8 (24)	9 (26)	17 (50)	34
Urban-oriented	8 (28)	8 (28)	13 (44)	29
Total	16 (25)	17 (27)	30 (48)	63

Chi-square, .20

Degrees of freedom, 2

Probability, 0.90<p<.95;

* One family headed by a woman whose urban experience is unknown has been omitted from this table.

TABLE 4
Low Caste Families by Combined type and Urban Experience of Family Head*

Family Head	*Nuclear*	*Supplemented Nuclear*	*Joint*	*Total*
Village-oriented	8 (42)	6 (32)	5 (26)	19
Urban-oriented	14 (56)	5 (20)	6 (24)	25
Total	22 (50)	11 (25)	11 (25)	44

Chi-square, 1.02

Degrees of freedom, 2

Probability, 0.50<p<0.70; when nuclear and supplemented nuclear are combined, 0.80<p<0.90

Two families headed by women whose urban experience is unknown have been omitted from this table.

Although the percentages of joint families in both tables are slightly higher for village-oriented men, there are no significant differences between families headed by urban-oriented and village-oriented men for either the high castes or the low.

Following a similar procedure, one can investigate the relationship of urban experience and family type while controlling to some extent the effects of landownership. Again, although there are slightly higher percentages of joint families among those headed by village-oriented men, the differences are not statistically significant. When the family types of landowning families are compared with regard to the urban experience of the family head, chi-square = 0.61 (0.70<p<0.80); the same comparison for landless families yields a chi-square of 0.56 (0.70<p<0.80).

If we consider only the families with illiterate family heads and compare their family types with regard to the urban experience of the family head, we find that chi-square = 1.77 (0.30<p<0.50). The same comparison for families with literate family heads yields a statistically significant difference at the 0.05 level: chi-square = 6.68 (0.02<p<0.05). This difference can be explored more fully by comparing families headed by village-oriented and urban-oriented men with both caste and literacy held constant. This has been done in Table 5.

TABLE 5
Families with Literate Family Heads by Combined Family Type, Caste, and Urban Experience of Family Head*

Family Head	*Nuclear*	*Supplemented Nuclear*	*Joint*	*Total*
High caste				
Village-oriented	3 (30)	0	7 (70)	10
Urban-oriented	4 (21)	8 (42)	7 (37)	19
Low caste				
Village-oriented	0	0	0	0
Urban-oriented	10 (77)	1 (8)	2 (15)	13
Total	17 (41)	9 (21)	16 (38)	42

* Families headed by individuals whose urban experience and/or literacy are unknown have been omitted from this table.

The most noteworthy features of this table are that all low-caste literate men are urban-oriented and only 15 per cent of them head joint families. Thus, the combination of low-caste status and literacy is correlated with a high proportion of nuclear families. The difference that we find in family type between families headed by literate urban-oriented men and literate village-oriented men, therefore, reflects caste differences as well as differences in urban experience among literate family heads.

In a study of another village in Delhi Union Territory, Yadav (1966: 27-28) presents data that show a relationship between family type and occupation, the occupational variables indicating whether the head of a household is following his traditional calling or is currently holding a non-traditional job that pays a cash income and provides him with relative economic independence. Yadava demonstrates that family heads following traditional occupations are much more likely to head joint families than those who hold non-traditional jobs paying a cash income; we have calculated the value of chi-square from Yadava's data, and the difference is highly significant ($p<0.001$). Although there are some dificulties in applying to the Shanti Nagar data the criterion of non-traditional jobs which pay a cash income and give a person considerable economic independence, we have classified the family heads of Shanti Nagar according to those who currently hold such jobs and those who follow traditional callings. We find a correlation between current employment and family type significant at the 0.05 level; family heads with traditional occupations are much more likely to head joint families than those with non-traditional jobs.

We believe, however, that this apparent relationship between type of current employment and family type is actually due to the age of a family head rather than to his type of employment. Men over 40 years of age are more likely to head joint families than the younger ones because a young man ordinarily will not have a son old enough to be married. The Shanti Nagar data with regard to age of family heads and family type are given in Table 6 where we note that the relationship is highly significant ($p < 0.001$). Since family heads less than 40 years of age are more likely to he employed for cash at non-traditional occupations than older men (Table 7), it is difficult to separate the effects of age from those of type of employment. The Shanti Nagar data most suitable for testing the relationship of type of employment and family type are the families headed by men younger than 40 years of age. When age is held relatively constant in this fashion, we found no difference in family type between families headed by men currently having non-traditional jobs paying cash and those whose heads follow traditional occupations (Table 8). Thus, the age of family heads does correlate with family type; but type of current employment and urbanization, as we have defined it, do not.

TABLE 6
Families by Combined type and Age of Family Head*

Family Head	*Nuclear*	*Supplemented Nuclear*	*Joint*	*Total*
39 years and younger	25 (61)	10 (24)	6 (15)	41
40 years and older	13 (20)	18 (27)	35 (53)	66
Total	38 (36)	28 (26)	41 (38)	107

Chi-square, 21.94

Degrees of freedom, 2

Probability, $p<0.001$

*Three families headed by women have been omitted from this table.

TABLE 7
Family Heads by Age and Occupation*

Family Head	*Non-Traditional Job, Cash Income*	*Traditional Job*	*Total*
39 years and younger	15 (37)	26 (63)	41
40 years and older	7 (11)	59 (89)	66
Total	22 (21)	85 (79)	107

Chi-square, 8.92

Degrees of freedom, 1

Probability, $0.001<p<0.01$

* The women who head families have been omitted from this table.

An examination of the residential arrangements of all the adult men of Shanti Nagar (family heads as well as adult men who do not head families) shows that there is no significant difference between village-oriented and urban-oriented men as regards, their combined family types. Breaking the group of adult men into smaller groups (high-caste, low-caste, literate, illiterate, landowning, and landless) and comparing urban and village-oriented within each of these groups shows no significant difference for any of them except for the illiterate men, where a significant difference exists at the 0.05 level;[5] therefore, five of six comparisons support the general conclusion that urban experience makes no difference in the combined family types of adult men.

TABLE 8
Families by Combined Type and Occupation of Family Head (20 to 39 Years of Age)

Family Head	*Nuclear*	*Supplemented Nuclear*	*Joint*	*Total*
Non-traditional job, cash income	9 (60)	4 (27)	2 (13)	15
Traditional	16 (62)	6 (23)	4 (15)	26
Total	25 (61)	10 (24)	6 (15)	41

Chi-square, 0.08

Degrees of freedom, 2

Probability, $0.95<p<0.98$

However, there is a significant difference at the 0.05 level with regard to the residential arrangements of urban and village-oriented adult men excluding family heads from the point of view of the urban experience of their family heads. Although urban-oriented men show only a slightly greater tendency (54 per cent) to live with urban-oriented family heads rather than with village-oriented family heads, village-oriented men have a rather strong tendency (74 per cent) to live with village-oriented family heads rather than with urban-oriented family heads (Table 9).

TABLE 9
Adult Men (Not Family Heads) by their own Urban Experience and the Urban Experience of their Family Heads

Family Men (Not Family Heads)	*Family Heads*		*Total*
	Urban-Oriented	*Village-Oriented*	
Urban-oriented	20 (54)	17 (46)	37
Village-oriented	9 (26)	25 (74)	34
Total	29 (41)	42 (59)	71

Chi-square, 4.50

Degrees of freedom, 1

Probability, $.02<p<0.05$

Other variables of possible significance in influencing family types are education, caste, and landownership. We find no correlation between education and family types. When the family types of literate and illiterate family heads are compared, chi-square=0.45 ($0.70<p<0.80$). This result depicts when family heads are broken down into smaller groups high-caste, low-caste, urban-oriented, village-oriented, landowning, and landless, and the comparison of family types by literate and illiterate family heads is made within each of these groups. Sen (1965: 10-11) also failed to find a relationship between education and family type.

The two variables that correlate with family type are caste and landownership (Tables 10 and 11). In both cases, the differences are significant at the 0.02 level. Joint families are more common among the high castes and the landowners; nuclear families predominate among the low castes and the landless. We can examine the data of Table 10 more closely by comparing family types of high and low castes within smaller groups—illiterate, literate, urban-oriented, and village-oriented family heads. The most noteworthy feature of this comparison is one that we have pointed out above, namely, that literate low-caste men are very likely to head nuclear families.

TABLE 10
Families by Combined type and High Low Caste

Caste	*Nuclear*	*Supplemented Nuclear*	*Joint*	*Total*
Low	24 (52)	11 (24)	11 (24)	46
High	17 (26)	17 (26)	30 (47)	64
Total	41 (37)	28 (26)	41 (37)	110

Chi-square, 8.57

Degrees of freedom, 2

Probability, $0.01<p<0.02$

TABLE 11
Families by Combined type and Ownership of Land

Landownership	*Nuclear*	*Supplemented Nuclear*	*Joint*	*Total*
Owns land	15 (25)	16 (27)	28 (48)	59
Landless	26 (51)	12 (24)	13 (25)	51
Total	41 (37)	28 (26)	41 (37)	110

Chi-square, 8.47

Degrees of freedom, 2

Probability, $0.01<p<0.02$

A similar analysis of the data given in Table 11 shows which literate landless men are very likely to head nuclear families (12 head nuclear families; 2, supplemented nuclear families and 2, joint families). Thus the data from Shanti Nagar lead us to the conclusions that family type is correlated with caste status and with landownership, and that literate low-caste or literate landless men are likely to head nuclear families. We note, however, that, in another village in Delhi Union Territory, Yadaya (1966: 24-25) presents data that show no significant correlation of landownership and family type; and Kolenda (1968: 384), after analysing data from five areas including the village of Rampur, Delhi studied by Oscar Lewis (1958), concludes that in general there does not appear to be a close relationship between family type and either landownership or caste rank.

It is impossible to separate the effects of caste from landownership in Shanti Nagar, for high-caste position is strongly correlated with the ownership of land, and low-caste position with being landless. Fifty-eight of 64 high-caste families own land; 45 of 46 low-caste families are landless. Thus, we cannot determine whether an apparent effect of caste is actually due to landownership or an appparent effect of landownership is actually due to caste.

We believe, however, that the effective variable is the ownership of land and not caste position. This conclusion seems reasonable to us because we can think of no reason why caste position *per se* should influence family type, but we can easily see a relationship between land, especially if a family cultivates the land itself, and family type. The separation of a joint family into its component nuclear families involves a division of property. As Mandelbaum notes (1968: 32-34) in an excellent general discussion of the breakup of joint families, the more property there is to divide, the more difficult the separation. Land is an inconvenient form of property to divide. A family's landholding is usually divided into a number of scattered plots. To divide each of these plots, as is usually done when a joint family separates, increases the labour and expense of cultivation; and to trade plots in order to achieve a significant degree of land consolidation involves difficult decisions for the individual farmer that he would prefer to avoid. Recent land reform legislation has effectively eliminated the possibility of a family's leasing its land and dividing the rent. The option of selling land and dividing the money does not really exist in Shanti Nagar and in most Indian villages. Land is too valuable: it is the best investment in rural India, for it is inflation-proof and land taxes are low; its ownership gives a man social standing that can be achieved in no other way; and the emotional implications of land to the Indian farmer are powerful. Thus, the ownership of land is the variable that seems to correlate significantly with family type. Landowning families, especially if they are also cultivators, are more likely to be joint than landless families because it is more difficult and takes longer to divide the property of a landowning family; and the greater resources of the joint family, especially the larger number of persons available for farm labour, make it a more efficient farming unit under the present conditions of village agriculture.

Sen (1965:8-10) has shown a relationship between land-related occupation, and family type. In the villages that he studied in West Bengal, owner-cultivators and sharecroppers had a higher proportion of joint families than people who followed other occupations. His data with regard to family type and caste lead him to the conclusion that those castes showing a higher proportion of joint families are the castes that are principally agriculturalists (Sen 1965:7-8). This support our interpretation of the Shanti Nagar data to the effect that the correlation of caste position and family type is really a correlation of landownership and family type. Both Sen (1965:11) and Bose (1966:168, 172) show that the proportion of joint families increases directly with the size of landholdings. The larger a family's landholding, the more likely the family will be joint. Our own data support this (Table 12).

TABLE 12

Landowning Families by Combined type and Size of Landholding

*Landowning (Acres)**	*Nuclear*	*Supplemented Nuclear*	*Joint*	*Total*
Less than 4.25	9 (45)	6 (30)	5 (25)	20
4.50-21	2 (9)	8 (36)	12 (55)	22
21.25-74	4 (23)	2 (12)	11 (65)	17
Total	15 (25)	16 (27)	28 (48)	59

* These intervals were selected so that they all would contain approximately the same number of families. They were originally expressed in the bigha, the Indian measure of land, and their conversion into acres accounts for the use of fractional parts of acres to separate intervals.

Type of house, whether it is made of mud or brick, appears to be related to type of family, although the correlation does not quite attain the 0.05 level (chi-square = 5.44, $0.05<p<0.10$). Families living in brick houses are more likely to be joint than those living in mud houses. However, we believe that this apparent relationship is primarily due to the fact that landowners are more likely to live in brick houses than landless families. Thus, the relationship of type of house to family type principally reflects the correlation between landownership and family type. When the families of Shanti Nagar are divided into landowning and landless families and the comparison of family types by house type is made within these two groups, the correlations fall far short of statistical significant.

Summary

With regard to the data from Shanti Nagar, there is no significant difference in family types between families headed by city-oriented men and those headed by village-oriented men. This result holds when caste, landownership, and literacy are held relatively constant. Type of family is correlated with the age of the family head: older men more likely to head joint families. Both the ownership of land and high and low-caste status correlate with family type. High-caste and landowning families are more likely to be joint than low-caste and landless ones. Our data do not permit us to analyse these variables separately, for most high caste families own land and all low-caste families but one are landless. We believe, however, that the effective factor is landownership and not caste position, for the inconvenience of dividing land, and a probable reduction in farming efficiency resulting thereby, clearly tend to keep families together; but there is nothing about caste position, other than the ownership of land that would seem to do so. Although we cannot demonstrate it with the Shanti Nagar data because almost all landowners are cultivators and only few landless persons are tenant-cultivators, we suggest that the correlation of landownership and family type may be strongest when landowners are also cultivators and that the family types of landless tenant-cultivators may resemble more closely those of landowning cultivators than those of landless people who are not cultivators. The Shanti Nagar data also indicate that literate landless (or literate low-caste) family heads are very likely to head nuclear families. Literacy, type of house, and type of current employment do not appear to be related to family type.

The foregoing conclusions should he viewed with some caution. The essential difference between urban-oriented and village-oriented men in Shanti Nagar is an average of 7.8 years of urban employment and/or residence. We found no correlation of family type and urban experience in Shanti Nagar; but a comparison in which the contrast between urban and non-urban is stronger than in Shanti Nagar could well show a correlation. Our finding that literate landless or literate low-caste men usually head nuclear families is based on relatively few cases. All of these problems are open to further investigation with larger samples and in a variety of rural and urban settings.

NOTES

1. We thank the Social Science Research Council and the National Science Foundation for the post-doctoral fellowships that supported our field research in India from 1957 to 1959; Mrs. Diana Kollmar of Hunter College of the City University of New York, who assisted us while supported by the Hunter College Work-Study Program financed jointly by Hunter College and The American Museum of Natural History; and Dr. Pauline M. Kolenda, University of Houston, and Dr. Joan P. Mencher, Herbert H. Lehman College of the City University of New York for reading and criticizing the manuscript.
2. We have no educational data for 13 adult men.
3. The chi-square test yields inexact probabilities when expected frequencies fall below 5 in 20 percent of the cells of a table or when an expected frequency is less than one. Such is the case in 2 of the tables, one of which can be brought closer to these guidelines by combining categories. We have reported which categories we have combined and the resultant value of chi-square at the bottom of this table (Table 4).
4. Sen (1965:13-14) investigated the relationship of family types to the "outside contacts" of the heads of families. Although Sen's category of outside contacts includes visits to cities, it is only very slightly comparable to our "urban experiences." Nonetheless, it is of some interest that Sen found no apparent relationship between outside contacts and family type.
5. Illiterate urban-oriented men have a higher proportion of both joint and nuclear families than do illiterate village-oriented men, the latter showing a much higher proportion of supplemented nuclear families. We can think of no satisfactory explanation for this other than that it is due to tolerance.

REFERENCES

Bose, A.B.: 1966: Rural Family Organisation in Western Rajasthan. *The Eastern Anthropologist* 19, pp. 163-75.

Freed, Stanley A.: 1963: An Objective Method for Determining the Collective Caste Hierarchy of an Indian Village. *American Anthropologist* 65, pp. 879-91.

Goode, William J.: 1963: *World Revolution and Family Patterns*. New York: The Free Press.

Gould, Harold A.: 1968: "Time-Dimension and Structural Change in an Indian Kinship System: A Problem of Conceptual Refinement," in *Structure and Change in Indian Society* (ed.by Milton Singer and Bemard S. Cohen), pp. 413-21. Viking Fund Publications in Anthropology, no. 47.

Kolenda, Pauline M.: 1968: "Region, Caste, and Family Structure: A Comparative Study of the Indian 'Joint' Family, in *Structure and Change in Indian Society* (ed. by Milton Singer and Bernard S. Cohen), pp. 339-96. Viking Publications in Anthropology, no. 47.

Lewis Oscar: 1958: *Village Life in Northern India*. Urbana: University of Illinois Press.

Mandelbaum, David G.: 1968: "Family, *Jati*, Village," in *Structure and Change in Indian Society* (ed. by Milton Singer and Bernard S. Cohen), pp. 29-50. Viking Publications in Anthropology, no. 47.

Marriott, McKim: 1968: "Caste Ranking and Food Transactions: A Matrix Analysis" in *Structure, and Change in Indian Society* (ed. by Milton Singer and Bernard S. Cohen), pp. 133-71. Viking Fund Publications in Anthropology, no. 47.

Sen, Lalit Kumar: 1965: "Family in Four Indian Villages". *Man in India* 45, pp. 1-16.

Singer, Milton: 1968: "The Indian Joint Family in Modern Industry", in *Structure and Change in Indian Society* (ed. by Milton Singer and Bernard S. Cohen), pp. 423-52. Viking Fund Publications in Anthropology, no. 47.

Yadava, Jaswant Singh: 1966: "Changing Family Structure in a Delhi Village.*The Anthropologist* 13, pp. 21-29.

14

Family Structure in Village Lonikand, India: 1819, 1958 and 1967*

Pauline Mahar Kolenda

In this essay, I compare statistics on family structure collected in 1819, 1958, and 1967 for the village of Lonikand, Haveli Taluka, Poona District, Maharashtra. The 1819 figures reported by Surgeon Thomas Coats represent a rare find (Coats 1823), brought to the attention of our generation by G.S.Ghurye in his book, *After a Century and a Quarter* (Ghurye 1960). It is the rareness, almost non-existence, of such data that has made it impossible to make statements with real certainty about the decline that is claimed for the "joint" family in India.

Various sociologists and anthropologists (Weber 1950; Parsons 1943, 1949, 1961; Wirth 1938; Ogburn and Nimkoff 1950; Burgess and Locke 1953; Linton 1952; Williams 1950; Goode 1963) have argued that the family type functionally consistent with a modern, urban industrial economy is the nuclear family, that composed of a couple and their unmarried children. As an economy is modernized, extended or "joint" families, if present, may be expected to break into their component nuclear units. Such hypotheses have stimulated discussion and research on family structure in various societies of the world (Nimkoff and Middleton 1960) including Japan (Johnson 1964), England (Young and

Wilmott 1957), China (Levy 1949), Barbados (Greenfield 1961), and India (Ross 1961; Desai 1964; Kapoor 1965; Orenstein and Micklin 1966; Orenstein 1961; Morrison 1959; Gore 1961; Sarma 1964; Shahani 1961). Earlier research in the United States (Litwak 1960a, 1960b; Streib 1958; Arensberg 1955, 1960; Sussman 1963) has developed to culminate in a series of works generally rejecting the model of the typical American family as an "isolated" nuclear one. (See the papers by Sussman, Belnkner, Kerckhoff, Litwak, Back, and Rosow, as well as the editors' introduction in Shanas and Streib 1965).

As William Goode (1963-4:1) has pointed out, studies of change in family structure are stymied by the paucity of historical data on family structure. It is hard to say how much the modern industrial economy has changed family structure in the United States, for example, since exact baseline data on family types prevalent before industrialization are lacking. Conrad Arensberg has even suggested that the small nuclear family presently prevalent in the United States is to be explained as a descendant of "the Anglo-Saxon, post-medieval, and Puritan small-family way" (1960: 72), rather than as a change from a large extended family type, in response to the demands of modern industrial conditions.

In India, it has been at least since the decennial censuses made by British officials in the latter quarter of the nineteenth century that observations of the "breakdown" of the Indian "joint" family have been avowed. There is little exact statistical data to support such claims, especially since the censuses up to 1961 did not report family structure, but only family size, and it remains unclear what the formula for the relationship between size and structure should be. Thus, a "joint" family may consist of as few as four person-parents with one married son and his wife, while a nuclear family may have from two up to ten or even more members depending upon the number of unmarried children present. Orenstein (1961) has summarized statistics on family size, the number of persons per household, from the Censuses of India from 1911 to 1951. He states that "contrary to expectation, there is no sign of a decrease in household size in the period 1911 to 1951. Data for earlier years are sporadic, but a review of them offers little that may contradict this" (Orenstein 1961: 346).

In recent anthropological reports, there are well-argued retrojections of earlier family structure in particular local caste groups or villages in India. John Hitchcock was able to make a retrospective estimate of family structure in 1901 for a section of a village *jati* of Rajputs (Hitchcock 1956:155) in western Uttar Pradesh. F.G. Bailey has logically reasoned that the Oriyas of Bisipara village in Phulbani district, Orissa, must have shifted from joint family living to nuclear family living over the past century as a market cash economy and modern salaried occupations became established in their way of life (Bailey 1957). S.T. Epstein has traced changes in family structure related to the shift from an agrarian subsistence economy to a cash economy (Epstein: 307). Changes in family law or legal practices relating to joint property are reported to have led to a breakdown in joint families among Naiars of Malabar (Mencher 1962:236-37; Gough 1952: 79, 81) and among villagers of Namhalli village, Mysore (Beals 1955: 86-87, 91-92). But in none of these studies are the substantiating statistics available for the earlier time periods with which the current period is compared.

Elsewhere (Kolenda 1968), I have presented a baseline of data on the structure of Indian families in various parts of India, data gathered by sociologists and anthropologists between 1949 and 1961. That comparison of twenty-six studies revealed marked regional differences in the prevalence of various types of family; I have also explored the cultural reasons for these regional differences (Kolenda 1967). While the baseline data of our earlier decade may be useful to investigators of the future, the statistical data necessary for measuring change in a longer-range period are lacking. Clearly, the identification of variables and specifications of hypotheses relevant to variations in family structure are more advanced than the accumulation of factual evidence that might test the hypotheses. Given this state of affairs, Surgeon Coats' competent 1819 report for a Poona village has a unique significance.

Lonikand, twelve miles north-east of the city of Pune, was described by Thomas Coats a year after the British had taken over the area from the Marathas' Peshwa. It was restudied by Ghurye's students – L. N. Chapekar in 1954, and M.G. Kulkarni in 1958. The latter took a twenty per cent sample of the families of Lonikand upon which Ghurye reported in his book, *After a Century and a Quarter*. The sample was, however, not a random representative one as Kulkarni himself has pointed out (Kulkarni 1960: 12). It was with Dr. Kulkarni's introduction to the village leaders who also helped me greatly, that I resurveyed Lonikand in January 1967, taking a full census.

In the remainder of this essay, I shall present the family types for Lonikand in the three time periods. The composition of various family types used in the comparisons appear as follows in Chart I.

Chart I
Composition of Family Types Used in Comparisions

1. Single-person household.
2. *Sub-nuclear family:* a fragment of a formerly complete nuclear family such as a widow with her unmarried children, or two unmarried, siblings living together.
3. *Supplemented subnuclear family:* a sub-nuclear family plus some unmarried, widowed or divorced relative(s) not part of the nuclear family. For example, a widow with her unmarried children plus her widowed mother-in-law.
4. *Nuclear family:* parents and their unmarried children.
5. *Supplemented nuclear family:* a nuclear family plus some unmarried widowed or divorced relative. For example: parents and unmarried children, plus the father's unmarried brother or widowed mother.
6. *Lineal joint family:* parents with their unmarried children plus a married son with his wife and unmarried children.
7. *Supplemented lineal joint family:* a lineal joint family plus some unmarried, widowed or divorced relative who is not a part of either of the component nuclear families such as older man's unmarried brother or widowed sister.
8. *Collateral joint family:* two or more married brothers, their wives and unmarried children.
9. *Supplemented collateral joint family:* two married brothers, their wives and unmarried children, plus some other unmarried, widowed or divorced relative not a part of either of the component nuclear families such as the brothers' widowed mother.
10. *Lineal-collateral joint family:* married brothers, their wives, and unmarried children, plus both parents and any of the Latters' unmarried children.
11. *Supplemented lineal-collateral joint family:* a lineal-collateral joint family supplemented by some unmarried, widowed, or divorced relative not a member of the component nuclear families.
12. *Polygynous:* a man with two wives plus unmarried children. (Other polygynous types may be devised such as supplemented polygynous–in which some other unmarried, widowed, or divorced relative resides with the polygynous

family, or sub-polygynous – in which the two wives both widowed live with their unmarried children).

13. *Other:* any household that cannot be categorized in the types above such as a grandmother living with her grandson, or a father-in-law living with his widowed daughter-in-law.

In July, 1819, Coats reported:

The number of houses is 107, in a few of which are more than one family; and the proportion of persons to each house is rather more than five. There are 130 married men, 11 or 12 of whom have two wives; and the total number of children is 203, which gives only one and a half to each family, which seems a small proportion (Coats 1823: 194).

The population of the village included 175 adult males, 187 adult females, 105 male children and 98 female children. (*Ibid*). There were residing in Lonikand 16 different castes, as well as 17 "Mohamedans". 11 "hired servants," and 18 "slaves". The caste and religion of the latter two categories were not identified. The hired servants came from outside the village since they were married men, seemingly unaccompanied by their wives or children, residing in Lonikand only temporarily (Coats: 239). The slaves, though perhaps descendants of captives of war, had all been born in the village itself (Coats: 240). Two Marwari shopkeepers, though married, lived alone, because, as Coats says: "Their women were sent away when the war with the Peshwa broke out and have not yet returned" (Coats: 236).

From Coats' data, it is possible to make estimates of the maximum number of joint families and supplemented nuclear families and the minimum number of nuclear families present in 1819. Coats' own table is reproduced as Table 1. In Table 2, the maximum numbers of joint families represent the number present if each were composed of only two nuclear families, either lineally or collaterally related. I have distributed the unmarried adult males and females, as well as the married male hired servants and the one slave whose wives and children were elsewhere, among the otherwise nuclear families. These, then, become supplemented nuclear families.

TABLE 1
Enumeration of the inhabitants of the township of Lony by Surgeon Coats–July 1819 (taken from Coats 1823: 194 with Corrections*)

	Houses	*No. of Families*	*Males*	*Females*	*Male Children*	*Female Children*	*Total Population*
Tulkarrees, or hereditary cultivators, including the Patails	47	50	55	73	51	38	217
Ooprees, or persons cultivating on lease	26	34	54	56	27	25	162
Brahmins, including the hereditary Accountant and Priest	3	3	6	5	3	7	21
12 Hereditary Servants of the Township							
Carpenter (Sutar)	1	1	1	1	2	—	4
Ironsmith (Lohar) non-resident	—	—	—	—	—	—	—
Washerman (Pareet)	1	1	1	2	—	—	3
Barber (Navee)	1	1	1	2	—	—	3
Potter (Koombar)	1	1	1	1	2	2	6
Silversmith and Treasurer (Sonar Potedar)	1	1	1	1	1	1	4
Dresser of Idols (Goorow)	1	1	1	1	1	1	4
Water-carrier (Kolee) lives in the house of a cultivator	—	1	1	1	2	—	4
Shoemaker and worker in leather (Chamar)	1	2	3	3	—	—	6
Ropemaker (Mang) non-resident	—	—	—	—	—	—	—
Watchman (Mhar)	13	13	16	16	9	7	48
Mahomedan Sacrificer	1	1	1	1	—	1	3
Jain Shopkeepers (Wanee)	2	3	4	8	2	7	21
Marwarree	1	2	2	—	—	—	2
Police Servants (Ramoossees)	3	3	4	3	1	3	11
Mahomedans	3	4	4	6	4	3	17
Hired Servants	—	—	11	—	—	—	11
Slaves	1	8	8	7	—	3	18
	107	130	175	187	105	98	565

* There were four mistakes of addition in Coats' table as published, plus the misplacement of the 11 hired servants under the female column rather than the

male column. Coats states clearly (Coats: 239) that the hired servants were male. I have taken the liberty of correcting these errors in the above table.

Coats said that of the eleven hired male servants: "The Brahmin employ two to cultivate their freeholds, and the rest are employed as labourers by the husbandmen ... They live under the same roof with their master, and their fare and clothing scarccely differ from his..." (Coats: 239).

I have accordingly assigned two of the hired men to Brahmin families and the rest to the Tulkarrees, the landed group among the Koonbee caste. (The tenant group among the Koonbees are called Ooprees.)

Except for one family of slaves which has its own house, the slaves also "are inmates with their masters; their treatment is very good; they are clad and fed in the same way as the members of the family, scarcely any difference being observable, except taking their meals apart" (Coats: 240).

Coats said that there were eleven or twelve polygynous families and that polygyny tended to be practiced by the rich (Coats: 212). I have assumed that there were twelve such families, and I have assigned six of the co-wives to the figures for married women among the Koonbee Tulkarrees and six to the Koonbee Ooprees.

Coats seems to have defined a family as a unit headed by a married man who was a native to the village, whose wife and children were or were not present in the village at the time of Coats' census. Thus, among the 130 married men, Coats spoke of the two Marwarree shopkeepers whose wives were sent away, as well as one slave man whose wife was not present. This I infer from the fact that there were 8 slave families, 8 adult males, but only 7 adult females present. The eleven hired men, all of whom were married, were not listed in the total of married men, presumably because they were not natives of Lonikand, but were residents only temporarily while they worked as servants.

While Coats focused more upon the married man in defining the family, I have taken the residential group or Coats' "house" to calculate the maximum numbers of joint and supplemented nuclear families and the minimum number of nuclear families that could have been present in Lonikand in 1819.

When one subtracts from Coats' figures for adult men and adult women the numbers of married men and married women, one is left with a pair of remainders of 34 unmarried males and 48 unmarried females. It seems unlikely to me that none of those unmarried adults lived in a house alone, so I also calculated the maximum number of joint and supplemented nuclear families, and the minimum number of nuclear families that would have been present if one-third of these unmarried men and women lived alone. Unfortunately, Coats did not say how he defined children as distinct from adults, so we do not know whether these 82 unmarried persons are largely older, still unmarried, adolescents, or whether they are largely widows and widowers. In 1967, of the eighty-eight widows living in Lonikand, only ten or eleven per cent lived alone. There were also fourteen widowers, only one of whom lived alone. An assumption that one-third of the unmarried adults lived alone in 1819 would, in comparison, seem to be amply high. The estimates of family types, given the condition that one-third of the unmarried adults lived alone, appear in Table 3.

In Table 4 appear the distributions of family types for Lonikand in 1819 under the two sets of conditions—when all unmarried adults live with a married couple, and when one-third of the unmarried adults lived alone.

In 1958, the population of Lonikand was 1404, about 250 per cent of the 1819 population of 565. Three hundred and six families lived in 247 houses. There were 403 adult males, 389 adult females, 550 children below the age of twelve, and 62 persons over 60 years old (Ghurye 1960: 14). M.G. Kulkarni collected information on a sample of 50 families which included 476 persons. Both a summary table (Ghurye: 80) and a descriptive chapter (Ghurye: 82-106) treat the composition of these 50 families. From these, I developed Table 5.

It was evident from the unusually large average size of the family in the 1958 sample—9.2 persons as compared to the average size for all families of 6.4 persons—that the sample over-represented large-sized families. The figures from the census made in 1967 suggests that it overrepresented joint families and under-represented single-person households. Since the 1958

TABLE 2

Estimates of the Maximum numbers of joint and supplemented nuclear famillies and the minimum number of nuclear families present in lonikand in 1819 (it is assumed that all unmarried adult males and females lived with at least one married couple

Caste	Hou-ses	Fami-lies	Md. Ms.	Md. Fs.	Unmd. Ms.	Unmd. Ps.	Servants Md. Ms.	Servants Md. Fs.	*** Sgl. Ms.	Max. Supp. Jt.	Max. Jt.	Max. Nuc.	Mn. Nuc. ***	Others
Koonbee-Tulkarrees	47	50	50	46	5	17	7	7	10	0	10	32	5	0
Koonbee-Ooprees	26	34	34	40	20	16	0	0	0	0*	8	18	0	0
Brahmans	3	3	3	3	3	2	0	0	2	0	0	3	0	0
Sutars	1	1	1	1	0	0	0	0	0	0	0	0	1	0
Pareets	1	1	1	1	0	1	0	0	0	0	0	1	0	0
Navees	1	1	1	1	0	1	0	0	0	0	0	1	0	0
Koombar	1	1	1	1	0	0	0	0	0	0	0	0	1	0
Sonar-Potedar	1	1	1	1	0	0	0	0	0	0	0	0	0	0
Goorow	1	1	1	1	0	0	0	0	0	0	0	0	1	0
Chamar	1	2	2	2	1	1	0	0	0	1	0	0	0	0
Mhars	13	13	13	13	3	3	0	0	0	0	0	6	7	0
Mulana	1	1	1	1	0	0	0	0	0	0	0	0	1	0
Wanees	2	3	3	3	1	5	0	0	0	1	0	1	0	0

Caste	Hou-ses	Fami-lies	Md. Ms.	Md. Fs.	Unmd. Ms.	Unmd. Ps.	Servants Md. Ms.	Servants Md. Fs.	*** Sgl. Ms.	Max. Supp. Jt.	Max. Jt.	Max. Nuc.	Mn. Nuc. ***	Others
Marwarrees	1	2	2	0	0	0	0	0	0	0	0	0	0	1
Ramoossees	3	3	3	3	1	0	0	0	0	0	0	1	2	0
Mahomedans	3	4	4	4	0	2	0	0	0	0	1	2	0	0
Slaves*	1	1	1	1	0	0	0	0	0	0	0	0	1	0
	107	129**	122	132	34	48	7	7	12	2	19	65	20	1

* Coats (Coats: 240) says that all the slaves except for one family which has its own house live with their masters. Six women and seven men are thus listed as servants in the households of Tulkarrees. See the first row of figures in the foregoing.

** This total includes the 7 married men and married women listed under the servant columns, six slave couples and one Kolee (watercarrier) couple, as well as the families of the two Marwarree shopkeepers whose wives and children were, in fact, absent.

*** Coats said that 11 or 12 men had two wives and that polygyny tended to be practised by the rich. Thus, six families among the Tulkarrees and six families among the Ooprees have been counted as polygynous.

**** These "single men" seem to have been married men, but the wives and children of the 11 hired men were in their home villages elsewhere, and the wife of one slave man was absent. The latter married man, however, was counted by Coats, in his total of 130 married men in the village.

TABLE 3

Estimates of the Maximum numbers of joint and supplemented nuclear famillies and the minimum number of nuclear families in lonikand in 1819 (it is asumed that about one-third of the unmarried adult males and females lived alone)

Caste	*Hou-ses*	*Fami-lies*	*Md. Ms.*	*Md. Fs.*	*Unmd. Ms.*	*Unmd. Ps. Fs.*	*Servants Md. Ms.*	*Servants Md. Fs.*	*Servants Sgl. Ms.* ****	*Max. Supp. Jt.*	*Max. Jt.*	*Max. Supp Nuc.*	*Max. Nuc.*	*Single Person*	*Others* ***
Koonbee-Tulkarrees	47	50	50	56	5	17	7	7	10	0	10	25	5	7	0
Koonbee-Ooprees	26	34	34	40	20	16	0	0	0	14	0	0	0	12	0
Brahmins	3	3	3	3	3	2	0	0	2	0	1	1	0	1	0
Sutars	1	1	1	1	0	0	0	0	0	0	0	0	1	0	0
Pareets	1	1	1	1	0	1	0	0	0	0	0	1	0	0	0
Navees	1	1	1	1	0	1	0	0	0	0	0	1	0	0	0
Koombar	1	1	1	1	0	0	0	0	0	0	0	0	1	0	0
Sonar-Potedar	1	1	1	1	0	0	0	0	0	0	0	0	1	0	0
Goorow	1	1	1	1	0	0	0	0	0	0	0	0	1	0	0
Chamar	1	2	2	2	1	1	0	0	0	1	0	0	0	0	0
Mhars	13	13	13	13	3	3	0	0	0	0	2	4	5	2	0
Mulana	1	1	1	1	0	0	0	0	0	0	0	0	1	0	0

Caste	*Hou-ses*	*Fami-lies*	*Md. Ms.*	*Md. Fs.*	*Unmd. Ms.*	*Unmd. Ps. Fs.*	*Servants Md. Ms.*	*Md. Fs.*	*Sgl. Ms.* ****	*Max. Supp. Jt.*	*Max. Jt.*	*Max. Supp Nuc.*	*Max. Nuc.*	*Single Person*	*Others* ***
Wanees	2	3	3	3	1	5	0	0	0	1	0	0	0	1	0
Marwarrees	1	2	2	0	0	0	0	0	0	0	0	0	0	0	1
Ramoossees	3	3	3	3	1	0	0	0	0	0	0	1	2	0	0
Mahomedans	3	4	4	4	0	2	0	0	0	1	1	0	0	1	0
Slaves*	1	1	1	1	0	0	0	0	0	0	0	0	1	0	0
	107	129**	122	132	34	48	7	7	12	17	14	33	18	24	1

* Coats (Coats: 240) says that all the slaves except for one family which has its own house live with their masters. Six women and seven men are thus listed as servants in the households of Koonbee-Tulkarrees. See the first row of figures above.

** This total includes the seven families of married men and married women listed under the servant columns, 6 slave couples and one Kolee (watercarrier) couple, as well as the two Marwarree shopkeepers whose wives and children were, in fact, were absent.

*** Coats said that eleven or twelve men had two wives and that polygyny tended to be practised by the rich. Thus, six families among the Tulkarrees and six families among the Ooprees have been counted as polygynous.

**** These single men seem to have been married men, but the wives and children of the eleven hired men were in their home villages elsewhere, while the wife of one slave man was absent. Coats, however , counted the latter married man in his total of 130 men in Lonikand.

sample seems clearly to be biased in the direction of over-representing large families and probably also joint families, we cannot place any confidence in representatives of the 1958 results.

TABLE 4

Maximum proportions of joint and supplemented nuclear families and minimum proportion of nuclear families in Lonikand in 1819 under two sets of assumptions

	1819 A		*1819 B*	
	Per cent		*Per cent*	
Supplemented joint family—supplemented with relatives	2	2	17	16
Joint (couples are relatives)	12	11	7	6.5
Joint (couples are master and servants)	7	6.5	7	6.5
Supplemented Nuclear-supplemented with relatives	53	49.5	22	20.5
Supplemented Nuclear-supplemented with servants	10	9	10	9
Supplemented Nuclear-supplemented with both relatives and servants	2	2	1	1
Minimum: Nuclear	20	19	18	17
Single person households	0	0	24	22.5
Other	1	1	1	1
	107	100	107	100

A–Assuming that all unmarried adults live with a married couple.

B–Assuming that one-third of these unmarried adults live alone.

	Summary of above Distributions *1819 A*		*1819 B*	
	Per cent		*Per cent*	
Joint Families	21	19.5	31	29
Supplemented Nuclear	65	60.5	33	30.5
Nuclear	20	19	18	17
Single person household	0	0	24	22.5
Other	1	1	1	1
	107	100 (per cent)	107	100 (per cent)

TABLE 5
Distribution of Family Types in a 20 per cent sample taken from Lonikand in 1958

Family Types	*Families*	*Per cent*		*Persons included*	*Per cent*	
Lineal Joint	6	12		45	9	
Supplemented lineal	2	4		22	5	
Collateral	2	4		25	5	
			50 %			67%
Supplemented Collateral	4	8		54	11	
Lineal-Collateral	7	14		95	20	
Supplemented lineal-Collateral	4	8		83	17	
Supplement nuclear	10	20		76	16	
Nuclear	12	24		68	14	
Subnuclear	2	4		4	1	
Other	1	2		4	2	
	50	100 %		476	100 %	

A comparison of Table 4 with Table 5 suggests that there were clearly more joint families in 1958 than in 1819 – 19.5 per cent or 29 per cent in 819 versus 50 per cent in 1958, but more supplemented nuclear families in 1819 than in 1958 – 60.5 per cent or 30.5 per cent in 1819 *versus* 20 per cent in 1958. It should be remembered that my estimates of family types in 1819 represented the most joint and supplemented nuclear families that could be present and the fewest nuclear families that could be present, so that we would expect that there were, in fact, more nuclear families and fewer joint families than estimated.

In Table 6 appears the distribution of family types for the entire population of Lonikand in January 1967.

Comparison of Table 6 and Table 4 suggests that in 1967 there was as large a proportion of joint families – 29 per cent – as there was in 1819 – calculated to be between 29 per cent and 19.5 per cent – or possibly even a lesser proportion of joint families at that time. There appear to have been a higher proportion of supplemented nuclear families in 1819, and a lower proportion of nuclear families than in 1967.

There are various types of non-comparability between the two sets of data. First of all, the figures for 1819 are only estimates, but they do represent estimates of the highest proportion of joint and supplemented families that could have been present, given the assumptions I have made. Thus, if in 1967 there appears to be as high a proportion of joint families, this evidence would support an argument that there has been no decrease in the proportions of joint families.

Secondly, the citizens of Lonikand in 1967 are not all descendants of those living in Lonikand in 1819. Of the fifty families in Kulkarni's sample, 28 claimed to have always resided in the village, while 22 had come between 25 and 90 years ago (Ghurye: 190). Ten of the 21 immigrant families claimed to have come from nearby villages and talukas (Ghurye: 71). Ghurye estimated that "not less than 40 per cent of the present population of Lonikand is the descendants of the immigrants who migrated to Lonikand 30 to 40 years after Coats' time" (Ghurye: 109-110).

One of the major differences in the composition of the population would appear to be the displacement of the Kunbis by Marathas and Malis. However, it seems likely, that the Kunbis changed their caste identification from Kunbi to Maratha. Irawati Karve has reported that Kunbis of western Maharashtra have changed their name to Maratha and raised their caste rank (1965: 175). Ghurye himself quoted a District Gazetter of Poona published in 1885 in which the author said it is difficult to draw a line between Kunbis and Marathas (Ghurye: 110). But, perhaps even more convincing evidence that the Marathas presently living in Lonikand are descendants, direct or distant, from the Tulkarrees of 1819 in the fact that some have the same surnames. Thus, Coats says: "Thirty-five of the Tulkarree families are branches of the Patail families of Scinde and Kund" (Coats: 240).

In Lonikand today, 17 families have the surname of Shinde, while 76 families have the surname, Kand.

Coats also lists some other surnames: "Jaddow, Gykwar, Powar, Cuddum, Kattee, Sandajee, Seetolee, Muggur, etc." (Coats: 216).

TABLE 6
Distribution of Family types in Lonikand in 1967

Family Types	*Families*			*Persons included*		
		Per cent			*Per cent*	
Lineal Joint	37	14	29%	284	16.4	45.6%
Supplemented lineal Joint	11	4		109	6.2	
Collateral Joint	6	2		57	3.3	
Supplemented Collateral	14	5		181	10.5	
Lineal-Collateral Joint	7	3		101	5.85	
Supplemented Lineal-Collateral	3	1		58	3.35	
Supplemented Polygynous	3	1		24	1.44	
Supplement Nuclear	53	20		327	19.00	
Nuclear	89	35		489	28.00	
Supplemented Sub-nuclear	5	2		28	1.6	
Sub-Nuclear	16	6		55	3.2	
Single person	16	6		16	.93	
Other	2	1		4	.23	
	262	100%		1733	100%	

Three of these eight surnames are presently represented in Lonikand: Yadav, Gaikwad, and Magar. Yadavs are all Marathas, but Gikwads appear both among the Marathas and among the Mahars (Coats: "Mhars"), and Magar appears both among the Marathas and among the Nhaviz (barbers; Coats' 'Navees'). Since it seems more likely that these citizens with the same surnames as some of Lonikand's denizens of 1819 are descendants of the latter and hence that they are more comparable with them, let us examine family types among Kands, Shindes, Magars, Gaikwads, and Yadavs. Table 7 presents these surname groups' family types as we found them in 1967.

In Table 8, we compare these groups with common surnames with the figures on joint family for the whole population of Lonikand.

We find that for all with the old surnames, 119 families and 815 persons, a somewhat higher proportion of the families, 32.3 per cent, are joint in structure as compared to the total population of Lonikand, 29 per cent of the families of which are joint in

TABLE 7
Distribution of Family types among Kands, Shindes, Yadavs, Gaikwads and Magars in Lonikand in 1967

Family Types	Shindes (Marathas,				Kands (Marathas)				Yadavs, Gaikwads, Magars				Gaikwads (Mahars)				Magars (Nhavis)				Totals			
	Families	Per cent	Persons	Per Cent	Families	Per cent	Persons	Per cent	Families	Per cent	Persons	Per cent	Families	Per cent	Persons	Per cent	Families	Per cent	Persons	Per cent	Families	Per cent	Persons	Per cent
Lineal Joint	1	6	8	6	11	15	85	16	3	25	30	39	2	25	14	33	—	—	—	—	17	14	137	16.8
Supplemented Lineal	—	—	—	—	5	6.5	48	9	—	—	—	—	—	—	—	—	—	—	—	—	5	4.6	—	—
Collateral	1	6	8	6	1	1	7	1	1	8	8	10.5	—	—	—	—	—	—	—	—	3	2.5	—	—
Supplemented Collateral	2	12	25	18	4	5.5	55	10	1	8	8	10.5	—	—	—	—	—	—	—	—	7	6	88	10.8
Lineal-Collateral	1	5	20	15	4	5.5	46	9	—	—	—	—	—	—	—	—	—	—	—	—	5	4	66	8.1
Supplemented Lineal-Colla-teral	—	—	—	—	1	1	19	3.5	—	—	—	—	—	—	—	—	—	—	—	—	1	1.2	19	2.3
Supplemented Polygynous	—	—	—	—	1	1	6	1	—	—	—	—	1	12.7	7	16	—	—	—	2	2	1.7	13	1.6
Supplemented nuclear	4	23	27	19	17	22	105	20	2	17	10	13	2	25	10	23	1	16.5	3	11.5	26	22	155	19
Nuclear	7	42	44	32	20	26	119	22	5	42	21	21	1	12.5	3	7	4	67	20	77	37	31	207	25.5
Supplemented Sub-Nuclear	—	—	—	—	4	5.5	25	5	—	—	—	—	—	—	—	—	—	—	—	—	4	3	25	3
Sub-Nuclear	1	6	5	4	4	5.5	13	2.5	—	—	—	—	2	25	9	21	1	16.5	3	11.5	8	7	30	3.7
Single Person	—	—	—	—	4	5.5	4	1	—	—	—	—	—	—	—	—	—	—	—	—	4	3	4	.5
Total	17	100	137	100	76	100	532	100	12	100	77	100	8	100	43	100	6	100	26	100	119	100	815	100

structure. The fluctuation between surname groups can be given little significance since the number of families among the Yadavs, Gaikwads and Magars in the Maratha caste, the Gaikwads in the Mahar caste, and the Magars in the Nhavi caste are small. Such an analysis does not suggest that those people who may be descendants of early villagers are significantly from the total population in adherence to joint family living.

One other source of non-comparability between the 1819 and the 1967 data lies in the differences in definition of the family that I have used. For the 1819 data, I have used the residential family as the unit for enumeration. For the 1967 data, I have used the hearth group or commensal family. Since there may be two or more hearth groups in a residence, and since we find as many or more joint families of the commensal. type in 1967 as compared to the residential families of 1819, we can be sure that there would be more residential joint families in 1967 as compared to 1819.

Lastly, we may consider the relationship between caste membership and joint family living. In 1819, the Koonbees-Tulkarrees and Ooprees – made up 67 per cent of the population (379 persons out of 565 persons) and contributed 85 per cent or 77 per cent of the estimated number of joint families; they were thus over-represented. This seems to have been especially the case for the Ooprees, who composed 28.53 per cent of the population, but contributed 38 percent or 45 per cent of the joint families.

TABLE 8

	Percentage of Joint Families	*Percentage of Population Living in Joint Families*
Lonikand Population 1967	29	45.6
Shindes	29	45.0
Kands	34.5	48.5
Yadav, Gaikwads, Magars in Maratha caste	41	60.0
Gaikwads among Mahars	25	33.0
Magars among Nhavis	0	0
All surnames listed above	32.3	48.6

The differences between proportions of the population and proportions of joint families contributed by each of the various caste groupings presented in Table 9 are otherwise small. The slaves and merchants, each making up a tiny proportion of the population, could have among them no joint families. The middle castes may be considered to be somewhat under-represented, and the Muslims somewhat over-represented. The counterpart table for 1967–Table 10 – shows no marked disproportions between population and joint families contributed by various caste groupings. This latter finding is particularly interesting in light of the statement often made that most joint families are found in high-ranking landed castes. In fact, most joint families are found in Lonikand among Marathas, but this is because most of the villagers are Marathas; joint families are found to be proportionate to the various representations of the caste groupings in the total population of the village.

Dr. Ghurye has detailed a great many of the changes in Lonikand over the century and a quarter between 1819 and 1958 (Ghurye 1960). Some of the most obvious differences include decline in isolation, increase in population, decline of the *baluta* system of services, increase in cultivated land, increase in proportion of children sent to school, and the high proportions of men now following non-traditional and non-agricultural occupations.

In 1819, as today, a highway passed through Lonikand, but in 1819 village roads were "seldom practicable for wheeled carriages and (were) never straight, but wind to avoid difficult places, and are often only known by the uncertain track of cattle and travellers" (Coats 1823: 184).

Today, scores of buses beep and roar through the village as they speed over the highway between Poona and Ahmednagar. Between ten and fifteen per cent of the Lonikand adult men take the bus daily to work in Poona.

Despite a population increase of 250 per cent by 1958, and 300 per cent by 1967, and the excellent transportation to outside points two-thirds of the men in 1958 (Ghurye 1960: 14) and 58 per cent in 1967 were still involved in agriculture. In 1967, an additional ten per cent combined agriculture with some other work. Eighteen men still did their traditional *baluta* service work in exchange for payments of grain and cash – six carpenters (*Sutars*) – three rope makers (*Mangs*) – and three leatherworkers (*Chambhars*) working full time, and one blacksmith (*Lohar*), five barbers (*Nhavis*) combining *baluta* work with agriculture. In 1819, twenty-seven men were baluta servants (Coats: 194). There were four male adults who were police servants or "Ramoossees"; in 1967, there was one man who was a police servant or Ramoshi. In the village in 1967, there were no Potters, Water-carriers, and Washermen, or Mahomedan Sacrificer present in 1819, but there was a resident Lohar and resident Mangs, absent in 1819 when their services were done by non-residents. There was a large Mahar community in Lonikand in 1967 – 82 persons. In 1819, there were 48, of whom the sixteen adult males were *baluta* servants – watchmen. The Mahars gave up their traditional *baluta* relationships, we were told, upon becoming Buddhists in recent decades. There has been a disastrous decline in the *baluta* system since 1819, it would appear.

TABLE 9

Comparison of proportions in population of various caste groupings and proportions of joint families contributed by each caste grouping in Lonikand in 1819

Caste Groupings	*Proportion of Total Population*		*Per cent Joint Families– 1819 A*		*Per cent Joint Families– 1819B*	
		Per cent		*Per cent*		*Per cent*
Kunbis-Tulkarrees	217	38.5	10	47	10	32.2
Kunbis-Ooprees	162	28.53	8	38	14	45
Brahmins	21	3.7	0	—	1	3.2
Middle castes*	62	10.91	1	5	1	3.2
Muslims	20	3.5	1	5	2	6.4
Servants	11	2.1	0	—	0	—
Slaves	18	3.2	0	—	0	—
Untouchables**	54	9.56	1	5	3	10
Total	565	100.00	21	100.00	31	100.00

*Middle castes include Sutars, Pareets, Navees, Koombars, Sonar-Potedar, Goorow, Kolee, Wanees, Marwarrees and Ramoossees.

** Untouchables include Mhars and Chamars.

TABLE 10

Comparison of proportions in population of various caste groupings and proportions of joint families contributed by each caste Grouping in 1967

Caste Groupings	*Proportion of Total Population*		*Proportion of Joint Families*	
	Per cent		*Per cent*	
Marathas	1085	63	53	67
Malis	347	20	15	19
Brahmans and Middle Castes*	156	9	5	6
Untouchables**	146	8	6	8
Total	1734	100	79	100

*Middle class include Guravs, Sutars, Lohars, Nhavis, Ramoshis, Sonars, Dongars, Pardeshis, Garudis, Chimpis, and Muslims.

** Untouchables include Chambhars, Mangs and Mahars – both Buddhist and Hindu Mahars.

The more popular non-agriculture jobs included having grocery, cycle, or tea shops (sixteen men), working in factories – *punkah* (fan) factory (eight men), munition factory (twelve men), other factories (six), driving trucks (eleven men), working for the Public Works Department (six men), or for the railways (four men), being teachers (five men), clerks (four men), and peons (five men). Some fifteen men cycled to Poona regularly to sell milk.

Ghurye reported that there had been a fifty per cent increase in the cultivated land of the village and a tripling of the number of animals (oxen, bulls, cows and buffaloes) (Ghurye: 18-21). He also said that about one-sixth of the families lived in the fields sometimes as much as one mile from the village (Ghurye 1960: 109). In 1967, about two-fifths of the population lived in hamlets or on farms some distance from the village cluster. Moving away from the village cannot be seen as a move to relieve population congestion, since the village was, in 1967, a shambles of deserted tumbled-down ruins of former homes (Coats suggested this was the case even in 1819) (Coats: 191). Settling in distant hamlets probably reflects the desire to be close to the fields for work, and also the passing away of the need to build homes, village walls and structures with an eye to defense (Coats: 191). Indeed in 1819, the "outcasts"–probably Mahars or Chamars – whose houses were outside the village walls were destroyed during the war between the British and Peshwa (Coats: 192).

The chief connection with the central government in 1819, besides the brutal contacts of war, was in the payment of taxes. Today, of course, Lonikand is part of a national democracy. During our field trip there in January 1967, representatives of various political parties stopped there on election campaigns. Lonikand is involved in village, taluka and district panchayats (self-governing bodies), and she is the recipient of various government improvement programmes. While in 1819 the Lonikand school was "only attended by the children of the Brahmins, shopkeepers and patails, so scarcely any of the cultivators can either read or write" (Coats: 204), today hundreds of Lonikand children are in school. On Republic Day, 1967, I counted over 300 children in the assembly at the Lonikand school. Scores more of Lonikand children go to high school in a nearby village, and some go on to still higher education.

There is no question that the quality of life in Lonikand has changed profoundly in the past century and a half. What our figures suggest, however, is that joint family living has not declined. In 1819, there were about the same and probably fewer joint families proportionately than in 1967. Our figures suggest that there were more supplemented nuclear families then and also fewer nuclear families then, than now, but I have manipulated the 1819 figures so as to minimise the number of nuclear families. What seems clear is that there were not more joint families in 1819 than in 1967.

NOTE

* In November, 1965 I read at the American Anthropological Association meetings in Denver, Colorado, a paper comparing the 1819 statistics on family structure in Lonikand with those published in 1958; that investigation stimulated me to survey the village in 1967.

I owe special thanks to Dr. M.G. Kulkarni of the Gokhale Institute of Politics and Economics, to Tukaram Ramji Tapkir of village Lonikand, and to Jyoti Subramaniam and Aguila Shaikh for their help with the January 1967 phase of the study of Lonikand. My research work was supported at that time by a Faculty Research

Fellowship of the American Institute of Indian Studies and by the National Science Foundation, Grant Ga-1961. I offer thanks to both foundations.

REFERENCES

Arensberg, Conrad, M.: 1955: "American Communities." *American Anthropologist*, 66, pp. 1143-62.

————: 1960: "The American Family in the Perspective of other Cultures". *The Nation's Children, 1: Family and Social Change* (Eli Ginzberg ed.), Washington, White House Conference.

Back, Kurt, W.: 1965: "A Social Psychologist Looks at Kinship Structure". *Social Structure and the Family: Generational Relations* (Ethel Shanas and Gordon F. Streib, eds.), Englewood Cliffs, New Jersey, Prentice-Hall, Inc., pp. 326-40.

Bailey, F.G.: 1957: *Caste and the Economic Frontier.* Manchester, Manchester University Press.

Beals, Alan, R.: 1955: "Interplay among Factors of Change in a Mysore Village." *Village India* (McKim Marriott ed.), Am. Anthropo. Assoc. Mem., 83, Vol. 57, No. 3, Part II, pp. 78-101.

Blenkner, Margaret: 1965: "Social Work and Family Relationships in Later Life With Some Thoughts on Filial Maturity." *Social Structure and the Family: Generational Relations* (Ethel Shanas and Gordon F. Streib, eds.), Englewood Cliffs, New Jersey, Prentice-Hall, Inc., pp. 46-59.

Burgess, E.W. and H.J. Locke: 1953: *The Family.* New York, American Book Company.

Coats, Thomas: 1823: "Account of the Present State of the Township of Lony." *Trans. Literary Soc.* Bombay, 3, pp. 172-64.

Desai, I.P.: 1964: *Some Aspects of Family in Mahuva*, New York, Asia Publishing House.

Epstein, T., Scarlett: 1962: *Economic Development and Social Change in South India.* Manchester, Manchester University Press.

Ghurye, G.S.: 1960: *After a Century and a Quarter.* Bombay, Popular Book.

Goode, William, J.:1963: *World Revolution and Family Patterns.* London, The Free Press of Glencoe, Collier Macmillan Limited.

————: 1963-64: "The Process of Role Bargaining in the Impact of Urbanization and Industrialisation on family systems." *Current Sociology*, Vol. pp. 1-15.

Gore, Madhav Sadashiv: 1961: "The Impact of Industrialization and Urbanization on the Aggarwal Family in Delhi Area", *Ph.D. Thesis*, Columbia University.

Gough, E. Kathleen: 1952: "Changing Kinship Usages in the Setting of Political and Economic Change among the Nayars of Malabar." *Journal of the Royal Anthropological Institute*, 82, pp. 71-88.

Greenfield, Sidney, M.: 1961: Industrialization and the Family in Sociological Theory. *American Journal of sociology*, 47, pp. 312-22.

Hitchcock, John T.: 1956: "The Rajputs of Khalapur: A Study of Kinship, Social Stratification and Politics", *Ph.D. Thesis*, Cornell University.

Johnson, Erwin.: 1964: "The Stem Family and its Extension in Present Day Japan." *American Anthropologist*, 66, pp. 839-51.

Karve, Irawati: 1965: *Kinship Organization in India*. Bombay, Asia Publishing House.

Kapoor, Saroj: 1965: "Family and Kinship Groups Among the Khatris in Delhi". *Sociological Bulletin*, 14, pp. 54-63.

Kerckhoff, Alan C.: 1965: "Nuclear and Extended Family Relationships: A Normative and Behavioral Analysis." *Social Structure and the Family: Generational Relations* (Ethel Shanas and Gordon F. Streib, eds.), Englewood Cliffs, New Jersey, Prentice-Hall, Inc., pp. 93-112.

Kolenda, Pauline: 1967: "Regional Differences in Indian Family Structure". *Regions and Regionalism in South Asian Studies: An Exploratory Study* (Robert Crane, ed.), Duke Univ. Prog. Comp. Studies on S. Asia, Monograph No. 5, pp. 147-226.

————: 1968: "Region, Caste and Family Structure: A Comparative Study of the Indian Joint Family" *Structure and Change in Indian Society* (Milton Singer and Bernard S. Cohn, eds.), Chicago, Aldine Press, pp. 339-96.

Kulkarni, M.G.: 1960: A Brief Review of Literature on Family Structure with Special Reference to Some Empirical Studies, Mimeo.

Levy, Marion J.: 1949: *The Family Revolution in China*. Cambridge, Harvard University Press.

Linton, Ralph: 1952: "Cultural and Personality Factors Affecting Economic Growth". *The Progress of Underdeveloped Areas* (Bert F. Hoselitz, ed.) Chicago, University of Chicago Press.

Litwak, Eugene: 1960a: "Occupations, Mobility and Family Cohesion". *American Sociological Review*, 25, pp. 9-20.

————: 1960b: "Geographical Mobility and Family Cohesion". *American Sociological Review*, 25, pp. 385-94.

———: 1965: "Extended Kin Relations in an Industrial Democratic Society". *Social Structure and the Family: Generational Relations* (Ethel Shanas and Gordon F. Streib, eds.), Englewood Cliffs, New Jersey, Prentice-Hall, Inc., pp. 290-323.

Mencher, Joan P.: 1962: "Changing Familial Roles Among South Malabar Nayars". *Southwestern Journal of Anthropology*, 18, pp. 230-45.

Morrison, William A.: 1959: "Family Types in Badlapur: An Analysis of a Changing Institution in a Maharashtrian Village". *Sociological Bulletin*, 8, pp. 45-67.

Nimkoff, M.F. and Russell Middleton: 1960: "Types of Families and Types of Economy". *American Journal of Sociology*, 66, pp. 215-25.

Ogburn, William F. and Meyer F. Nimkoff: 1950: *Sociology*, Boston, Houghton Mifflin.

Orenstein, Henry: 1961: "The Recent History of the extended Family in India". *Social Problems*, 8, pp. 341-53.

Orenstein, Henry and Michael Micklin: 1966: " The Hindu Joint Family: The Norms and the Numbers". *Pacific affairs*, 39, pp. 314-25.

Parsons, Talcott: 1943: "The Kinship System of the Contemporary United States." *American Anthropologist*, 45, pp. 22-38.

———: 1949: "The Social Structure of the Family". *The Family: Its Function and Destiny* (Ruth N. Anshen, ed.), New York, Harper & Row, pp. 173-201.

———: 1961: Introduction to Part two: "Differentiation and Variation in Social Structures". *Theories of Society* (Talcott Parsons, Edward Shils, Kaspar D. Naegele, Jesse R. Pitts, eds.), New York, Froo Press of Glencoe, p. 257.

Rosow, Irving: 1965: "Intergenerational Relationships: Problems and Proposals". *Social Structure and the Family: Generational Relations* (Ethel Shanas and Gordon F. Streib, eds.), Englewood Cliffs, New Jersey, Prentice-Hall, Inc., pp. 341-78.

Ross, Aileen D.: 1961: *The Hindu Family in its Urban Settitng*. Toronto, University of Toronto Press.

Sarma, Jyotimoyee: 1964: "The Nuclearization of Joint Family Households in West Bengal". *Man in India*, 44, pp. 193-206.

Shahani, Savitri: 1961: "The Joint Family: A Case Study", *Economic Weekly*, 13, pp. 823-1828.

Shanas, Ethel and Gordon F. Streib (eds.): 1965: *Social Structure and the Family: Generational Relations*. Englewood Cliffs, New Jersey, Prentice-Hall, Inc.

Streib, Gordon, F.:1958: "Family Patterns in Retirement", *Journal of Social Issues*, 14, pp. 46-60.

Sussman, Marvin B.: 1963: " The Isolated Nuclear Family: Fact or Fiction?". *Sourcebook in Marriage and the Family* (Marvin B. Sussman, ed.), Boston, Houghton Mifflin, pp. 48-53.

————: 1965: "Relationships of Adult Children with their Parents in the United States". *Social Structure and the Family: Generational Relations* (Ethel Shanas and Gordon F. Streib, eds.)., Englewood Cliffs, New Jersey, Prentice-Hall, Inc., pp. 62-92.

Weber, Max: 1950: *General Economic History*, Glencoe, Illinois, Free Press.

Wirth, Louis: 1938: "Urbanism as a Way of Life". *American Journal of Sociology*, 40, pp. 1-24.

Young, Michael and Peter Willmott: 1957: *Family and Kinship in East London*, London: Routledge and Kegan Paul.

15

Family Structure and Classes in Four Villages

Pradip Kumar Bose

Abstract

The study of family so far concentrated on investigating relationship between caste and family types. The present essay based on the study of four Bengal villages, and attempts to analyse the relationship of family structure with the classes and economic activity of the peasants and labourers. Since in the villages lower caste being lower economic class also, the study of family structure only on the basis of caste gives a partial view of the reality unless the economic status of the villagers is taken into account. This present essay shows that there exists a strong relationship between class status and family structure.

In the study of family, in India, the caste and its relationship with the family, has been one of the recurring issues; and one of the principal focus of analysis has been the way caste is supposed to have affected the household structure. Though it has often been shown that untouchables are more likely to have nuclear families (Kolenda, 1968: 391; Shah, 1974) but little attempt has been made to relate the family types with economic activity of untouchable or to that effect any caste whatsoever. For instance, Kolenda (1976: 214) though found that those families with least land are less likely to maintain joint households, but she pays little attention to this phenomenon and instead asks 'Is the joint family more characteristic of higher castes than lower castes?' 'Is the joint family more characteristic of landed castes than of landless castes?' (1968: 390).

But another and closely related issue is the way family types are related to the economic structure of the society and the way it responds to economic changes. More specifically, the question may be posed as whether, for instance, untouchables, have nuclear families because they belong to a particular caste or because they are related in a certain way to organization of production and consequently perform a specific type of economic activity.

The association between nuclear family type and modern industrial society has been hypothesized by many sociologists (Weber, 1950; Linton 1951) and according to Goode (1963) predominant family type in future will be nuclear family. The predominance of extended families in traditional agrarian societies has been noted by sociologists, but it has also been found that predominance of nuclear families is associated with societies where hunting and gathering are dominant occupations (Nimkoff and Middleton, 1960). In India also nuclear family existed in traditional peasant societies and as Singh (1973: 175) points out, the lower caste families where the chief occupation was agricultural labour were mostly nuclear and this nuclearity was related to "absence of landed property, lack of sufficient and stable means of livelihood and shifting mode of occupation". Dube (1969: 203) also points out that in rural India "contrary to common belief the basic unit of social organization.. is not the large joint family but the nuclear family .. Recent village studies have shown that large joint families are relatively few in number and they too are largely confined to upper, i.e. priestly, trading and agricultural castes".

What is the explanation of the existence or predominance of nuclear families in villages which are isolated from the mainstream of urban-industrial life? In villages, what are variables that affect the family structure? The different studies indicate that the economic factors like landownership and occupation are quite important in this respect. Sen (1965) in a study of four Bengal villages, found that in those villages, nuclear families are more predominant than extended families, and there exists a significant relationship between family types and occupation, landownership.

According to Sen (1965: 15) "non-cultivating owners, day labourers, and non-agriculturists have a very large proportion of nuclear families as compared to the owner-cultivators and sharecroppers. This indicates the fact that differences in occupation and subsistence pattern within the same society will also explain the distribution of the nuclear and extended families among the various sections of the population". Sarma (1963) in a similar study of Bengal villages, arrived at the same conclusion as above. Gough (1956) in her study of Kumbapettai village found the Brahmans, who are large landowners, do no manual work and are totally dependent on land have extended families while the landless labourers known as Adi-Dravidas, live in nuclear families. Cohn (1963) in Senapur village also found that among Chamars, most of whom are landless labourers, there were only 42 joint families out of 122 Chamar households in the village, and principal reason for this according to Cohn is the poverty of the Chamar landless labourers. It is evident from the above studies that there is a relationship between social class and family types and the family structure is related to the economic activity of the members.

Kolenda (1967) in her study of thirteen regions of India based on thirty-two publications, attempted an analysis of factors influencing the family types, but she concludes, that there is no universal association with any of the factors like landownership, caste identity, etc. and the prevalence of joint or nuclear families. She relates the pattern of family structure in different regions with the process of family breakup. According to her (1957: 166-67) "where the nuclear family in India is most prevalent, it is not the result of the natural death of the older generation, but is the result of breakup before the peasants' death. Furthermore, where the joint families are most prevalent the death of the progenitor does not result in either the immediate or somewhat delayed breakup of the joint family. Three different patterned timings for breakup emerge from the studies of Indian rural areas. First is the patterned breakup within a few months of years of marriage of the sons... The second pattern is the breakup of married brothers upon or shortly after the fathers death ...A third pattern is the breakup of the joint family when it is headed by married brothers who have lived together with their families for some years, or even when the family is headed by male first cousins".

Though the studies summarized by Kolenda exhaust the possible correlations of the family structure and change, but she was unable to examine the individual cases in detail and made broad generalizations on the basis of existing studies. Hence, the possibilities of other variables affecting the family structure cannot be totally ruled out, and in this context one can ask whether the causes family breakups are, as Kolenda suggests, high divorce and marriage rates, bride wealth and dowry payment and usorilaterality versus virilaterality or the causes lie much deeper in the infrastructural sphere of property relations, poverty and wealth, the partial replacement of traditional economic relationship, and the changing economic activity of the peasants?

In this essay we have attempted to analyse the family structure in four villages in terms of classes and tried to find out whether or not subsistence pattern, modes of livelihood, landownership or lack of it affect the family structure.

Villages. The three villages (the names of the villages are fictitious), namely Azadpur, Kanchanpur and Birpur are in the district of Birbhum and the fourth village Tusugaon is in the district of Purulia. The villages Azadpur and Tusugaon are non-irrigated villages, whereas Kanchanpur and Birpur are fully irrigated and partially irrigated villages respectively. The distance of three villages in Birbhum from the nearest town Bolpur is six to eight kilometres and all the three villages are connected by buses. Tusugaon is an interior village, not connected by *pukka* road or buses and its distance from the nearest town Jhalda is twenty-two kilometers. Inspite of irrigation facilities available in two of the villages, all the four villages yield one crop a year and the economy still remains at subsistence level, agricultural practice still being traditional with traditional implements and animal and human labour used as sources of power. But in terms of communication, school, etc., the Birbhum villages are comparatively more modernized than the village Tusugaon.

Collection of Data. The fieldwork was conducted in these four villages from October 1974 to January, 1976. All the heads of the households in four villages were interviewed, a household being defined as those who live under one roof and take food cooked at common hearth. Total household in the four villages is 483. Besides, ascertaining the family structure, information about the respondents' economic position, landholding, occupation of the various members of the household, migration of the members of the household, etc., was gathered. On the basis of the data, the households were classified in twelve family types following Kolenda (1968) and five classes on the basis of economic position of the members of the households.

Social Classes. The households in the four villages have been stratified into five classes, viz. (1) Landlord, (2) Rich Peasant, (3) Middle Peasant, (4) Poor Peasant and (5) Agricultural Labourers. The stratification is based on primarily three criteria: (1) Those who possess and those who do not possess means of production. (2) Those who work and those who do not work and (3) Those who hire labour and those who do not (Ossowski, 1969). On the basis of the combination of all the criteria, the five classes are defined as follows:

1. Landlords: Who own land but do not engage in any kind of labour. They completely depend on hired labourers or tenants.

2. The Rich Peasants: They own land but themselves engage in labour, also depend on hired labourer to a large extent.

3. The Middle Peasants: They own land but not of sufficient quantity or just as much, they usually depend on family labour, and do not employ hired labourers unless extremely necessary.

4. The Poor Peasants: They own very little land or no land at all and/or rent land for cultivation and in general they hire out themselves as wage labourers.

5. The Agricultural Labourers: They are landless and own very little or no farm implements. They depend wholly or mainly on selling out their labour power alone.

Family types To analyse the family structure in four villages and to find its relationship with classes we have adopted Kolenda's typology, which she prepared on the basis of family structures in thirteen regions of India (1968: 346-47) and can be put to comparative use.

(1) Single person household.

(2) Subnuclear family: a fragment of former nuclear family such as widowed or divorced parent with unmarried children, or unmarried, widowed or divorced siblings living together or widowed mother and married son without his family.

(3) Supplemented subnuclear family: a subnuclear family plus some other unmarried, widowed or divorced relative(s) who are not a part of the original nuclear family. For example, a widow with her unmarried children plus her dead husband's brother's widow.

(4) Nuclear family: couple and their unmarried children.

(5) Supplemented nuclear family: a nuclear family plus some other widowed, divorced or unmarried relative(s) such as the husband's widowed mother or his unmarried brother or sister.

(6) Lineal joint family: parents with unmarried children plus one married son and his wife and unmarried children.

(7) Supplemented lineal joint family: a lineal joint family plus some other unmarried, divorced or widowed relative(s) such as the widowed sister of the older man or his unmarried brother.

(8) Collateral joint family: two or more married brothers with their wives and unmarried children.

(9) Supplemented collateral joint family: a collateral joint family plus some other unmarried, widowed or divorced relative(s), such as the widowed mother, widowed father or unmarried brother or sister of the married brothers.

(10) Lineal collateral joint family: parents, their unmarried children plus two or more married sons with their wives and children.

(11) Supplemented lineal collateral joint family: a lineal collateral joint family plus some other relative(s) who is (are) not (a) member(s) of any of the nuclear families involved. For example, a wife's widowed brother or the eldest male's unmarried brother.

Though nuclear family according to the definition consists of the couple and their unmarried children, but the concept of family as nuclear should not be confused with the use of the concept in the Western sense. Structurally the nuclear family in the villages is about the same as in the West but in terms of social and ritual ties with the parent family there are some differences (Desai 1955, 1964; Dube 1969; Sen 1965). The nucleated units maintain varying degrees of ritualistic obligation with the parent family and are involved in sentiments and relationship of jointness.

In this essay we have only analysed the structural correlates of the family, and not the social ties or sentiments of jointness. The nucleated units maintain economic independence, but social and ritual dependence. The nuclear family in the villages has to be understood in this context to avoid confusion.

Family structure and classes. The distribution of families shows that in all the villages nuclear families are much more numerous than joint families—and in the non-irrigated and backward villages the percentage of nuclear families is higher than the partially irrigated villages and irrigated villages (Table 1). This is contrary to general notion that in peasant societies the predominant family type is the extended or joint family and that the nuclear families are result of industrialization and technological development.

What are the reasons for this large number of nuclear families? Is caste related to family structure? As there exists a relationship between caste and class (r-.68 s-.001) because members of lower class come mainly from lower castes, so to find out the contribution of caste on family structure, the low castes and tribes are stratified into five classes. Table 2 shows that even among the lower castes the family structure is related to their class status. When the high castes are similarly stratified the same results are found. But, when a particular class is stratified into caste group no such relationship is observed.

The large proportion of nuclear families, we find, then is neither related to the technological aspect of the village economic structure as the village economy is still traditional and consumption-oriented nor related to the caste. The reasons for the large number of nuclear families are to be investigated in the internal differentiation of classes within the village.

From Tables, 3, 4, 5 and 6 we find that agricultural labourers have the highest percentage of nuclear families. The poor peasants and middle peasants have generally nuclear families; but in the villages, these classes also have supplemented nuclear families and joint families. The big landowners like rich peasants and landlords usually live in joint families. The sharecroppers who belong to the poor peasants usually have the joint or supplemented nuclear families. The reason for this is that the sharecroppers and the middle peasants, to reduce the cost of hired labour, prefer family labour and hence joint families or supplemented nuclear families. On the other hand, large landowners prefer to keep their property under joint control and live in joint families. Their large ownership of land can also support greater number of people.

The higher percentage of nuclear families among agricultural labourers can be explained by their absence of landownership and the type of livelihood in which they receive wages in cash or kind. The cash earning independently without any help of family members makes them free of obligation from the family. Another factor that affects the family types among the agricultural labourers, is the contribution of women a wage earners in the family. If wife is a wage earner, the couple breaks away from the family sooner than if she is not.

On the other hand, the members of poor peasant and middle peasant families prefer to remain in joint families for greater economic security. For example in the village Azadpur, during the survey, a sharecropper had a lineal collateral joint family with three married sons and their children. He was evicted from land during my presence in the village and all the family members turned into agricultural labourers. The sons continued to remain in the joint family till the family grain stocks and sales proceedings from cattle could maintain themselves and soon after they broke away and formed separate nuclear families. The reason was clear, all the sons have then to depend upon their own income from labour and family could not provide the economic security which was available earlier.

The reasons of family partition are mainly quarrels over distribution of food and income. As cohn (1963: 1053) has pointed out, "a brother with one small child does not see, why he should share his meagre earnings with a brother who has three small children and hence gets a larger share of the household food supply". Such tendencies are observed among agricultural labourers much more than peasants, because in a labourer's family father loses his authority when he becomes old and is not able to earn as a labourer what his grown up sons earn. Among the large landowners, the older men retain their authority, firstly because of their ownership of property and secondly due to their managerial functions. The joint families among the upper classes can be explained, by the fact that since they supervise the cultivation and own large amounts of land, they need considerable amount of labour and want their sons to help them. Again besides cultivation they have other occupations like running of grocer's shop, moneylending business, etc., which are managed by family members. On the other hand, the non-cultivating owner, i.e., the owner who has leased out his land to sharecropper, receives his annual share from the sharecropper and usually "does not contribute to the maintenance or improvement by investment on the land in any way. So, the pooling of resources is not necessary in his case. In cases where the nucleated parts of a previous joint family have common ownership on a piece of land, they divide the annual share among themselves. There is no need to keep the total income under joint control" (Sen, 1965: 9).

The actual frequency distribution of rich peasants and landlords being few in the four villages, the pattern of family types among these classes, though statistically does not point out to a conclusive direction, but we find, that among these classes the type of family differs according to the economic factors mentioned above, i.e., the leasing out of land, diversification of economic interests and activities, labour resources and its management, etc. The sons of these landowners take part in various economic activities like trade, teaching, moneylending, etc. and under the overall control of father remain in joint families. After the death of the head of household, the sons retain the joint family if agriculture remains the principal source of livelihood, but if sons are not dependent on agriculture but are employed in other occupations they partition the family. As Bailey (1957: 92) points out "while the family are agriculturists pure and simple, family economics can be efficiently managed by one man. Whatever the rivalries and tensions between brothers their economic interests is directed to the same end making the estate produce as much as possible. But when one brother gets an income from trade and another is a policeman and third is a carter and the fourth and fifth remain on the land; and when the trader and the policeman and the carter refuse to put their earnings into the common pool, as they are permitted to do in certain conditions; and when they demand a share of the estate so that they may sell it and use the money to finance other undertakings–then all the brothers are glad to partition and go their own way. The joint family cannot survive divergent interests and disparate income among its members". These are the various factors, which contributes towards existence/non-existence of joint families among big landowners who belong to upper classes.

Among the agricultural labourers, we have seen the predominance of nuclear families mainly depends on their modes of livelihood and hence their class position. The relationship between classes and family types shows that in three comparatively backward villages, the relationship is significant (Tables 3, 5, 6), while in the irrigated village Kanchanpur this is not so (Table 4). This points out that agricultural technology affects only marginally the family forms. Orenstein (1960) in survey of fifty-nine villages of Poona district found that there were less number of joint families in those villages that had most acreage per family under irrigation. According to him, families with irrigated land get more of their income in cash and both cash and irrigated lands are readily divisible, hence the members partition the family quickly, because money income leads to arguments. Epstein (1962: 177-78) also suggests two hypothesis of a similar nature: (1) "In a subsistence economy the joint family is associated with joint estates; correspondingly, if a family in this type of economy does not own an estate, it cannot expand beyond the elementary size; (2) if a cash crop is introduced into a society of subsistence farmers holding estates on the basis of joint families, the conversion of the subsistence into cash economy will necessarily produce competition between the component families and lead to the breaking of wider kinship ties". But we find that in the two non-irrigated villages Azadpur and Tusugaon, the relationship between classes and family types is stronger than the village, which is partially irrigated, and the village, which is fully irrigated. In the non-irrigated villages the percentage of nuclear families are higher than that of irrigated villages, contrary to Orenstein's findings. The explanation may be that in village Kanchanpur, though irrigated, the economy still remains a subsistence economy, as it mainly yield one crop, and cash crops are not cultivated on a large scale. But the irrigation facility has given the peasants an amount of economic security and the poor and middle peasants, to cultivate the land with their own family labour, prefer joint families. Secondly, as the cash economy has not penetrated to a large extent in this village, the problem of divisibility of income has not arised. On the other hand, the poor peasants, who own very little land in the non-irrigated villages, have comparatively less work to do in the land as they cultivate paddy only and the amount of land they own is much below their subsistence level. As a result they hire out themselves as agricultural labourers. This makes them prefer nuclear families or supplemented nuclear families where one or two grown up relatives are given shelter in the family to work as family labour. Hence, we find in Tusugaon and Azadpur more than 60 per cent of the poor peasants have nuclear families, the comparative figure in Kanchanpur is 35.7 per cent. The poor peasants of non-irrigated villages have a greater need to work as labourers as the productivity of their land is low, and being partly agricultural labourers, i.e., preference for nuclear families. On the other hand, the poor peasants who have irrigated land try to maintain themselves from land, whose productivity is higher, by cultivating a few other vegetables with their family labour. Though these poor peasants also hire out themselves but their income from land being secured, as they get water from canal, rain or no rain, they can afford to have a bigger family with larger number of family labours.

The above analysis shows that, lower castes have nuclear families not because they are low castes but because most of them are involved in specific kind of economic activities as agricultural labourers and belong to lower class.

The poor peasants, when they have a certain amount of economic security, prefer supplemented nuclear family or joint family to add to their family labour force. But in cases where the poor peasant has to work for most of the time as agricultural labourer, he more often lives in nuclear families.

The middle peasants and rich peasants, as they are directly involved in cultivation, prefer supplemented nuclear family or joint family for the extra family labour. In these two classes we also find that the percentage of nuclear families is more in underdeveloped villages like Azadpur and Tusugaon than the developed villages. This is because the middle peasant families find agriculture not so productive due to uncertainty of rainfall and feel no need to keep family income under control. It is only those who have irrigation facilities that prefer to live in a joint family.

TABLE 1
Family Structure in Four Village

Village	Family Type	Single Person	Sub-nuclear	Sup. Sub-nuclear	Nuclear	Sup. Nuclear	Lineal Joint	Sup. Lineal Joint	Colla-teral Joint	Sup. Colla-teral Joint	Lineal Colla-teral Joint	Sup. Lineal Colla-teral Joint	Total
Azadpur	No	4	6	1	60	15	8	1	1	3	4	1	104
	Per cent	3.8	5.8	1.0	57.7	14.4	7.7	1.0	1.0	2.9	3.8	1.0	100.0
Kanchanpur	No.	6	13	2	66	35	13	5	1	5	3	—	149
	Per cent	4.0	8.7	1.3	44.3	23.5	8.7	3.4	0.7	3.4	2.0		100.00
Birpur	No.	5	4	1	41	19	5	—	1	—	2	—	78
	Per cent	6.4	5.1	1.3	52.6	24.4	6.4		1.3		2.6		100.0
Tusugaon	No.	6	10	2	95	18	10	—	1	4	6	—	152
	Per cent	3.9	6.6	1.3	62.5	11.8	6.6		0.7	2.6	3.9		100.0
Total	No.	21	33	6	262	87	36	6	4	12	15	1	483
	Per cent	4.3	6.8	1.2	54.2	18.0	7.4	1.2	0.8	2.5	3.1	0.2	100.00

Table 2
Family Types among Low Castes/Tribes in Four Villages

Family Type	*Single Person*	*Sub-nuclear*	*Sup. Sub-nuclear*	*Nuclear*	*Sup. Nuclear*	*Lineal Joint*	*Sup. Lineal Joint*	*Collateral Joint*	*Sup. Colla-teral Joint*	*Lineal Colla-teral Joint*	*Total*
Middle Peasant										1	1
Poor Peasant				9	3	5	1		1	1	20
Agricultural Labourer	9	17	3	90	26	13	3	1	3	1	166
Total	9	17	3	99	29	18	4	1	4	3	187

Chi² — 74.90 df — 18

Cramer's V — .447 Contingency Coeff (C) — .534

Table 3
Family Types and Class in Azadpur

Family Type	*Single Person*	*Sub-nuclear Family*	*Sup. Sub-nuclear Family*	*Nuclear Family*	*Sup. nuclear Family*	*Lineal Joint Family*	*Sup. Lineal Joint Family*	*Collateral Joint Family*	*Sup. Colla-teral Joint Family*	*Lineal Colla-teral Joint Family*	*Sub. Lineal Colla-teral Joint Family*	*Total*
Landlord				1	1				1			3
Rich Peasant				1				1				2
Middle Peasant		1		2						1	1	5
Poor Peasant	2	1		20	3	1			1	2		30
Peasant Proletariat	2	4	1	36	11	7	1		1	1		64
Total	4	6	1	60	15	8	1	1	3	4	1	104

Chi^2 — 96.773 df — 40

C — .694 V — .482

Table 4
Family Types and Classes in Kanchanpur

Family Type	*Single Person*	*Sub-nuclear*	*Sup. Sub-nuclear*	*Nuclear*	*Sup. Nuclear*	*Lineal Joint*	*Sup. Lineal Joint*	*Collateral Joint*	*Sup. Colla-teral Joint*	*Lineal Colla-teral Joint*	*Total*
Landlord				2	4	1				1	8
Rich Peasant				3	1				1		5
Middle Peasant		1		6	4	1	1		1		14
Poor Peasant		2		10	9	4	2			1	28
Peasant Proletariat	6	10	2	45	17	7	2	1	3	1	94
Total	6	13	2	66	35	13	5	1	5	3	149

Chi^2 — 29.125 df — 36

C — .404 V — .221 Value of P — .784

Table 5
Family Types and Classes in Birpur

	Single Person	*Sub-nuclear*	*Sup. Sub-nuclear*	*Nuclear Family*	*Sup. Nuclear*	*Lineal Joint*	*Collateral Joint*	*Lineal Colla-teral Joint*	*Total*
Landlord				2		21			3
Rich Peasant					1	1			2
Middle Peasant	2		1	8	7	1		2	21
Poor Peasant	1	1		5	4	1			12
Peasant Proletariat	2	3		26	7	2			40
Total	5	4	1	41	19	5	1	2	78

Chi^2 — 48.972 df — 28
C — .621 V — .396
— .0084

Table 6
Family types and Classes in Tusugaon

	Single Person	Sub-nuclear	Sup. Sub-nuclear	Nuclear	Sup. Nuclear	Lineal Joint	Collateral Joint	Sup. Colla-teral Joint	Lineal Colla-teral Joint	Total
Rich Peasant				2		2	1		1	6
Middle Peasant	1	1		29	5	4		4	4	48
Poor Peasant	3	8	2	48	13	4			1	79
Peasant Proletariat	2	1		16						19
Total	6	10	2	95	18	10	1	4	6	152

Chi^2 — 63.07 df — 24
C — .541 V — .372
— .0000

Among landlords, as we have mentioned earlier, those who have leased out their land, do not feel necessary to keep joint families as they can divide the share of the produce among themselves. On the other hand those who supervise the cultivation and take greater direct interest in farm management prefer to keep the property under joint control.

Thus, the change in family structure is related to the economic activity of the different classes and infrastructural development. It is not only technological development which gives rise to nuclear families, but technological facilities when related to various classes, produces different family forms depending upon the productive and consumptive needs of the various classes.

REFERENCES

Bailey, F.G.: 1957: *Caste and the Economic Frontier.* Manchester University Press.

Cohn, Bernard S.: 1963: Chamar Family in a North Indian Village. *Economic Weekly*, XIII.

Desai, I.P.: 1955: Symposium on Caste and Joint Family. Sociological Bulletin, IV (2).

Desai, I.P.: 1964: *Some Aspects of Family in Mahuva. Bombay*: Asia Publishing House.

Dube, S.C.: 1969: Social Structure and Change in Indian Peasant Communities. In A.R. Desai (ed.), *Rural Sociology in India.* Bombay: Popular Prakashan.

Epstein, T. Scarlett: 1962: *Economic Development and Social Change in South India*. Manchester: Manchester University Press.

Goode, William, J.: 1963: *World Revolution and Family Pattern*. London: Free Press of Glenco, Collier–Macmillan.

Gough, R. Kathleen: 1956: Brahmin Kinship in a Tamil Village. *American Anthropologist*, Vol. 58.

Kolenda, Pauline M.: 1967: Regional Differences in Indian Family Structure. In R. I. Crane (ed.), *Regions and Regionalism in South Asian Studies: An Exploratory Study*. Durham, N.C.: Duke University Program in Comparative Studies on Southern Asia Monograph No. 5.

Kolenda, Pauline M.: 1968: Region, Caste and Family Structure: A Comparative Study of Indian Society. In Milton Singer and Bernard

S. Cohn (eds.), *Structure and Change in Indian Society*. Chicago: Aldine Publishing Company.

Linton, Ralph: 1952: Culture and Personality Factors Affecting Economic Growth. In Bert F. Hoselitz (ed.), *The Progress of Underdeveloped Areas*. Chicago: University of Chicago Press.

Namkoff, M. F. and Russell Middleton. 1960. Types of Family and Types of Economy. American Journal of Sociology, LXVI (November).

Orenstein, Henry: 1960: Irrigation, Settlement Pattern and Social Organization. In Anthony F.C. Wallace (ed.), *Selected Papers of the Fifty International Congress of Anthropological and Ethnological Sciences*. Philadelphia: University of Pensylvania Press.

Ossowski, S.: 1969: Old Nations and New Problems; Interpretation of Social Structure in Modern Society. In Andre Beteile (ed.), *Social Inequality*. London: Penguin Books.

Sarma, Jyotirmoyee: 1963: The Nuclearization of Joint Family Households in West Bengal. *Man in India*, Vol. 44 (July-September).

Sen, Lalit Kumar: 1965: Family in Four Indian Villages. *Man in India*, Vol. 45 (January-March).

Shah, A.M.: 1974: *The Household Dimension of the Family in India: A Field Study of Gujarat Village and a Review of Other Studies*. Berkeley, University of California Press.

Singh, Yogendra: 1973: *Modernization of Indian Tradition*. Delhi: Thomson Press (India) Ltd.

Weber, Max: 1950: *General Economic History*. Glencoe: Free Press.

16

Some Aspects of Household Organization and Family Structures in Calcutta

Prafulla Chakrabarty and Samita Bhowmick

Introduction

Although the system of kinship and family in India has drawn considerable attention of social scientists of various disciplines, not much emphasis has perhaps been given as yet on analysing the household formation and family structures in the Indian metropolis. The researches conducted earlier on city families are mostly by-products of other studies on urban communities, and hence lack proper representation and coverage (Ross 1961; Sharma 1964; Bose 1964; Gore 1968). We have, of course, some excellent works on town families, e.g., Navsari (Kapadia 1955), Mahuva (Desai 1964), Dharwar (Conklin 1976), etc., but the extent to which the family patterns observed in these towns conform to that of the large cities cannot be ascertained from these.

Family studies in India stinted, by and large, confusing concepts and definitions. While reviewing the literature on the subject a number of scholars (Dube 1974; Shah 1974; Desai 1980) have pointed out how our understanding of this basic social unit has been restricted by the subjective procedures adopted by the individual researchers. The controversy lies also in the levels of interpretations and generalizations made in individual cases. For example, while a group of scholars (Goode 1963; Ross 1961) assert that the family in a metropolitan complex individualistic society is shorn of its all other functions and attributes, and is reduced to mean a 'group defined by a sex relationship sufficiently precise and enduring to provide for the procreation and upbringing of children', (cf. Kulkarni 1962), others hold an entirely opposite view. For example, Desai (1980: 44) notes that the present economic system is unable to provide basic conditions for a 'small-nuclear family', and it generates a process which compels families to depend on traditional social kin-groups, as well as to evolve justifications for older values and norms.

Many researchers, on the other hand, strongly assert a rural-urban difference in household organization and family structures according to their locale; but Conklin (1976), from his study of Dharwar finds in contrast a homogeneity in the family patterns of the two locations. It appears, therefore, that our knowledge of Indian family structures, particularly, in urban locations, suffers from both methodological and conceptual limitations. An understanding of the composition of urban households in metropolitan areas is of crucial importance because under the economic and housing conditions in which the families have to live in metropolitan areas, family life is bound to be affected and would differ from what it may be in smaller towns and villages. This calls for a systematic study and appraisal of the patterns and structures in urban areas of different sizes and categories. This essay makes an attempt in this direction by analysing household organizations and family patterns in Calcutta.

The main objective of this essay is to examine the variations in family structures and study their interrelationships with certain sociocultural and economic variables. It seeks to show how family in a metropolitan urban complex adapts itself to different societal situations while retaining its basic structural characteristics.

The Study

The study is based on the data collected in connection with a survey on some aspects of family planning in Calcutta by the Indian Statistical Institute during 1973-74. A two-stage stratified sample design was adopted with block as the first stage and the household as the second stage of sampling. The sample frame consisted of 3870 Urban Frame Blocks of Calcutta city. The blocks were stratified into 4 strata on the joint consideration of locality, type and religious composition of the area. A sample of 64 blocks was selected with probability proportional to number of sample households in 1970 from the master sample of 304 blocks. A total of 1417 households were so selected randomly from 64 blocks as to make the design self-weighted (for details of sampling design see: Sarkar 1977). All households of sample blocks were stratified into three strata according to certain demographic characteristics, like presence or absence of married females belonging to the age up to 49 years, incidence of live birth, and so on. The households referred to were mutually distinguished, coresident commensal kin group who usually lived together and ate from the same kitchen.

For the present analysis, a systematic classification of the households was made in relation to kinship ties, which bound the constituents together in locally functioning families units. Ultimately, a sample of 1573 families and non-familial units were identified from the surveyed households by the criterion of kinship relation.

On the basis of intra-family relations the family units were next grouped into two types: (1) nuclear and (2) extended. The nuclear type includes members who are related with one another by conjugal, parental or sibling relationships. But those containing members who are related among themselves lineally or affinally, with or without the simultaneous presence of nuclear relations in the unit, had been labelled as extended. The extended family type was again classified into three sub-types: (i) lineal joint, and (ii) collateral joint and (iii) 'complex', from the point of view of 'inclusiveness of membership'. The criterion of collaterality had been ascertained in terms of the 'heads' (or Ego) of the family, and 'complex' through 'adhesions' i.e., those kins or affines who cannot trace their lines of descent among themselves and do not belong usually to the basic structures according to the patri-virilocal norm of residence (Mukherjee 1962, Pakrashi 1962, Chakrabarti 1981).

We have examined the internal variations in the family structures by nature of intra-familial relations, couple, and generations, and the external variations by state of origin, community, education, occupation, and age. Since the data were of secondary nature having very little qualitative information, no attempt was made for any causal explanation of the variations noted in course of this analysis.

Findings

From the analysis of the sample households in Calcutta, the following characteristics of the city families have been noticed:

General

(i) The single-number households, i.e., the non-familial units accounted for 18.11 per cent of the city household in 1973-74.

(ii) Compared to extended families, the incidence of nuclear family was relatively higher for 45.33 per cent of the city families were nuclear while the percentage of extended families was 36.56.

(iii) The difference between the nuclear and extended family units gradually narrowed down when the non-familial units were excluded. The ratio of the two types was 13:12.

(iv) Among the extended families, the lineal joint type outnumbered the 'complex' type which was followed by the collateral type. The respective percentages of the three types of extended families were 16, 11 and 9.

It has been noticed that mainly the male immigrants constitute the non-family units. Most of them are married and thus, living away from their family consorts. The female non-familial units comprising one-third of the total, on the contrary, are mostly composed of widowed or divorced persons in the older age groups.

Characteristics of Nuclear Families

For examining the nature of formation of nuclear families, we have classified these units according to the presence or the absence of conjugal, parental, and sibling relations. This would provide us not only an indication of completeness or incompleteness of nuclear family structures but also with their internal variations in the city (Table 1).

The overwhelming majority of nuclear families in Calcutta are complete as they contain all the three possible kinship relations. These are formed by parents with their unmarried children. The incidence of incomplete nuclear families is noticed in 12 per cent cases only, three-fourth of which are formed by the conjugal relations, i.e., husband and wife. There are very few families formed on the basis of parental and sibling relations, and those containing sibling relations only, occur in rare cases. These families, therefore, tend to register a partial disintegration of nuclear families.

Characteristics of Extended Families

An examination of the characteristics of the extended family structures shows that the majority of these families contain all the five intra-familial relations: lineal, affinal, conjugal, parental and sibling (Table 2). Nearly 81 per cent of them are formed by these 5 specific relations. Despite the fact that 24 combinations are possible as per the five relations, only 17 combinations have been discerned, among them 10 occur in less than one per cent cases. In fact, about 95 per cent of the total extended structures have been accounted for by five combinations only. This indicates that the extended families in Calcutta are not unpatterned. They conform to a pattern that does not suggest their structural disintegration.

The structural variations in extended families can be examined in the light of number of couples, generational depth, membership size, and many other variables. Since we did not find much variations by size, and as we lacked other variables like head's familial role, status, etc., this analysis has been made in terms of two variables: (i) number of couples and (ii) generational depth (Table 3).

It is noticed that two or more couple families are preponderant in the lineal joint structures whereas the majority of one couple families go to form the collateral joint structures. The 'complex' families, however, show a tendency to accommodate more than one couple in them. Generationally also three varieties of extended families differ with one another. The collateral variety, for example, is restricted by two-generation structure in depth while greater depth can be marked in the lineal variety. Though few in number, the four-generational structures occur more in the "complex" families.

Some Inter-relationships

Having thus analyzed the internal characteristics of the non-familial and family units, we may now examine their nature of relationships with some sociocultural and economic variables.

State of Origin and Family Type

To begin with, we shall ascertain whether the people of various states who have come to the city differ in their family organization. For this we have examined the state of origin of the heads of units by their family types (Table 4).

Apparently, there seems to be very little difference between the West Bengal and the non-West Bengal people in respect of the percentage distribution of broad family units, except in the case of having a relatively higher proportion of nuclear families by the former group and of 'complex' families by the latter group. But within the immigrant section, there is some difference that deserves our notice. For example, the non-familial unit appears to be fairly high among the people who came from Bihar and Orissa while it is distinctly low among the Bangladesh and Uttar Pradesh people living in Calcutta. Similarly, the nuclear family occurs relatively more among those coming from Assam, Kerala, Andhra Pradesh whom we have included in the category 'others' and among the Bangladesh, Uttar Pradesh and Orissa immigrants, whereas its incidence is found to be relatively less among the Bihar and Orissa people. The percentage of lineal joint family again is distinctly lower among the Orissa and Bihar households in Calcutta compared to the households from other States of India and Bangladesh. The incidence of collateral joint family, however, is relatively higher among the former than the latter groups. The 'complex' family occurs not at all or very insignificantly among the households from Orissa and other States. The table, therefore, confirms the view that family structures vary by region (Kolenda 1968) and it can be noticed even in a metropolitan setting.

Community: Religious-caste/group and Family Type

Community-wise also we notice, a variation in the structural articulations of the city families (Table 5). It is among the Muslims that the non-familial units are minimum and the 'complex' families are maximum in number. Among the Christians and other non-

Hindu communities, the nuclear families occur in the maximum, with the corresponding minimum occurrence of extended families. Compared to the high and the scheduled caste Hindus, the incidence of patrilineal joint families appears to be high in the other Hindu group, which includes mainly the clean castes.

Education and Family Type

Education is usually assumed to play an important role in shaping the structure of a family. As such, to what extent it is related to the formation of different types of families in the city may be noteworthy. For this purpose, the maximum levels of education attained by the members of the families have been categorized broadly into three categories: (a) low—having education below the level of primary or none, (b) medium—covering primary and above but below the level of school final, (c) high—including the education level of school final and above. The family types have been examined in the light of these education levels (Table 6).

It is found that low education is highly pronounced among the non-familial units. The nuclear families, on the other hand, are characterised mostly by the medium level education, while the converse relationship holds good for the extended structures. The table tends to suggest that education and extended structure have a positive relationship and this appears true for all the sub-types of extended structures.

Occupation and Family Type

On the basis of nature of principal household occupation, the non-familial and family units were examined in terms of four categories: (i) professional-managerial and technical, (ii) clerical, (iii) trade and commerce, and (iv) manual, semi- and unskilled type of jobs (Table 7).

The non-famlllal units are mainly engaged in the manual activities, while the majority of the nuclear families are employed in the clerical, technical, and other non-manual jobs. The trading or commercial activities occur relatively more in the extended families irrespective of their types. Occupationally, therefore, the city families show a positive association.

Age of Head and Family Type

In every family, it is the 'head' who plays a vital role in its decision making, management and organizational process. The variations in family structures, as Mukherjee (1977) noted earlier, "can be accounted for by the kind of family organization sponsored by the 'heads' of families in course of their life-spread." The structure of family, therefore, depends considerably on 'head's' characteristics of which the demographic variable, 'age', is one. Consequently, we have examined the interrelationship of age and family structure to assess the nature of variations (Table 8).

We find that the non-familial units are mostly represented by the young aged people, while the 'heads' of the city families are the older people. But compared to nuclear families, the incidence of older 'heads' (in the age group of 60 years or above) in the extended structure is maximum. Within the extended structure, the patrilineal joint families have more elderly 'heads' relatively, than the non-patrilineal families. And within the joint families, the 'heads' of collateral joint families are comparatively young in age.

Discussion and Conclusion

In the preceding pages, we have examined some internal characteristics of Calcutta families and analysed their structures in terms of certain socio-cultural and economic variables.

We noticed that the single-member households account for only about one-fifth of the total households in Calcutta. This indeed is a very low figure compared to what one finds in Sen's survey of 1954-55 which revealed that 57.4 per cent households in the city are single-member households (Sen 1961: 164).

Such a reduction in the proportion of single-number units, even after a period of two decades, seems impossible because of the fact that there has not been any foreseeable reasons, like improvement in the living condition during these years which might have inspired these individuals to bring their left-out members from their places of origin to this city. If we attribute this reduction to urban-rural migration that would also be a far-fetched assumption for urban-rural migration, so far as the available literature shows, has not acquired such a proportion at any period during this time due to improvement of village economy which could draw these people back and to alter the content of any location. The large difference in the proportional incidence of single-number households needs, therefore, some other explanation.

One reason that can perhaps explain the phenomenon is the differential nature of the design adopted for the study. We mentioned earlier that the data that have been used here were meant originally to study the fertility behaviour of Calcutta couples. Hence, it is not unlikely that those areas or blocks in the city where the single-member households were concentrated have been excluded from the scope of the sampling, resulting therefore to an underestimation of such households. But Mukherjee's (1977) study of family structures conducted more or less in the same period (in the city of Calcutta and Howrah) also revealed a figure much below than what we notice in Sen's survey. The study showed that 33 per cent of the total non-familial and family units of the city were single-member units. From the census reports of Calcutta arid reports from other metropolitan cities like Delhi (Rao and Desai 1965), Bombay (Bulsura 1970), Madras (Balakrishna 1961), etc., we find the percentages of single-member households vary in the range of 11-16 only. These findings while tilt the balance in our favour and also suggest that Calcutta has a relatively large percentage of single-member households, it is certainly not to that extent which might give an impression that it is a city of lonely individuals!

As far as the family units are concerned, the study has not revealed any indication that can suggest the incompatibility of the city environment for sustaining extended kinship ties. The majority of the families, as we have noticed, are complete in their structural articulations and do not lead us any indication of their structural possible disintegration. The variations, that we notice, occurred possibly due to demographic process of birth, death and marriage. Considering the internal characteristics of Calcutta families, can it be said that the existing physical, economic and social systems create such a situation that induce more and more families to get attached with their traditional social kins? Otherwise, how can we explain the formation of so many 'complex' structures in the city?

Enough evidence has been given to indicate that there is a close connection between family structure and nature of the ethnicity, occupation, education and religious community. We have seen that the single-member units occur relatively more among those who came from Orissa but less among the immigrants from Bihar and Uttar Pradesh. Orissa being relatively closer to Bengal and as majority of the people from Orissa engage in unorganized sector like plumbing, cooking, small trade, etc. (Bose 1964) they possibly find no interest in setting family life in the city in view of the acute shortage of accommodation and high cost of living. The people from Bihar and Uttar Pradesh are employed mostly in factories and manufacturing concerns and also in other manual jobs. Being employed in organized sectors, they usually get quarters from their employers where they usually live with their family members in security. This is, however, not to suggest that they always set up families with wives and children. In many cases, we found several married brothers without wives lived together with nephews or cousins.

However, among all communities, the incidence of nuclear families is maximum among the Christians, Muslims, and Scheduled Castes. The white-collar, technical and professional jobholders seem to favour this type of family. The motive and reasons, however, could not be investigated in the present study. For the community-wise variation in family organization we may guess that cultural and economic factors have a role to play. With regard to the extended families, we noticed that the middle caste Hindus having education School Final level and above, and pursuing business and independent non-manual occupations show a tendency to form this type families. This is a finding, which corroborates with the experience of Gore (1968) from Delhi and Balakrishna (1970) from Madras. The higher incidence of non-patrilineally extended families among the Muslims seems to have taken place due to the prevalence of cousin-marriage and the higher rate of divorce among them—as discussed in a separate paper (Chakrabarti 1981).

To sum up, the present study has shown that the households in Calcutta follow a cyclic process of growth and the internal variations in family structures are less prominent and most of the external variations can be accounted for by age, education and ethnicity and occupation.

TABLE 1
Intra-Family Relations in Nuclear Families

Completeness	*Intra-family relations*	*Composition*	*Percentage to total*
(1)	*(2)*	*(3)*	*(4)*
Complete	Conjugal, Parental sibling	Husband, wife, unmarried children	69.43
	Conjugal, parental	Husband, wife, unmarried child	18.37
Incomplete	Conjugal	Husband, wife	9.26
	Parental, sibling	Father/mother, unmarried cildren	1.12
	Parental	Father/mother, unmarried child	1.12
	Sibling	Brother(s) and/or sister(s)	0.70
	Total		100.00
	Sample		(713)

TABLE 2
Kinship Relations in Extended Families

Kinship relations	*Type of extended family*			
	Patrilineal joint		*Non-patri-lineal joint 'complex'*	*Total*
	Lineal	*Collateral*		
(1)	*(2)*	*(3)*	*(4)*	*(5)*
Affinal, lineal, conjugal parental sibling	82.29	84.26	75.43	80.70
Affinal conjugal, parental, sibling	7.48	4.79	4.57	5.92
Affinal, lineal, conjugal, parental	3.54	0.68	5.72	3.48
Lineal, conjugal, parental, sibling	0.39	0.68	4.57	1.74
Affinal, lineal, conjugal, sibling		0.68		0.17
Affinal, lineal, parental, sibling			0.57	0.17
Affinal, conjugal, sibling		6.86	2.29	2.44
Affinal, lineal, conjugal	3.54			1.57

(1)	*(2)*	*(3)*	*(4)*	*(5)*
Affinal, conjugal, parental	1.97		0.57	1.04
Lineal, parental, sibling		1.37	1.71	0.87
Conjugal, parental, sibling			2.29	0.70
Lineal, conjugal, parental			0.57	0.17
Lineal, conjugal, sibling			0.57	0.17
Lineal, sibling	0.79			0.35
Lineal, conjugal			0.57	0.17
Lineal, parental			0.57	0.17
Affinal		0.68		0.17
Total Sample	100.00 (254)	100.00 (146)	100.00 (175)	100.00 (575)

TABLE 3
Per cent Distribution of Couple and Generation in Extended Family

Number of couple/ generation	*Lineal*	*Type of extended family* *Patrilineal joint collateral*	*Total*	*Non-Patrilineal 'complex'*	*Total (sample)*
(1)	*(2)*	*(3)*	*(4)*	*(5)*	*(6)*
			Couple		
0				100.00	100.00 (1)
1	10.74	52.07	62.81	37.19	100.00 (121)
2	56.68	16.61	73.29	26.71	100.00 (337)
3	45.57	18.99	64.56	35.44	100.00 (79)
4 or above	37.84	32.43	70.27	29.73	100.00 (37)
			Generation		
1		73.33	73.33	26.67	100.00 (15)
2	18.33	50.56	68.89	31.11	100.00 (180)
3	59.13	11.99	71.12	28.88	100.00 (367)
4 or above	30.77		30.77	69.23	100.00 (13)
Total	44.17	25.39	69.56	30.44	100.00 (575)

TABLE 4
Per cent Distribution of Households by State of Origin and Family Type

Family type	*State of Origin*					
	West Bengal	*Bihar*	*Orissa*	*Uttar Pradesh*	*Bangla-desh*	*Others*
(1)	*(2)*	*(3)*	*(4)*	*(5)*	*(6)*	*(7)*
Non-familial unit	18.89	30.69	38.24	13.60	11.50	12.82
Nuclear family	42.51	37.57	47.06	50.00	49.20	58.12
Lineal joint family	15.38	10.58	2.94	16.95	21.39	16.24
Collateral joint family	8.91	12.70	11.76	9.32	8.29	8.55
'Complex' family	14.31	8.46	—	10.17	9.62	4.27
Total (Sample)	100.00 (741)	100.00 (189)	100.00 (34)	100.00 (118)	100.00 (374)	100.00 (117)

TABLE 5
Per cent Distribution of Household by Religions-caste Community and Family Type

Family type	*Religious-Caste Community*					
	Hindu			*Total*	*Muslims*	*Christian and others*
	High caste	*Scheduled caste*	*Other caste*			
(1)	*(2)*	*(3)*	*(4)*	*(5)*	*(6)*	*(7)*
Non-familial unit	21.16	16.67	20.51	20.23	5.93	27.27
Nuclear family	42.76	48.10	42.31	43.56	51.48	51.96
Lineal joint family	16.48	16.19	18.27	16.88	14.44	10.39
Collateral joint family	10.37	9.05	9.62	9.95	7.41	5.19
'Complex' family	9.23	10.00	9.29	9.38	20.75	5.19
Total (Sample)	100.00 (704)	100.00 (210)	100.00 (312)	100.00 (1226)	100.00 (270)	100.00 (77)

TABLE 6
Per cent Distribution of Households by Maximum Level of Education and Family Type

Family type	*Maximum Level of Education*		
	Illiterate or below primary	*Primary or below School Final*	*School Final or above*
(1)	*(2)*	*(3)*	*(4)*
Non-familial unit	44.28	7.80	5.87
Nuclear family	34.75	51.02	48.53
Lineal joint family	9.53	18.98	18.98
Collateral joint family	3.81	10.68	12.72
'Complex' family	7.63	11.53	13.89
Total (Sample)	100.00 (472)	100.00 (590)	100.00 (511)

TABLE 7
Per cent Distribution of Households by Nature of Occupation and Family Type

Family type	*Nature of Occupation*			
	Professional/ technical	*Clerical*	*Trade/ Comm-erce*	*Manual and allied*
(1)	*(2)*	*(3)*	*(4)*	*(5)*
Non-familial unit	11.90	7.27	11.64	30.94
Nuclear family	51.14	57.46	46.86	34.87
Lineal joint family	14.18	12.73	21.38	16.24
Collateral joint family	12.91	11.27	7.23	7.01
'Complex' family	9.87	11.27	12.89	10.94
Total (Sample)	100.00 (395)	100.00 (275)	100.00 (318)	100.00 (585)

TABLE 8
Per cent Distribution of Age of Head of Households and Family Type

Family type	*Age-group of head of households (in years)*			
	29 or less	*30-44*	*45-59*	*60 or above*
(1)	*(2)*	*(3)*	*(4)*	*(5)*
Non-familial unit	56.43	12.77	9.92	8.48
Nuclear family	24.90	54.24	51.22	21.22
Lineal joint family	7.47	12.93	15.18	44.85
Collateral joint family	7.47	12.04	7.69	5.45
'Complex' family	3.73	8.02	15.99	20.00
Total (Sample)	100.00 (241)	100.00 (673)	100.00 (494)	100.00 (165)

REFERENCES

Balakrishna, R.: 1961: *Report on the Economic Survey of Madras City*. Delhi: Publication Division, Government of India.

Bose, N. K.: 1964: *Calcutta: 1964; A Social Survey*. Calcutta: Lalvani Publishing House.

Bulsura, J.F.: 1970: *Patterns of Social Life in Metropolitan Areas (with particular reference to Greater Bombay)*. New Delhi: Research Programmes Committee.

Chakrabarti, P.: 1981: "Some Aspects of 'Complex' Families in Calcutta" (Mimeo.). Calcutta. *Sociological Research Unit*, Indian Statistical Institute, pp. 1-24.

Conklin, G.H.: 1976: "Family Structure, Caste and and Economic Development: An Urban-rural Comparison from Dharwar", in Giri Raj Gupta, (ed). *Family and Social Change in Modern India*, Main Currents in Indian Sociology-II. New Delhi: Vikas Publishing House, pp. 19-35.

Desai, A.R.: 1980: *Urban Family and Family Planning in India*. Bombay: Popular Prakashan.

Desai, I.P.: 1964: *Some Aspects of Family in Mahuva*. Bombay: Asia Publishing House.

Dube, L.: 1974: "Sociology of Kinship: A Trend Report", in Indian Council of Social Science Research (ed.) *A Survey of Research in*

Sociology and Social Anthropology, Vol. II. Bombay: Popular Prakashan.

Goode, W.J.: 1963: *World Revolution and Family Patterns*, New York: Free Press.

Gore, M.S.: 1968: *Urbanization and Family Change*. Bombay: Popular Prakashan.

Kapadia, K.M.: 1955: "Changing Patterns of Hindu Marriage and Family III", *Sociological Bulletin*, Vol. 4. No. 2.

Kolenda, P.M.: 1968: "Region, Caste and Family Structure: A Comparative Study of the Indian 'Joint Family'", in Singer, M. and Cohn, B.S. (eds.) *Structure and Change in Indian Society*. Chicago: Aldine Publishing, Co., pp. 339-90.

Kulkarni, M.G.: 1962: "The Family–A Perspective" (mimeo.), Seminar paper, Poona: Gokhale Institute of Economics and Politics.

Mukherjee, R.: 1962: "On the Classification of Family Structure", in Madan, T.N. and Sarana, G. (eds.), *Indian Anthropology: Essays in Memory of D.N. Majumdar*, Bombay: Asia Publishing House. pp. 352-98.

————: 1977: *West Bengal Family Structures: 1946-66*. New Delhi: Macmillan & Co.

Pakrashi. K.: 1962: "A Study of Some Aspects of Household Types and Family Organisation in Rural Bengal, 1946-47", *Eastern Anthropologist*, Vol. 15, pp. 55.63.

Ross, A.D.: 1961: *The Hindu Family in an Urban Setting*. Toronto: Oxford University Press.

Sarkar, B.N.: 1977: *Awareness and Practice of Family Planning in Calcutta*. Calcutta: Demographic Research Centre, Indian Statistical Institute.

Sen, S.N.: 1961: *The City of Calcutta: A Socio-Economic Survey 1954-55 to 1957-58*. Calcutta: Bookland Private Ltd.

Shah, A.M.: 1974: *The Household Dimension of the Family in India*. New Delhi: Orient Longman.

Sharma, J.: 1964: "Nuclearization of Joint Family Households in West Bengal", *Man in India*, Vol. XLIV, pp. 193-206.

Bibliography

Abbi, B.L.: 1969: "Urban family in India". *Contributions to Indian Sociology*, New Series, No. 3, pp. 116-27.

Acharya, H.: 1955: "Caste and joint family in an immigrant community". *Sociological Bulletin*, Vol. 4, pp. 129-38.

———: 1974: "Some possible variations in family types in Gujarat". pp. 179-90 in G. Kurien (ed.), *Family in India: A Regional View*, The Hague, Mouton.

Agarwala, B.R.: 1955: "Caste and joint family in a mobile community". *Sociological Bulletin*, Vol. 4, pp. 138-146.

———: 1961: "Nature and extent of social change in a mobile commercial community (Study of change in family and marriage patterns)". *Sociological Bulletin*, Vol. 11, Nos. 1-2, pp. 141-46.

———: 1962: "Nature and extent of social change in a mobile commercial community" *Sociological Bulletin*, Vol. 11, pp. 141-45.

Agarwal, C.B.: 1968: "Family organisation and authoritarian personality". *Journal of Social Research*, Vol. 11, pp. 7-26

Ahmad, I.: 1976: *Family, Kinship, and Marriage among Muslims in India*. Columbia: South Asia Books.

Ahuja, R.: 1966: "Family pattern among Bhils". *Eastern Anthropologist*, Vol. 19, pp. 29-43.

Aiyappan, A.: 1955: "Caste and joint family in Tamil Nadu." *Sociological Bulletin*, Vol. 4, pp. 117-22.

Aiyar, C.S.R.: 1921-22: "The Hindu joint family". *Hindu Law Journal*, Vol. 3, 4.

Aldous, J. and R. Hill: 1966: *International Bibliography of Research in Marriage and the Family*: 1900-64. Minneapolis: University of Minnesota Press.

Ames, M.M.: 1969: "Modernisation and social structure: Family, caste and class in Jamshedpur". *Economic and Political Weekly*, Vol. 4, Special Number (Nos. 28, 29, 30), pp. 1217-24.

————: 1973: "Structural dimensions of family life in the steel city of Jameshedpur". In M. Singer (ed), *Entrepreneurship and Modernisation of Occupational Cultures in South Asia*. Duke University, Durham, N.C.

Augustine, J.S.: 1982: *The Indian Family in Transition*. New Delhi: Vikas Publishing House.

Bailey, F.G.: 1957: *Caste and the Economic Frontier*. Manchester: Manchester University Press.

————: 1960: "The joint family in India". *Economic Weekly*, Vol. 20 (February), pp. 345-52.

Baksi, B.K.: 1965: "Changing Indian family". *Social Welfare*, Vol. 12, pp. 1-3.

Bandyopadhyay, S. and K. Chattopadhyay: 1964: "A method of classifying family structures". *Indian Sociological Bulletin*, Vol. 11, pp. 22-23.

Banerjee, B.: 1966: *Marriage and kinship of the Gangadikara Vokkaligas of Mysore*. Deccan College Reserarch Institute, Poona.

Banerjee, M.N.: 1944-45: "Hindu family and Freudian theory". *Indian Journal of Social Work*, Vol. 5, pp. 180-87.

Banerjee, S.: 1963: "Pnar kinship system". *Bulletin of the Anthropological Survey of India*, Vol. 12 (3 and 4).

————: 1964: "Residence pattern among the Pnar". *The Bulletin of the Anthropological Survey of India*, Vol. 13, Nos. 1-2.

Barnabas, A.P.: 1955: "Patterns of rural family". *Bulletin of the Christian Institute for the Study of Society*, Vol. 4 (September), pp. 16-25.

Barua, I: 1979: "Some aspects of kin relationship in an Ahom village". *Eastern Anthropologist*, Vol. 32, No. 1 (January-March), pp. 1-12.

Bawa, M.: 1967: "Role analysis of fictive kinship in a Kumaoni society". *Anthropos*, Vol. 62, pp. 898-906.

Beals, A.R.: 1955: "Interplay among factors of change in a Mysore village". pp. 78-102 in McKim Marriott (ed.), *Village India*. Chicago: Chicago University Press.

Behura, K.K.: 1965: "Aspects of Bod Bhatia kinship in an Orrissa village". *Man in India*, Vol. 45, No. 1, pp. 37-49.

Beteille, A.: 1961: "Family and social change in India and other South Asian countries". *Economic Weekly*, Vol. 16, pp. 237-44.

———: 1992: "Caste and family representations of Indian family". *Anthropology Today*, Vol. 8, No. 1 (February), pp. 13-18.

Bhadra, R.K.: 1977: "Some observations on the study of family change in India". *Man in India*, Vol. 57, pp. 44-59.

Bhandari, J.S.: 1962: "The family organisation of the Mishing (Miri) of Assam". *Bulletin of the Department of Tribal Culture and Folklore Research*, Gauhati, Assam: Gauhati University.

———: 1963: "Kinship structure among the Rajputs of Baila– a polyandrous village of Jaunsar Bawar". *Bulletin of the Anthropological Survey of India*, Vol. 12, pp. 7-21.

———: 1965: "Kinship, marriage and family among the Korwa Dudhi (Mirzapur, U.P.)". *Eastern Anthropologist*, Vol. 16, pp. 79-106.

Bharat, S.: 1986: "Single-parent family in India:Issues and implications". *Indian Journal of Social Work*, Vol. 47, No. 1, (April), pp. 55-65.

Bose, A.B.: 1963: "The structure and composition of rural families". *Indian Journal of Social Work*, 23, pp. 352-58.

———: 1963: "The size and composition of households in dispersed dwellings". *Journal of Family Welfare*, Vol. 10, pp. 24-31.

———: 1964: "Age of head and composition of rural joint

households". *Indian Journal of Social Research*, Vol. 5, pp. 229-38.

———: 1964: "Composition of rural households in Rajasthan". *Indian Journal of Social Research*, Vol. 5, pp. 299-308.

———: 1965: "Some characteristics of rural nuclear households". *Man in India*, Vol. 45, pp. 195-200.

———: 1966: "Rural family organization in Western Rajasthan". Eastern Anthropologist, Vol. 21, pp. 163-75.

Bose, A.B., S.P. Malhotra and L.P. Bharara: 1963: "Socio-economic difference in dispersed dwellings". *Man in India*, Vol. 43, No. 2, pp. 119-30.

Bose, A.B. and P.C. Saxena: 1964: "Composition and size of rural households in Rajasthan (Studies in Households III)". *Indian Journal of Social Research*, Vol. 5, No. 2, pp. 299-308.

———: 1965: "Composition and size of rural joint household (Studies in Households IV)". *Indian Journal of Social Research*, Vol. 6, No. 1, pp. 30-40.

———: 1966: "Some characteristics of nuclear households". *Man in India*. Vol. 45, No. 3, pp. 195-200.

———: 1966: "Marriage and family in Western Rajasthan". *Proceeding of the International Conference on the Family*, New Delhi.

Bose, N.K.: 1928: "Marriage and kinship among the Juanga". *Man in India*, Vol. 8, No. 4, pp. 233-42.

Bose, P.K.: 1978: "Family structure and classes in four villages". *Man in India*, Vol. 58, pp. 151-170.

Bott, E.: 1971: *Family and Social Network*. London: Tavistock Publications (originally published, 1954).

Brara, R.: 1996: "Family, kinship and marriage in India". (Book review: P. Uberoi, ed. Family, Kinship and Marriage in India), *Contribution to Indian Sociology*, Vol. 30, No. 2, (July—December), p. 327.

Bryce, L.W.R.: 1937: "The Changing Family in India". *Unpublished Ph.D. Dissertation*, Toronto University.

Buradkar, M.P.: 1940: "Kinship among the Gonds". *Nagpur University Journal*, pp. 147-80.

———: 1964: *Rengsanggri: Family and Kinship in a Garo Village. Philadelphia*: University of Pennsylvania Press.

Caldwell, J.C., P.H. Reddy and P. Caldwell: 1984: "The determinants of family structure in rural south India". *Journal of Marriage and the Family*, Vol. 46, pp. 215-29.

Carroll, J.J.: 1975: "Field research on urbanization and family change in India". *Man in India*, Vol. 55 (October-December), pp. 339-54.

Carroll, L.: 1983: "The Muslim family in India: Law, custom, and empirical research". *Contributions to Indian Sociology*, Vol. 17, No. 2 (July-December), pp. 205-22.

Chakrabarty, P. and S. Bhowmick: 1983: "Some aspects of household organization and family structures in Calcutta". *Eastern Anthropologist*, Vol. 36, pp. 31-44.

Chakrabarti, P.: 1985: "Some aspects of 'complex' families in Calcutta–A research note". *Journal of Comparative Family Studies*, Vol. 16 (Autumn), pp. 377-86.

Chandrasekhar, S.: 1943: "The Hindu joint family". *Social Forces*, Vol. 21, (March), pp. 328-33.

Chatterjee, M.: 1974: "Kinship in an urban low caste locality." Eastern Anthropologist, Vol. 27 (October- December), pp. 337-49.

———: 1977: "Conjugal roles and social networks in an Indian urban sweeper locality". *Journal of Marriage and the Family*, Vol. 39 (February), pp. 193-202.

Chattopadhyay, G.: 1964: "Kinship and marriage among the Hos". *Bulletin of the Cultural Research Institute*, Vol. 3, pp. 13-26.

Chattopadhyay, K.P.: 1921: "Some Malayalam Kinship Terms". Man in India, Vol. 1, No. 2, pp. 141-43.

———: 1922: "Levirate and kinship in India". *Man*, Vol. 22, No. 25, pp. 36-41.

———: 1939-40: "Kinship in the Vedic period". *Journal of the Indian Anthropological Institute*, Vol. 2.

———: 1941: "Kashi kinship and social organization". Calcutta University Anthropology Papers, No. 6, pp. 1-39.

———: 1961: "A study of Santal family size". *Journal of National Institute of Science.* Silver Jubilee Volume.

———: 1961: "On definitions, mainly of family types".In R.N. Saxena (ed.), *Social Research and Social Problems in India*. Bombay: Asia Publishing House.

———: 1962: "On terms of kinship and social relationship". In T.N. Madan and Gopala Sarana (eds.), *Indian Anthropology*. Bombay: Asia Publishing House.

Chauhan, B.R.: 1960: "Family and household in a Rajasthan village". *Indian Sociologist*, Vol. 2, No. 3, pp. 36-40.

Chekki, D.A.: 1962: "The study of kinship in Anthropology". *Journal of Karnatak University (Humanities),* Vol. 7, pp. 133-44.

———: 1969: "Social legislation and kinship in India: A socio-legal study". *Journal of Marriage and the Family*, Vol. 31, No. 1, pp. 165-72.

———: 1974: *Modernization and Kin Network*. Leiden: E.J. Brill.

———: 1986: "The Lingayat family and community in transition". *Paper presented at the XI World Congress of Sociology*, New Delhi, August, 18-22, pp. 1-29.

———: 1988: "Recent directions in family research: India and North America". *Journal of Comparative Family Studies*, Vol. 22 (Summer)", pp. 171-86.

———: 1988: "Family in India and North America: Change and continuity among the lingayat families". *Journal of Comparative Family Studies*, Vol. 19 (Summer), pp. 329-43.

———: 1996: "Family values and family change". *Journal of Comparative Family Studies*, Vol. 27, No. 2, (Summer), pp. 409-13.

Cohn, B.S.: 1965: "Chamar family in a north-Indian village". *Economic Weekly*, Vol. 13, pp. 1051-55.

Conklin, G.H.: 1968: "The family formation process in India: An overview". *Journal of Family Welfare*, Vol. 14, pp. 28-37.

———: 1969: "Social change and the joint family: the causes of research biases". *Economic and Political Weekly*, Vol. 4, pp. 1445-48.

———: 1973: "Emerging conjugal role patterns in a joint family system: correlates of social change in Dharwar, India". *Journal of Marriage and the Family*, Vol. 35 (November), pp. 742-48.

———: 1974: "The extended family as an independent factor in social change". *Journal of Marriage and the Family*, Vol. 36 (November), pp. 798-804.

———: 1976: "The household in urban India". *Journal of Marriage and the Family*, Vol. 38 (November), pp. 771-79.

———: 1976: "Family structure; caste and economic development: An urban-rural comparison from Dharwar, Karnataka." pp. 19-35 in G. R. Gupta (ed.), *Family and Social Change in India*, Main Currents in Indian Sociology-II, New Delhi: Vikas Publishing house.

———: 1977: "Family modernization values and factory employment: An example from South India". *Journal of Comparative Family Studies*, Vol. 8 (Autumn), pp. 315-26.

———: 1987: "The influence of economic development on patterns of conjugal power and extended family residence in India". *Journal of comparative Family Studies*, Vol. 19 (Summer), pp. 187-205.

Dandekar, V. M. and V. Pethe: 1960: "Size and composition of rural families". Artha Vijnana, Vol. 2, pp. 189-99.

Das, A.K. and S.K. Banerjee: 1966: "The family of tribals of West Bengal static and dynamic aspects of composition". *Bulletin of the Cultural Research Institute*, Vol. 2, No. 1, pp. 12-20.

Das, B.M.: 1955: "Rabha kinship terms". *Man in India*, Vol. 35, No. 1, pp. 52-57.

———: 1957: "Family structure of the Rabhas of Assam". *Man in India*, Vol. 37, pp. 119-24.

Das, Man Singh and V.K. Gupta (eds.): 1996: *Changing Family Roles and Feminism*. New Delhi: M.D. Publications.

Das, R.K.: 1972: "Marriage and kinship among the Kabu Nagasa of Manipur". *Man in India*, Vol. 52, No. 3, (July-September), pp. 228-34.

Dasgupta, M.: 1965: "Changes in the joint family in India". *Man in India*, Vol. 45 (October-December), pp. 283-88.

———: 1966: "An approach to the study of structure of descent, marriage and kinship in India". *Journal of the Indian Anthropological Society*, Vol. 1, pp. 197-203.

Dasgupta, P.K.: 1966: "Family among the War Khasi". *Journal of the Indian Anthropological Society*, Vol. 1, No. 2.

Datta, J.M.: 1961: "On disintegration of joint families". *Modern Review*, Vol. 109, pp. 275-80.

Datta Choudhury, R.: 1957: "Joint family system: Its present and future". *Economic Weekly*, Vol. 9, pp. 1233-37.

Davis,K.: 1942: "Changing modes of marriage: contemporary family types". In H. Becker and R. Hill (eds.), *Marriage and the Family*, New York: D.C. Heath.

Davis, M.: 1976: "The politics of family life in rural West Bengal". Ethnology, Vol. 15, No. 2, (April), pp. 189-200.

———: 1977: "Rank and rivalry in the Bengal Hindu family". *Eastern Anthropologist*, Vol. 30, No. 1, (January- March), pp. 67-87.

Derrett, J. Duncan M.: 1960: "Law and the predicament of the Hindu family". *Economic Weekly*, Vol. 12, pp. 305-11.

———: 1962: "The history of the jurisdical framework of the joint Hindu family". Contributions to Indian Sociology, Vol. 6, pp. 17-47.

Desai, G.H.: 1932: *Hindu Families in Gujarat: Being An Account of Their Domestic, Social and Economic Life*. Baroda: Baroda State Press.

Desai, I.P.: 1954: "Caste and family". *Economic Weekly*, Vol. 6, pp. 249-54.

———: 1955: "An analysis. In symposium: caste and joint family". *Sociological Bulletin*, Vol. 4, pp. 97-117.

———: 1956: "The joint family in India: an analysis". *Sociological Bulletin*, Vol. 5, pp. 144-56.

———: 1961: "Effects of changes in occupations on social relationships with special reference to family". *Journal of the Maharaja Sayajirao*, University of Baroda, Vol. 10, pp. 1-11.

———: 1964: *Some Aspects of Family in Mahuva*. New York: Asia Publishing House.

Desai, N.C.: 1936: *Report on the Hindu Joint Family: Its Economic and Social Aspects.* Baroda: Baroda State Press.

Devanandan, P.D. and M.M. Thomas: 1966: *The changing pattern of family in India*. Bangalore: Christian Institute of Study of Religion and Society.

Driver, E.D.: 1962: "Family structure and socio-economic status in central India". *Sociological Bulletin*, Vol II, pp. 112-20.

———: 1984: "Social class and marital homogamy in urban South India". *Journal of Comparative Familiy Studies*, Vol. 15, pp. 195-210.

Driver, E.D. and A.E. Driver: 1988: "Social and demographic correlates of consanguineous marriages in South India". *Journal of Comparative Family Studies*, Vol. 19 (Summer), pp. 229-44.

D'Souza, Victor and Sethis, Raj Mohini: 1972: "Social class and occupational prestige in India: a case study". *Sociological Bulletin*, Vol. 21: (March).

Dube, L.: 1974: *Sociology of Kinship: An Analytical Survey of Literature*. Bombay: Popular Prakashan.

———: 1997: *Women and Kinship:Comparative Perspectives on Gender in South and South-East Asia*. Tokyo:United Nations University Press.

Dube, S.C.: 1963: "Men's and women's roles in India: A sociological review". In B. Ward (ed.), *Women in the New Asia*. UNESCO.

Dubey, S.M.: 1965: "Role of kinship and ideology in rural factionalizm". Eastern Anthropologist, Vol. 18, pp. 22-33.

Dubey, S.M. and M. Moore: 1983: "On kinship structure, female autonomy, and demographic behaviour in India".

Population and Development Review, Vol. 9, No. 1, (March);35-60.

————: 1980: "Family, marriage and Social change on the Indian fringe", in S.M. Dubey, P.K. Bordoloi and B.N. Borthakur (eds), Family, Marriage and Social Change on the Indian Fringe, New Delhi, Cosmo Publications.

Dumont, L.: 1951: "Kinship and alliance among the Pramalai Kallar". *Eastern Anthropologist*, Vol. 4, pp. 3-26.

————: 1953: "The Dravidian kinship terminology as an expression of marriage". Man, Vol. 54, pp. 34-39.

Dumont, L.and D. Pocock: 1957: "Kinship". *Contributions to Indian Sociology*, Vol. 1, pp. 43-64.

————: 1964: "Marriage in India: the present state of the question; postcript to part one". *Contributions to Indian Sociology* 7, pp. 77-98.

Durham, M.: 1973: "Experiments in marriage". In A.A. Khatri and E. Porterfield (eds.), *Perspectives on Marriage and the Family: A Reader Lexington*, Mass.: Xerox.

Dyson, T. and M. Moore: 1983: "On kinship structure, female autonomy, and demographi behaviour in India". *Population and Development Review*, Vol. 9, No. 1 (March), pp. 35-60.

Ehrenfels, U.R. von: 1952: "Matrilineal family background in South India". *Madras University Journal*, Vol. 3, pp. 38-43.

————: 1971: "Matrilineal joint family patterns in India". *Journal of Comparative Family Studies*, Vol. 2 (Spring), pp. 54-56.

Elder, J.W.: 1967: "Regional differences in family and caste attitudes: North and South India". In Robert I. Crane (ed.), *Region and Regionalism in South Asian Studies: An Exploratory Study*. Duke University Program in Comparative Studies on Southern Asia, No. 5.

Epstein, T.S.: 1962: *Economic Development and Social Change in South India*. Manchester: Manchester University Press.

Fernandez, M.: 1997: "Domestic violence by extended family members in India: Interplay of gender and generation".

Journal of Interpersonal Violence, Vol. 12, No. 3 (June); pp. 433-55.

Fonseca, M.B.: 1963: "Family disorganization and divorce in Indian communities". *Sociological Bulletin*, 12, pp. 14-33.

Freed, S.: 1963: "Fictive kinship in a north Indian village". *Ethnology*, Vol. II, pp. 86-104.

Freed, S.A. and R.S. Freed: 1969: "Urbanization and family types in a north Indian village". *Southwestern Journal of Anthropology*, Vol. 25 (Winter), pp. 342-59.

———: 1982: "Changing family types in India". *Ethnology*, Vol. 21 (July), pp. 189-202.

———: 1983: "The domestic cycle in India: natural history of a will-o'-the-wisp". *American Ethnologist*, Vol. 10, pp. 310-27.

Gangrade, K.D.: 1960: "Dynamics of the Indian family". *Journal of Family Welfare*, Vol. 7, pp. 1-5.

Ganesh, K.: 1994: "Crossing the threshold of numbers: The hierarchy of gender in the family in India". *Indian Journal of Social Sciences*, Vol. 7, No. 2-3, (July-December), pp. 355-62.

Ghosh, B.R.: 1974: "Changes in the size and composition of the household brought about by urbanization in Delhi area" pp. 249-261 In G. Kurian (ed), *The Family in India: A Regional View*, The Hague.

Ghosh, D.: 1964: "Notes on the family among the Dimasa Kachari". *Man in India*, Vol. 45, pp. 17-27.

Ghurye, G.S.: 1952-54: "Social change in Maharashtra". *Sociological Bulletin*, Vol. 1.1 and 3.1.

———: 1955: *Family and Kin in Indo-European Culture*. Bombay: Oxford University Press.

Gist, N.P.: 1954: "Occupational differentiation in South India". *Social Forces*, Vol. 33, pp. 129-33.

Goode, W.J.: 1963: *World Revolution and Family Patterns*. New York: The Free Press of Glencoe.

Gore, M.S.: 1961: "The Impact of Industrialization and Urbanization on Aggarwal Family in Delhi Area". *Unpublished Ph.D. Thesis, Columbia University.*

———: 1962: "The husband-wife and the mother-son relationships". *Sociological Bulletin*, Vol. II, pp. 91-102.

———: 1963: "Kinship structure and attitudes to wealth: In R.D. Lambart and B.F. Hoselitz (eds), *The Role of Savings and Wealth in Southern Asia and the West*, UNESCO, Paris.

———: 1965: "The traditional Indian family". pp. 209-31 in M.F. Nimkoff (ed.), *Comparative Family Systems*, Boston: Houghton Mifflin.

———: 1968: *Urbanization and Family Change*. New York: Humanities Press.

Gough, E.K.: 1952: "Changing kinship usages in the setting of political and economic change among the Naiars of Malabar". *Journal of the Royal Anthropological Institute*, Vol. 82, pp. 71-88.

———: 1955: "Brahman kinship in a Tamil village". *American Anthropologist*, Vol. LVIII, pp. 826-53.

———: 1967: "Inter-personal kinship relations". In D.M. Schneider and E.K Gough (eds.), *Matrilineal Kinship*, Berkeley: University of California Press.

———: 1971: "The origin of the family". *Journal of Marriage and the Family*, Vol. 33 (November), pp. 760-71.

———: 1975: "Changing households in Kerala". In D.Narain (ed.), *Exploration and the Family and other Essays*, Bombay: Thacker and Co.

Gould, H.A.: 1968: "Time dimension and structural change in an Indian kinship system: A problem of conceptual refinement", pp. 413-21 in M. Singer and B.S. Cohn (eds.), *Structure and Change in Indian Society*, Chicago: Aldine.

Guha, A.: 1989: "Bengali kinship: A preliminary enquiry into the native categories". *Journal of the Indian Anthropological Society*, Vol. 24, No. 3 (November), pp. 232-43.

Gulat, I.S. and K.S. Gulati: 1964: *The Undivided Hindu Family: Its Tax Priviledges*. Bombay: Asia Publishing House.

Gulati, L.: 1983: "Impact of the development process on the Indian family". *Kerala Sociologist*, Vol. 11, pp. 7-36.

Gupta, B.: 1994: "Modernity and Hindu joint family system: A problcmatic interaction". *International Journal of World Peace*, Vol. 11, No. 4 (December), pp. 37-60.

Gupta, G.R.: 1974: *Marriage, Religion and Society: Patterns of Change in an Indian village*. New York: Halsted Press.

———: 1976: *Family and Social Change in Modern India*. New Delhi: Vikas

Gupta, K.: 1973: "Structure and organization of Indian family: The emerging patterns". *International Journal of Contemporary Sociology*, Vol. 10 (October), pp. 163-82.

———: 1981: "Structural functional role strain theory of family system in India." *Indian Journal of Social Research*, Vol. 22, pp. 210-29.

———: 1982: "Female sociologists and family sociology in India". *Indian Journal of Social Research*, Vol. 23, pp. 220-44.

———: 1982: "Jointness of Indian family". *Sociological Perspective*, Vol. 1, pp. 1-8.

Gupta, S; S.K. Santra and M.N. Malty: 1971: "Types of Poundra family of lower Bengal". *Society and Culture*, Vol. 2 (January), pp. 69-73.

Gupta, T.R.: 1968: "Rural family status and migration: Study of a Punjab village". *Economic Weekly*, Vol. 13, pp. 1597-1603.

Haider, S.: 1997: "An ethnographic profile of family and kinship among eastern Uttar Pradesh Chamar migrants in a Delhi squatter settlement". *Guru Nanak Journal of Sociology*, Vol. 18, No. 2 (October), pp. 1-32.

Hallen, G.C. and G.A. Theodorson: 1961: "Change and traditionalism in Indian family". *Indian Journal of Social Research*, Vol. 2, pp. 51-59.

————: 1963: "Change and traditionalism in the Indian family". *Indian Journal of Social Research* 4, pp. 105-10.

Hallen, G.C.: 1982: "Family theory in India; some strategies". *Indian Journal of Social Research*, Vol. 23, pp. 991-96.

————: 1982: "Family Researches in India: Some Strategies". Meerut: *Indian Journal of Social Research Publication.*

Hate, C.: 1969: *The Changing Status of Women in Post-independent India.* Bombay: Allied Publishers Private Ltd.

Hershman, P.: 1981: *Punjabi Kinship and Marriage.* Delhi: Hindustan.

Hitchcock, J.T.: "The Rajputs of Khalapur: A Study of Kinship, Social Stratification and Politics". *Unpublished Ph.D. Thesis*, Cornell University.

Hobson, S.: 1978: *Family Web: A Story of India.* London: J. Murray.

Hsu, Francis L.K.: 1965: "The effect of dominant kinship relations on kin and non-kin behaviour". American Anthropologist, Vol. 67, No. 3, pp. 638-61.

Hughes, A.L.: 1988: "Kin networks and political leadership in a stateless society: The Toda of South India". *Ethnology and Sociobiology*, Vol. 9, No. 1, pp. 29-44.

Indiradevi, M.: 1988: *Women, Education, Employment, Family Living: A Study of Emerging Hindu Wives in Urban India.* Delhi: Gian Publishing House.

Inkeles, A.: 1969: "Making men modern". *American Journal of Sociology*, Vol. 75 (September), pp. 208-25.

————: 1971: "Joint family: still strong". *Indian Institute of Public Opinion.* Monthly Public Opinion Survey, Vol. 16 (May), pp. 28-34.

Ishwaran, K.: 1965: "Kinship and geographical distance in Indian village". *International Journal of Comparative Sociology*, 6.

————: 1974: "The interdependence of elementary and extended family". pp. 163-77 in G. Kurian (ed.), *The Family in India-A Regional View.* The Hague.

Jain, R.K.: 1958: "Features of kinship in an Asur village". *Eastern Anthropologist*, Vol. 12, No. 1, pp. 25-41.

Jha, J.C. and B.B. Chatterjee: 1969: "Changing family in a Polyandrous community". Eastern Anthropologist, Vol. 18, No. 2, pp. 64-72.

Kaldate, S.: 1961: "Urbanization and disintegration of rural joint family". *Sociological Bulletin*, II, pp. 103-12.

Kannan, C.T.: 1963: *Intercaste and Intercommunity Marriage in India*. Bombay: Allied Publishers.

Kanter, R.M.: 1973: "Communes". In A.A. Khatri and E. Potterfield (eds.), *Perspectives on Marriage and the Family*. Lexington, Mass.: Xerox.

Kapadia, K.M.: 1947: Hindu Kinship: *An Important Chapter In Hindu Social History*. Bombay: The Popular Book Depot.

————: 1954-55: "Changing pattern of Hindu marriage and family". *Sociological Bulletin*, Vol. 3 (1, 2) and Vol. 4 (2).

————: 1956: "Rural family patterns: A study in urban-rural relations". *Sociological Bulletin*, Vol. 5, pp. 111-26.

————: 1958: *Marriage and Family in India*. Second Edition. London: Oxford University Press.

————: 1959: "The family in transition". *Sociological Bulletin*, Vol. 8, pp. 68-99.

————: 1966: *Marriage and Family in India*. Third Edition. Bombay: Oxford University Press.

Kapoor, D.: 1957: "The kinship system of the non-polyandrous Kanets of Mahasu". *The Anthropologist*, Vol. 5, No.1-2, pp. 19-31.

Kapoor, S.: 1965: "Family and kinship groups among the Khatris in Delhi". *Sociological Bulletin*, Vol. 14, pp. 54-63.

Kapur, P.: 1970: *Marriage and the Working Women in India*. Delhi: Vikas Publishing House.

————: 1971: "Roles and relationships with special reference to the changing role and status of women". *Paper read at the All India Seminar on the Indian Family in the Change and Challenge of the 70's*. Delhi, November 28-December 2.

————: 1974: *The Changing Status of Working Women in India*. Delhi: Vikas Publishing House.

Kapur, R.: 1969: "Role conflict among employed housewives". Indian Journal of Industrial Relations, Vol. 5 July.

Karvey, I.: 1940: "Kinship terminology and kinship usages on the Maratha country". *Bulletin of Deccan College Research Institute*, Vol. 1, No. 2-4.

————: 1941: "Kinship system and kinship usages in Maharashtra". *Twenty-eighth Indian Science Congress.*

————: 1942: "Kinship terminology and kinship usages in Gujarat and Kathiawad". *Bulletin of Deccan College Research Institute*, Vol. 4, No. 3.

————: 1950: "The system and kinship terms in Karnatak". *Bulletin of Deccan College Research Institute*, Vol. 10, No. 1, pp. 49-61.

————: 1953: *Kinship Organization in India*. Deccan College Research Institute, Poona, Bombay: Asia Publishing House.

————: 1963: "Family through six generations". In Bala Ratnam (ed.), *Anthropology on the March*, Madras: The Book Centre and the Social Sciences Association.

————: 1964: "Family in India". In Baidyanath Varma (ed.), *Contemporary India*, Bombay: Asia Publishing House.

————: 1967: "Analysis of jointness and non-jointness of family". *The Anthropologist*, Vol. 14, No. 1.

————: 1968: *Kinship Organization in India*. Bombay: Asia Publishing House, 3rd edition.

Kashyap, L.D.: 1993: Family interactions". *Indian Journal of Social Work*, Vol. 54, No.1, (January), pp. 23-29.

Kattakayam, J.J.: 1996: "Marriage and family among the tribals of Kerala: A study of Mannans of Idukky district". *Journal of Comparative Family Studies*, Vol. 27 (Autumn), pp. 545-58.

Khan, N.A.: 1963: "Emerging new pattern of family in India". *Indian Journal of Social Research*, Vol. 4, pp. 88-96.

Khatri, A.A.: 1961: "Some neglected approaches and problems in the study of family in India". *Sociological Bulletin*, Vol. 10, pp. 75-81.

———: 1962: "Social change in the Hindu family and its possible impact on personality and mental health". *Sociological Bulletin*, Vol. II, pp. 146-65.

———: 1963: "Rationale for a scale to measure jointness-nuclearity of families". *A paper presented at the Indian Science Congress*, Delhi.

———: 1963: "Social change in the Hindu family and its possible impact on mental health". *Vidya* 6, pp. 65-77.

———: 1965: "Changing family and personality of Hindus: A few broad hypotheses". *Vidya*, Vol. 8, pp. 112-33.

———: 1966: "Marriage and family in India: An overview of researches". *Researches in Child Development, Marriage and Family Relations Done in Indian Institutions of Teaching and Research*. Baroda: Department of Child Development, Faculty of Home Science, University of Baroda.

———: 1970: "Personality and mental health of Indians (Hindus) in the context of their changing family organization". In E.J. Anthony and C. Koupernik (eds.), *The Child in His Family*. New York: John Wiley.

———: 1970: "Marriage and family relationships in Gujarati fiction". *Unpublished Ph. D. Thesis*, University of London.

———: 1971: *Manual of the Scale to Measure Jointness of Families in India*. Ahmedabad, India: B.M. Institute.

———: 1972: "The Indian family: An empirically derived analysis of shifts in size and types". *Journal of Marriage and the Family*, Vol. 34 (3), pp. 725-34.

———: 1973: "Decision-making and mutual consultation among patrilineally related families in India". *Mimeographed*.

———: 1974: "Understanding changes in the family in contemporary India: A few hypotheses". Presented at the Family Research Committee of the International Sociological Association, *the VIII World Congress of Sociology*, Toronto, Canada, during August.

———: 1975: "The adaptive extended family in India today". *Journal of Marriage and the Family*, Vol. 37 (August), pp. 633-42.

———: 1983: *Marriage and Family Relations Through Literature*. Scintilla Publications, India, Distributors, New York: General Hall.

———: 1988: "Some dimensions of Asiatic family: A quantitative evaluation". *Journal of Comparative Family Studies*, Vol. 19 (Summer), pp. 261-72.

Khatri, A.A. and E. Porterfield (Eds.): 1973: *Perspective on Marriage and the Family*. Lexington, Mass.: Xerox.

Khatri, A.A. and R.R. Sutaria: 1973: "Family types and lineality-collaterality in families in India-glimpses into their jointness". *Mimeographed*.

Kochar, V.K.: 1963: "Kinship terms and usages among the Santals of Bolpur area, Birbhum". *Bulletin of Anthroplogical Survey of India*, Vol. 12, No. 1-2, pp. 47-56.

———: 1963: "Size and composition of families in a Tharu village". Vanyajati, Vol. 11, No. 3, pp. 99-106.

———: 1965: "Fission and segmentation process in the joint families of a Tharu village". *Vanyajati*, Vol. 13, No. 1, pp. 3-8.

Kolenda, P.: 1967: "Regional differences in Indian family structure", pp. 147-226 in R. Crane (Ed.), *Regions and Regionalizm in South Asian Studies: An Exploratory Study*. Duke Univ. Prog. Comp. Studies on South Asia, Monograph No. 5.

———: 1968: "Region, caste and family structure: A comparative study of the Indian joint family" pp. 339-96 in M. Singer and B.S. Cohn (Eds.), *Structure and Change in Indian Society*. Chicago: Aldine.

———: 1970: "Family structure in village Lonikand, India: 1819, 1958 and 1967". *Contributions to Indian Sociology*: New Series, Vol. 4, pp. 50-72.

———: 1987: *Regional Differences of Family Structures in India*. Jaipur: Rawat Publications.

———: 1994: "Family, kinship and marriage". (book review: Author: P. Uberoi, ed. 'Family and Kinship and Marriage in India'), *The Journal of Asian Studies*, Vol. 53, No. 3 (August), p. 980.

Kulkarni, M.G.: 1960: "Family patterns in Gokak Taluka". *Sociological Bulletin*, Vol. 9, pp. 60-81.

Kulkarni, M.G.: 1960: "A Brief Review of Literature on Family Structure with Special Reference to Some Empirical Studies", Mimeo.

Kuppuswami, B.: 1957: *Study of Opinion Regarding Marriage and Divorce*. Bombay: Asia Publishing House.

Kurian, G.: 1961: *The Indian Family in Transition*. The Hague: Mouton.

————: 1974: *The Family in India: A Regional View*. The Hague: Mouton.

Kurian, G. and R. Ghosh: 1978: "Changing authority within the context of socialization in Indian families". *Social Science*, Vol. 53 (Winter), pp. 24-32.

Kurian, G.: 1979: "Marriage in transition: A comparison of India and China". *International Journal of Critical Sociology*, Vol. 3, pp. 60-69.

Kutty, K.: 1960: "The Indian joint family: Comment". *Economic Weekly*, Vol. 12, pp. 763.

Lakshminarayana, H.D.: 1963: "Rhythm in joint family". *Indian Journal of Social Research*, Vol. 4, pp. 97-98.

————: 1969: "Family patterns in Mysore village". *Economic and Political Weekly*, Vol. 4, pp. 845-47.

————: 1982: "The rural family in transition", in *The Indian Family in Transition*, edited by J. Augustine, Delhi: Vikas Publishing House.

Lal, A.K.: 1976: "Locus of power in the family". *Indian Journal of Social Work*, Vol. 37, no. 2, pp. 187-93.

Lambert. R.D.: 1963: *Workers, Factories and Social Change in India*. Princeton: Princeton University Press.

Lemercinier, G.: 1979: "Kinship relations and religious symbolism among the clans of Kerala during the Sangan period (First century A.C.)". *Social Compass*, Vol. 26, No. 4, pp. 461-89.

Leonard, K.: 1975: "Women and social change in modern India". *Feminist Studies*, Vol. 3 (Spring-Summer), pp. 117-30.

Lewis, O.: 1958: *Village Life in Northern India*. Urbana: University of Illinois Press.

Madan, T.N.: 1953-54: "Kinship terms used by the Pandits of Kashmir". *Eastern Anthropologist*, Vol. 7, pp. 37-46.

———: 1962: "The Hindu joint family". *Man*, Vol. LXII, pp. 88-89.

———: 1962: "The joint family: A terminological clarification". *International Journal of Comparative Sociology*, Vol. 3, pp. 7-16.

———: 1965: *Family and Kinship: A Study of the Pandits of Rural Kashmir*. New York: Asia Publishing House.

———: 1968: "The Hindu family and economic development". Planning for Social Change, *Proceedings of a Seminar*, Council for Social Development, India International Centre, New Delhi.

———: 1976: "The Hindu family and development". *Journal of Social and Economic Studies*, Vol. IV (September), pp. 211-31.

Mahapatra, L.K.: 1968: "Ritual kinship in Orissa". *Proceedings of the 8th International Congress of Anthroplogical and Archaeological Sciences*.

Majumdar, D.N.: 1923: "A few remarks on the Sema Naga kinship terms". *Man in India*, Vol. 4, Nos. 2-3, pp. 198-208.

———: 1930: "Social organization amongst the Korwas". Man in India, Vol. 10, Nos. 2-3, pp. 104-05.

———: 1954: "Family and marriage in a polyandrous society". Eastern Anthropologist, Vol. 8, No.2, pp. 86-110.

———: 1960: *An Introduction to Social Anthropology*, Bombay: Asia Publishing House. Ch. IV (The Family).

Malhotra, S.P. and M.L. Sen: 1964: "A comparative study of the socio-economic characteristics of nuclear and joint households". *Journal of Family Welfare*, pp. 21-32.

Mamdani, M.: 1972: "The myth of population control: Family, caste and class in an Indian village". *Monthly Review Press*, New York.

Mancher, J.P.: 1962: "Changing familial roles among south Malabar Naiars". *Southwestern Journal of Anthropology*, Vol. 18, pp. 230-45.

Mandelbaum, D.G.: 1948: "The family in India". *Southwestern Journal of Anthropology*, Vol. 4, pp. 123-39.

———: 1949: "The family in India". In R.N. Anshen (Ed.), *The Family Its Function and Destiny Harper and Brothers*, New York.

———: 1957: "The family in India". In Introduction to Civilization of India: *Changing Dimensions of Indian Society and Culture*. Chicago: University of Chicago Press.

———: 1968: "Family, jati, village". pp. 29-50 in M. Singer and B.S. Cohn (Eds.), *Structure and Change in Indian Society*, Chicago: Aldine.

Mayer, A.C.: 1960: *Caste and Kinship in Central India: A Village and it Regions*. London: Routledge and Kegan Paul.

Mehta, S.: 1934: *Marriage and Family in Gujarat*. Ahmedabad: Gujarat Vidya Saba.

———: 1973: "Is the joint family breaking up". *The Illustrated Weekly of India*, Sept. 23, pp. 6-8.

Merchant, K.T.: 1935: *Changing Views on Marriage and Family*. Madras: B.G. Paul.

Miller, K.A.: 1984: "The effects of industrialization on men's attitudes toward extended family and women's rights: A cross-national study" *Journal of Marriage and the Family*, Vol. 46 (February), pp. 153-60.

Minault, G.(ed.): 1981: *The Extended Family: Women and Political Participation in India and Pakistan*. Columbia, Miss.: South Asia Books.

Misra, R.: 1949: "Status of the Joint Family in the Lower Middle Class in Lucknow". *Unpublished Ph.D. Dissertation*, University of Lucknow.

Mistry, J.P.: 1955: "The Family as a Unit of Study". *Unpublished Ph.D. Dissertation*, University of Bombay.

Morrison, W.A.: 1959: "Family types in Badlapur: An analysis of a changing institution in a Maharashtrian village". *Sociological Bulletin*, Vol. 8, pp. 45-67.

Mukherjee, B.: "Garo Family". *Eastern Anthropologist*, Vol. 11, No. 1, pp. 25-31.

————: 1961: "Comparative study of the kinship systems of six matrilineal tribes". *Eastern Anthropologist*, Vol. 14, No. 3, pp. 216-29.

————: 1962: "Rajbashi kinship system". *Bulletin of the Anthropological Survey of India*, Vol. 11, No. 1, pp. 47-56.

————: 1963: "Comparative study of kinship systems of two polyandrous communities". *Eastern Anthropologist*, Vol. 16, No. 2, pp. 75-78.

Mukherjee, R.K.: 1959: "A note on the classification of family structures". *Regional Seminar on Techniques of Social Research: Proceedings and Papers*. Calcutta: UNESCO Research Centre, pp. 133-43.

————: 1962: "On the classification of family structures". In T.N. Madan and Gopala Sarana (Eds.), *Indian Anthropology: Essays in Memory of D.N. Majumdar*, Bombay: Asia Publishing House, pp. 352-98.

————: 1964: "A note on the measurement of kinship distance". *Indian Journal of Social Research*, Vol. 4, No. 1, pp. 12-14.

————: 1971: "Family in India: A perspective". *The Indian Journal of Public Administration*, Vol. 8, pp. 41-106.

————: 1972: "Concepts and methods for the secondary analysis of variations in family structures". *Current Anthropology*, Vol. 13, pp. 3-6.

————: 1976: "Family in India", pp.1-64 in *Explorations in the Family and Other Essays*. Edited by D. Narain, Bombay: Thacker.

————: 1977: *West Bengal Family Structure*, pp. 1946-66. New Delhi: Macmillan and Company.

Mullatti, L.: 1995: "Families in India: Beliefs and Realities". *Journal of Comparative Family Studies*, Vol. 26, (Spring), pp. 11-25.

Mukopadhya, C.C.: 1995: "Family, kinship and marriage in India".

(book review), *American Ethnology*, Vol. 22, No. 3, p. 642.

Murmu, D.: 1982: "The tribal family in transition", in J.S. Augustine (ed.), *The Indian Family in Transition*, New Delhi, Vikas Publishing House.

Nag, M.K.: 1956: "Family structure of the Kanikkar and the Urali of Travancore". *Man in India*, Vol. 36, No. 3, pp. 219-24.

Nag, N.G.: 1960: "Family and marriage in Lahaul Valley". *Eastern Anthropologist*, Vol. 13, No. 4, pp. 185-202.

Naik, R.D.: 1981: "An analysis of change in family composition". *Indian Journal of Social Work*, Vol. 42, No. 1 (April), pp. 27-32.

Naik, T.B.: 1953: "Family in Gujarat". *Journal of Gujarat Research Society*, Vol. 15, pp. 117-37.

———: 1959: "Kinship terms among the Bhils of Malwa". *Bulletin of the Tribal Research Institute*, Vol. 1, No.1

Nakane, C.: 1963: "The Naiar family in a disintegrating matrilineal system". In J. Mogey (Ed.), *Family and Marriage*, Leiden: E.J. Brill. Leiden.

Narain, D.: 1970: "Interpersonal Relationships in the Hindu Family". In *Families in East and West* Edited by R. Hill and R. Konig, Paris:Mouton.

———: 1975: *Explorations in the Family and Other Essays*. Bombay: Thacker and Co. Ltd.

Nicholas, R.W.: 1961: "Economics of family types in two West Bengal villages". *Economic Weekly*, Vol. 13, pp. 1057-60.

Nimkoff, M.F.: 1959: "Family in India: Some problems concerning research on the changing family in India". *Sociological Bulletin*, Vol. 8, pp. 32-39.

Nimkoff, M.F. and M.S. Gore: 1959: "Social bases of the Hindu joint family". *Sociology and Social Research* XLIV, pp. 27-36.

Nimkoff, M.F.: 1960: "Is the joint family an obstacle to industrialization?" *International Journal of Comparative Sociology*, Vol. 1, pp. 109-18.

Oommen, T.K.: 1982: "The urban family in transition". In *The Family in Transition*, edited by J. Augustine, Delhi: Vikas Publishing House.

Orenstein, H.: 1960: "Irrigation, settlement pattern and social organization", pp. 318-23 in A.F.C. Wallace (ed.), *Selected Papers of the Fifth International Congress of Anthropological and Ethnological Sciences*, Philadelphia: University of Pennsylvania Press.

————: 1961: "The recent history of the extended family in India". *Social Problems*, Vol. VIII, pp. 341-50.

Orenstein, H. and M. Micklin: 1966: "The Hindu joint family: The norms and the numbers". *Pacific Affairs*, Vol. 39, pp. 314-25.

Ostar, A., L. Fruzzetti and S. Barnett: *Concepts of Persons: Kinship, Caste, and Marriage in India*. Cambridge, Mass.: Harvard University Press.

Owens. R.: 1971: "Industrialization and the Indian joint family". *Ethnology*, Vol. 10 (April), pp. 223-50.

Pakrasi, K.: 1962: "A study of some aspects of household types and family organization in rural Bengal, 1946-1947". *Eastern Anthropologist* 15, pp. 55-63.

————: 1965: "On some aspects of family structure of the refugees of West Bengal". *Sociological Bulletin*, Vol. 14, pp. 13-20.

————: 1967: "Occupation, class, migration and family structure among the refugees of West Bengal". *Man in India*, Vol. 47, pp. 200-13.

Palriwala, R.: 1996: "Negotiating patriliny: Intra-household consumption and authority in Northwest India". In R. Palriwala and C. Risseeuw (eds.), *Shifting Circles of Support: Contextualising Kinship and Gender in South Asia and Sub-Saharan Africa*, Walnut Creek, CA: Alta Mira.

Panikar, K.M.: 1938: *The Origin and Evolution of Kinship in India*. Baroda.

Parasuraman, S.: 1985: "Migration and its effect on the family". *Indian Journal of Social Work*, Vol. 47, No. 1, (April), pp. 1-14.

Parmar, S.B. Singh: 1979: "Jointness and nuclearity of the Hindu family in rural settings". *Eastern Anthropologist*, Vol. 32, 3 (July-September), pp. 193-99.

Pethe, V.P.: 1962: "Life cycle of families in an urban community". *Sociological Bulletin*, Vol. 12, No. 1, pp. 39-46.

Phadke, S.: 1967: "Special problem of the education of women". In M.S. Gore, I.P. Desai and S. Chintis (eds.), *Papers on the Sociology of Education in India*, Delhi: National Council of Research and Training.

Prasad, R.: 1981: "Family as a support in crisis situation in clinical settings". *Indian Journal of Social Research*, Vol. 22 (December), pp. 278—U4.

Puthenkalan, J.: 1966: "The family organization in the Southwest of India." *Sociological Bulletin*, Vol. 15, pp. 1-27.

Queen, S.A. and R.W. Habenstein: 1952: "The Polyandrous Toda family" In S.A. Queen and R.W. Habenstein, *The Family in Various Cultures*, Philadelphia: J.B. Lippincott Company.

Raha, M.K.: 1988: "Kinship and marriage among the Karens of Andaman Island". *Journal of the Indian Anthropological Society*, Vol. 24, No. 2 (July), pp. 111-20.

Ramanujan, B.K.: 1971: "The Indian family in transition:Changing role and relationships". *Social Action*, Vol. 22, No.1, pp 16-25.

Ramu, G.N.: 1972: "Family and Caste in Urban India". *Unpublished Ph.D. Dissertation*, University of Illinois.

————: 1972: "Researchs on the family in India". *Man in India*, Vol. 52, pp. 212-27.

————: 1972: "Geographic mobility, kinship and the family in South India". *Journal of Marriage and the Family 34*, pp. 147-52.

————: 1973: "Family structure and entrepreneurship: An Indian case". *Journal of Comparative Family Studies*, Vol. 4 (Autumn), pp. 240-56.

————: 1974: "Urban kinship ties in South India". *Journal of Marriage and the Family*, Vol. 36 (August), pp. 619-27.

———: 1979: Family and Caste in Urban India. Delhi: Vikas Publishing House.

———: 1987: "Indian husbands: their role perceptions and performance in single-and-dual-earners families". *Journal of Marriage and the Family*, Vol. 49 (November), pp. 903-15.

———: 1989: "Marital roles and power: Perceptions and reality in the urban setting". *Journal of Comparative Family Studies*, Vol. 21 (Summer), pp. 207-27.

Rao, A. Ramachandra and S. Bandyopadhyay: 1986: "Measures of reciprocity in a social network: A study of some villages in India". *International Sociological Association*. (Paper presented at the International Sociological Association, 1986).

Rao, G.R.S.: 1965: "Emerging role pattern of women in family". *Indian Journal of Social Work*, Vol. 26, pp. 239-42.

Rao, M.S.A.: 1955: "Caste and joint family in Kerala". *Sociological Bulletin*, Vol. 4, pp. 122-129.

———: 1968: "Occupational diversification and joint household organization". *Contributions to Indian Sociology*, Vol. 2 (December), pp. 98-111.

Rao, N.J. Usha: 1973: "Family patterns in an urban setting: A case study in 'Pataliputra Colony', Patna (Bihar)". *Journal of Social Research*, Vol. 16 (September), pp. 35-52.

Rao, V.N. and V.V.P. Rao: 1973: "An analysis of the employed mother in India". *International Journal of Sociology of the Family*, Vol. 3 (September).

Rao, V.V.P. and V.N. Rao: 1979: "An evaluation of the Bardis familism scale in India". *Journal of Marriage and the Family*, Vol. 41 (May), pp. 417-421.

———: 1980: "The dowry system in Indian marriages: attitudes, expectations and practices". *International Journal of Sociology of the Family*, Vol. 10, No. 1 (January-June), pp. 99-113.

———: 1982: *Marriage, The Family and Women in India*. Columbia, Missouri: South Asia Books.

Rawat, P.S.: 1985: "Fluidity in joint family structure: Some theoretical issues. *Guru Nanak Journal of Sociology*, Vol. 6, No. 2 (October), pp. 97-106.

———: 1987: "Migration and fluidity in family structure: A case study of rural society of Garhwal". *International Journal of Sociology of the Family*, Vol. 16, no. 1, (Spring), pp. 143-57.

Rivers, W.H.R.: 1921: "Kinship and marriage in India". *Man in India*, Vol. 1, pp. 6-11.

Ross, A.D.: 1955: "An approach in symposium on caste and joint family". *Sociological Bulletin*, Vol. 4, pp. 85-96.

———: 1959: "Education and family change". *Sociological Bulletin*, Vol. 8, pp. 39-44.

———: 1961: *The Hindu Family in its Urban Setting*. Toronto: University of Toronto Press.

———: 1977: "Some comments on the home roles of businesswomen in India, Australia and Canada". *Journal of Comparative Family Studies*, Vol. 8 (Autumn), pp. 327-40.

Roy, D. and Rustum: 1975: "Is monogamy outdated?" In G.J. Wells (ed.), *Current Issues in Marriage and the Family*. New York: Macmillan.

Roy, P.K.: 1974: "Industrialization and the 'fitness' of nuclear family". *Journal of Comparative Family Studies*, Vol. 5 (Spring), pp. 74-86.

———: 1975-76: "Socio-economic impact of industrialization on the Indian family: A case study in Ranchi, India". *Anthropological Forum*, Vol. IV, pp. 97-109.

———: 1983: "The structure and change of the family in India: A review of research and theory". *International Journal of Asian Studies*, Vol. 3, pp. 22-33.

Roy, S.C.: 1920: "Kinship organisation, marriage and inheritance among the Pahri Bhuiyas". *Journal of Bihar and Orissa Research Society*, Vol. 6, pp. 69-92.

———: 1920: "Kinship and marriage organisation of the Paharias". *Journal of the Bihar and Orissa Research Society*, Vol. 7, pp. 25-32.

———: 1921: "Khasi kinship terms". *Man in India*, Vol. 1, No. 3, pp. 233-38.

Sarana, G.: 1955: "Kinship among the Chamars of Dhanaura". *Agra University Journal of Research*, Vol. 3, pp. 148-57.

Sarma, J.: 1951: "Formal and informal relations in the Hindu joint household of Bengal" *Man in India*, Vol. 31, pp. 51-71.

———: 1964: "The nuclearization of joint family households in West Bengal". *Man in India*, Vol. 44, pp. 193-206.

Sastray, J.: 1998: "Household structure, satisfaction and distress in India and the United States: A comparative cultural examination". *Journal of Comparative Family Studies*, Vol. 30, no. 1, pp. 135-52.

Schlesinger, B.: 1961: "The changing patterns in the Hindu joint family system of India". Marriage and Family Living, Vol. 23 (May), pp. 170-75.

Schneider, D.M. and E.K. Gough (Eds.): 1963: *Matrilineal Kinship*, Berkeley: University of California Press.

Sekhar, T.V.: 1996: "Male emigration and changes in the family: Impact on female sex roles". *Indian Journal of Social Work*, Vol. 57, No. 2, (April), pp. 277-94.

Sen, L.K.: 1965: "Family in four Indian villages". *Man in India*, Vol. 45, pp. 1-16.

Sengupta, P.: 1970-71: "Woman power: The neglected infrastructure". *Today, Magazine of the YWCA of India Winter*.

Sengupta, S.K.: 1958: "Family organization in West Bengal: Its nature and dynamics". *Economic Weekly*, Vol. X, pp. 384-89.

Shah, A.M.: 1964: "Basic terms and concepts in the study of family in India". *Indian Economic and Social History Review*, Vol. 1, pp. 1-36.

———: 1968: "Changes in the Indian family: An examination of some assumptions". *Economic and Political Weekly*, Vol. III, pp. 127-34.

———: 1968: "Family and kinship among the Pandits of rural Kashmir: A review". *Eastern Anthropologist*, Vol. 21, pp. 305-17.

————: 1974: *The Household Dimension of the Family in India*. Berkeley: University of California Press.

————: 1997: *The Family in India: Critical Essays*. New Delhi: Orient Longman.

Shahani, S.: 1961: "The joint family: A case study". *Economic Weekly*, Vol. 13, pp. 823-28.

Sharma, A. and S. Rajlakshmi: 1979: "Opinions of married couples regarding the selection of marriage partner: A study of couples responding in Broda". *Sociological Bulletin*, Vol. 28, 1-2 (March-September), pp. 71-82.

Sharma, P.K.: 1990: "The changing role of the head of the joint family in rural Chhattisgarh". *The Journal of Sociological Studies*, Vol. 9, (January), pp. 31-44.

Shastri R.R.: 1955: "The Hindu family". *Agra University Journal of Research*, Vol. 3, pp. 88-90.

Singer, M.: 1968: "The Indian joint family in modern industry", pp. 423-452 in M. Singer and B. Cohn (eds.), *Structure and Change in Indian Society*, Chicago: Aldine.

Singh, H.: 1980: "Kin, caste and Kisan movement in Marwar: Some questions to the conventional sociology of kin and caste". *Journal of Peasant Studies*, Vol. 7, No.1 (October), pp. 101-18.

Singh, K.P.: 1998: "The Demography of families: An Indian historical perspective". (Book review:Author: A. Maharatna), *Sociological Bulletin*, Vol. 46, No. 2, (September), pp. 271-72.

Singh, R.A.P.: 1984: "The joint family in the agrarian setting". *Eastern Anthropologist*, Vol. 37 (January-March), pp. 49-55.

Singh, R.D.: 1962: "Family Organization in a North Indian Village: A Study in Culture Change". *Ph.D. Dissertation*, Cornell University.

Sinha, D.: 1983: "Some recent changes in the Indian family and their implications for socialisation". *Indian Journal of Social Work*, Vol. 45, No. 3 (October), pp. 271-86.

Sinha, Ramesh P.: 1977: "Indian joint family: An attempt toward taxonomic refinement". *Man in India*, Vol. 57 (January-March), pp. 60-68.

Sontheimer, G.D.: 1977: *The Joint Hindu Family: Its Evolution as a Legal Institution*. New Delhi: Munshiram Manoharlal Publishers.

Srinivas, M.N.: 1942: *Marriage and Family in Mysore*. Bombay: New Book Company.

———: 1952: "A joint family dispute in a Mysore village". *Journal of M.S. University of Baroda*, Vol. 1, pp. 7-31.

Srivastasava, K.: 1986: *Social Class and Family Life in India*. Delhi:Chugh Publishers.

Straus, M.A. and D. Winkelmann: 1969: "Social class, fertility and authority in nuclear and joint households in Bombay". *Journal of Asian and African Studies*, Vol. 9, pp. 61-74.

Straus, M.A.: 1975: "Husband-wife interaction in nuclear and joint households". In D. Narain (ed), *Explorations in the Family and other essays*. Bombay: Thacker and Co. Ltd.

Surya, N.C.: 1969: "Ego structure in the Hindu joint family: Some considerations", pp. 381-92 in W. Caudill and T. Lim (Eds.), *Conference on Mental Health Research in Asia and the Pacific*. Honolulu.

Talwar, P.: 1997: "A study of familial and non-familial influences in aggression among adolescents". *Indian Journal of Social Work*, Vol. 56, No. 4 (October), pp. 467-75.

Taylor, W.S.: 1943: "Behaviour disorders and the breakdown of the orthodox Hindu family system". *Indian Journal of Social Work*, Vol. 4, pp. 162-70.

Tewari, D.N.: 1951: "Changes in the Family Among the AgriculturalClass in few Rural Areas of Lucknow," *Unpublished Ph.D. Dissertation*, University of Lucknow, India.

Trautman, T.R.: 1981: *Dravidian Kinship*. Cambridge: Cambridge University Press.

Tripathi, B.D.: 1969: "Hindu family system and family planning". *Religion and Society*, Vol. 16, pp. 1-8.

Tzeng, J.M.: 1999: "The family in India: Critical essays".(Book review: Author: A.M. Shah, The Family in India), *Journal of Comparative Family Studies*, Vol. 30, No. 2, pp. 329-30.

Uberoi, P.: 1993: *Family, Kinship, and Marriage in India*, Delhi: Oxford University Press.

Vatuk, S.J.: 1969: "Reference, address and fictive kinship in urban north India". *Ethnology*, Vol. 8, pp. 255-72.

———: 1971: "Trends in north Indian urban kinship: The 'matrilateral asymmetry' hypothesis". *Southwestern Journal of Anthropology*, Vol. 27, pp. 287-307.

———: 1978: *Kinship and Urbanization*. Berkeley: University of California Press.

———: 1991: "The cultural construction of shared identity: A South Indian family history". *Social Analysis*, Vol. 28, (July), pp. 114-31.

Vidyarthi, L.P.: 1969: *Cultural Configuration of Ranchi: Survey of an Emerging Industrial City of Tribal Bihar*. Calcutta: Bookland.

Vijayalaxmi, A.H.M. and K. Saroja: 1992: "Changes in kinship adjustment of mixed and intracaste married working women". *International Journal of Sociology of the Family*, Vol. 22, No. 2 (Autumn), pp. 61-68.

Viswananathan, N. and M.M. Desai: 1966: "Housing and family life". *Indian Journal of Social Work*, Vol. 26 (January), pp. 393-405.

Wood, M.R.: 1972: "Women in Urban Gujarat". *Paper presented at the Canadian Society of Asian Studies*. Ottawa, May 26.

Yadava, J.S.: 1966: "Changing family structure in Delhi village". *The Anthropologist*, Vol. 13, pp. 21-29.

———: 1970: "Kinship groups in a Haryana village". *Ethnology*, Vol. 8, No. 4, pp. 494-502.

Zimmerman, C.C.: 1953: "Nature of the family". *Sociological Bulletin*, Vol. 2, pp. 103-17.

————: 1954: "Family and social change". *Sociological Bulletin*, Vol. 3, pp. 1-27.

————: 1955: "Family cultural cause types". *Sociological Bulletin*, Vol. 4, pp. 1-3.

Index

Absent, family members/wives, 79-80
Adaptive Extended Family (AEF) features of, 191, 199
Addition of relationships, 101
Advantage of joint family, 128
Age and attitude towards family, 30
    rise in family heads, 123
    of family head and family type, 293
    occupation, 294
Aggarwal families and nuclear family norms, 22
    traditional occupation, 22-23
Agricultural technology relationship to family type, 5
Ancient literature's contribution to students of Indian family, 104
Assumptions about Indian family examination, beliefs, 99-100
Attitudes towards family size, 28-29
Authority pattern and role relations, 154
    structure and collective decision making, 265-66

Baluta system of service, 321-22
    followers of, 322
Baniyas proportion of joint families in, 47
Beginning of family in branched and unbranched families, 91
Bengal village study of family structure/economic activity correlations, 329, 332
    villages description, 332
    social classes/family types in villages, 333-34
    family structure and classes, 335-40
Bilateral kinship norms, 230
Branched family, 82
Break-up of family description of Mahisya non-entrepreneuer and economic factors influencing, 172
    and family structure, 331
Breakdown of joint family observations, 304
Bride selection/seeing of (ritual) Howrah, 182

Calcutta household structures, 349
Caste (High/Low) and family type, 296
Caste status and family type, 10
Category of family types, 40
Census Commissioner's Reports, 270
    Schedule and data on households, 106
Chamar joint families and exodus of wage earners, 169-70
    households and nuclear families, 331

Changes in family causes of, different schools of thought, 3-4
  areas of, 194
Changing family types analysis of Shanti Nagar, 115, 118
China joint family system in, 66
Chulhas as basis of joint family, 52, 79, 262
Circumstantial problems in distinction of residential groups, 80
Classification of family Kulkarni's, 41
  Leela Dube's, 41
  Driver's, 42
  Ross, 66
  Basu, 42
  Bandyopadhyay and Chattopadhyay, 44
  Pakrasi, 44
  Madan, 45, 66
  Murdock, 66
  Meyer, 46
  Sengupta, 46
  Gough & Ray, 47
  Shahani, 47
  Gore, 66
Clothing Styles changes in, 182
Collateral joint family, 172, 334
  relationships, 39
  classification, 47, 116
Combined Family Types (Shanti Nagar), 119
Community/religious caste organization and family type, 354
Commensal family, 156
  definition, relations with coparcenary, 157
  and family income, 163
  and property sharing and skills, 169
  and causes of jointness and break-up, 185
Comparative statistics (family structure) village Lonikand, 303
Common Family Property, Accounts, Cooking factor, 79
Complex or joint household, 101
Conjugal pattern and family system, 20
  and extended kinship lines, 9
  family-emergence of in India, 139, 268
  trends in India, 191
Conflicts (family), 70
Coparceners/Coparcenary Family, 157
  and ancestral property, 261
  and business successes, 9
Co-residence and patrilateral trends, 238
Correlation/Correlational approach to joint family controversy, 114
  between industrialization and joint family, 153
Criticism of assumption of large to small families, 99

Dayabhaga definition of, 104
  law of ownership, 263-64
  legal system (Bengal, Assam), 172
Death of Family Head, 87-88
Decision making and family types, 195
Demographic factors influence on family types, 126-27
Determinants of developmental process, 102
Developmental cycle-stages, 73-74
Dharma influence on family, 128-29
Dharwar (case study), 140
Different type of households percentage in towns/villages, 38-39
Differentiation between joint and nuclear families, 42
Distribution of combined family types Shanti Nagar, 122
  size of Family-rural and urban sectors, 29

immigrant/urban people, 30
Dinner relations, 217
Disintegration of joint family, 270
Division of property statistics, 142-44
Domestic cycle, 74, 86, 88
Life cycle-relationship, 90
concept of, 75
end of, 90
Domestic groups, changes in, 73

Eating and living arrangements separation of, 181
Earlier (1871) Census–drawbacks, 108
Economic advantage and kinship structure, 275
development–effect on family life, 129
factors influencing joint families, 173
rationality and cooperation, 148
progress and joint family, 21-22
in living jointly, 168
Education and size of the family, 5, 139
and new goals, 148
impact of, 273
and family type, 355
Ego based kin behaviour (case study Kolar Gold fields), 212
Employment and attitude of family, 30
Entrepreneurs/non-entrepreneurs comparison, 154
Extended Family identification, 26
and rural areas, 70
type-classification, 351
characterise, 353
Extension classification according to, 48
Indian form, 113
definition use of term, 37
European countries and population per household, 108
Evidence about changes in Indian family–interpretation of, 193
case study (sample findings), 194-97

Family identification–concept, meaning of, 26, 261
definition, 78
definition used in analysies, 116
preference, 61
studies in India–controversis, 350
groupings, 351
Family maintenance costs/variables–urban/rural comparison, 170
Family structure and class/economic activity relationship, 329
Family Planning aspects in Calcutta (Statistics), 350
Family types study of:
Changing structure, 1-2
relations and social change, 3
factors affecting, schools of thought, 19
relation with variables, correlations, 281
and castes statistics (Shanti Nagar), 287
Flexibility aspect of nuclear families, 138

Geographical distance and extended family, 27
Generations family classifications according to, 45
Ghar Jamai (matrilocally resident makes), 235
Ghurye's report on Lonikand village and family types, 306-07, 321
Groupings among joint/nuclear families, 39-40
Growth injoint families, 119
Gujarat (villages) and case of joint living of married sons, 103
households, anaysis, 107

Heads of family village/urban orientations, 288
Heriditar occupation and economic development, 265
Henry Summer Maine's view on Indian society, 257-58
High fertility and living levels, 267
Hindu family and Economic Development, 263
 Succession Act, 1956, 249
Historical evidence of joint family, 65
Hospitality of son-in-law non-acceptance trend, 247
Household/family similarity and distinction, 260
Howrah case study, 154
 industry, 155-56
Husbands separated from family, 166
Hypothesis from nuclear to joint families supporters, 114
 of breakdown in joint family due to industrialization, 281-82

Ideal family type, 287
Ideal/real family structure, 178-79
 adjustment–ways, 182
Identification of family (Sarma's), 44
Impact of economic changes on family structure, 269
 urbanization on kinship, 272
Industrialization and urbanization and nuclear family, 20, 23, 109-10
 and family identification, 25, 50-51, 60, 192, 268
 impact on family, 6
Industrialists and joint family, 7
Indian definition of family, 138
indological idea of joint family, 105-106
Indian Domestic Cycle, 81
Inhabitants of Lonikand family types (enumeration 1819), 308
 (enumeration 1958), 316
 (enumeration 1967), 318-19
Inter household relationships, 53
Interactional dimensions of family life, 211
Institutionalization of kin relationship, 214
Interactional dimensions of family life, 211
Inter-generational household sharing, 237
Interrelationships of family structure with socio-cultural and economic variables, 350
Intra family relations in Nuclear families, 354

Japan traditional families, 21
Jati identities (KGF), 213
Jointness and family income, 163
 and traditional occupation, 5
 practise of, 22
 features, study, 50
Joint families study in villages, 23
 classification, 39
 term, 64, 67, 304
 definition, 105
 and caste memberships, 320
 controversy, 114-15
 decline, 137
 aspects of, 137
 among entrepreneurs/non-entrepreneurs statistics, 165
 attitude towards, 197
 correlates to caste eco-structure, 330
Joint and separated families differences, 41
 patterns (14), 41

Karl Marx's views on Indian society, 257
Karta decisions–case studies, 158-59

authority loosening of, 182-83
selection of ideal/actual basis, 184-85
role of, 187
Key concepts in literature on family, 193
Kin Networks study of decline–Ranchi, 25
loose knit, 27
Kinship ties nature of (case study–Kolar Gold Fields), 212
Kin households and social change, 141
Kin interaction, 214
universe, 215-16
geographical dimension, 215
Kinship composition, 272
in Mahuva (Gujarat), 272
relations in extended families, 359
Kolar Gold Fields (case study), 212

Landwnring families (by size of holding) and family type, 298
Large Joint Families, 62
Later Census–advantages, 108
Legal changes and disintegeration of families, 305
Letter writing frequency among kin, 225-26
Levels of operation of Hindu family, 262
Lineal joint family, 172, 181, 285, 334
collateral joint family, 334
relationship, 39
classification, 47, 116
collateral families, 285
Literacy and natal kin contact, 249
Lonikand village study, 303
changes observed in family over century, 321
and caste/joint family, 322-23
Loose knit kinship networks, 27
Madan's classification of Kashmiri families, 64
Madras industrial leaders–trends of family, 274
Mahuva (Gujarat) study of joint family, 22
Mahabharata and joint family, 65
Mahisya entrepreneurs of Howrah case study, 158
living arrangements, 63, 180
Male Household heads composition in India, 141
Market cash economy as factor of disintegration (Orissa), 305
Married woman's residential incorporation, 231-32
Matrilateral asymmetary, 9, 229
and kinship practices, 9-10
trend towards, 229, 236-37
Matrilocal residence, 231, 238
Matrilaterality till towards (KGF), 219
Meerut study of kin relations, 236-37
Membership composition (KGF), 220
Methods and techniques of data collection, 70
Metropolitan urban complex family in, 350
Migration rural-urban, 4
Mitakshara definition of coparcenary, 104
and family types, 113
succession, 91
law of ownership and inheritance, 263-64
Modern forces effect of on nuclear and extended families, 21
Monetary Aid (give and take) among KGF respondents, 221
Monthly income statistics of commensal families (1963), 164
Most important relative choice, 217
Mutual Aid among kin, 222-24

Nairs of Malabar and disintegration of family, 305
Natal home visits, 248
New generations feelings for joint family, 22
New family beginning stage determination, 89
application of formula, 90
Non-cultivator owners vs cultivators and nuclear families, 331
Non-economic factors of survival/ break-up of joint families, 178
North-Indian urban kinship, 229
Nuclear family definition, 116
reasons for choosing, characteristics of, 31, 352-53
classification, 39, 46
term, 63
in villages (trend), 272, 330
in India and conjugal family USA (differences), 202
incidents among different communities, 358
Nuclearization of joint family, 60
denial of, 60-61
studies on, 60

Occupational mobility and extended family identification, 25-26
Occupation of head of family and family type, 294
and family type, 355
Okhla industrial entrepreneurs and family trend, 274
Orissa village changes in, 4, 305
Orientation of family head (urban/ village) and family type, 290
in low caste families, 291
literate/high/low castes, 292
and adult men in family, 295
Overpopulation and women's status/ role, 265
Ownership of land and family type, 10, 296
urban business and house (joint), 186

Parent children relationship, 53
inlaws non-residence in same city, 246
and daughters (nuclear households) visitations, 244-45
Patrilateral emphasis, 235
trend towards, 235
Patidars and proportion of joint families, 47
Pattern of family, 49, 52
kin interaction, 221
Patrilineal/patrilocal families, 49
descent, 231
Patrilocal residence, 231, 286
Paternal authority acceptance of, 138
Permanent jobs and kinship networks, 27
Pihar concept of reisdence, 243
and *sasural* structural separation, 232-33
Polygynous family, 77-78, 116, 285
Preference in family size, 30
Pre-industrialized period and family type, 25
Pre-British Society, 59
Principles of Aggregation, 102
residential unity of patri-kin, 102-103
Principles regarding family type, 77
Property ownership and jointness, 6
types–commensal families, 167
rights (Dayabhaga), 172
rights, 262
Propositions regarding ideal/conjugal joint family, 195
Pune factory worker study, 273
Punjab villge-trends in, 275

Ram Mohan Roy on Hindu family institutions, 263
Ranchi as study setting, 24
Regional differences in family types, 305
Relationship factors for type of family, 39
Relatives (non-member) residing of, 80
Relative living in separate household, 218
Residence of widows, 239-40
    pattern and interaction with patrilateral and matrilateral kin, 248
Residential proximity of kins, 240
Role expectation, 53
    changes in, 53
Ross' classification of types A-D families, 62
Rural people and joint families, 7
    /urban difference in household organization, 144, 350
    /urban differences in household structure (Dharwan), 144
    property and commensal jointness, 175
Sample of study, 24
Sanskritization of a caste, 103
Sasural (conjugal home) residence patterns, 242-43
Security of income and ties with family, 171
Separation of potential joint families factors conducive to, 174-75
Separate families, 41
Separated joint families, 166
Sequence of changes undergone by family, 6
Setting of present study, 24
Shanti Nagar case study, 75-76, 117, 282
    location, 117, 282
Sharing of Property (case studies), 145-47
Shraddha rituals and property rights, 105
Sharing of households with kinsmen, 238-39
Size of family property owned, 168
Single member households (Calcutta), 351
    reasons, 357
Small hosueholds, 39
Small nuclear family, 350
Socio-economic status and attitude towards joint families, 197
Social institutions and economic development, 257
    system in western civilization, 269
Sons living away/within family (statistics), 142
State of origin and family type, 351
Standard model and family type, 129
Stimulating factors–joint to nuclear families, 113

Subsistence to cash economics and break of households, 269
Sub-nuclear family, 334
Supplemented
    collateral joint family, 334
    joint families, 334
    lineal collateral
    lineal joint family, 334
    nuclear family, 288, 344
    polygynous family, 116
    sub-nuclear family, 344
Sweetser's hypothesis, 230
Symbolic Act of property sharing, 145

Ties within joint families commonality factors, 194
Traditional and rational decisions (dichotomy), 267

Transitional family unit, 67-68
Trend towards nuclear families, 50-51, 259
  factors related to, 51
  larger/smaller joint families, 51
Trends in (possible) Indian/American families, 201
  AEF, 201, 203
Tribal families classification of, 43
Types of family as per relationship among kin, 39, 62-63

Unbranched family, 81
  sequences of in Shanti Nagar, 83
Understanding of household life, 101
Units of joint families, 48
  nuclear families, 48
Universal applicability of methods, 69
Urbanization, 4
  impact on joint family, 61, 137, 268
Urban joint family, 140
  effect of family head, 289

Variations in family types, 10
  in family structure, 350
Vama distribution of respondents, 214
Vertical mobility characteristics and aspects, 26
Village studies, 40
  connection with different categories of respondents (Howrah), 176
Virilocal marriges, and women residence, 286
Visiting married daughter low trends, 246-47
Visiting pattern among kins, 225

Wasteful expenditures in rituals, 265
Western family and role of kin, 21
Western model of conjugal family, 191
  core characteristics and ideal type, 192
Western society and matrilateral asymetry, 229
  social systemin, 264
Wife's kin emphasis/trend towards, 230
Wife's absence from village, 285
Women in formulation of domestic cycle, 91
Women's share in property, 250